CONSUMER INVOLVEMENT IN PRIVATE EU COMPETITION LAW ENFORCEMENT

Consumer Involvement in Private EU Competition Law Enforcement

MARIA IOANNIDOU

Great Clarendon Street, Oxford, OX2 6DP,
United Kingdom

Oxford University Press is a department of the University of Oxford.
It furthers the University's objective of excellence in research, scholarship,
and education by publishing worldwide. Oxford is a registered trade mark of
Oxford University Press in the UK and in certain other countries

© Oxford University Press 2015

The moral rights of the author have been asserted

First Edition published in 2015

All rights reserved. No part of this publication may be reproduced, stored in
a retrieval system, or transmitted, in any form or by any means, without the
prior permission in writing of Oxford University Press, or as expressly permitted
by law, by licence or under terms agreed with the appropriate reprographics
rights organization. Enquiries concerning reproduction outside the scope of the
above should be sent to the Rights Department, Oxford University Press, at the
address above

You must not circulate this work in any other form
and you must impose this same condition on any acquirer

Crown copyright material is reproduced under Class Licence
Number C01P0000148 with the permission of OPSI
and the Queen's Printer for Scotland

Published in the United States of America by Oxford University Press
198 Madison Avenue, New York, NY 10016, United States of America

British Library Cataloguing in Publication Data

Data available

Library of Congress Control Number: 2015948052

ISBN 978–0–19–872643–2

Links to third party websites are provided by Oxford in good faith and
for information only. Oxford disclaims any responsibility for the materials
contained in any third party website referenced in this work.

Acknowledgements

This book is a revised and updated version of my DPhil thesis defended in May 2012, at the University of Oxford. It is the outcome of a long journey that has been made possible due to the support of many people and different institutions, both on a personal and an academic level, for which I am very grateful. In reality, I am grateful to many more people and far more grateful than I could ever express in this note...

To my supervisor Ariel Ezrachi I am immensely indebted for his continuous support, guidance, and encouragement throughout the completion of this project and beyond. He has allowed me ample room to develop my ideas while always instilling an optimistic account of every perceived problem. I would also like to express my warmest thanks to my DPhil examiners, Philip Marsden and Aidan Robertson, for their very helpful comments and for making the viva such an enjoyable experience. Invaluable advice and comments have been provided by many people at different stages of the project, especially Stephen Weatherill, Barry Rodger, and Caron-Beaton Wells.

This book would not have been made possible without the generous financial support of IKY, the Hellenic State Scholarships Foundation, and the Leventis Foundation. Special thanks are owed to all the staff at the Bodleian Law Library and the Law Faculty, University of Oxford, for their continuous support, especially Geraldine Malloy, for having an answer to every question. Corpus Christi College has provided a particularly stimulating and supportive environment throughout my time in Oxford. Liz Fisher, Lucia Zedner, Sanja Bogojević, and Louis Karaolis have played an important role in this regard.

Rethinking of this project took place in Brussels and I would like to thank in particular Julian Ellison for being such a wonderful person to work with, as well as Luiza Wojciszke, Ed McNeill, Tania Patsalia, and Elissavet Karaiskou for being excellent colleagues and friends. Part of the re-writing of this book was done at the University of Surrey and the Queen Mary University of London and it was made much easier and enjoyable by many colleagues, especially Theodore Konstadinides, Kanstantsin Dzehtsiarou, Filippo Fontanelli, Anastasia Karatzia, Ioannis Kokkoris, Eyad Dabbah, Spyros Maniatis, and Valsamis Mitsilegas. The help of the people at OUP in bringing this project into fruition is much appreciated.

Many people have contributed in many different and unique ways to this project—from my first MJur/BCL year in Oxford back in 2007. I am really happy that I met such great people. It is the people you meet and the friends you make that define an unforgettable journey. Thank you for all the funny, unique, and memorable times we had. Seb Grifnee you have been a big part of this journey and you will always be remembered.

I would also like to thank my closest friends from Oxford, London, Athens, and beyond for making my life so much better and easier; Dimitrios Moraitis, Andriani Fili, Vassia Balafa, Vanessa Tzoannou, Strati Sakellariou, Elmina Chadio, Konstanti Ioannidou, Eugenia Bouvi, Antonios Kouroutakis, Michalis Risvas, Eliza Kazili, Elena Siskou, Pantelis Aivaliotis, Katerina Virvidaki, Lily Kotsana, Deni Mantzari, Christina Moutsiana, and Kalliope Vounisea.

My interest in competition law and the long library days would not have been the same had it not been for Vasiliki Brisimi, Julian Nowag, and Pablo Marquez. It has been a real privilege working (and living) with such great people and I still miss it.

This book is dedicated to my family: my parents, Anna and Charalambos, and little brother, Diomedes, for always being there for me, especially when I am often not.

Contents

Table of Cases	xi
Table of Legislation	xxiii
List of Abbreviations	xxix

1. Introduction	1
1. Background	1
2. Nature of the Subject Matter	2
2.1 EU competition law enforcement: A fused approach	3
2.2 The consumer's role in EU competition law enforcement	3
2.3 Function of tort law	4
2.4 Harmonization: Unity or diversity?	4
3. Methodology and Terminological Clarifications	5
4. Structure	7

PART A: NORMATIVE APPROACH TO CONSUMER PARTICIPATION

2. 'Consumer Interest' and the Aims of EU Competition Law	11
1. Introduction	11
2. The Interplay between Competition Law and Consumer Law	12
3. Multiple Aims and the 'Consumer Interest'	15
3.1 Multiplicity of aims	15
3.2 'Consumer welfare' in EU competition law	22
3.3 'Consumer interest' in EU competition law	24
4. The Role of the 'Consumer Interest'	25
4.1 'Consumer welfare': Commission 'rhetoric'	26
4.2 'Consumer interest': Insights from EU jurisprudence	28
5. Embracing 'Consumer Interest' in EU Competition Law	42
6. Conclusion	44
3. Normative Justifications for Increased Consumer Involvement	47
1. Introduction	47
2. Endemic/Functional Aims of Private Competition Law Enforcement	48
2.1 Private enforcement of EU law	48
2.2 Private enforcement of EU competition law: EU institutions' approach	52
2.3 Scepticism as to the deterrent function of (follow-on) damages actions	62
2.4 Ranking the endemic aims	66

Contents

   3. Ancillary Institutional Benefits   67
      3.1 Proliferation of information—contributing to consumer education and empowerment   67
      3.2 Legitimization of EU policies   68
   4. Conclusion   72

PART B: PRACTICAL APPROACH TO CONSUMER PARTICIPATION

4. Improving Consumers' Role: 'Standing' and 'Access to Evidence'   75

   1. Introduction   75
   2. Characteristics of Consumer Claims: Justifying a More 'Enabling' Approach   75
   3. Consumer Standing and Passing-on   79
      3.1 A theoretical account: SCOTUS approach   80
      3.2 The European Court's approach   83
      3.3 Legislative solution   86
   4. Access to Evidence   90
      4.1 Disclosure of evidence: Promoting stand-alone consumer claims   90
      4.2 Promoting follow-on consumer claims—preserving the effectiveness of public enforcement   94
   5. Conclusion   104

5. Improving Consumers' Role: Collective Actions   107

   1. Introduction   107
   2. EU Developments on Collective Redress: A Historical Account   108
   3. Demarcating Collective Action Mechanisms in the Field of Competition Law   111
      3.1 Individual v collective consumer interest   111
      3.2 'Access to justice' for consumer claims in competition law   115
   4. Structural Characteristics of a Model Collective Action   117
      4.1 Structuring the group: Opt in v opt-out   118
      4.2 Standing to bring claims: Consumer representatives   120
      4.3 Funding of actions   124
      4.4 Distribution of the damages award   125
      4.5 Synopsis   126
   5. Structural Characteristics of Member States' Collective Action Mechanisms   126
      5.1 Furthering individual consumers' interests   127
      5.2 Furthering the collective consumer interest   132
      5.3 Synopsis   136
   6. Structuring the Appropriate EU Collective Action Mechanism   137
      6.1 Standing: Lead plaintiff, public body, or consumer organization   138
      6.2 Forming the group: Opt-in v opt-out   141
      6.3 Distribution of the damages award   142
      6.4 Costs and funding of collective actions   144
   7. Conclusion   147

6. Consumer Involvement in Public Competition Law Enforcement: Towards Acceptable Alternatives — 151

   1. Introduction — 151
   2. Fused Approach to Enforcement: The Benefits — 152
      2.1 Rethinking the deterrence—Compensation dichotomy — 152
      2.2 Ancillary institutional benefits — 155
   3. Current Avenues for Consumer Participation: Public Enforcement *Stricto Sensu* — 156
      3.1 Complaints to the Commission — 156
      3.2 Making complaints to the Commission more effective — 162
      3.3 Sector inquiries — 163
      3.4 Improvements to sector inquiries: Priorities, structure, and outcome — 165
      3.5 'Super-complaints': The European way — 166
      3.6 Other participation avenues: Intervention — 170
   4. Public Enforcement *Lato Sensu*: Towards a Mixed Approach to Competition Law Enforcement — 171
      4.1 Instances of 'public compensation' — 172
      4.2 Categorization of cases — 175
      4.3 Institutionalizing a public compensation approach — 176
      4.4 Serving the collective consumer interest — 179
   5. Conclusion — 180

7. Overcoming Institutional and Political Limitations: Appropriate Instruments for the Introduction of European-Wide Measures — 181

   1. Introduction — 181
   2. Enhancing Consumer Participation: Political Obstacles and the Proposed Measures — 182
      2.1 Political obstacles and the Directive on Damages Actions — 182
      2.2 Content of the proposals — 184
   3. Implementing the Proposals — 186
      3.1 Justifying a competition-specific harmonization of procedural rules for consumer claims — 186
      3.2 In search of an adequate legal base — 189
      3.3 In search of the most appropriate legislative instrument — 199
   4. Implementing Remaining Public Enforcement Proposals — 200
   5. Conclusion — 202

8. Concluding Remarks — 205

Selected Bibliography — 209
Index — 245

Table of Cases

COURT OF JUSTICE (EU)

(Alphabetical table)

Aalborg Portland and Others v. Commission of the European Communities
(Joined Cases C-204/00 P, C-205/00P, C-211/00P, C-213/00P, C-217/00P
and C-219/00P) [2004] ECR I-123 82
Amministrazione delle Finanze dello Stato v SpA San Giorgio (Case 199/82)
[1983] ECR 3595 .... 50, 85
AEPI v Commission (Case C-425/07P) [2009] ECR I-3205 .... 160, 161
Albany (Case C-67/96) [1999] ECR I-5751 .... 18, 19, 20
Allianz Hungária Biztosító Zrt. and Others v Gazdasági Versenyhivatal
(Case C-32/11) [2013] 4 CMLR 25 30
Amministrazione delle Finanze dello Stato v Simmenthal (Case 106/77)
[1978] ECR 629 50
Andrea Francovich and Others v Italian Republic (Joined Cases C-6/90 and
9/90) [1991] ECR I-5357 .... 50, 55, 56
AOK Bundesverband (Case 264/01 etc) [2004] ECR I-2491 19
Belgische Radio en Televisie and Societe belge des auteurs, compositeurs
et editeurs v SV SABAM and NV Fonior 'BRT I' (Case 127/73)
[1974] ECR 51 .... 49, 52, 55
Brasserie du Pêcheur SA v Federal Republic of Germany (Joined Cases
C-46/93 and 48/93) [1996] ECR I-1029 .... 50, 72
Britannia Alloys & Chemicals v Commission (Case C-76/06P) [2007] ECR I-4405 152
British Leyland Plc v Commission (Case 226/84) [1986] ECR 3263 35
Bundeswettbewerbsbehörde v Donau Chemie AG and Others (Case C-536/11)
[2013] 5 CMLR 19 .... 58, 59, 94, 102–4
Carmine Antonio Russo v AIMA (Case 60/75) [1976] ECR 45 50
CILFIT and Lanicio di Gavardo SpA v Ministry of Health (Case 283/81) [1982]
ECR 3415 15
Comet v Produktschap voor Siergewassen (Case 45/76) [1976] ECR 2043 .... 50, 193
Commission v Agrofert (Case C-477/10P) [2012] 5 CMLR 9 96
Commission v Alrosa (Case C-441/07P) [2010] ECR I-5949 177
Commission v Council (Case 45/86) [1987] ECR 1493 191
Commission v Council (Case C-300/89) [1991] ECR I-2867 191
Commission v Council (Case C-338/01) [2004] ECR I-4829 191
Commission v Council (Case C-94/03) [2006] ECR I-1 191
Commission v Council (Case C-176/03) [2005] ECR I-7879 196
Commission v Editions Odile SAS (Case C-404/10P) [2012] 5 CMLR 8 96
Commission v EnBW Energie Baden-Württemberg AG (Case C-365/12P)
[2014] 4 CMLR 30 .... 58, 94–6, 99
Commission v Otis NV and Others (Case C-199/11) [2013] 4 CMLR 4 58
Commission v SGL Carbon AG (Case C-301/04P) [2006] ECR I-5915 91
Commission v Technische Glaswerke Ilmenau GmbH (Case C-139/07P) [2010]
ECR I-5885 96
Commission v Volkswagen (Case C-74/04P) [2006] ECR I-6585 158
Competition Authority v Beef Industry Development Society (Case C-209/07)
[2008] ECR I-8637 .... 23, 31

Consiglio nazionale dei geologi v Autorità garante della concorrenza e del mercato (CNG)
  (Case C-136/12) [2013] 5 CMLR 40..19
Costa v ENEL (Case 6/64) [1964] ECR 585..55
Courage Ltd v Bernard Crehan and Bernard Crehan v Courage Ltd
  and Others (Case C-453/99) [2001] ECR I-6297 ....48, 53, 55–8, 60, 70, 78, 84, 193
Dansk Rørindustri and Others v Commission (Joined Cases C-189/02P,
  C-202/02P, C-205-208/02P and C-213/02P) [2005] ECR I-5425 ....176, 203
Deutsche Telekom v Commission (Case C-208/08P) [2010] ECR I-955 ....39, 40
Dole Food v Commission (Case C-286/13P), 19 March 2015......................................29
Eco Swiss China Time Ltd v Benetton International NV (Case C-126/97)
  [1999] ECR I–3055...17, 23, 55
ETA Fabriques d' Ebauches v SA DK Investment (Case 31/85) [1985] ECR 3933............33
Établissements Consten S.à.R.L. and Grundig-Verkaufs-GmbH v Commission
  (Joined Cases 56/64 and 58/64) [1966] ECR 299........................... 17, 31, 32
Europemballage Corporation and Continental Can Company Inc v Commission
  (Case 6/72) [1973] ECR 215 ....18, 35, 37, 38, 42
Europese Gemeenschap v Otis NV and Others (Case C-199/11) [2013]
  4 CMLR 4..58
Federicco Cipolla v Rosaria Fazari et al (Joined Cases C-94/04 and
  C-202/04) [2006] ECR I-11421 ....41, 145
FEDESA (Case C-331/88) [1990] ECR 4023.......................................190
FNV Kunsten Informatie en Media v Netherlands (Case C-413/13) [2015]
  4 CMLR 1..20
Football Association Premier League Ltd (Joined Cases C-403/08 and C-429/08)
  [2011] ECR I-9083 17
Ford of Europe Incorporated and Ford Werke AG v Commission (Joined
  Cases 228 and 229/82) [1984] ECR 1129......................................170
Gema v Commission (Case 125/78) [1979] ECR 3173............................160
General Motors Continental NV v Commission (Case 26/75) [1975] ECR 1367.............35
Germany v European Parliament and Council (Case C-376/98) [2000] ECR I-8419 ....190, 192
GlaxoSmithKline Services v Commission (Case C-501/06P) [2009] ECR I-9291 ....23, 32
Greenpeace v Commission (Case C-321/95P) [1998] ECR-I 1651 158
Groupement des Cartes Bancaires v Commission (Case C-67/13) [2014] 5 CMLR 22 30
GT-Link AC v De Danske Statsbaner (Case C-242/95) [1997] ECR I-4349 ....53, 187
Guerin Automobiles v Commission of the European Communities
  (Case C-282/95P) [1997] ECR I-1503...53
H J Banks & Co v British Coal Corporation (Case C-128/92) [1994] ECR I-1209 ....49, 55
Hans Just v Danish Ministry for Fiscal Affairs (Case 68/79) [1980] ECR 501 85
Hoefner and Elser v Macrotron GmbH (Case C-41/90) [1991] ECR I-1979 19
Humblet (Case 6/60) [1960] ECR 559 50
IECC v Commission (Case C-449/98P) [2001] ECR I-3875 161
IMS Health GmbH and Co OHG v NDC Health GmbH and Co KG
  (Case C-418/01) [2004] ECR I-5039..38
Kapniki Mikhailidis AE v Idryma Koinonikon Asfaliseon (Joined Cases C-441/98
  and 442/98) [2000] ECR I-7145 85
Kone AG and Others v ÖBB Infrastruktur AG (Case C-557/12) [2014]
  5 CMLR 5..59, 60
Konkurrensverket v TeliaSonera AB (Case C-52/09) [2011] ECR I-527 ....21, 23, 35, 40
Koppensteiner GmbH v Bundesimmobiliengesellschaft mbH (Case C-15/04)
  [2005] ECR-I-4855...189
Lord Bethell v Commission (Case 246/81) [1982] ECR 2277.........................158
Marshall v Southampton and South-West Hampshire Area Health Authority
  (Case C-271/91) [1993] ECR I-4367..51

Table of Cases

Marty v Estée Lauder (Case 37/79) [1980] ECR 2481...................................53
MasterCard Inc v Commission (Case C-382/12P) (judgment of 11 September 2014) 164
Masterfoods Ltd v HB Ice Cream Ltd (Case C-344/98) [2000] ECR I-11369 160
Meca-Medina (Case C-519/04P) [2006] ECR I-6991..............................19, 20
Metro (I) (Case 26/76) [1977] ECR 1875...20
Muñoz Cia SA and Superior Fruiticola Ltd and Redbridge Produce Marketing Ltd
  (Case C-253/00) [2002] ECR I-7289 51
Musique Diffusion Française and others v Commission (Joined Cases 100/80 to
  103/80) [1983] ECR 1825 152
NV Algemene Transport—en Expeditie Onderneming van Gend en Loos and
  Nederlandse Administratie der Belastingen (Case 26/62) [1963] ECR 1 ....49, 50, 55
Opinion 2/94 (Accession to the ECHR) [1996] ECR I-1759 198
Opinion 2/00 (Cartagena Protocol) [2001] ECR I-9713.........................190, 191
Ordem dos Técnicos Oficiais de Contas v Autoridade da Concorrência (OTOC)
  (Case C-1/12) [2013] 4 CMLR 20..19
Orkem v Commission (Case 374/87) (1989) ECR 3283...............................91
Oscar Broenner v Mediaprint (Case C-7/97) [1998] ECR-I 7791.......................38
Otto BV v Postbank NV (Case C-60/92) [1993] ECR I-5683 91
Parliament v Council (Case C-436/03) [2006] ECR I-3733..........................191
Parliament v Council (Case C-155/07) [2008] ECR I-7879 191
Pavlov (Case C-180/98 etc) [2000] ECR I-6451 19
Pfleiderer AG v Bundeskartellamt (Case C-360/09) [2011] ECR I-5161............ 52, 58, 59,
                                                                          94, 101–4, 202, 203
Portugal v Council (Case C-268/94) [1996] ECR I-617.............................191
Post Danmark A/S v Konkurrencerådet (Case C-209/10) [2012] 4 CMLR 23......23, 35, 39, 40
R (on the application of Alliance for Natural Health and Nutri-Link Ltd)
  v Secretary of State for Health, R (on the application of National Association
  of Health Stores and Health Food Manufacturers Ltd) v Secretary of State
  for Health and National Assembly for Wales (Joined Cases C-154/04 and
  C-155/04) [2005] ECR I-6451 192
R v Secretary of State for Transport, ex p Factortame Ltd (Case C-213/89) [1990]
  ECR I-2433..50
R and others, Suiker Unie v Commission (Case 41/73) [1973] ECR 1465 171
Republik Oesterreich v Martin Huber (Case C-336/00) [2002] ECR I-7699.............191
Rewe Handelsgesellschaft Nord mbH and Rewe-Markt Steffen v Hauptzollamt Kiel
  (Case 158/80) [1981] ECR-1805 49
Rewe v Landwirtschaftskammer fuer das Saarland (Case 33/76) [1976] ECR 1989....49, 50, 193
RTE and ITP v Commission (Joined cases C-241/91 and 242/91P) [1995] ECR I-743 38
Societe Comateb and others v Directeur General des Douanes et Droits Indirects
  (Joined Cases C-192/95 to 218/95) [1997] ECR I-165 85
Sot Lelos kai Sia EE v GlaxoSmithKline AEVE (Joined Cases C-468/06 to 478/06)
  [2008] ECR I-7139 39
Spain v Council (Case C-350/92) [1995] ECR I-1985..............................192
Spain v Council (Case C-36/98) [2001] ECR I-779 191
Stergios Delimitis v Henninger Braue AG (Case C-234/89) [1991] ECR I-935 53
Sweden v Commission and My Travel Group (Case C-506/08P) [2011] ECR I-6237 96
SYFAIT v GlaxoSmithKline Plc (Case C-53/03) [2005] ECR I-4609 ....23, 39
T-Mobile Netherlands BV v Raad van Bestuur van de Nederlandse Mededingingsautoriteit
  (Case C-8/08) [2009] ECR I-4529 ....23, 29, 30, 32, 51, 187
Telefónica and Telefónica de España v Commission (Case C-295/12P)
  (judgment of 10 July 2014) 135
Tepea v Commission (Case 28/77) [1978] ECR 1391.................................24
Tetra Pak v Commission (Case C-333/94P) [1996] ECR I-5951.......................19

Tomra Systems and Others v Commission (Case C-549/10P) [2012] 4 CMLR 27 . . . . 40, 41
Ufex v Commission (Case C-117/97P) [1999] ECR I-1341 160
Unibet (London) Ltd and Unibet (International) Ltd v Justitiekanslern
 (Case C-432/05) [2007] ECR I-2271 49
United Brands Company and United Brands Continental BV v Commission
 (Case 27/76) [1978] ECR 207 . . . . 35, 36
Vincenzo Manfredi and Others v Lloyd Adriatico Assicurazioni SpA and Others
 (Joined Cases C-295/04 to 298/04) [2006] ECR I-6619 . . . . . . 48, 51, 56–8, 61, 70, 78, 84, 193
Vodafone and others v Secretary of State (Case C-58/08) [2010] ECR I-4999 . . . . 190, 192
Von Colson and Kamann v Land Nordrhein—Westfalen (Case 14/83) [1984]
 ECR 1891 51
Walt Wilhelm v Bundeskartellamt (Case 14/68) [1969] ECR 1 . . . . 18, 187
Weber's Wine World Handels-GmbH v Abgabenberufungskommission Wien
 (Case C-147/01) [2003] ECR I- 11365 85
Wouters (Case C-309/99) [2002] ECR I-1577 . . . . 19, 20
Yassin Abdullah Kadi and Al Barakaat International Foundation v Council of the European
 Union and Commission of the European Communities (Joined Cases
 C-402/05P and C-415/05P) [2008] ECR I-6351 198
Zuckerfabrik AG v Hauptzollamt (Joined cases C-143/88 and 92/89)
 [1991] ECR I-415. 54

(Chronological table)
6/60 Humblet [1960] ECR 559 50
26/62 NV Algemene Transport—en Expeditie Onderneming van Gend en
 Loos and Nederlandse Administratie der Belastingen [1963] ECR 1 . . . . 49, 50, 55
6/64 Costa v ENEL [1964] ECR 585 55
56/64 and 58/64 Établissements Consten S.à.R.L. and Grundig-Verkaufs-GmbH
 v Commission [1966] ECR 299 . . . . 17, 31, 32
14/68 Walt Wilhelm v Bundeskartellamt [1969] ECR 1 . . . . 18, 187
6/72 Europemballage Corporation and Continental Can Company Inc
 v Commission [1973] ECR 215 . . . . 18, 35, 37, 38, 42
41/73 R and others, Suiker Unie v Commission [1973] ECR 1465 171
127/73 Belgische Radio en Televisie and Societe belge des auteurs, compositeurs
 et editeurs v SV SABAM and NV Fonior 'BRT I' [1974] ECR 51 . . . . 49, 52, 55
26/75 General Motors Continental NV v Commission [1975] ECR 1367 35
60/75 Carmine Antonio Russo v AIMA [1976] ECR 45 50
26/76 Metro (I) [1977] ECR 1875 20
27/76 United Brands Company and United Brands Continental BV v Commission
 [1978] ECR 207 . . . . 35, 36
33/76 Rewe v Landwirtschaftskammer fuer das Saarland [1976] ECR 1989 . . . . 49, 50, 193
45/76 Comet v Produktschap voor Siergewassen [1976] ECR 2043 . . . . 50, 193
28/77 Tepea v Commission [1978] ECR 1391 24
106/77 Amministrazione delle Finanze dello Stato v Simmenthal [1978] ECR 629 50
125/78 Gema v Commission [1979] ECR 3173 160
37/79 Marty v Estée Lauder [1980] ECR 2481 53
68/79 Hans Just v Danish Ministry for Fiscal Affairs [1980] ECR 501 85
100/80 to 103/80 Musique Diffusion Française and others v Commission
 [1983] ECR 1825 152
158/80 Rewe Handelsgesellschaft Nord mbH and Rewe-Markt Steffen v Hauptzollamt
 Kiel [1981] ECR-1805 49
246/81 Lord Bethell v Commission [1982] ECR 2277 158
283/81 CILFIT and Lanicio di Gavardo SpA v Ministry of Health
 [1982] ECR 3415 15
199/82 Amministrazione delle Finanze dello Stato v SpA San Giorgio [1983] ECR 3595 . . . . . . 50, 85

Table of Cases

228 and 229/82 Ford of Europe Incorporated and Ford Werke AG v Commission
  [1984] ECR 1129..170
14/83 Von Colson and Kamann v Land Nordrhein—Westfalen [1984] ECR 1891 51
226/84 British Leyland Plc v Commission [1986] ECR 3263............................35
31/85 ETA Fabriques d' Ebauches v SA DK Investment [1985] ECR 3933..................33
45/86 Commission v Council [1987] ECR 1493......................................191
374/87 Orkem v Commission (1989) ECR 3283 91
C-143/88 and 92/89 Zuckerfabrik AG v Hauptzollamt [1991] ECR I-415..................54
C-331/88 FEDESA [1990] ECR 4023...190
C-213/89 R v Secretary of State for Transport, ex p Factortame Ltd [1990]
  ECR I-2433..50
C-234/89 Stergios Delimitis v Henninger Braue AG [1991] ECR I-935....................53
C-300/89 Commission v Council [1991] ECR I-2867 191
C-6/90 and 9/90 Andrea Francovich and Others v Italian Republic [1991]
  ECR I-5357..50, 55, 56
C-41/90 Hoefner and Elser v Macrotron GmbH [1991] ECR I-1979......................19
C-241/91 and 242/91P RTE and ITP v Commission [1995] ECR I-743 38
C-271/91 Marshall v Southampton and South-West Hampshire Area Health
  Authority [1993] ECR I-4367..51
C-60/92 Otto BV v Postbank NV [1993] ECR I-5683.................................91
C-128/92 H J Banks & Co v British Coal Corporation [1994] ECR I-1209..............49, 55
C-350/92 Spain v Council [1995] ECR I-1985......................................192
C-46/93 and 48/93 Brasserie du Pêcheur SA v Federal Republic of Germany
  [1996] ECR I-1029 ....50, 72
C-268/94 Portugal v Council [1996] ECR I-617 191
C-333/94P Tetra Pak v Commission [1996] ECR I-5951 19
C-192/95 to 218/95 Societe Comateb and others v Directeur General des
  Douanes et Droits Indirects [1997] ECR I-165..................................85
C-242/95 GT-Link AC v De Danske Statsbaner [1997] ECR I-4349.................53, 187
C-282/95P Guerin Automobiles v Commission of the European Communities
  [1997] ECR I-1503...53
C-321/95P Greenpeace v Commission [1998] ECR-I 1651............................158
C-67/96 Albany [1999] ECR I-5751 ....18, 19, 20
C-7/97 Oscar Broenner v Mediaprint [1998] ECR-I 7791 38
C-117/97P Ufex v Commission [1999] ECR I-1341 160
C-126/97 Eco Swiss China Time Ltd v Benetton International NV [1999]
  ECR I–3055..17, 23, 55
C-36/98 Spain v Council [2001] ECR I-779..191
C-180/98 Pavlov [2000] ECR I-6451 19
C-344/98 Masterfoods Ltd v HB Ice Cream Ltd [2000] ECR I-11369....................160
C-376/98 Germany v European Parliament and Council [2000] ECR I-8419 ....190, 192
C-441/98 and 442/98 Kapniki Mikhailidis AE v Idryma Koinonikon Asfaliseon
  [2000] ECR I-7145...85
C-449/98P IECC v Commission [2001] ECR I-3875.................................161
C-309/99 Wouters [2002] ECR I-1577..19, 20
C-453/99 Courage Ltd v Bernard Crehan and Bernard Crehan v Courage Ltd
  and Others [2001] ECR I-6297....................48, 53, 55–8, 60, 70, 78, 84, 193
C-204/00 P, C-205/00P, C-211/00P, C-213/00P, C-217/00P, and C-219/00P Aalborg
  Portland and Others v Commission of the European Communities [2004] ECR I-123....... 82
C-253/00 Muñoz Cia SA and Superior Fruiticola Ltd and Redbridge Produce
  Marketing Ltd..51
C-336/00 Republik Oesterreich v Martin Huber [2002] ECR I-7699 191
C-147/01 Weber's Wine World Handels-GmbH v Abgabenberufungskommission
  Wien [2003] ECR I- 11365..85

C-264/01 AOK Bundesverband [2004] ECR I-2491 19
C-338/01 Commission v Council [2004] ECR I-4829 191
C-418/01 IMS Health GmbH and Co OHG v NDC Health GmbH
  and Co KG [2004] ECR I-5039 38
C-189/02P, C-202/02P, C-205-208/02P, and C-213/02P Dansk Rørindustri
  and Others v Commission [2005] ECR I-5425 .... 176, 203
C-53/03 SYFAIT v GlaxoSmithKline Plc [2005] ECR I-4609 .... 23, 39
C-94/03 Commission v Council [2006] ECR I-1 191
C-176/03 Commission v Council [2005] ECR I-7879 196
C-436/03 Parliament v Council [2006] ECR I-3733 191
C-15/04 Koppensteiner GmbH v Bundesimmobiliengesellschaft mbH [2005]
  ECR-I-4855 189
C-74/04P Commission v Volkswagen [2006] ECR I-6585 158
C-94/04 and C-202/04 Federicco Cipolla v Rosaria Fazari et al [2006]
  ECR I-11421 .... 41, 145
C-154/04 and C-155/04 R (on the application of Alliance for Natural
  Health and Nutri-Link Ltd) v Secretary of State for Health, R (on the application
  of National Association of Health Stores and Health Food Manufacturers
  Ltd) v Secretary of State for Health and National Assembly for Wales [2005]
  ECR I-6451 192
C-295/04 to 298/04 Vincenzo Manfredi and Others v Lloyd Adriatico
  Assicurazioni SpA and Others [2006] ECR I-6619 .... 48, 51, 56–8, 61, 70, 78, 84, 193
C-301/04P Commission v SGL Carbon AG [2006] ECR I-5915 91
C-519/04P Meca-Medina [2006] ECR I-6991 .... 19, 20
C-402/05P and C-415/05P Yassin Abdullah Kadi and Al Barakaat International
  Foundation v Council of the European Union and Commission of the
  European Communities [2008] ECR I-6351 198
C-432/05 Unibet (London) Ltd and Unibet (International) Ltd v Justitiekanslern
  [2007] ECR I-2271 49
C-76/06P Britannia Alloys & Chemicals v Commission [2007] ECR I-4405 152
C-468/06 to 478/06 Sot Lelos kai Sia EE v GlaxoSmithKline AEVE [2008] ECR I-7139...... 39
C-501/06P GlaxoSmithKline Services v Commission [2009] ECR I-9291 .... 23, 32
C-139/07P Commission v Technische Glaswerke Ilmenau GmbH [2010] ECR I-5885 96
C-155/07 Parliament v Council [2008] ECR I-7879 191
C-209/07 Competition Authority v Beef Industry Development Society
  [2008] ECR I-8637 .... 23, 31
C-425/07P AEPI v Commission [2009] ECR I-3205 .... 160, 161
C-441/07P Commission v Alrosa [2010] ECR I-5949 177
C-8/08 T-Mobile Netherlands BV v Raad van Bestuur van de Nederlandse
  Mededingingsautoriteit [2009] ECR I-4529 .... 23, 29, 30, 32, 51, 187
C-58/08 Vodafone and others v Secretary of State [2010] ECR I-4999 .... 190, 192
C-208/08P Deutsche Telekom v Commission [2010] ECR I-955 .... 39, 40
C-403/08 and C-429/08 Football Association Premier League Ltd [2011] ECR I-9083 17
C-506/08P Sweden v Commission and My Travel Group [2011] ECR I-6237 96
C-52/09 Konkurrensverket v TeliaSonera AB [2011] ECR I-527 .... 21, 23, 35, 40
C-360/09 Pfleiderer AG v Bundeskartellamt [2011] ECR I-5161 .... 52, 58, 59, 94,
                                                                      101–4, 202, 203
C-209/10 Post Danmark A/S v Konkurrencerådet [2012] 4 CMLR 23 .... 23, 35, 39, 40
C-404/10P Commission v Editions Odile SAS [2012] 5 CMLR 8 96
C-477/10P Commission v Agrofert [2012] 5 CMLR 9 96
C-549/10P Tomra Systems and Others v Commission [2012] 4 CMLR 27 .... 40, 41
C-32/11 Allianz Hungária Biztosító Zrt. and Others v Gazdasági Versenyhivatal
  [2013] 4 CMLR 25 30
C-199/11 Europese Gemeenschap v Otis NV and Others [2013] 4 CMLR 4 58

Table of Cases xvii

C-536/11 Bundeswettbewerbsbehörde v Donau Chemie AG and Others
[2013] 5 CMLR 19 .... 58, 59, 94, 102–4
C-1/12 Ordem dos Técnicos Oficiais de Contas v Autoridade da Concorrência
(OTOC) [2013] 4 CMLR 20 19
C-136/12 Consiglio nazionale dei geologi v Autorità garante della concorrenza
e del mercato (CNG) [2013] 5 CMLR 40 19
C-295/12P Telefónica and Telefónica de España v Commission (judgment
of 10 July 2014) 135
C-365/12P Commission v EnBW Energie Baden-Württemberg
AG [2014] 4 CMLR 30 .... 58, 94–6, 99
C-382/12P MasterCard Inc v Commission (judgment of 11 September 2014) 164
C-557/12 Kone AG and Others v ÖBB Infrastruktur AG [2014] 5 CMLR 5 .... 59, 60
C-67/13 Groupement des Cartes Bancaires v Commission [2014] 5 CMLR 22 30
C-286/13P Dole Food v Commission, 19 March 2015 29
C-413/13 FNV Kunsten Informatie en Media v Netherlands [2015] 4 CMLR 1 20

GENERAL COURT (EU)

(Alphabetical table)
AEPI v Commission (Case T-229/05) [2007] ECR II-84 .... 160, 161
Agrofert v Commission (Case T-111/07) [2011] 4 CMLR 6 96
AKZO Nobel v Commission (Case T-345/12) [2015] 4 CMLR 12. .... 101, 105
Archer Daniels Midland Co v Commission (Case T-59/02) [2006] ECR II-3627 173
Association belge des consommateurs test-achats ASBL v Commission
(Case T-224/10) [2011] ECR II-7177 25
Atlantic Container Line AB v Commission (Case T-395/94) [2002] ECR II-875 .... 55, 177
Automec srl v Commission (Case T-24/90) [1992] ECR I-2223 .... 160, 161
Automobiles Peugeot SA and Peugeot SA v Commission (Case T-9/92) [1993]
ECR II-493 171
BEMIM v Commission (Case T-114/92) [1995] ECR II-147 .... 158, 160
BEUC and NCC v Commission (Case T-37/92) [1994] ECR II-285 .... 161, 162
British Airways Plc v Commission (Case T-219/99) [2003] ECR II-5917 .... 38, 41
CDC Hydrogen Perogide v Commission (Case T-437/08) [2011]
ECR –II 8251 .... 59, 92, 96, 98–100
CEAHR v Commission (Case T-427/08) [2011] 4 CMLR 14. 162
Der Grüne Punkt—Duales System Deutschland GmbH v Commission
(Case T-151/01) [2001] ECR II-1607. 35
Éditions Jacob v Commission (Case T-237/05) [2010] ECR II-2245 96
EnBW Energie Baden-Württemberg AG (Case T-344/08) [2012]
5 CMLR 4. .... 58, 94, 99, 100, 105
European Night Services v Commission (Case T-374/94) [1998] ECR II-3141 32
Franchet and Byk v Commission (Joined Cases T-391/03 and T-70/04) [2006]
ECR II-2023 96
GlaxoSmithKline Services v Commission (Case T-168/01) [2006]
ECR II-2969 .... 23, 24, 30, 31, 32
Hilti AG v Commission (Case T-30/89) [1991] ECR II-1439 .... 19, 44
IMS Health Inc v Commission (Case T-184/01R) [2001] ECR II—3193. 38
Intel v Commission (Case T-286/09) (judgment of 12 June 2014) 41
Koelman v Commission (Case T-575/93) [1996] ECR II-1. 161
Ladbroke Racing v Commission (Case T-74/92) [1995] ECR II-115. 160
Ladbroke Racing v Commission (Case T-548/93) [1995] ECR-II 2565 160
Mannesmannröhren-Werke AG v Commission (Case T-112/98) (2001)
ECR II-729 91

MasterCard Inc v Commission (Case T-111/08) [2012] 5 CMLR 5 164
MasterCard Inc v Commission (Case T-516/11) (judgment of 9 September 2014) 96
Matra Hachette v Commission (Case T-17/93) [1994] ECR-II 595 .... 20, 32
Métropole télévision (M6) v Commission (Case T-112/99) [2001]
    ECR II-2459 34
Microsoft Corp v Commission (Case T-201/04) [2007] ECR II- 3601.................. 23, 83
My Travel v Commission (Case T-403/05) [2008] ECR II-2027 96
Netherlands v Commission (Case T-380/08) (judgment of 13 September 2013) 99
O2 (Germany) v Commission (Case T-328/03) [2006] ECR II-1231..................... 33
Oesterreichischer Postsparkasse AG v Commission (Joined Cases T-213/01
    and T-214/01) [2006] ECR II-1601.. 24, 158
Pergan Hilfsstoffe v Commission (Case T-474/04) [2007] ECR II-4225 104
Raiffeisen Zentralbank Oesterreich AG v Commission (Joined Cases T-259/02 to
    T-264/02 and T-271/02) [2006] ECR II-5169...................................... 24
Schenker AG v European Commission (Case T-534/11) (judgment
    of 7 October 2014) 100
Scippecercola and Terzakis v Commission (Case T-306/05) [2008] ECR II-4 160
Sumitomo Chemicals v Commission (Joined Cases T-22/02 and 23/02) [2005]
    ECR II-4065 51
Telefonica and Telefonica de Espana v Commission (Case T-336/07) [2007]
    OJ C269/55.. 171
Tomra Systems and Others v Commission (Case T-155/06) [2010]
    ECR II-4361 .... 40, 41
Verein für Konsumenteninformation v Commission (Case T-2/03)
    (2005) ECR II-1121... 94, 96, 97, 99
Volkswagen v Commission (Case T-208/01) [2003] ECR II–5141 159

(Chronological table)
T-30/89 Hilti AG v Commission [1991] ECR II-1439 .... 19, 44
T-24/90 Automec srl v Commission [1992] ECR I-2223 .... 160, 161
T-9/92 Automobiles Peugeot SA and Peugot SA v Commission [1993]
    ECR II-493... 171
T-37/92 BEUC and NCC v Commission [1994] ECR II-285...................... 161, 162
T-74/92 Ladbroke Racing v Commission [1995] ECR II-115 160
T-114/92 BEMIM v Commission [1995] ECR II-147....................... 158, 160
T-17/93 Matra Hachette v Commission [1994] ECR-II 595..................... 20, 32
T-548/93 Ladbroke Racing v Commission [1995] ECR-II 2565...................... 160
T-575/93 Koelman v Commission [1996] ECR II-1 161
T-374/94 European Night Services v Commission [1998] ECR II-3141.................. 32
T-395/94 Atlantic Container Line AB v Commission [2002] ECR II-875 .... 55, 177
T-112/98 Mannesmannröhren-Werke AG v Commission (2001) ECR II-729 91
T-112/99 Métropole télévision (M6) v Commission [2001] ECR II-2459.................. 34
T-219/99 British Airways Plc v Commission [2003] ECR II-5917 .... 38, 41
T-151/01 Der Grüne Punkt—Duales System Deutschland GmbH v Commission
    [2001] ECR II-1607... 35
T-168/01 GlaxoSmithKline Services v Commission [2006]
    ECR II-2969 .... 23, 24, 30, 31, 32
T-184/01 R IMS Health Inc v Commission [2001] ECR II—3193................... 38
T-208/01 Volkswagen v Commission [2003] ECR II–5141 159
T-213/01 and T-214/01 Oesterreichischer Postsparkasse AG v Commission
    [2006] ECR II-1601 .... 24, 158
T-22/02 and 23/02 Sumitomo Chemicals v Commission [2005] ECR II-4065 51
T-59/02 Archer Daniels Midland Co v Commission [2006] ECR II-3627................ 173

Table of Cases   xix

T-259/02 to T-264/02 and T-271/02 Raiffeisen Zentralbank Oesterreich AG
v Commission [2006] ECR II-5169...24
T-2/03 Verein für Konsumenteninformation v Commission [2005] ECR II-1121......94, 96, 97, 99
T-328/03 O2 (Germany) v Commission [2006] ECR II-1231...........................33
T-391/03 and T-70/04 Franchet and Byk v Commission [2006] ECR II-2023...............96
T-201/04 Microsoft Corp v Commission [2007] ECR II- 3601.......................23, 83
T-474/04 Pergan Hilfsstoffe v Commission [2007] ECR II-4225.......................104
T-229/05 AEPI v Commission [2007] ECR II-84...............................160, 161
T-237/05 Éditions Jacob v Commission [2010] ECR II-2245...........................96
T-306/05 Scippecercola and Terzakis v Commission [2008] ECR II-4..................160
T-403/05 My Travel v Commission [2008] ECR II-2027..............................96
T-155/06 Tomra Systems and Others v Commission [2010] ECR II-4361...............40, 41
T-111/07 Agrofert v Commission [2011] 4 CMLR 6.................................96
T-336/07 Telefonica and Telefonica de Espana v Commission [2007] OJ C269/55..........171
T-111/08 MasterCard Inc v Commission [2012] 5 CMLR 5.........................164
T-344/08 EnBW Energie Baden-Württemberg AG [2012] 5 CMLR 4.......58, 94, 99, 100, 105
T-380/08 Netherlands v Commission (judgment of 13 September 2013).................99
T-427/08 CEAHR v Commission [2011] 4 CMLR 14..............................162
T-437/08 CDC Hydrogen Perogide v Commission [2011] ECR II 8251......59, 92, 96, 98–100
T-286/09 Intel v Commission (judgment of 12 June 2014).............................41
T-224/10 Association belge des consommateurs test-achats ASBL
v Commission [2011] ECR II-7177...25
T-516/11 MasterCard Inc v Commission (judgment of 9 September 2014).................96
T-534/11 Schenker AG v European Commission (judgment of 7 October 2014)...........100
T-345/12 AKZO Nobel v Commission [2015] 4 CMLR 12......................101, 105

COMMISSION DECISIONS

1998 Football World Cup (Case IV/36.888) Commission Decision 2000/12/EC
[2000] OJ L5/55...36
Airfreight (Case COMP/39258) Commission decision of 9 November 2010...............100
Asahi [1994] OJ L 354/87..20
BPCL/ICI (Case IV/30.863) Commission Decision 84/387 [1984] OJ L212/1..............34
British Leyland Plc (Case IV/30.615) Commission Decision 84/379/EEC [1984]
OJ L 207/11...35
CECED [2000] OJ L 187/47...20
Chiquita (Case IV/26.699) Commission Decision 76/353/EEC [1976] OJ L95/1...........35
Deutsche Bahn I (Case COMP/AT.39678) Commission Decision
of 18 December 2013..173, 174, 179
Deutsche Bahn II (Case COMP/AT.39731)...............................173, 174, 179
Deutsche Post (Case COMP/C-1/36.915) Commission Decision
2001/892/EC [2001] OJ L331/40...35, 36
DSD (Case COMP D3/34493) Commission Decision 2001/463 [2001] L166/1............35
DSD (Commission Decision 2001/837) [2001] OJ L 319/1...........................20
EBU/Eurovision (Case IV/32.150) Commission Decision 93/404/EEC [1993]
OJ L179/23...34
Exxon-Shell [1994] OJ L144/21...20
Ford/Volkswagen (Case IV.33.814) Commission Decision 93/49 [1993]
OJ L20/14..20
General Motors Continental (Case IV/28.851) Commission Decision 75/75/EEC
[1975] OJ L29/14..35, 172, 174
Greek Ferries (Case IV/34.466) Commission Decision 1999/271/EC [1999]
OJ L 109/24..157

Hydrogen Peroxide and Perborate (Case COMP/F/38.620) Commission
  Decision of 5 June 2006, C(2006) 1766 final....................................64
Lombard Club (Case COMP 36.571/D-1) Commission Decision 2004/138/EC
  [2004] OJ L56/1..97
MasterCard, EuroCommerce and Commercial Cards (Case COMP/34.579,
  36.518 and 38.580) Commission Decision of 17 December 2007
  [2009] OJ C 264/8...164
Microsoft (Case COMP/C-3/37.792) Commission Decision of 24/3/2004,
  C(2004) 900 final..38
Peugeot (Cases COMP/E2/36623, 36820 and 37275) Commission Decision
  2006/431/EC [2006] OJ L173/20...157
Philips/Osram (Case IV/34.252) Commission Decision 94/986/EC [1994]
  OJ L378/37..20, 34
Pre-Insulated Pipe Cartel (Case No IV/35.691/E-4) Commission
  Decision 1999/60/EC [1999] OJ L24/1.....................................172, 174
Stichting Baksteen [1994] OJ L 131/15...20, 158
Synthetic Fibres (Case IV/30.810) Commission Decision 84/380/EEC
  [1984] OJ L207/17..20, 34
Volkswagen (Case COMP/F-2/36.693) Commission Decision 2001/711/EC
  [2001] OJ L 262/14..159
Wanadoo España v Telefonica [Case COMP/38.784] Commission Decision of
  July 04 July 2007 [2007] OJ C269/55...135

GERMANY

Amtsgericht Bonn, decision of 18 January 2012, case No 51 Gs 53/09 (Pfleiderer II)
  (January 2012)...94
Oberlandesgericht Düsseldorf, decision of 22 August 2012, case No B-4
  Kart 5/11 (OWi)..94

IRELAND

Competition Authority v O'Reagan and Others [2007] IESC 22.......................41

ITALY

Unipol judgment of the Italian Supreme Court (Corte di Cassazione,
  Decision No.2207/2005)...78

UNITED KINGDOM

2Travel Group PLC (in Liquidation) v Cardiff City Transport Services Ltd [2012]
  CAT 19...57
Association of Convenience Stores v OFT [2005] CAT 36..........................169
Attheraces Ltd v The British Horseracing Board Ltd and BHB Enterprises plc
  [2007] UKCLR 309...35
Black v Sumitomo [2001] EWCA Civ 1819...90
Burgess v OFT [2005] CAT 25...41, 171
Consumers' Association v JJB Sports Plc (Case No1078/7/9/07) [2009] CAT 2...128, 129
Cooper Tire and Rubber Company v Shell Chemicals UK [2010] EWCA Civ 864.........63
Deutsche Bahn AG and others v Morgan Crucible Company plc [2014] UKSC 24........64

Table of Cases

Devenish Nutrition Ltd v Sanofi-Aventis SA (France) [2008]
EWCA Civ 1086, [2009] 3 All ER 27...89
Emerald Supplies Ltd v British Airways Plc [2010] EWCA Civ 1284,
[2011] 2 WLR 203...131
Emerald Supplies Ltd v British Airways Plc [2014] EWHC 3513 (Ch)..................103–5
Hutchison 3G UK Ltd v O2 Ltd and others [2008] EWHC 55 (Comm)....................90
Napp Pharmaceuticals Holdings Ltd v Director General of Fair Trading
[2002] CAT 1..35
National Grid Electricity Transmission Plc v ABB Ltd [2011] EWHC 1717 (Ch)...........102
National Grid Electricity Transmission Plc v ABB Ltd [2012] EWHC 869 (Ch)............94
National Grid plc v Gas and Electricity Markets Authority [2009] CAT 21................41
Nokia AU Optronics and others [2012] EWHC 731 (Ch)..............................63
Provimi Ltd v Aventis Animal Nutrition SA and others [2003] 2 All ER 683...............63
Prudential Assurance Co Ltd v Newman Industries Ltd [1981] Ch.229, [1980]
2 WLR 339...131
R v Secretary of State for Transport, ex p Factortame Ltd [1991] 1 AC 693 (HL)..........50
Toshiba Carrier UK Ltd v KME Yorkshire Ltd [2012] EWCA Civ 1190...................63
Trouw UK Ltd v Mitsui & Co (UK) plc [2007] EWHC 863 (Comm)....................90

UNITED STATES OF AMERICA

Amchem v Windsor Products 117 SCt 2231 (1997)...................................113
Bell Atlantic Corp et al v Twombly et al 550 US 127 SCt 1955 (2007)....................90
Blue Shield of Virginia v McCready 457 US 465 (1982)...............................114
Brunswick Corp v Pueblo Bowl-O-Mat, Inc 429 US 477 (1977).........................114
California v ARC America Corp 490 US 93, 109 SCt 1661 (1989).......................81
Deposit Guarantee Bank v Roper, 445 US 326 (1980)................................113
Eisen v Carlisle, 417 US 156 (1974)...119
Hanover Shoe, Inc v United Shoe Machinery Corp 392 US 481,
88 SCt 2224 (1968)...80, 81
Hawaii v Standard Oil and Co 405 US 251-254 (1972)...............................123
Illinois Brick Co v Illinois, 431 US 720, 97 SCt 2061 (1977).....................80–3, 121
Mitsubishi Motors Corp v Soler Chrysler Plymouth 473 US 614 (1985)..................114
Ortiz v Fibreboard 119 SCt 2295 (1999)...113
Phillips Petroleum Co v Shutts 472 US 797 (1985)...................................113
Verizon Communications Inc v Law Offices of Curtis V Trinko,
LLP 540 US 398, 407, 124 SCt 872 (2004)....................................35

Table of Legislation

TREATIES AND CONVENTIONS

Charter of Fundamental Rights of the
    European Union
    Art 38 25
    Art 41 163
    Art 42 95
    Art 43 160
    Art 47 .58, 67, 142
Convention on Access to Information,
    Public Participation in
    Decision-Making and Access to
    Justice in Environmental Matters
    (Aarhus Convention). 139
CJEU Statute
    Art 40(2) 170
    Art 53(1) 170
European Convention on Human
    Rights and Fundamental Freedoms
    Art 6 . . . . 22, 66, 142
    Art 13 22
Lisbon Treaty 2007 . . . . .18, 21, 186
Protocol (No 21) on the position of the
    United Kingdom and Ireland in
    respect of the Area of Freedom,
    Security and Justice. 197
Protocol (No 27) on the Internal
    Market and Competition. 18, 21
Protocol (No 25) on the Exercise of
    Shared Competence. 186
Treaty establishing the European
    Community (TEC)
    Art 2 18
    Art 3 18
    Art 65 . . . . .190, 196
    Art 95 190
    Art 175(1) 190
    Art 255 95
Treaty of Amsterdam. 13, 197
Treaty on European Union
    (Maastricht Treaty) 13
Treaty on European Union
    (Lisbon Treaty) (TEU)
    Art 3 18
    Art 3(3) 18
    Art 4(3) 41, 50, 56
    Art 5(1) 190

Art 5(2) 190
Art 5(3) 186
Art 10(3) 69
Art 11 69
Art 11(4) 72
Art 19(1) 50
Art 51 21
Treaty on the Functioning of the
    European Union (TFEU)
    Art 1(1) 190
    Art 3(1)(b) 186
    Art 7 18
    Art 9 18
    Art 11 18
    Art 12 . . . . .18, 25
    Art 15(3) 95, 96
    Art 26 192
    Art 81 . . . . 190, 194, 196–8
    Art 81(2) 196
    Art 101 . . . . 1, 6, 15, 21, 26, 28, 32,
                    34, 42, 43, 54, 55, 57, 171,
                    174, 194, 195, 200
    Art 101(1). 19, 20, 26, 28–34, 195
    Art 101(2) 47
    Art 101(3) 19, 20, 23, 24, 26, 28,
                    32, 34, 195
    Art 102 . . . . 1, 6, 15, 16, 19, 26, 35–42,
                   55, 171, 173, 194, 195, 200
    Art 102(b) 26
    Art 102(c) 36
    Art 103 . . . . 190–2, 194–6, 198–201
    Art 103(1) 191, 195
    Art 103(2) 195
    Art 103(2)(a) 195
    Art 103(2)(e) 194
    Art 114. . . . . .190–4, 197, 198
    Art 147(2) 18
    Art 167(4) 18
    Art 168(1) 18
    Art 169 198
    Art 169(2) 190
    Art 169(2)(a) 198
    Art 169(2)(b) 198
    Art 175 18
    Art 192(1) 190
    Art 208 18
    Art 263(4) 160

Art 265 160
Art 288 ....111, 160, 202
Art 289(1) 190
Art 289(2) 191
Art 294 190
Art 352 ....190, 191, 198, 200

EU INSTRUMENTS

EU REGULATIONS

Regulation No 17/62: First Regulation
  Implementing Articles 85 and 86
  of the Treaty [1962] OJ Spec Ed 87
Art 9(1) 52
Art 12 164
Regulation No 123/85 on the application
  of Article 81(3) of the Treaty
  to certain categories of motor
  vehicle distribution and servicing
  agreements [1985] OJ L15/16........157
Regulation No 2790/1999 on the
  Application of Article 81(3) of the
  Treaty to Categories of Vertical
  Agreements and Concerted Practices
  [1999] OJ L 336/21 20
Regulation No 44/2001 on Jurisdiction
  and the Recognition and
  Enforcement of Judgments in
  Civil and Commercial Matters
  [2001] OJ L12/1 ....133, 188
Regulation No 1049/2001 regarding
  public access to European
  Parliament, Council and
  Commission documents [2001]
  OJ L145/43 ....94, 95, 97, 99, 105
Recitals 1-4 95
Art 4 96
Art 4(1)(b) 98
Art 4(2) 96–9
Art 4(3) 96
Art 6(3) 98
Regulation No 1206/2001 on Cooperation
  between Courts of the Member States
  in the Taking of Evidence in Civil
  and Commercial Matters [2001]
  OJ L174/1 188
Regulation No 1/2003 on the
  Implementation of the Rules on
  Competition Laid Down in
  Articles 81 and 82 of the Treaty
  [2003] OJ L1/1 .... 1, 20, 43, 47,
                     53, 70, 95, 96, 101, 158, 163,
                     165, 166, 169, 187, 200–2

Recital 5.........................187
Recital 8....................162, 194
Recital 9........................195
Recital 15.......................162
Recital 18..................162, 163
Recital 23 91
Art 2 187
Art 3 ....162, 189, 194
Art 7 177
Art 7(2) 158, 163
Art 9 ....173, 179
Art 11 ....162, 201
Art 13 170
Art 16(1) 97
Art 17 163
Art 23(2) 178
Art 23(3) 178
Art 27 .... 95, 99
Art 27(1) 159
Art 27(3) 170
Art 28 .... 95, 99
Art 33 201
Regulation No 139/2004 on the
  Control of Concentrations Between
  Undertakings [2004] OJ L24/1
Recitals 2-3 200
Recitals 5-7 200
Recital 7........................ 200
Regulation No 773/2004 relating to the
  Conduct of Proceedings by
  the Commission pursuant to
  Articles 81 and 82 of the
  EC Treaty [2004] OJ L123/18....... 95,
                      160, 163, 201, 202
Recital 11.......................170
Art 5(1) 159
Arts 6-8........................159
Art 7 201
Art 13(1) 170
Art 13(3) 171
Art 15.......................... 95, 99
Art 16 .... 95, 99
Regulation No 802/2004 implementing
  Council Regulation (EC)
  No 139/2004 on the control of
  concentrations between
  undertakings [2004] OJ L 133/1
Art 11(c)........................170
Regulation No 2006/2004 on
  cooperation between national
  authorities responsible for the
  enforcement of consumer
  protection laws [2004] OJ L364/1
Art 1 112

Art 2(4) 112
Art 3(k) 112
Regulation No 1367/2006 on the
  Application of the Provisions
  of the Aarhus Convention on
  Access to Information, Public
  Participation in Decision Making and
  Access to Justice in Environmental
  Matters to Community
  Institutions and Bodies [2006]
  OJ L264/13 ....105, 140
  Recital 15 105
  Art 6(1) 105
  Art 11 140
Regulation No 861/2007 on the
  European Small Claims Procedure
  [2007] OJ L199/1 188
  Art 16 146
Regulation No 622/2008 amending
  Regulation (EC) No 773/2004,
  as regards the conduct of
  settlement procedures in cartel
  cases [2008] OJ L171/3
  Recital 4 178
Regulation No 1217/2010 on the
  application of Article 101(3) of
  the Treaty on the Functioning of
  the European Union to certain
  categories of research and development
  agreements [2010] OJ L335/36
  Recital 10 26
Regulation No 1218/2010 on the
  application of 101(3) of the Treaty
  on the Functioning of the European
  Union to certain categories of
  specialisation agreements [2010]
  OJ L335/43
  Recital 6 26
  Recital 10 26
Regulation No 1250/2012 on
  jurisdiction and the recognition
  and enforcement of judgments
  in civil and commercial matters
  (recast) [2012] OJ L351/1 ......88, 133
  Art 30 88
Regulation No 524/2013 on online
  dispute resolution for consumer
  disputes and amending Regulation
  (EC) No 2006/2004 and Directive
  2009/22/EC [2013] OJ L165/1 70
Regulation No 254/2014 on a multiannual
  consumer programme for the years
  2014-20 and repealing Decision No
  1926/2006/EC [2014] OJ L84/42

Art 2 67
Art 3(1)(b) 67
Art 5 146

EU DIRECTIVES

Directive 98/6/EC on Consumer
  Protection in the Indication
  of Prices of Products Offered to
  Consumers [1998] OJ L80/27 198
Directive 98/27/EC on Injunctions
  for the Protection of Consumers'
  Interests [1998] OJ L166/51
  Art 1 112
Directive 1999/34/EC amending
  Council Directive 85/374/EEC on
  the approximation of the laws,
  regulations and administrative
  provisions of the Member States
  concerning liability of defective
  products 188, 197
Directive 2002/8/EC of 27 January 2003
  to Improve Access to Justice in
  Cross-border Disputes by
  Establishing Minimum Common
  Rules Relating to Legal Aid for
  Such Disputes [2003] OJ L 26/41 188
Directive 2004/35/EC of 21 April 2004
  on environmental liability with
  regard to the prevention and
  remedying of environmental damage
  [2004] OJ L 143/56 ....70, 188,
                                190, 197
Directive 2004/48/EC on the
  enforcement of intellectual property
  rights [2004] OJ L 195/16 ......188, 193
  Recital 3 193
  Recital 8 193
  Recital 9 193
  Art 14 146
Directive 2007/66/EC amending
  Council Directives 89/665/EEC
  and 92/13/EEC with regard to
  improving the effectiveness of
  review procedures concerning the
  award of public contracts [2007]
  OJ L335/31 188
Directive 2009/22/EC on Injunctions
  for the Protection of Consumers'
  Interests (codified version) [2009]
  OJ L110/30 ....122, 140
  Recital 3 112
  Art 1 ....112, 123

Art 3 140
Art 4(3) 140
Directive 2011/83/EU of the
European Parliament and the
Council on Consumer Rights'
[2011] L 304/64
Art 2 24
Directive 2013/11/EU on Alternative
Dispute Resolution for
Consumer Disputes and
Amending Regulation (EC) 2006/
2004 and Directive 2009/22/EC
[2013] L165/63 69
Directive 2014/104/EU of the European
Parliament and of the Council of
26 November 2014 on Certain
Rules Governing Actions for
Damages Under National Law for
Infringements of the Competition
Law Provisions of the Member
States and of the European Union
[2014] OJ L 349/1 ..... 1, 3, 5, 47, 57, 59,
    63, 70, 75, 91, 94, 104, 110, 111,
    182, 184, 187, 190, 191, 205, 206
  Recital 1 61
  Recital 3 61
  Recital 5 178
  Recital 6 63
  Recital 7 192
  Recital 8 192
  Recital 12 57
  Recital 15 .... 92, 93
  Recital 16 92
  Recital 18 92
  Recital 25 105
  Recital 40 86
  Recital 54 195
  Art 1(1) 195
  Art 2(20) 79
  Art 3 57
  Art 3(1) 84, 86
  Art 5 91
  Art 5(1) 91
  Art 5(2) 92
  Art 5(3) 92, 102
  Art 5(4) 92
  Art 5(5) 92
  Art 5(6) 93
  Art 5(7) 93
  Art 5(8) 93
  Arts 5–7 182
  Art 6 102
  Art 6(5) 102, 105
  Art 6(6) 64, 102
  Art 7(1) 91, 102
  Art 7(2) 91, 103
  Art 7(3) 91, 103
  Art 9 97
  Art 9(2) 97
  Art 11(4) 64
  Art 12(1) 86
  Art 12(3) 86
  Arts 12–14 182
  Art 13 88
  Art 14(1) 87
  Art 14(2) 87
  Art 15(1) 88, 89
  Art 15(2) 88
  Art 16 87
  Art 18(3) 178

EU RECOMMENDATIONS

Commission (EU) Recommendation
of 11 June 2013 on common
principles for injunctive and
compensatory collective redress
mechanisms in the Member
States concerning violations
of rights granted under Union
Law [2013] OJ L 201/60 .... 2, 5,
    94, 107, 110, 116, 138, 139, 141,
    144, 145, 179, 182, 185, 186, 197

EU NOTICES

Commission (EC) Notice on Cooperation
Between National Courts and the
Commission in applying Articles 85
and 86 of the EEC Treaty [1993]
OJ C39/6 53
Commission (EC) Notice on
Cooperation within the Network
of Competition Authorities [2004]
OJ C101/43 .... 3, 163
Commission (EC) Notice on the
conduct of settlement procedures
in view of the adoption
of Decisions pursuant to Article 7
and Article 23 of Council
Regulation (EC) No 1/2003 in cartel
cases [2008] OJ C167/1 .... 103, 178

Commission (EC) Notice on the
 Cooperation Between the
 Commission and the Courts of
 the EU Member States in the
 Application of Articles 81 and 82
 EC [2004] OJ C101/54 . . . . 3, 53, 95
Commission (EC) Notice on the
 Handling of Complaints by the
 Commission under Articles 81
 and 82 of the EC Treaty [2004]
 OJ C101/65 . . . . 3, 53, 156, 158, 159,
 160, 161, 163
Commission (EC) Notice on the
 Rules for Access to the Commission
 File [2005] OJ C325/7. 95
Commission (EU) Notice on Best
 Practices for the Conduct
 of Proceedings Concerning
 Articles 101 and 102 TFEU [2011]
 OJ C 308/6 170
Commission (EU) Notice on Immunity
 from fines and reduction of fines
 in cartel cases [2006]
 OJ C298/17. . . . . .95, 103
Commission (EU) Notice on the conduct
 of settlement procedures in view of
 the adoption of Decision pursuant to
 Article 7 and Article 23 of Council
 Regulation (EC) No 1/2003 in cartel
 cases [2008] OJ C 167/1 95
Commission (EU) Notice published
 pursuant to Article 27(4) of Council
 Regulation (EC) No 1/2003 in
 Case COMP/C- 3/39.530 — Microsoft
 (Tying) [2009] OJ C 242/20. 24

EU GUIDELINES

Commission (EC) Guidance on the
 Commission's Enforcement
 Priorities in Applying Article 82 EC
 of the EC Treaty to Abusive
 Exclusionary Conduct by Dominant
 Undertakings [2009] OJ C45/7. 24
Commission (EC) Guidelines on the
 Application of Article 81 of the
 EC Treaty to Technology Transfer
 Agreements [2004] C101/02 . . . . . .17, 26
Commission (EC) Guidelines on the
 Application of Article 81(3) of the
 Treaty [2004] OJ C101/08 . . . . . . 17, 20,
 23–6, 29, 32, 33, 34

Commission (EC) Guidelines on the
 assessment of horizontal mergers
 under the Council Regulation on the
 control of concentrations between
 undertakings [2004] OJ C 31/5. 24
Commission (EC) Guidelines on the
 Method of Setting Fines Imposed
 Pursuant to Article 23(2) (a)
 of Regulation No 1/2003 [2006]
 OJ C210/2. 152
Commission (EC) Guidelines on
 Vertical Restraints (Notice) [2000]
 OJ C 291/01 . . . . 20, 26
Commission (EU) Guidelines on the
 Applicability of Article 101 of the
 Treaty on the Functioning of the
 European Union to Horizontal
 Co-operation Agreements [2011]
 OJ C 11/1 . . . . 26, 33
Commission (EU) Guidelines on the
 Application of Article 101 of the
 Treaty on the Functioning of
 the European Union to Technology
 Transfer Agreements [2014] C 89/3 26
Commission (EU) Guidelines on
 Vertical Restraints [2010]
 OJ C 130/1 . . . . .17, 26, 33

NATIONAL LEGISLATION

France
Consumer Code 130
 Article L 422-1 127
Law No 2014-344 130
 Art L423-1. 130
 Art L423-3–5 130
 Art L423-10. 130
 Art L423-17. 130

Germany
Act Against Restraints of Competition Art
 33(3) 83

Greece
Consumer Code .131
L2251/1994
 Art 10(16) 132
 Art 10(20) 132
L3587/2007. 131

Spain
Civil Procedure Act 2000 134

Competition Act 15/2007 of 3 July
  Art 64(3)(c) 178

Sweden
Group Proceedings Act 2002 129

United Kingdom
Competition Act 1998 .... 135, 155
  s 47B 128
  s 47B(2) 135
  s 47B(5) 135, 136
  s 47B(6) 136
  s 47B(7) 136
  s 47B(10) 136
  s 47B(11) 136
  s 47C(2) 136
  s 47C(3) 136
  s 47C(5) 136
  s 47C(6) 136
  s 47C(8) 136
  s 47C(9)(b) 136
  s 49A 136
  s 49B 136
  s 49C 136
  s 60 189
Consumer Rights Act 2015 135,
                             142, 155, 179
  s 81 135
  Sch 8 .... 135, 155
Courts and Legal Services Act 1990
  s 53AA(3) 136
Civil Procedure Rules 1998
  r 19.6 131
  r 31.16 90
Enterprise Act 2002 .... 166, 167
  s 11(1) 167, 201
  s 11(2) 168
  s 11(9)(a) 167
  s 131(2) 167
  s 205 167
Enterprise Act 2002 (Super-complaints
  to Regulators) Order 2003
  (SI 2003/1368) 167
Enterprise and Regulatory Reform
  Act 2013 166
Financial Services Act 2012
  s 40 168
Financial Services and Markets
  Act 2000
  s 234C 168
Legal Services Act 2007
  s 194(8) 136
Legal Services Act 2007
  (Prescribed Charity) Order
  2008 (SI 2008/2680) 136

United States
Class Action Fairness Act, Pub L
  109–2, 119 Stat 4
  (18 Feb 2005) 121
Federal Rules of Civil Procedure
  r 23 142
  r 23(a) 119
  r 23(b)(1) 113
  r 23(b)(2) 113
  r 23(b)(3) 113, 119
  r 23(c)(2)(b) 119
  r 23(e)(1) 119
  r 23(e)(4) 119
  r 23(g)(1) 120
Hart Scott Rodino Antitrust
  Improvements Act of 1976,
  Pub L No 94–435, 90
  Stat 1383 (1976) 123

List of Abbreviations

AG	Attorney General
AJCL	American Journal of Comparative Law
ALI	American Law Institute
AMC	Antitrust Modernization Commission
ASCOLA	Academic Society for Competition Law
BA	British Airways
BDI	Bundesverband der Deutschen Industrie
BERR	Department for Business, Enterprise and Regulatory Reform
BEUC	The European Consumer Organisation
BIS	Department for Business, Innovation & Skills
CA	Competition Act
CAFA	Class Action Fairness Act
CAT	Competition Appeal Tribunal
CBI	Confederation of British Industry
CC	Competition Commission
CDC	Cartel Damage Claims
CEPR	Centre for Economic Policy Research
CJC	Civil Justice Council
CJEU	Court of Justice of the European Union
CJQ	Civil Justice Quarterly
CLES	Centre for Law, Economics and Society
CLJ	Cambridge Law Journal
CMA	Competition and Markets Authority
CMLR	Common Market Law Reports
Comp L Rev	Competition Law Review
CMLRev	Common Market Law Review
CPI	Competition Policy International
CPN	Competition Policy Newsletter
CPR	Civil Procedure Rules
CPRev	Consumer Policy Review
DB	Deutsche Bahn
DBA	Damages-Based Agreements
DG SANCO	Directorate General for Health & Consumers
DTI	Department of Trade and Industry
EA	Enterprise Act
EBLR	European Business Law Review
EBOR	European Business Organization Law Review
EC	European Community
ECCG	European Consumer Consultative Group
ECHR	European Convention on Human Rights
ECJ	Court of Justice
ECLR	European Competition Law Review
ECN	European Competition Network

List of Abbreviations

ECR	European Court Reports
ECtHR	European Court of Human Rights
EEA	European Economic Area
EESC	European Economic and Social Committee
ELI	European Law Institute
ELJ	European Law Journal
EP	European Parliament
ERPL	European Review of Private Law
ERRA	Enterprise and Regulatory Reform Act
ESC	Economic and Social Committee
EU	European Union
EUI	European University Institute
EUMR	European Merger Regulation
EWCA Civ	Court of Appeal Civil Division
EWHC (Ch)	High Court (Chancery Division)
FCA	Financial Conduct Authority
FIDE	International Federation for European Law
FRCP	Federal Rules of Civil Procedure
GC	General Court
GCLR	Global Competition Litigation Review
GLO	Group Litigation Order
GM	General Motors
GP	Green Paper
GWB	Gesetz gegen Wettbewerbsbeschränkungen
IAR	Impact Assessment Report
IBA	International Bar Association
ICLQ	International and Comparative Law Quarterly
ICN	International Competition Network
ICON	International Journal of Constitutional Law
IE	Instituto de Empresa Business School
ILSA	International Law Students Association
IP	Intellectual Property
JAE	Journal of Antitrust Enforcement
JCLE	Journal of Competition Law and Economics
JCP	Journal of Consumer Policy
JECLAP	Journal of European Competition Law & Practice
JEPP	Journal of European Public Policy
JITE	Journal of Institutional and Theoretical Economics
JLEO	Journal of Law, Economics & Organization
LCD	Liquid-Crystal Display
LQR	Law Quarterly Review
LS	Legal Studies
LT	Lisbon Treaty
MLR	Modern Law Review
NCA	National Competition Authority
NGO	Non-governmental Organization
ODR	Online Dispute Resolution
OECD	Organisation for Economic Co-operation and Development
OFCOM	Office of Communications

OFGEM	Office of Gas and Electricity Markets
OFT	Office of Fair Trading
OJ	Official Journal
OJLS	Oxford Journal of Legal Studies
PCA	Personal Current Account
PIN	Personal Identification Number
SCOTUS	Supreme Court of the United States
SMEs	Small and Medium-sized Enterprises
SWD	Staff Working Document
SWP	Staff Working Paper
TEC	Treaty establishing the European Community
TEU	Treaty on European Union
TFEU	Treaty on the Functioning of the European Union
UK	United Kingdom
UKCLR	United Kingdom Competition Law Reports
US	United States
USC	United States Code
VKI	Verein für Konsumenteninformation
WP	White Paper
YEL	Yearbook of European Law

1
Introduction

1. Background

The past 15 years have seen radical changes in EU competition law enforcement, both substantive and procedural. The European Commission's (Commission) efforts to imbue EU competition law with a more economic approach began in the late 1990s; these efforts were successful with regard to the enforcement of Article 101 of the Treaty on the Functioning of the European Union (TFEU) and merger control but remained sketchy in relation to Article 102 TFEU. A recurring theme in the Commission's past efforts has been a rhetorical emphasis on consumer welfare and competition law's potential to promote consumer interest. In fact, the 'more economic approach' was hailed for its potential to bring more benefits to consumers.

At about the same time, the Commission embarked on a substantial procedural reform. Regulation 1/2003 changed the enforcement landscape,[1] strengthening the role of national actors: national competition authorities (NCAs) and courts. Central to these attempts was the aim to strengthen private competition law enforcement alongside the primary public enforcement model in the EU.

The debate on the inadequacy of private enforcement was reinvigorated with the publication of the Ashurst study in 2004,[2] following which the Commission led the debate regarding improvement of the conditions for bringing damages claims in Europe. Consumers' inability to raise damages claims in competition law often emerged as a recurring problem during this debate. A decade later, the EU Directive on Damages Actions has finally been adopted.[3] This is a welcome development, although the adopted legislation is a watered-down version of previous proposals and does not contain binding provisions on collective actions.

---

[1] Council Regulation (EC) 1/2003 on the Implementation of the Rules on Competition Laid Down in Articles 81 and 82 of the Treaty [2003] OJ L1/1.

[2] D Waelbroeck, D Slater, and G Even-Shoshan, 'Study on the Conditions of Claims for Damages in Case of Infringement of EC Competition Rules' (Comparative Report) (Ashurst Study) (31 August 2004) <http://ec.europa.eu/competition/antitrust/actionsdamages/comparative_report_clean_en.pdf> accessed 30 June 2014.

[3] Directive 2014/104/EU of the European Parliament and of the Council of 26 November 2014 on Certain Rules Governing Actions for Damages Under National Law for Infringements of the Competition Law Provisions of the Member States and of the European Union [2014] OJ L349/1.

The latter are discussed in the Commission Recommendation,[4] which discusses non-binding common principles that will arguably prove inadequate for the bringing of collective actions for competition law violations. As such, recent developments in private enforcement of EU competition law render questionable whether they can improve the consumer's role therein.

The central tenet of this book is located at this juncture, as it explores the role of consumer interest and consumer participation in EU competition law enforcement. It focuses on the private enforcement of competition law and aims to examine the importance of consumer interest in EU competition law with a view to reshaping the enforcement mechanisms in the competition law field. It discusses the justifications for more active consumer participation as well as the necessary remedial and procedural tools to facilitate such participation. The structure and methodology are prescribed by two factors, namely the reported shift in EU competition law towards a consumer welfare-oriented approach (policy and substantive factors) and the EU debate on private competition law enforcement and consumer collective redress procedures (procedural factor).

Building on the identified policy, substantive, and procedural factors, a two-part structure is employed incorporating the individual chapters. The first normative part essentially builds the framework upon which the book is premised. It deals with policy implications and normative justifications for increased consumer involvement in competition law. After the first part has formulated the normative framework and placed the whole debate regarding consumer involvement in competition law in a wider EU law perspective, the second practical part moves on to address the remedial and procedural measures necessary to allow such involvement.

2. Nature of the Subject Matter

This book deals with consumer participation in private EU competition law enforcement. Its subject matter is addressed primarily from an EU competition law perspective, but in reality it is much broader and has to tackle many challenging issues from the wider EU law discipline. This explains why some broader themes, not confined to EU competition law, recur throughout the analysis. Some of these points concern consumer participation in general, whereas others pertain to the relevant consumer participation either in private or public competition law enforcement. However, all of these aspects help to locate the book's central topic within the wider contemporary EU law debates. These recurring themes are introduced briefly here, in order to show the wide variety of complex issues involved when trying to justify increased consumer participation in EU

---

[4] Commission (EU), 'Recommendation of 11 June 2013 on Common Principles for Injunctive and Compensatory Collective Redress Mechanisms in the Member States Concerning Violations of Rights Granted under Union Law' [2013] OJ L201/60.

Nature of the Subject Matter

competition law enforcement and formulate appropriate measures for facilitating such participation.

2.1 EU competition law enforcement: A fused approach

The first contentious issue concerns the different approaches to the enforcement system in EU competition law, which is comprised of both public and private mechanisms.[5] The most pronounced aims of the EU competition law enforcement system are deterrence and compensation.[6] While the traditional view suggests a clear attribution of these functions to public and private enforcement respectively, this book advocates a fused and integrated approach to competition law enforcement, as the analysis in the individual chapters will reveal. This approach reinforces the underlying substantive aims of EU competition law, acknowledges the importance of private actors and private claims in the EU legal order, and justifies the increased consumer participation in EU competition law enforcement advocated herein.

2.2 The consumer's role in EU competition law enforcement

The consumer's role is influenced by the fused approach to EU competition law enforcement that was briefly described above. This book does not treat the consumer as a self-interested motivated individual seeking to redress damage flowing from EU competition law violations. On the contrary, the consumer's role is systemic. In this book, the assumption is that competition law is relevant to consumers, and that consumers are equally relevant to competition law. Through appropriately formulated enforcement mechanisms, consumers could assume an instrumental role in competition law enforcement, further promoting the aims of the system as a whole. Arguments to this end are first drawn from the contemporary debates in EU consumer and competition law. Consumers not only stand to benefit from well-functioning markets but also assume a more active role in promoting and sustaining them. Their participation both in private enforcement and in EU competition law enforcement in general could be viewed as a means

---

[5] Regulation 1/2003 (n 1); see also Commission (EC), 'Notice on Cooperation within the Network of Competition Authorities' [2004] OJ C101/43; Commission (EC), 'Notice on the Handling of Complaints by the Commission under Articles 81 and 82 of the EC Treaty' [2004] OJ C101/65; Commission (EC), 'Notice on the Cooperation between the Commission and the Courts of the EU Member States in the Application of Articles 81 and 82 EC' [2004] OJ C101/54.

[6] Regarding the aims of the EU competition law enforcement system see W Wils, 'The Relationship between Public Antitrust Enforcement and Private Actions for Damages' (2009) 32 W Comp 3, 5. See also A Komninos, 'Relationship between Public and Private Enforcement: Quod Dei Deo, Quod Caesaris Caesari' in P Lowe and M Marquis (eds), *European Competition Law Annual 2011* (Hart 2014) 141, 141–142. To the deterrence and compensatory elements Wils also adds the task of law clarification: see W Wils, *Efficiency and Justice in European Antitrust Enforcement* (Hart 2008) 50.

to achieve this end and fits well with proposals and efforts to increase consumer empowerment.[7]

2.3 Function of tort law

Another, related, contentious issue is whether the fused approach to competition law enforcement and the functional consumer role therein can be reconciled with the principal compensatory function of tort law.[8] Notwithstanding its principal function, tort law is also attributed a deterrent function.[9] In fact, neither compensation nor deterrence can solely explain the multiple applications of tort law.[10] Ideally the two functions should be reconciled but, even in the case of conflict, it is possible that deterrence may be the preferred function for certain forms of economic behaviour. This book argues in favour of a primary deterrent function of damages actions for low-value consumer claims that further allows a partial fulfilment of the compensatory function. Arguments to that effect are drawn from the EU institutions' approach to private EU competition law enforcement, as well as from the nature of consumer claims.

2.4 Harmonization: Unity or diversity?

The pertaining different Member States' approaches towards tort law and civil procedure raise the issue of how much harmonization is permissible or even desirable. Even if the relevant need is identified and the legal issue of the EU's competence to introduce harmonized measures on consumer participation in private competition law enforcement is resolved, the different approaches of national legal systems with regard to remedies and procedures remain a significant issue. One is then confronted by bottom-up pressures exerted by individual Member States claiming that they are protecting their national legal systems and opposing any harmonized measures proposed. Part of this opposition could be seen as an attempt to protect national legal systems in their cultural context, and much has

---

[7] Commission (EU), 'EU Consumer Policy Strategy 2007–2013' COM(2007) 99 final, 5; Commission (EU), 'Single Market Act—Twelve Levers to Boost Growth and Strengthen Confidence' (Communication) COM(2011) 206 final, para 2.4; see Commission (EU), 'Consumer Empowerment in the EU' (Staff Working Paper) SEC(2011) 469 final.

[8] W van Gerven, J Lever, and P Larouche, *Tort Law* (Hart 2000) 19, 30, 740. The main opposing approaches to tort law theory stem from the law and economics school of thought and from justice-driven theories. For two interesting collections of essays on these different approaches to tort law see E Weinrib (ed), *Tort Law* (Ashgate 2002); D Owen (ed), *Philosophical Foundations of Tort Law* (Clarendon Press 1995). On the law and economics approach see W Landes and R Posner, *The Economic Structure of Tort Law* (Harvard University Press 1987). For a concise presentation of these two approaches and their main representatives see G Schwartz, 'Mixed Theories of Tort Law: Affirming Both Deterrence and Corrective Justice' (1997) 75 Texas L Rev 1801, 1802–1811.

[9] S Deakin, A Johnston, and B Markesinis, *Markesinis and Deakin's Tort Law* (Clarendon 2008) 50–52; P Cane, *The Anatomy of Tort Law* (Hart 1997) 217–225.

[10] *Schwartz* (n 8) 1801; I England, 'The Idea of Complementarity as a Philosophical Basis for Pluralism in Tort Law' in Owen (ed), *Philosophical Foundations of Tort Law* (Clarendon Press 1995) 183.

been written on the culturally embedded nature of legal systems and the impossibility of successful legal transplants.[11] At the same time, however, part of this opposition is an expression of political opportunism. Ultimately, how to satisfy this opposition is a complex political matter that may, at times, impede the adoption of effective legal solutions.

3. Methodology and Terminological Clarifications

In developing a theoretical framework on consumer involvement in EU private competition law enforcement and suggesting remedial and procedural measures for its realization, this book examines both EU institutions' and individual Member States' approaches. It also takes due account of the opinions of other stakeholders, such as businesses and consumer organizations. The aim is to address the diverse legal and political hurdles that permeate the analysis.

First, the relevant EU legal sources and policy documents are reviewed. EU legislation and the relevant EU case law, as well as the Commission's approaches to date, are also examined. The Commission's past efforts in advancing private enforcement of EU competition law, culminating in the adoption of the EU Directive on Damages Actions, can serve as a useful starting point, since these show a tendency to adopt modest measures and may well influence future initiatives in this field. The Commission's Recommendation in the field of collective redress can also be read in this vein. The measures proposed in this book reflect the approaches of the Union's institutions with regard to the aims and functions of private competition law enforcement.

At the same time, however, any proposed measures need to attract Member States' consent; if they do not, any proposals to adopt harmonized legislation will be doomed to fail. Therefore, the analysis also takes into account Member States' approaches towards remedial and civil procedure rules, as well as the US federal class action model. However, it does not present itself as a comparative venture. It draws upon publicized materials on private competition law enforcement and collective redress, comprising Commission reports, national reports, stakeholder comments, and other academic reports that present quantitative and qualitative data on Member States' legal systems and litigation levels. In addition, personal contacts with consumer organizations are helpful in discerning the consumer view. The aim is to unravel different national trends that could potentially serve as examples and guidance for future steps to be taken at the EU level.

---

[11] P Legrand, *Fragments on Law as Culture* (W.E.J. Tjeenk Willink 1999); P Legrand, 'European Legal Systems are not Converging' (1996) 45 ICLQ 52; P Legrand, 'The Impossibility of Legal Transplants' (1997) 4 Maastricht J Eur & Comp L 111; G Teubner, 'Legal Irritants: Good Faith in British Law or How Unifying Law Ends Up in New Divergencies' (1998) 61 MLR 11. For the opposite view see A Watson, *Legal Transplants: An Approach to Comparative Law* (2nd edn, University of Georgia Press 1993).

Furthermore, some terminological clarifications are needed. This book often refers to the consumer role in competition law *enforcement* and the formulation of the necessary facilitating *remedial* and *procedural measures*. A broad approach to 'enforcement' encompasses mechanisms and procedures that permit the application of the substantive competition law rules (Articles 101 and 102 TFEU and their national equivalents) by public authorities and national courts (*procedural enforcement*), as well as the actual enforcement standard itself (*substantive enforcement*). The enforcement standard refers to the fulfilment of the aims of EU competition law (retaining a competitive market structure, market integration, consumer welfare, etc).[12] Unless otherwise stated, in this book 'enforcement' refers to the former, and encompasses both public mechanisms (Commission and NCA actions) and private mechanisms (damages claims before national courts).

Clarifying the content of procedural measures and distinguishing them from remedial measures is a complex task.[13] A 'right' constitutes a legal position that a person, recognized as such by law, may have and which can be enforced by that person by means of 'remedies' according to the relevant 'procedures' intended to make such remedies operational.[14] The distinction between rights and remedies has a common law flavour in the sense that, in civil law countries such as Germany, once a person is granted a legal right this also entails the power to pursue the enforcement of that right.[15] Remedies are inalienable from rights.[16] The category of procedural rules is narrower, and encompasses rules on judicial organization, jurisdiction, and the rules of procedure before the courts.[17] When reference is made in this book to 'remedial and procedural' measures, this is to

---

[12] See Chapter 2 ('Consumer Interest' and the Aims of EU Competition Law), text to nn 17–61.
[13] W van Gerven, 'Of Rights, Remedies and Procedures' (2000) 37 CMLRev 501. On the difficulties in distinguishing between procedural, remedial, and substantive rules see also FG Jacobs and T Deisenhofer, 'Procedural Aspects of the Effective Private Enforcement of EC Competition Rules: A Community Perspective' in CD Ehlermann and I Atanasiu (eds), *European Competition Law Annual 2001: Effective Private Enforcement of EC Antitrust Law* (Hart 2003) 187, 188. The difficulties in distinguishing between rights and remedies are further aggravated by the different common and civil law approaches: see S Prechal, 'Does Direct Effect Still Matter?' (2000) 37 CMLRev 1047, 1053–1054. See also J Jolowicz, *On Civil Procedure* (CUP 2000) 60, 61, 65–69, which points to difficulties in distinguishing procedural law, proceedings, and substantive law.
[14] Van Gerven (n 13) 502. See also T Tridimas, *The General Principles of EU Law* (2nd edn, OUP 2006) 500–501, where he notes that based on the *ubi jus, ibi remedium* maxim, 'the value of a right is determined by the legal consequences which ensue from its violation, namely the remedies available from its enforcement'.
[15] M Ruffert, 'Rights and Remedies in European Community Law: A Comparative View' (1997) 34 CMLRev 307, 332–333. As common law countries emphasize remedies as rights protected by a cause of action, they seem to arrive at the same conclusion: Prechal (n 13) 1053–1054.
[16] See van Gerven (n 13) 503 in a similar vein, who points to the Latin maxim *ubi ius, ibi remedium* as enshrined in the EU law principle of access to a court, which is also reflected in Articles 6 and 13 ECHR. Contra JS Delikostopoulos, 'Towards European Procedural Primacy in National Legal Systems' (2003) 9 ELJ 599, 611, arguing that 'the fact that remedial rights are often—but not always—determined not by their own nature but by the nature of right which they serve to protect does not lead to a conceptual identity between right and remedy'.
[17] M Tulibacka, 'Europeanization of Civil Procedures: In Search of a Coherent Approach' (2009) 46 CMLRev 1527, 1532 with further references to M Storme (ed), *Approximation of Judiciary Law in the European Union* (Kluwer Rechtswetenschappen 1994) 1; Jolowicz (n 13) 61.

distinguish these rules from the directly effective EU competition rules and the substantive rights granted by them. The challenge is to formulate 'remedial and procedural' rules to permit the application of substantive EU competition rules before the national courts.

4. Structure

In Chapter 2 the following questions are addressed: Who is the consumer and what is meant by 'consumer interest' in the context of EU competition law? How is 'consumer interest' depicted in the substantive competition law analysis? The chapter first addresses the relationship between consumer and competition law. A consideration of the role of competition law vis-à-vis consumer law facilitates the subsequent discussion on 'consumer interest' in EU competition law. In relation to 'consumer interest' it points to the inconsistencies between its frequent presence in the Commission's policy documents and its rather limited role in the Court of Justice of the European Union (CJEU)[18] case law and the Commission's substantive enforcement practice. This finding points to the need for more active consumer involvement in actual competition law enforcement as an alternative route for bringing consumer interests to the fore. In addition, it links the policy and substantive elements with the advancement, in Chapter 3, of concrete normative justifications for increased consumer involvement.

The analysis in Chapter 3 first discusses the 'endemic/functional' aims of damages actions as these are discerned in the CJEU jurisprudence and Commission policy documents. These 'endemic/functional' aims comprise deterrence and compensation and are reflected in the structure of the procedural mechanisms for bringing damages actions. It is argued that even though they both constitute equally valued objectives, in the case of conflict, deterrence should be ranked first. This is supported by the CJEU case law; a closer reading of the respective case law, together with the Commission's early statements, also advocates in favour of ranking deterrence first when formulating the procedural measures. Provided that a correct balance is achieved between the 'endemic/functional' aims, consumer damages actions may account for wider institutional benefits, contributing to consumer empowerment and the legitimization of EU competition policy.

Chapters 2 and 3 thus provide the theoretical justifications for the increased consumer participation advocated herein. Chapters 4 and 5 then move on to formulate practical proposals that could enable consumers to assume a more active role—or, to put it in accurate terms, which would actually allow consumers to assume a role in private competition law enforcement. The analysis in Chapter 4 embarks on a discussion of the characteristics of consumer claims, as opposed to

---

[18] The CJEU includes the Court of Justice, the General Court, and specialized courts. See Article 19(1) of the Treaty on European Union (TEU). In this book 'CJEU' refers only to the Court of Justice (ECJ) and the General Court (GC).

customers' and competitors' claims, which justify a more enabling approach in the formulation of procedural measures for the bringing of such actions. The procedural measures discussed in the chapter concern offensive and defensive passing on and access to evidence problems.

In Chapter 5 the formulation of effective collective action procedures for low-value consumer claims is addressed and the difficulties in reaching a political consensus for the adoption of such a solution by individual Member States are also underlined. Thereafter, Chapter 6 examines alternative consumer participation avenues in the field of public enforcement that could potentially be more acceptable to the Member States as well as EU institutions. Finally, the analysis in Chapter 7 examines whether a legal basis exists in the Treaty for the introduction of the measures proposed herein. In addition to the partial harmonization of civil procedural rules (strict approach), it addresses alternative soft law instruments that have the potential to increase the role of consumer interest and consumer participation in competition law enforcement.

Through discussion of the normative grounds for consumer participation, this book highlights how consumer involvement advances the aims of EU competition law enforcement and wider EU aspirations. At the same time, the formulation of practical measures shows that *de lege ferenda* such participation is possible. However, because the book acknowledges the relevant institutional and political limitations, it also examines the possibilities for consumer involvement in the course of public competition law enforcement. It aspires to reveal that the line between public and private enforcement mechanisms and the respective roles of the different actors is somewhat blurred. This 'blurring' may be of benefit to both competition law enforcement and the protection of the 'consumer interest'. In a multi-level system, as in the case of the EU, it is vital to consider the emplacement of new modes of enforcement and governance in order for the desired policy ends to be achieved[19] and, most importantly, to attain acceptance from the ultimate addressees of competition policy.

---

[19] 'Multi-level' governance refers to the vertical relations between different levels of government. It also includes a 'horizontal' component, namely the relationship between private and public actors. S Smismans, 'Civil Society and European Governance: From Concepts to Research Agenda' in S Smismans (ed), *Civil Society and Legitimate European Governance* (Edward Elgar 2006) 3, 8.

PART A

NORMATIVE APPROACH TO CONSUMER PARTICIPATION

2
'Consumer Interest' and the Aims of EU Competition Law

1. Introduction

This chapter introduces the main variables which influence the analysis undertaken, namely the 'consumer', 'consumer interest', and 'consumer welfare'. First, the relationship and interplay between competition and consumer law is examined and their respective potential to cater for different consumer needs is addressed. This analysis points to potential spillover effects between the two disciplines and the limits of competition law enforcement in endorsing different consumer interests (section 2). The accommodation of consumer interests in competition law analysis depends on the aims of the competition law regime. Section 3 discusses the multiplicity of aims in EU competition law and argues that the protected 'consumer interest' under EU competition law is directly related to its respective aims. If EU competition law is to place increased emphasis on 'consumer welfare', then the meaning attributed to this term, whether broader or narrower, permits a more consumer-oriented enforcement of competition law.

Section 4 moves on to discuss the role of consumer welfare in EU competition law. It identifies an increased emphasis on consumer welfare in the Commission rhetoric and questions whether this is mirrored in the CJEU jurisprudence. The discussion examines the perception of the consumer interest (or the dearth thereof) in decisional practice, and points to inconsistencies between the rhetoric and practice. In the past, the Commission and the CJEU have neither addressed consumer interest in a consistent manner nor developed a clear notion of consumer benefit/detriment.[1] The aim is to show that competition law analysis should take the interests of final consumers into account more explicitly, in line with the relevant policy pronouncements and its underlying aims. However, as discussed in section 5, in light of the multitude of aims accommodated under EU competition law and the multifaceted notion of consumer welfare, consumer interest is unlikely to assume a more important role in the analysis. This conclusion serves as

---

[1] N Reich, 'Competition Law and the Consumer' in L Gormley (ed), *Current and Future Perspectives on EC Competition Law* (Kluwer Law 1997) 126, 137; M Hutchings and P Whelan, 'Consumer Interest in Competition Law Cases' (2006) 16 CPRev 182, 186.

the springboard for suggesting increased consumer participation as an alternative to strengthening consumer interest and links the analysis with the discussion in Chapter 3, which builds a normative framework in favour of increased consumer involvement in EU competition law enforcement.

2. The Interplay between Competition Law and Consumer Law

Policymakers often point to the interdependencies between competition and consumer law and their potential to deliver the maximum benefit for consumer welfare and productivity growth.[2] Competition law safeguards consumer choice, while consumer law ensures that consumers have all of the necessary information to choose between the different available products and services.[3]

Consumers not only stand to benefit from competitive markets but also play a role in generating them.[4] Consumer preferences shape firms' market strategies and consumer law has a definite role to play in this area. Consumer education is vital so that consumers can choose products that better suit their needs and are able to avoid being exploited, not only to their own disadvantage but also to the detriment of the competitive process.[5]

The prevailing assumption in consumer law is that consumers act rationally so that, when they have the necessary information, they will act in their own

---

[2] OECD, 'The Interface Between Competition and Consumer Policies' (Policy Roundtables) DAF/COMP/GF(2008) 10; OFT, 'Joining up Competition and Consumer Policy' (OFT 1151) (December 2009), para 1.2; See also OFT, 'Interactions between Competition and Consumer Policy' (OFT 991) (April 2008); L Sylvan, 'Activating Competition: The Consumer Protection—Competition Interface' (Speech delivered at the University of South Australia Trade Practices Workshop, 29 October 2004) <http://www.accc.gov.au/system/files/20041029%20SA%20Uni%20Trade%20Practices%20Workshop.pdf> accessed 14 June 2014. For a thorough analysis of the relationship between consumer and competition law see K Cseres, *Competition Law and Consumer Protection* (Kluwer Law International 2005) especially ch 7.

[3] This essentially reflects Averitt and Lande's 'consumer sovereignty' theory: N Averitt and R Lande, 'Using the "Consumer Choice" Approach to Antitrust Law' (2007) 74 Antitrust LJ 175; N Averitt and R Lande, 'Consumer Sovereignty: A Unified Theory of Antitrust and Consumer Protection Law' (1997) 65 Antitrust LJ 713. N Averitt, 'Protecting Consumer Choice: Competition and Consumer Protection Together' in J Drexl and others (eds), *More Common Ground for International Competition Law?* (Edward Elgar 2011) 36. Nihoul comments that this is, indeed, the approach adopted in the EU. See P Nihoul, 'Is Competition Law Part of Consumer Law?' in J Drexl and others (eds), *More Common Ground for International Competition Law?* (Edward Elgar 2011) 46, 46.

[4] G Howells and S Weatherill, *Consumer Protection Law* (2nd edn, Ashgate 2005) 48; DTI, 'Extending Competitive Markets: Empowered Consumers, Successful Business' (June 2005) <http://www.berr.gov.uk/files/file23787.pdf> accessed 14 June 2014; OFT, 'Assessing the Effectiveness of Potential Remedies in Consumer Markets' (OFT 994) (April 2008), para 1.1.

[5] The Commission pointed to the importance of consumer education. See Commission (EC), 'EU Consumer Policy Strategy 2007–2013' (Communication) COM(2007) 99 final, para 4. However, the importance of consumer education should not be confined only to consumer policy. See J Davies, *The European Consumer Citizen in Law and Policy* (Palgrave Macmillan 2011) 43–45, on the importance of consumer education for advancing the 'consumer citizen'.

best interests. However, new insights from behavioural economics challenge that assumption.[6] Securing the information flow to consumers is not enough;[7] rather, more pervasive measures are needed in order to tackle consumers' irrational decisions. Therefore, there is a need to move from a liberal model of consumer protection, which emphasizes information disclosure, to a 'quasi-paternalistic' model, in which more active interventionist measures are employed.[8] Furthermore, choosing a 'model' consumer (in terms of education, income, and potential for rational decision-making) for the purposes of consumer law analysis is in itself a difficult balancing exercise[9] that might adversely impact on competition policy.

The Commission acknowledged early on the potential of competition law to tackle consumer problems.[10] This is evident from the insertion of a section on

---

[6] See OECD, 'Roundtable on Demand-side Economics for Consumer Policy: Summary Report' DSTI/CP(2006)3/FINAL (20 April 2006), 11; C Jolls, C Sunstein, and R Thaler, 'A Behavioral Approach to Law and Economics' (1998) 50 Stan L Rev 1471; T Ulen, 'Information in the Market Economy—Cognitive Errors and Legal Correctives' in S Grundmann, W Kerber, and S Weatherill (eds), *Party Autonomy and the Role of Information in the Internal Market* (De Gruyter 2001) 98. See C Camerer and others, 'Regulation for Conservatives: Behavioural Economics and the Case for Asymmetric Paternalism' (2003) 151 U Pa L Rev 1211, 1247 for an attempt to reconcile the rationality assumption with the insights of behavioural economics. Behavioural economics recently attracted attention in competition law analysis. See, for example, Stucke, 'Behavioral Economics at the Gate: Antitrust in the Twenty-First Century' (2007) 38 Loyola U Chi LJ 513; M Stucke, 'Am I a Price Fixer? A Behavioral Economic Analysis of Cartels' in C Beaton-Wells and A Ezrachi (eds), *Criminalising Cartels: A Critical Interdisciplinary Study of an International Regulatory Movement* (Hart 2011) 263; A Tor, 'A Behavioural Approach to Antitrust Law and Economics' (2004) 14 CP Rev 18. For a criticism see J Wright, 'Nudging Antitrust? Commissioner Rosch's Weak Case for Behavioral Antitrust' (July 2010) <http://truthonthemarket.com/2010/07/12/nudging-antitrust-commissioner-roschs-weak-case-for-behavioral-antitrust-part-1/> accessed 15 June 2014; OFT 1151 (n 2), para 3.9.

[7] J Gans, 'Protecting Consumers by Protecting Competition: Does Behavioural Economics Support this Contention' 12 (Melbourne Business School, 31 May 2005) <http://www.accc.gov.au/system/files/Joshua%20Gans%20(paper)%20-%20Protecting%20consumers%20by%20protecting%20competition_%20Does%20behavioural%20economics%20support%20this%20contention.pdf> accessed 15 June 2014; I McAuley, 'Behavioural Economics and Public Policy: Some Insights' (Working Paper, February 2007) <http://www.home.netspeed.com.au/mcau/academic/bepubpol.pdf> accessed 14 June 2014, 12; S King and R Smith, 'Does Competition Law Adequately Protect Consumers?' (2007) 7 ECLR 412.

[8] See Cseres (n 2) 170–192 for a concise presentation of models for consumer protection. See also N Reich, 'Diverse Approaches to Consumer Protection Philosophy' (1992) 14 JCP 257, 258–261, 267.

[9] Davies (n 5) 32–42; E Hondius, 'The Notion of Consumer: European Union versus Member States' (2006) 28 Syd L Rev 89, 93–97; J Stuyck, 'The Notion of Empowered and Informed Consumer in Consumer Policy and How to Protect the Vulnerable Under Such a Regime' in G Howells and others (eds), *Yearbook of Consumer Law 2007* (Ashgate 2007) 167; S Weatherill, 'Who is the Average Consumer?' in S Weatherill and U Bernitz (eds), *The Regulation of Unfair Commercial Practices under EC Directive 2005/29: New Rules and New Techniques* (Hart 2007) 115. M Everson, 'Legal Constructions of the Consumer' in F Trentmann (ed), *The Making of the Consumer* (Berg 2006) 99, 108, 115 explores the question of whether EU law has managed to establish a coherent construction of the consumer from a legal perspective.

[10] Competition law provisions have been present in the Treaty since its inception, while specific provisions on consumer protection were inserted in 1992 by the Maastricht Treaty and were further modified by the Treaty of Amsterdam. This, however, did not prevent the formation of a European consumer policy, albeit of a more 'indirect' nature. European consumer policy was advanced through the application of free movement and competition law provisions. See S Weatherill, *EU Consumer Law and Policy* (2nd edn, Edward Elgar 2013) 1–33; N Reich, 'Protection of Consumers'

'consumer protection' in the first two Commission Reports on Competition Policy.[11] The following abstract from the Commission's First Report on Competition Policy (1972) is germane:

> An active competition policy…makes it easier for the *supply and demand structures* continually to adjust to technological developments…competition enables enterprises continuously to improve their efficiency, which is the *sine qua non* for *a steady improvement in living standards* and employment prospects within the countries of the Community…competition policy is an essential means of satisfying the *individual and collective needs of our society*.[12]

Competition policy can, thus, be viewed as a form of consumer policy,[13] but it has its limits. First, consumers may face problems in competitive markets.[14] For example, this might be in relation to markets of complex goods or services in which consumers cannot readily process the information (eg financial services or credence goods).[15] It may also arise in newly liberalized telecoms or energy markets in which the opening of these markets to competition has not yielded the desired results.[16] Second, competition law caters only for specific aspects of the consumer interest, namely only those that can be accommodated under competition law

---

Economic Interests by the EC' (1992) 14 Syd L Rev 23; Cseres (n 2) 193–240; C Twigg-Flesner, 'UK and EU Consumer Law' in C Twigg-Flesner and others (eds) *Yearbook of Consumer Law 2008* (Ashgate 2008) 365 for the evolution of consumer protection policy in the EU. See J Stuyck, 'European Consumer Law After the Treaty of Amsterdam: Consumer Policy in or Beyond the Internal Market?' (2000) 37 CMLRev 367.

[11] Commission (EEC), First Report on Competition Policy (Brussels, Luxembourg 1972) <http://ec.europa.eu/competition/publications/annual_report/ar_1971_en.pdf> accessed 15 June 2014, 187–200; Commission (EEC), Second Report on Competition Policy (Brussels, Luxembourg 1973) <http://ec.europa.eu/competition/publications/annual_report/ar_1972_en.pdf> accessed 15 June 2014, 163–171.

[12] First Report on Competition Policy (n 11) (emphasis added) 11.

[13] Commission (EC), XXIInd Report on Competition Policy 1992 (Brussels, Luxembourg 1993) <http://bookshop.europa.eu/is-bin/INTERSHOP.enfinity/WFS/EU-Bookshop-Site/en_GB/-/EUR/ViewPublication-Start?PublicationKey=CM7693689> accessed 15 June 2014, para 74; Howells and Weatherill (n 4) 518; S Weatherill, 'The Links between Competition Policy and Consumer Protection' in G Howells and others (eds), *Yearbook of Consumer Law 2007* (Ashgate 2007) 187; J Vickers, 'Healthy Competition and its Consumer Wins' (2002) 12 CP Rev 142. See also ESC, 'Opinion on the Twenty-second Competition Report' in Commission (EC), XXIIIrd Report on Competition Policy 1993 (Brussels, Luxembourg 1994) < http://bookshop.europa.eu/is-bin/INTERSHOP.enfinity/WFS/EU-Bookshop-Site/en_GB/-/EUR/ViewPublication-Start?PublicationKey=CM8294650> accessed 15 June 2014, Annex I, 368.

[14] N Howell and T Wilson, 'The Limits of Competition: Reasserting the Role for Consumer Protection and Fair Trading Regulation in Competitive Markets' in D Parry and others (eds), *Yearbook of Consumer Law 2009* (Ashgate 2009) 147.

[15] Credence goods are defined as goods whose quality is difficult to test even after they have been bought and consumed. Averitt and Lande, 'Using the "Consumer Choice" Approach to Antitrust Law' (n 3) 207.

[16] M Giulietti, C Waddams Price, and M Waterson, 'Consumer Choice and Competition Policy: A Study of UK Energy Markets' (2005) 115 Econ J 949; K Cseres, 'What Has Competition Done for Consumers in Liberalised Markets?' (2008) 4 Comp L Rev <http://www.clasf.org/CompLRev/Issues/Vol4Iss2Art1Cseres.pdf> accessed 15 June 2014, 77. For different situations where competition law needs to be complemented by consumer law measures see M Armstrong, 'Interactions Between Competition and Consumer Policy' (2008) 4 CPI 97, 106–132.

analysis and the respective aims of EU competition law. The following analysis of these aims fleshes out the consumer interests protected in EU competition law.

3. Multiple Aims and the 'Consumer Interest'

3.1 Multiplicity of aims

Reaching a consensus on 'the' goal of competition law presents a task of increased complexity. Economists and lawyers have argued in favour of a single goal in competition law.[17] However, the reality of competition law enforcement is more complex and different competition law systems have embraced different goals, from *core competition objectives* to *public interest objectives*, while observing *different grey zones* in between.[18] EU competition law is no exception.

The Commission has noted that 'competition policy cannot be pursued in isolation, as an end in itself, without reference to the *legal, economic, political* and *social context*'.[19] Thus, the multifaceted context within which EU competition policy operates has influenced its goals, which include the protection of the competitive market structure, the protection of economic freedom, advancing market integration, and promoting efficiency and consumer welfare. At the same time, different public policy goals have influenced EU competition law analysis, although they have not been officially elevated to aims of EU competition law.

The following analysis presents the influential variables for EU competition law and discusses these in the light of the three identified categories of competition

---

[17] Oduduu and Easterbrook support a unitary goal. See F Easterbrook, 'The Limits of Antitrust' (1984) 63 *Texas Law Review* 1; O Odudu, *The Boundaries of EC Competition Law* (OUP 2006) 159. See also R Blair and D Sokol, 'The Rule of Reason and the Goals of Antitrust: An Economic Approach' (2012) 78 Antitrust LJ 471, 472; In contrast, Stucke argues that a single well-defined objective for competition law is unrealistic: M Stucke, 'Reconsidering Antitrust Goals' (2012) 53 *Boston College Law Review* 551.

[18] OECD, 'The Objectives of Competition Law and Policy' (29 January 2003) CCNM/GF/COMP(2003) 3 <http://www.oecd.org/dataoecd/57/39/2486329.pdf> accessed 15 June 2014, paras 20–22. See also ICN, *Report on the Objectives of Unilateral Conduct Laws, Assessment of Dominance/Substantial Market Power, and State Created Monopolies* (May 2007) <http://internationalcompetitionnetwork.org/uploads/library/doc353.pdf> accessed 15 June 2014, 2. See also ICN, Unilateral Conduct Workbook, Chapter 1: 'The Objectives and Principles of Unilateral Conduct Laws' (April 2012). On the sponge-like qualities of competition law see A Ezrachi, 'Sponge' (2015) Working Paper CCLP (L) 42 <http://papers.ssrn.com/sol3/papers.cfm?abstract_id=2572028> accessed 5 May 2015.

[19] XXIInd Report on Competition Policy 1992 (n 13) 13 (emphasis added). See also R Whish and D Bailey, *Competition Law* (7th edn, OUP 2012) 20; R Posner, *Antitrust Law* (2nd edn, University of Chicago Press 2001) 286; Case 283/81 *CILFIT and Lanicio di Gavardo SpA v Ministry of Health* [1982] ECR 3415, para 20. See P Marsden, 'Checks and Balances: European Competition Law and the Rule of Law' (2009) 22 Loyola Consumer L Rev 51, 59 quoting Judge Cooke, the Judge Rapporteur in *Microsoft*, who stated that 'these Article [101 and 102 TFEU] cases are 20 percent fact, 20 percent law and 60 percent policy'. See also B Van Rompuy, *Economic Efficiency: The Sole Concern of Modern Antitrust Policy? Non-efficiency Considerations under 101 TFEU* (Kluwer Law International 2012) 23, in which he identifies political factors, economic learning, institutional actors, and jurisprudence as the four interrelated factors influencing antitrust enforcement.

law objectives. The aim is to show that EU competition law has not embraced a unitary goal and therefore attempts to gear competition law enforcement towards a more consumer welfare-oriented rationale are fraught with difficulties.

3.1.1 EU core competition objectives

Promoting the competitive process and attaining economic efficiency have been identified as the two core objectives of competition law, although the notion of these aims varies widely across different jurisdictions.[20]

In EU competition law, *the promotion of the competitive process* as a core aim can be traced back and attributed to its ordoliberal underpinnings. From a historical perspective, EU competition law was not adopted on a clean slate. On the contrary, it was influenced, to some extent, by US antitrust law and,[21] most importantly, by the ordoliberal Freiburg school of thought.[22] The ordoliberals were sceptical of private economic power and their concern was to eliminate this or, at least, to prevent its harmful effects.[23] Thus, they focused more on the structure of the market, the protection of the economic freedom of market players, and competition as a process as ends in themselves. Even today, it remains debatable as to whether EU competition law can be emancipated from this ordoliberal tradition.[24]

Aside from the protection of economic freedom advocated by the ordoliberals, economic efficiency has been a consideration in EU competition law, even though this was only highlighted more recently. Following the increased attention

---

[20] OECD (n 18) para 20.

[21] B Leuchts and M Marquis, 'American Influences on EEC Competition Law—Two Paths, How Much Dependence' in K Patel and H Schweitze (eds), *The Historical Foundations of EU Competition Law* (OUP 2013) 125. For Giocoli, the 'canonical narrative' about the roots of EU competition law is that it has been modelled upon US antitrust law, although he disagrees with this view: N Giocoli, 'Competition versus Property Rights: American Antitrust Law, the Freiburg School and the Early Years of EU Competition Policy' (2009) 5 JCLE 747, 763–768.

[22] H Buxbaum, 'German Legal Culture and the Globalisation of Competition Law: A Historical Perspective on the Expansion of Private Antitrust Enforcement' (2005) 23 Berkley J Int'l L 101, 106; D Gerber, 'Constitutionalising the Economy: German Neo-liberalism, Competition Law and the "New" Europe' (1994) 42 AJCL 25, 64; Contra P Akman, 'Searching for the Long-Lost Soul of Article 82 EC' (2009) 29 OJLS 267; P Akman, 'The Role of Freedom in EU Competition Law' (2013) 34 LS 183, 213. On the different influences in EU competition law and distinguishing between the political (both ordoliberal and Keynesian) and the judicial arena see S Ramirez Perez and S van de Scheur, 'The Evolution of the Law on Articles 85 and 86 EEC [Articles 101 and 102 TFEU]—Ordoliberalism and its Keynesian Challenge' in K Patel and H Schweitze (eds), *The Historical Foundations of EU Competition Law* (OUP 2013) 19, 21, 37. For a detailed account of the history and development of EU competition law see D Gerber, *Law and Competition in Twentieth Century Europe: Protecting Prometheus* (OUP 2001). A Weitbrecht, 'From Freiburg to Chicago and Beyond: The First 50 Years of European Competition Law' (2008) 29 ECLR 81.

[23] Gerber (n 22) 49–56; Gerber (n 22) ch 7; C Ahlborn and C Grave, 'Walter Eucken and Ordoliberalism: An Introduction from a Consumer Welfare Perspective' (2006) 2 CPI <https://www.competitionpolicyinternational.com/walter-eucken-and-ordoliberalism-an-introduction-from-a-consumer-welfare-perspective/> accessed 15 June 2014, 197 for an overview of the main concepts of ordoliberalism. See also W Möschel, 'The Proper Scope of Government Viewed from an Ordoliberal Perspective: The Example of Competition Policy' (2001) 157 JITE 3, 4.

[24] See text to nn 155–187 on the application of Article 102 TFEU.

attributed to economics in EU competition law analysis, the Commission emphasized the importance of considering economic factors, *such as efficiency and consumer welfare*.²⁵ To some extent, this can be seen as an attempt to synchronize EU competition law with its US counterpart in an international marketplace, as well as incorporating insights from economic theory.²⁶

In EU competition law *market integration* can also be listed as a core objective.²⁷ The drafters of the Treaty viewed competition law as a tool to open up the then fragmented national markets.²⁸ Thus, market integration was considered (and still is)²⁹ an important goal in EU competition law. ³⁰ For example, the Guidelines on Vertical Restraints mention market integration as one of the important factors in assessing vertical agreements. Market integration, however, is not a stand-alone objective but, rather, a means to promote competition within the EU.³¹ In this sense, market integration is an economic objective. However, in the short and medium term, market integration may conflict with economic efficiency goals also pursued by competition policy, a fact that highlights the political nature of this goal as well.³² The unification of competition and the internal market into

---

²⁵ Commission (EC), 'Green Paper on Vertical Restraints in EC Competition Policy' COM(96) 721 final, para 180; Commission (EC), 'Guidelines on the Application of Article 81(3) of the Treaty' [2004] OJ C101/08, Guidelines on Art [101(3)] TFEU paras 13, 33. For similar quotes see Commission (EC), 'Guidelines on the Application of Article 81 of the EC Treaty to Technology Transfer Agreements' [2004] C101/02, paras 5, 7; DG Competition, 'Discussion Paper on the Application of Article 82 of the Treaty to Exclusionary Abuses' (December 2005), para 4.
²⁶ See W Kovacic, 'Competition Policy in the European Union and the United States: Convergence or Divergence?' in X Vives (ed), *Competition Policy in the EU: Fifty Years on from the Treaty of Rome* (OUP 2009) 314, 329–333 on the forces fostering convergence between the two systems.
²⁷ OECD (n 18) n 2 lists 'market integration' as a public interest objective. However, in this book, 'market integration' is recognized as a core objective, in the light of its significance in EU competition law.
²⁸ Information Service High Authority of the European Community for Coal and Steel Luxembourg, 'The Brussels Report on the General Common Market' (June 1956) (Spaak Report); D Gerber, 'The Transformation of European Community Competition Law?' (1994) 35 Harvard Intl LJ 97, 102.
²⁹ Despite the Commission's overt shift towards a more efficiency based approach. See Commission (EC), 'White Paper on the Modernisation of the Rules Implementing Articles 85 and 86 of the EC Treaty' [1999] OJ C132/1, para 8.
³⁰ Joined Cases 56/64 and 58/64 *Établissements Consten S.à.R.L. and Grundig-Verkaufs-GmbH v Commission* [1966] ECR 299, 340; Case C-126/97 *Eco Swiss China Time Ltd v Benetton International NV* [1999] ECR I-3055, para 36; Joined Cases C-403/08 and C-429/08 *Football Association Premier League Ltd* [2011] ECR I-9083, paras 139–140; First Report on Competition Policy (n 11) 13; Commission (EC), XXth Report on Competition Policy (Brussels, Luxembourg 1991) <http://bookshop.europa.eu/is-bin/INTERSHOP.enfinity/WFS/EU-Bookshop-Site/en_GB/-/EUR/ViewPublication-Start?PublicationKey=CM6091410> accessed 15 June 2014, 11; Commission (EC), XXIst Report on Competition Policy 1991 (Brussels, Luxembourg 1992) <http://bookshop.europa.eu/is-bin/INTERSHOP.enfinity/WFS/EU-Bookshop-Site/en_GB/-/EUR/ViewPublication-Start?PublicationKey=CM7392247> accessed 15 June 2014, paras 43–44; Commission (EC), 'White Paper on the Completion of the Internal Market' COM(85) 310 final, para 19; CD Ehlermann, 'The Contribution of EC Competition Policy to the Single Market' (1992) 29 CMLRev 257; A Albors-Llorens, 'Competition Policy and the Shaping of the Single Market' in C Barnard and J Scott (eds), *The Law of the Single European Market* (Hart 2002) 311.
³¹ Commission (EU), 'Guidelines on Vertical Restraints' [2010] OJ C 130/1, para 7.
³² CD Ehlermann and L Laudati, Introduction in Ehlermann and Laudati (eds) *European Competition Law Annual 1997: the Objectives of Competition Policy* (Hart 1998) x.

a single protocol in the Lisbon Treaty (LT) seems to highlight the importance of competition rules for the internal market and emphasize their potential to promote market integration.[33] In this way, it eschews a US-inspired enforcement standard based solely on efficiency considerations.[34]

3.1.2 Public interest objectives

The influence of public interest considerations in competition law enforcement varies across different jurisdictions.[35] In general, a shift away from public interest objectives towards the core competition objectives has been identified,[36] and this holds true for EU competition law. However, EU competition law analysis has also occasionally embraced public policy considerations.[37] This is explicable in the light of the purposive interpretation adopted by the ECJ[38] in applying the competition provisions in conjunction with Articles 2 and 3 TEC[39] and the existence of integration clauses for a number of EU policies.[40] Public policy considerations have been taken into account

---

[33] Protocol (No 27) on the Internal Market and Competition [2008] OJ C115/309.

[34] P Marsden and P Whelan, 'The "Consumer Welfare" Standard as a Form of Substantive Protection for Consumers under European Competition Law' (2009) in A Ezrachi and U Bernitz (eds), *Private Labels, Brands and Competition Policy* (OUP 2009) 353, 360. For a discussion on EU competition law enforcement post the Lisbon Treaty see A Riley, 'The EU Reform Treaty and the Competition Protocol: Undermining EC Competition Law' (2007) 28 ECLR 703, 705; A Komninos, 'Continuity and Change in EU Competition Policy' (February 2010) CPI <https://www.competitionpolicyinternational.com/continuity-and-change-in-eu-competition-policy/> accessed 15 June 2014, 6. J Drexl, 'Competition Law as Part of the European Constitution' in A von Bogdandy and J Bast (eds), *Principles of European Constitutional Law* (2nd edn, Hart 2009) 659, 697. I Lianos, 'Some Reflections on the Question of the Goals of EU Competition Law' in I Lianos and D Geradin (eds), *Handbook on European Competition Law* (Edward Elgar 2013) 47–52.

[35] OECD (n 18), para 21.   [36] Ibid, para 4.

[37] DG Competition, 'The Application of Articles 85 and 86 of the EC Treaty by National Courts in the Member States' (Brussels, July 1997) (Braakman Report), para 148 for references to relevant case law; G Monti, 'Article 81 EC and Public Policy' (2002) 39 CMLRev 1057, 1069–1078; C Townley, *Article 81 and Public Policy* (Hart 2009); W Sauter, *Competition Law and Industrial Policy in the EU* (Clarendon Press 1997); S Kingston, *Greening EU Competition Law and Policy* (CUP 2012); G Amato, *Antitrust and the Bounds of Power* (Hart 1997); H Vedder, 'Of Jurisdiction and Justification. Why Competition is Good for "Non-Economic Goals" but May Need to be Restricted' (2009) 6 Comp L Rev <http://www.clasf.org/CompLRev/Issues/Vol6Issue1Article3Vedder.pdf> accessed 15 June 2014, 51. H Schweitzer, 'Competition Law and Public Policy: Reconsidering an Uneasy Relationship: The Example of Art. 81' (2007) (EUI WP Law 2007/30) <http://papers.ssrn.com/sol3/papers.cfm?abstract_id=1092883> accessed 15 June 2014, 2–8.

[38] Case 14/68 *Walt Wilhelm v Bundeskartellamt* [1969] ECR 1, 14; Case 6/72 *Europemballage Corporation and Continental Can Company Inc v Commission* [1973] ECR 215, paras 23–25; Case C-67/96 *Albany* [1999] ECR I-5751, para 54.

[39] After the adoption of the LT, Articles 2 and 3 TEC were repealed. The objectives of the Union are now to be found in Article 3 TEU. However, the reference to a system of undistorted competition has been deleted. For the potential effect of this removal see text to n 56.

[40] On the integration clauses in the LT see Article 7 TFEU, Article 9 TFEU (on adequate social protection); Article 11 TFEU (on the environment), Article 12 TFEU (on consumer protection), Article 147(2) TFEU (on employment), Article 167(4) TFEU (on culture), Article 168(1) TFEU (on health protection), Article 175 TFEU (on economic, social, and territorial cohesion) and Article 208 TFEU (on development cooperation). On the impact of the broader integration clauses in the LT in conjunction with Article 3(3) TEU see Lianos (n 34) 55–60. On the argument that policy linking clauses permit public policy considerations to be taken into account in competition law analysis see

at three distinct levels: when ruling on the existence of an 'undertaking'; in the analysis of Article 101(1) TFEU; and in the analysis of Article 101(3) TFEU.[41]

EU competition law is applicable to undertakings, namely entities that engage in economic activities regardless of their status or the way they are financed.[42] The approach to the term 'undertaking' is a functional one and excludes from its scope non-commercial activities in the public interest, acting as a jurisdictional threshold for the application of EU competition rules. When ruling on the existence of an undertaking, public policy arguments are employed in order to take a given practice outside the scope of EU competition law, thereby implying that EU competition law is not an appropriate tool to regulate activities in the public interest. Nonetheless, public interest considerations have at times influenced the substantive competition law analysis.

In the analysis of Article 101(1) TFEU public interest considerations such as the integrity of the legal profession in *Wouters*[43] and the proper conduct of sports in *Meca-Medina*[44] have been taken into account and prevented a certain practice from being classified as a restriction of competition. These cases concerned a practice of self-regulation adopted by collective bodies and the restriction on the freedom to compete was inherent in the proper organization of the regulated activity.[45] In *Wouters*, the Court considered that an activity that restricts freedom of action is not necessarily caught by Article 101(1) TFEU, since regard must be had first of all to the overall context of the agreement and its objectives and second to whether these consequential anti-competitive effects are inherent in the pursuit of those objectives. Finally, the restrictions should not go beyond what is necessary for the objective being pursued.[46] This approach was recently followed in *OTOC* in relation to the quality of chartered accountant services with the aim of attaining sound administration of companies' accounting and taxation issues and *CNG* in relation to guaranteeing the quality of services offered by geologists to final consumers.[47] Furthermore, in *Albany*, the Court exempted collective labour

---

Townley (n 37) 102–3; For the opposite view see O Odudu, 'The Wider Concerns of Competition Law' (2010) OJLS 1, 8–9.

[41] See also C Semmelman, 'The Future of the Non-competition Goals in the Interpretation of Article 81 EC' (2008) 1 Global Antitrust Rev 15, 19; Another possible route would have been in the context of objective justifications under Article 102 TFEU, but the CJEU has not been receptive to these arguments. Case T-30/89 *Hilti AG v Commission* [1991] ECR II-1439, paras 115–19; Case C-333/94 *P Tetra Pak v Commission* [1996] ECR I-5951, paras 36–37.

[42] Case C-41/90 *Klaus Höfner and Fritz Elser v Macrotron GmbH* [1991] ECR I-1979, para 21; Case C-180/98 etc *Pavlov* [2000] ECR I-6451, para 75; Case 264/01 etc *AOK Bundesverband* [2004] ECR I-2491, paras 46–47. For a rich discussion on the notion of undertaking see Odudu (n 17) 23–56.

[43] C-209/00 *Wouters* [2002] ECR I-1577, para 97.

[44] C-519/04P *Meca-Medina* [2006] ECR I-6991, paras 42–45.

[45] Schweitzer (n 37) 3. This is termed 'regulatory ancillarity'. See Whish and Bailey (n 19) 132.

[46] *Wouters* (n 43) paras 97, 107–109; *Meca-Medina* (n 44) paras 42, 47.

[47] Case C-1/12 *Ordem dos Técnicos Oficiais de Contas v Autoridade da Concorrência (OTOC)* [2013] 4 CMLR 20, paras 93–96. In this case the restriction of competition was not considered necessary for attaining the objective pursued. Ibid, para 98; Case C-136/12 *Consiglio nazionale dei geologi v Autorità garante della concorrenza e del mercato (CNG)* [2013] 5 CMLR 40, paras 52–54.

agreements from the scope of Article 101(1) TFEU since their social policy objectives would be undermined if management and labour were subject to Article 101(1) TFEU when seeking jointly to adopt measures to improve conditions of work and employment.[48]

Inasmuch as the practice adopted in *Wouters* and *Meca-Medina* resembled state regulation, it has been suggested that the Court applied the free movement justifications to the sphere of competition without inferring a general rule for transferring public policy justifications from the area of free movement to that of competition law.[49] Therefore, these cases can be seen as a separate category in which EU competition law is influenced by free movement considerations. This approach does not suggest that various public policy considerations are elevated to EU competition law aims, but rather that EU law and the Treaty scheme occasionally permit wider objectives to permeate the analysis.

More commonly, public policy justifications have been addressed under Article 101(3) TFEU when evaluating the pro-competitive effects of the agreement. Some examples include environmental,[50] employment,[51] and consumer considerations.[52] Despite the fact that these considerations may have heavily influenced the Commission's analysis in exempting the agreement, the Commission was cautious to address them in conjunction with the core competition objectives.[53]

The Commission, following the modernization of EU competition law, has refined its approach when considering public policy considerations as part of the Article 101(3) TFEU analysis.[54] Public policy considerations can be taken into account as long as they can be subsumed under the four conditions of Article 101(3) TFEU and this is now the prevailing approach in EU competition law.[55]

---

[48] *Albany* (n 38), paras 59–60. On this case see P Camesasca and R van den Bergh, 'Irreconcilable Principles? The Court of Justice Exempts Collective Labour Agreements From the Wrath of Antitrust' (2000) 25 ELRev 492. See also Case C-413/13 *FNV Kunsten Informatie en Media v Netherlands* [2015] 4 CMLR 1, paras 22, 23, 25, 41.

[49] Schweitzer (n 37) 3. For the opposite argument inferring a general rule termed as 'European rule of reason' see Monti (n 37) 1088–90. See also J Baquero Cruz, *Between Competition and Free Movement, The Economic Constitutional Law of the European Community* (Hart 2002) 151–153.

[50] See for example, *CECED* [2000] OJ L187/47, paras 30–37, 48, 51–57; *DSD* (Commission Decision 2001/837 EC) [2001] OJ L319/1, paras 143–145; *Exxon-Shell* [1994] OJ L144/21, paras 67–68; *Philips-Osram* [1994] OJ L378/37, para 25.

[51] *Ford/Volkswagen* (Case IV.33.814) Commission Decision 93/49/EEC [1993] OJ L20/14, para 36; On appeal Case T-17/93 *Matra Hachette v Commission* [1994] ECR-II 595, para 96; *Stichting Baksteen* [1994] OJ L131/15, paras 27–28; *Synthetic Fibres* [1984] OJ L207/17, para 37.

[52] *Asahi* [1994] OJ L354/87.   [53] Monti (n 37) 1078–79.

[54] Modernization refers to the changes in competition law enforcement brought about by Council Regulation (EC) 1/2003 on the Implementation of the Rules on Competition Laid Down in Articles 81 and 82 of the Treaty [2003] OJ L1/1. However, modernization may also be linked to the desirable changes in substantive application of EU competition law towards a more effects-based 'consumer welfare' approach, commencing with Commission Regulation (EC) 2790/1999 on the Application of Article 81(3) of the Treaty to Categories of Vertical Agreements and Concerted Practices [1999] OJ L336/21; Commission (EC), 'Guidelines on Vertical Restraints' (Notice) [2000] OJ C291/01, paras 7, 102.

[55] White Paper on Modernisation (n 29), para 57; Guidelines on Art [101(3)] TFEU (n 25) para 42. In its Guidelines the Commission makes further references to the following cases: *Matra Hachette* (n 51), para 139 and Case 26/76 *Metro (I)* [1977] ECR 1875, para 43. See also J Venit, 'Brave New World: The Modernization and Decentralization of Enforcement Under Articles 81

Different views were expressed in relation to the LT, allowing for an increased role for industrial and social policy considerations in the enforcement of competition law provisions,[56] but the ECJ in *TeliaSonera* suggested that the approach to EU competition policy would not change post the LT.[57]

3.1.3 'Grey zone' objectives

'Grey zone' objectives include the protection of fair competition, the protection of SMEs' interests and the prevention of an undue concentration of economic power.[58] The promotion of fair competition is relevant for traders' dealings with consumers and aims at protecting consumers as the weaker party in the transaction.[59] Thus, it has a different function from that of the protection of free competition. Nonetheless, fair competition has been promoted in the enforcement of Article 101 TFEU incidentally and this is an area where the complementary relationship between consumer and competition law is evident.[60]

The protection against undue concentration of economic power and safeguarding SMEs' interests as a 'grey zone' objective is close to the protection of the competitive process, which has been identified as a 'core objective' given the ordo-liberal influence in EU competition law. Protecting the competitive process is not necessarily synonymous with protecting competitors, although it could lead to the same outcome.

---

and 82 of the EC Treaty' (2003) 40 CMLRev 545, 579; Odudu (n 17) ch 7; A Witt, 'Public Policy Goals under EU Competition Law—Now is the Time to Set the House in Order' (2012) 8 Euro CJ 443, 462–463.

[56] The LT, in Article 3(3) TEU embraced a 'highly competitive social market economy' and the objective of undistorted competition was moved from its introductory provisions into Protocol No 27. Protocols form an integral part of the Treaties, enjoying the same legal validity (Article 51 TEU). On these changes see Riley (n 34) 704 quoting Petite, the Director General of the European Commission's Legal Service, who views competition as a means, rather than an objective, of the Union; Contra R Barents, 'Constitutional Horse Trading: Some Comments on the Protocol on the Internal Market and Competition' in M Bulterman (ed), *Views of European Law from the Mountain: Liber Amicorum for Piet Jan Slot* (Kluwer Law International 2009) 123, 127 arguing that 'there is no strict hierarchy in the sense of objectives and means since both provisions constitute the foundations of the EC'; C Townley, 'Is There (Still) Room for Non-Economic Arguments in Article 101 TFEU Cases?' in C Heide-Jorgensen and others (eds), *Aims and Values in Competition Law* (DJØF 2013) 115, 132–140; R Lane, 'EC Competition Law Post Lisbon: A Matter of Protocol' in M Bulterman (ed), *Views of European Law from the Mountain: Liber Amicorum for Piet Jan Slot* (Kluwer Law International 2009) 167, 176; C Semmelman, 'The European Union's Economic Constitution under the Lisbon Treaty: Soul-Searching Shifts the Focus of Procedure' (2010) 35 ELRev 516, 524 argues that the LT will not change the approach to EU competition policy but, at the same time, she points to the need for clarification of EU competition policy.

[57] Case C-52/09 *Konkurrensverket v TeliaSonera AB* [2011] ECR I-527, para 20. See Whish and Bailey (n 19) 50. Questioning this view, see Townley (n 56) 140.

[58] OECD (n 18) para 5.

[59] P Nebbia, 'Standard Form Contracts Between Unfair Contract Control and Competition Law' (2006) 31 ELRev 102, 103.

[60] For example, on the discussion as to whether unfair standard contract terms constitute a competition law problem see P Nebbia (n 59) 110; G Monti, 'The Revision of the Consumer Acquis From a Competition Law Perspective' [2007] ERCL 295, 307–310.

In the light of the multiplicity of aims in EU competition law, the analysis would be greatly facilitated if one of them were to be accorded priority, especially in cases in which different goals could lead to different outcomes. However, EU competition law enforcement to date has allowed for the accommodation of a plurality of goals and therefore attempts to rank the respective goals remain largely an academic exercise.[61] Embarking from this pragmatic observation, it is preliminarily submitted that the protection of consumer interests in EU competition law is directly influenced by all of the goals discussed. This is not to say that the protected 'consumer interest' should embrace wider public policy considerations. On the contrary, this should be viewed more narrowly in the light of the consumer welfare aim.

3.2 'Consumer welfare' in EU competition law

Consumer welfare constitutes one of the core objectives of EU competition law, although its content and role in EU competition law analysis remains nebulous.[62] Confusion regarding the notion of 'consumer welfare' can be partly attributed to the proponents of the Chicago school.[63] Bork equated consumer welfare with total welfare.[64] Kirkwood and Lande commented that, in so doing, 'Bork used "consumer welfare" as an Orwellian term of art that has little or nothing to do with the welfare of true consumers'.[65] Choosing between the consumer welfare standard and the total welfare standard is important because they may lead to different outcomes in certain cases; for example, when collaboration between competitors results in higher prices for consumers but lowers production costs.[66]

EU jurisprudence is of little assistance in searching for the meaning of 'consumer welfare' in EU competition law, since this term has appeared very rarely and

---

[61] On the difficulties in ranking competition law aims see L Parret, 'Shouldn't we Know what we are Protecting? Yes we Should! A Plea for a Solid and Comprehensive Debate about the Objectives of EU Competition Law and Policy' (2010) 6 Euro CJ 339, 375.

[62] On 'consumer welfare' see ICN, 'Competition Enforcement and Consumer Welfare' (2011) <http://www.internationalcompetitionnetwork.org/uploads/library/doc857.pdf> accessed 5 May 2015. On the different perceptions of 'consumer welfare' by economists, lawyers, and courts see B Orbach, 'The Antitrust Consumer Welfare Paradox' (2010) JCLE 133, 137.

[63] R Posner, 'The Chicago School of Antitrust Analysis' (1979) 127 U Pa L Rev 925.

[64] R Bork, *The Antitrust Paradox* (2nd edn, Maxwell Macmillan International 1993) 91; D Ginsburg, 'Judge Bork, Consumer Welfare, and Antitrust Law' (2008) 31 Harv JL & Pub Pol'y 449. Bork also employed a historical analysis and attributed consumer welfare (with the meaning of efficiency) as the Sherman Act's goal since its inception, a finding rebutted by Lande who argued, to the contrary, that the legislative intent embraced the redistribution of wealth. See R Bork, 'Legislative Intent and the Policy of the Sherman Act' (1966) 9 JL & Econ 7; R Lande, 'Wealth Transfers as the Original and Primary Concern of Antitrust: The Efficiency Interpretation Challenged' (1982) 34 Hastings LJ 65; R Lande, 'Proving the Obvious: The Antitrust Laws Were Passed to Protect Consumers (Not Just to Increase Efficiency)' (1999) 50 Hastings LJ 959, 961 on this debate.

[65] J Kirkwood and R Lande, 'The Fundamental Goal of Antitrust: Protecting Consumers not Increasing Efficiency' (2008) 84 Notre Dame L Rev 191, 199.

[66] J Brodley, 'The Economic Goals of Antitrust: Efficiency, Consumer Welfare and Technological Progress' (1987) 62 NYU L Rev 1020, 1034.

its content has never been formulated.⁶⁷ Contrary to Bork's definition of consumer welfare, it is generally accepted that 'consumer welfare' can be defined (in economic terms) as consumer surplus.⁶⁸ Improvement in consumer welfare is synonymous with providing consumers with access to a range of competitively priced goods and services.⁶⁹ This is consistent with Article 101(3) TFEU, which, arguably, excludes a neo-classical interpretation of consumer welfare and incorporates distributive elements, since the exempted agreement should '[allow] consumers a fair share of the resulting benefit'.⁷⁰ Very early on, the Commission seems to have opted for the adoption of 'consumer welfare', in the above-mentioned sense, as opposed to 'total welfare'. Note, for example, that in the 'First Report on Competition Policy' it stated that:

such a [competition] policy encourages the best possible use of productive resources for the greatest possible benefit of the economy as a whole and for the benefit *in particular of the consumer*.⁷¹

This raises the further question of when these resulting benefits should accrue for consumers; is long-term or short-term consumer welfare the appropriate standard? It has been recognized that if only short-term consumer benefits are accounted for, this will have a detrimental impact on firms' incentives to promote innovation and dynamic efficiencies.⁷² This approach seems to be in line with the Commission's rhetoric.⁷³ In its Guidelines on Article 101(3) TFEU it is stated that 'the fact that pass-on to consumers occurs within a certain time lag does not in itself exclude the application of [Article 101(3)]'.⁷⁴ Thus, the Commission does not, in principle, reject a long-term consumer welfare standard, since it accepts

---

⁶⁷ See the 'consumer welfare' reference in Case C-8/08 *T-Mobile Netherlands BV v Raad van Bestuur van de Nederlandse Mededingingsautoriteit* [2009] ECR I-4529, Opinion of AG Kokott, para 59 only to reject T-Mobile's argument; Case T-201/04 *Microsoft Corp v Commission* [2007] ECR II-3601, para 41 only when reiterating the Commission's decision; Case T-168/01 *GlaxoSmithKline Services v Commission* [2006] ECR II-2969, para 118; Case C-501/06P *GlaxoSmithKline Services v Commission* [2009] ECR I-9291, para 49 referring to GSK's argument; Case C-53/03 *SYFAIT v GlaxoSmithKline Plc* [2005] ECR I-4609, Opinion of AG Jacobs, para 91; Case C-209/07 *Competition Authority v Beef Industry Development Society* [2008] ECR I-8637, Opinion of AG Trstenjak, paras 56–57; *Eco Swiss* (n 30), Opinion of AG Saggio, para 42 referring to the well-being of consumers. See also *TeliaSonera* (n 57) para 22, which, oddly, refers to the well-being of the European Union; Case C-209/10 *Post Danmark A/S v Konkurrencerådet* [2012] 4 CMLR 23, para 42.
⁶⁸ M Motta, *Competition Policy: Theory and Practice* (CUP 2004) 18.
⁶⁹ K Cseres, 'Competition and Consumer Policies: Starting Points for Better Convergence' (2009) Amsterdam Center for Law & Economics Working Paper No 2009/06 <http://ssrn.com/abstract=1379322> accessed 15 June 2014, 4.
⁷⁰ Monti (n 37) 1065; Cseres (n 2) 252, 253.
⁷¹ First Report on Competition Policy (n 11) 12 (emphasis added).
⁷² Brodley (n 66) 1036; R Adhar, 'Consumers, Redistribution of Income and the Purpose of Competition Law' (2002) 23 ECLR 341, 350; S Bishop and M Walker, *The Economics of EC Competition Law: Concepts, Application and Measurement* (3rd edn, Sweet and Maxwell 2010) para 2.19.
⁷³ See XXIIIrd Report on Competition Policy 1993 (n 13) para 82; Commission (EC), XXXth Report on Competition Policy 2000 SEC (2001) 694 final <http://ec.europa.eu/competition/publications/annual_report/2000/en.pdf> accessed 15 June 2014, 42.
⁷⁴ Guidelines on Art [101(3)] TFEU (n 25), para 87.

that it is not necessary for the benefits to be passed on to consumers immediately. It points, though, to the fact that 'the greater the time lag, the greater must be the efficiencies to compensate also for the loss to consumers during the period preceding the pass-on'.[75]

3.3 'Consumer interest' in EU competition law

The multiplicity of aims accommodated in EU competition law and the interpretation of 'consumer welfare' allude to its potential to promote 'consumer interest' and suggest that competition law primarily accommodates the economic interests of consumers. This is so, as consumer welfare can in principle cater for lower consumer prices, wider choice, and better quality products.

However, in competition law the term 'consumer' refers not only to final consumers but also direct and indirect users of the product affected by the anti-competitive conduct or agreement.[76] Thus, the competition law notion of consumers is broader than that used in consumer law[77] and, therefore, the protective scope of competition law cannot (and should not) be limited to the protection of final consumers.[78] Competition law is not just an instrument of consumer policy, nor is it just about consumer protection.[79] That said, however, while competition law is aimed at enhancing consumer welfare, and the notion of consumer embraces a wider variety of stakeholders, final consumers are also included in that category and, for that reason, competition law definitely has a role to play. This is evident in judgments in which particular emphasis was given to the interests of final consumers.[80] Therefore, 'consumer interest' as synonymous with lower prices, better quality, and wider choice for final consumers presents a narrow

---

[75] Ibid. In favour of balancing benefits between present and future consumers see C Townley, 'Inter-generational Impacts in Competition Analysis: Remembering Those Not Yet Born' (2011) ECLR 580, in which he discusses an OFT Discussion paper on Article 101(3) TFEU. See OFT, 'Article 101(3)—A Discussion of Narrow Versus Broad Definition of Benefits' (Discussion Note for OFT Breakfast Roundtable, London, May 2010) para 1.8 and section 5.

[76] Commission (EC), 'Guidance on the Commission's Enforcement Priorities in Applying Article 82 EC of the EC Treaty to Abusive Exclusionary Conduct by Dominant Undertakings' [2009] OJ C45/7, para 19, fn 15; Guidelines on Art [101(3)] TFEU (n 25), para 84; Commission (EC), 'Guidelines on the Assessment of Horizontal Mergers under the Council Regulation on the Control of Concentrations between Undertakings' [2004] OJ C31/5, para 79.

[77] A general definition is provided in Directive 2011/83/EU of the European Parliament and the Council on Consumer Rights' [2011] L304/64, Article 2.

[78] K Cseres, 'The Controversies of the Consumer Welfare Standard' (2007) 3 Comp L Rev <http://www.clasf.org/CompLRev/Issues/Vol3Issue2Art1Cseres.pdf> accessed 15 June 2014, 121, 133.

[79] H Vedder, 'Competition Law and Consumer Protection: How Competition Law Can Be Used to Protect Consumers Even Better—Or Not?' (2006) 17 EBLR 83, 87.

[80] Case 28/77 *Tepea v Commission* [1978] ECR 1391, paras 56, 66–67; Case T-168/01 *GlaxoSmithKline Services* (n 67) para 118; Joined Cases T-213/01 and T-214/01 *Österreichischer Postsparkasse AG v Commission* [2006] ECR II-1601, para 115; Joined Cases T-259/02 to T-264/02 and T-271/02 *Raiffeisen Zentralbank Österreich AG v Commission* [2006] ECR II-5169, para 99; Commission (EU), Notice published pursuant to Article 27(4) of Council Regulation (EC) No 1/2003 in Case COMP/C-3/39.530—*Microsoft (Tying)* [2009] OJ C242/20, para 8.

approach to consumer welfare and should be distinguished from 'consumer welfare'. 'Narrow consumer welfare' corresponds to 'consumer interest' in competition law and forms part of 'consumer welfare' that embraces a wider variety of stakeholders.

Far from the narrow approach to consumer welfare, the influence of public interest considerations in EU competition law allowed some leeway for the non-economic interests of consumers to form part of the promoted 'consumer interest' in EU competition law. Nonetheless, public interest concerns such as the environment or health and safety considerations can only be accommodated in EU competition law if they can be translated in economic terms.[81] Finally, the market integration objective of EU competition law impacts upon the protected 'consumer interest' in EU competition, since it allows consumers to shop cross border thereby lowering prices and increasing choice. However, as will be discussed below, the promotion of market integration as a political objective may account for adverse effects on consumers.[82]

The above presents a legitimate interpretation of the consumer integration clause (Article 12 TFEU), which the LT placed amongst the introductory provisions of the Treaty and which provides that 'consumer protection requirements shall be taken into account in defining and implementing other Union policies and activities'.[83] If the consumer integration clause were to be interpreted more broadly, competition law enforcement would turn into a paternalistic system, promoting any kind of consumer interest over efficient market structures. The challenge is to encapsulate consumer interest within competition law analysis.

4. The Role of the 'Consumer Interest'

In this section, the Commission's rhetorical emphasis on consumer welfare as the preferred aim is discussed (part 1) in order to ascertain whether this overt emphasis on consumer welfare is matched by the substantive enforcement of competition law (part 2). This analysis allows for a comparison to be drawn between the role of 'consumer interest' (narrow approach to consumer welfare) in the Union institutions' rhetoric and its relevant role in the enforcement of EU competition provisions by the Commission and the CJEU.

---

[81] Guidelines on Art [101(3)] TFEU (n 25) paras 33, 42, 44, 49, 57, 59, 85.
[82] See text to nn 111–122 and 127.
[83] Article 12 TFEU (together with Article 38 Charter of Fundamental Rights) has been mentioned in Case T-224/10 *Association belge des consommateurs test-achats ASBL v Commission* [2011] ECR II-7177, para 43. It has been suggested that the mentioning of consumer protection in the introductory provisions of the Treaty and in the Charter may contribute to a more consistent consideration of consumer interests in other EU policy areas. See I Benoehr, *EU Consumer Law and Human Rights* (OUP 2014) 41. On Article 38 Charter of Fundamental Rights see S Weatherill, 'Article 38—Consumer Protection' in S Peers and others (eds), *The EU Charter of Fundamental Rights—A Commentary* (Hart 2014) 1005, 1025 arguing that Article 38 is unlikely to bring any significant change.

4.1 'Consumer welfare': Commission 'rhetoric'

The importance of consumer welfare in EU competition law can primarily be deduced from EU legislation and soft law instruments.[84] The wording of Articles 101 and 102 TFEU, as well as the way in which they are interpreted by the Commission, seems to attribute particular emphasis to the impact of certain conduct on consumers.[85] According to Article 101(3) TFEU, an otherwise anti-competitive agreement, caught by Article 101(1) TFEU, can be exempted from the scope of EU competition law if it is beneficial in terms of production, distribution, or technical and economic progress, as long as it provides consumers with a fair share of this benefit (and provided, of course, that the two residual conditions of this Article are met). In fact, this condition of passing on efficiencies to consumers is reiterated in EU legislation and Commission documents.[86] It is also expressly stated that 'the objective of Article [101 TFEU] is to protect competition on the market as a means of enhancing consumer welfare and of ensuring an efficient allocation of resources'.[87]

According to Article 102(b) TFEU, conduct is abusive when it limits production, markets, or technical development to the detriment of consumers. Indeed, in its 'Guidance on the Commission's Enforcement Priorities', the Commission attributes increased attention to 'likely consumer harm'.[88] Similar statements are to be found in the 'Discussion Paper on the Application of Article 82 of the Treaty on Exclusionary Abuses'.[89] Thus, the ultimate aim is the protection of consumer welfare while the competitive process serves as a means to that end, rather than being an aim in itself.[90]

---

[84] However, Drexl argues that the Treaty provisions do not support 'consumer welfare' as the goal of EU competition law and that reference to consumers in EU competition provisions only helps to define anti-competitive behaviour, and not the aim of the EU competition law system. Drexl (n 34) 686.

[85] Commission (EC), XXXIst Report on Competition Policy 2001 (Brussels, Luxembourg 2002) <http://ec.europa.eu/competition/publications/annual_report/2001/en.pdf> accessed 15 June 2014, 19–21 presenting Commission decisions that provide evidence of the direct impact of competition policy on consumer welfare.

[86] See, for example, Commission Regulation (EU) 1218/2010 on the application of Article 101(3) of the Treaty on the Functioning of the European Union to Certain Categories of Specialisation Agreements [2010] OJ L335/43 recitals 6, 10; Commission Regulation (EU) on the Application of Article 101(3) of the Treaty on the Functioning of the European Union to Certain Categories of Research and Development Agreements' [2010] OJ L335/36 recital 10; Guidelines on Vertical Restraints [2000] (n 54) para 136; Guidelines on Vertical Restraints [2010] (n 31) para 122; Guidelines on Art [101(3)] TFEU (n 25), para 85.

[87] Guidelines on Art [101(3)] TFEU (n 25) paras 13, 33; Commission (EC), 'Guidelines on the Application of Article 81 of the EC Treaty to Technology Transfer Agreements' [2004] C101/02, paras 5, 7; Commission (EU), 'Guidelines on the Applicability of Article 101 of the Treaty on the Functioning of the European Union to Horizontal Co-operation Agreements' [2011] OJ C11/1, para 269; Commission (EU), 'Guidelines on the Application of Article 101 of the Treaty on the Functioning of the European Union to Technology Transfer Agreements' [2014] C 89/3, paras 5, 7.

[88] Guidance Paper (n 76), para 19. [89] Discussion Paper (n 25) paras 1, 4.

[90] Commission (EC), Report on Competition Policy 2006 (2007) <http://ec.europa.eu/competition/publications/annual_report/2006/en.pdf> accessed 15 June 2014, 3 (Foreword); P Lowe, 'Consumer Welfare and Efficiency—New Guiding Principles of Competition Policy' (13th International Conference on Competition and 14th European Competition Day, Munich, 27 March 2007) <http://ec.europa.eu/competition/speeches/text/sp2007_02_en.pdf> accessed

The Role of the 'Consumer Interest' 27

After the modernization of EU competition law, 'consumer welfare' was bestowed a higher status, a fact which can be deduced from the Commissioners' speeches and other Commission initiatives.[91] The dedication to promoting private enforcement of competition law was, to a large extent, grounded on the potential for competition law to promote the interests of final consumers.[92] Furthermore, the Commission has undertaken a number of initiatives aimed at raising the awareness and involvement of European consumers in EU competition policy; hence the launching of European Competition Days[93] and the appointment of the Consumer Liaison Officer, responsible for taking complaints from end-users.[94]

The repeated statements in favour of the consumer welfare standard can be seen as an attempt by the Commission to increase consumers' confidence in competition policy and gain political support.[95] The 2008 Commission Report on Competition Policy[96] features, as its central focus, the topic 'Cartels and Consumers', while specifically mentioning the benefits for final consumers of a properly functioning competition regime. According to the Report:

> The fight against cartels is central to ensuring that the benefits of a properly functioning competition regime are offered to the final consumer in a given market for products or services...Cases such as the Banana cartel show that the impact of the cartel on final consumers may be direct when they are purchaser or user of a product or service.[97]

---

14 June 2014; contra T Eilmansberger, 'Dominance—The Lost Child? How Effects-based Rules Could and Should Change Dominance Analysis' (2006) 2 Euro CJ 15, 18; O Andriychuk, 'Can We Protect Competition Without Protecting Consumers?' (2009) 6 Comp L Rev <http://www.clasf.org/CompLRev/Issues/Vol6Issue1Article4Andriychuk.pdf > accessed 2 June 2014, 77.

[91] For example, see M Monti, 'Competition in a Social Market Economy' (Conference of the European Parliament and the European Commission on 'Reform of European Competition Law', Freiburg, 9–10 November 2000) <http://ec.europa.eu/competition/speeches/text/sp2000_022_en.pdf> accessed 14 June 2014; N Kroes, 'Delivering Better Markets and Better Choices' (European Consumer and Competition Day, London, 15 September 2005, Speech/05/512) <http://ec.europa.eu/competition/speeches/text/sp2007_11_en.pdf> accessed 14 June 2014; N Kroes, 'Competition Policy and Consumers' (General Assembly of BEUC, Brussels 16 November 2006, Speech/06/691) <http://europa.eu/rapid/pressReleasesAction.do?reference=SPEECH/06/691&format=HTML&aged=0&language=EN&guiLanguage=en> accessed 14 June 2014. See also P Lowe, 'Preserving and Promoting Competition: A European Response' [2006] 2 CPN 1; P Lowe, 'The Design of Competition Policy Institutions for the 21st Century—the Experience of the European Commission and DG COMP' [2008] 3 CPN 1, 6.

[92] Commission (EC), 'Damages Actions for Breach of the EC Antitrust Rules' (Green Paper) COM(2005) 672 final, para 2.5; Commission (EC), 'Damages Actions for Breach of the EC Antitrust Rules' (White Paper) COM(2008) 165 final, 4.

[93] XXXth Report on Competition Policy (n 73) 23; S Norberg, 'Competition Policy of the European Commission: In the Interest of Consumers?' (Leuven, 20 June 2003) <http://ec.europa.eu/competition/speeches/text/sp2003_021_en.pdf> accessed 15 June 2014.

[94] Commission (EC), Report on Competition Policy 2008, COM(2009) 374 final, para 109; Commission (EC), XXXIII Report on Competition Policy 2003, SEC(2004) 658 final, 16. Discussing the appointment of the Consumer Liaison Officer and its shortcomings as an under-resourced body, O Dayagi-Epstein, 'Representation of Consumer Interest by Consumer Associations—Salvation for the Masses?' (2007) 3 Comp L Rev <http://www.clasf.org/CompLRev/Issues/Vol3Issue2Art3DayagiEpstein.pdf> accessed 15 June 2014, 209, 217.

[95] Cf Cseres (n 69) 5. [96] Report on Competition Policy 2008 (n 94).

[97] Ibid, paras 5–6. See also Commission (EU), 'Staff Working Paper Accompanying the Report from the Commission on Competition Policy 2008' COM(2009) 374 final, for example, para 325.

The Commission has stressed that 'consumers' concerns [are] at the heart of its competition activities and considers it essential that the main thrust of competition policy should be on maximising consumer welfare'.[98] It is vital that end consumers benefit from a functioning competition regime.[99] Such statements suggest that the Commission accepts a narrow consumer welfare standard corresponding to the promotion of 'consumer interest' in EU competition law. However, despite the Commission's overt dedication to 'consumer interest', it seems questionable as to whether the CJEU and the Commission itself are indeed prepared to adopt this standard.

4.2 'Consumer interest': Insights from EU jurisprudence

In what follows, selected cases are analysed, with a focus on cases that are indicative of the inconsistency between the rhetoric and substantive EU competition law enforcement.[100] In the selected cases a conflict can be discerned between the narrow consumer welfare aim and other EU competition law aims (market integration, economic freedom, and competitive market structure). Furthermore, these cases are relevant to the interests of 'final' consumers and the analysis will seek to show how these interests have affected the substantive enforcement of EU competition law.

4.2.1 Consumer interest and Article 101 TFEU

The bifurcated structure of Article 101 TFEU (prohibition—exemption) allows consumer interest to be taken into account at two different stages of the analysis: first, in finding that an agreement has, as its *object* or *effect*, the *restriction of competition* (Article 101(1) TFEU); and second, in ruling that this agreement is, nonetheless, not caught by Article 101 TFEU, since it *improves the production* or *distribution of goods* or *promotes technical and economic progress* while allowing *consumers a fair share of the resulting benefit* and does not impose restrictions that are not indispensable to the attainment of these objectives and does not afford the possibility of eliminating competition in respect of a substantial part of the products in question (Article 101(3) TFEU).

a. Consumer interest in Article 101(1) TFEU

The interpretation of the object and effect categories, as well as the notion of restriction of competition, links back to the multiplicity of aims in EU competition law. If consumer welfare is the preferred standard for EU competition law

---

[98] Report on Competition Policy 2008 (n 94), para 108.
[99] SWP to 2008 Report (n 97), para 355.
[100] See E Buttigieg, *Competition Law—Safeguarding the Consumer Interest: A Comparative Analysis of US Antitrust Law and EC Competition Law* (Kluwer Law International 2009) for a detailed analysis of this issue.

over, for example, economic freedom or market integration as a political objective, then the interpretation of restriction of competition is different.[101]

1. Object restrictions and consumer interest

This section focuses on cases where the ECJ resorted to a formalistic approach to the object category and refused to take into account the lack of potential adverse impact on consumer interests as part of its analysis. These cases can be read in the light of the traditional approach to object cases;[102] however, a closer look suggests that the outcome may have been different had the ECJ followed a narrow consumer welfare standard and interpreted the restriction of competition as the possible adverse impact on the latter rather than as a restriction on the economic freedom of other market participants.

T-Mobile concerned an exchange of confidential information between the five mobile telephone operators in the Netherlands. The ECJ was asked to give a preliminary ruling on whether this practice constituted an object restriction. The referring court suggested that, because the direct object of this practice was not the determination of prices for post-paid subscriptions in the retail market, its actual detrimental effects on competition could not be unmistakably inferred so as to qualify as an object restriction.[103] The ECJ, in line with its case law on object restrictions, opined that 'the concerted practice must simply be capable in an individual case, having regard to the specific legal and economic context, of resulting in the prevention, restriction or distortion of competition within the common market and…it is not possible on the basis of the wording of Article [101(1) TFEU] to conclude that only concerted practices which have a direct effect on the prices paid by end users are prohibited'.[104] The ECJ endorsed AG Kokott's Opinion and stressed that 'Article [101 TFEU], like the other competition rules of the Treaty, is designed to protect not only the immediate interests of individual competitors or consumers but also to protect the structure of the market and thus competition as such'.[105]

The ECJ in *T-Mobile* disregarded the absence of a direct link between the practice and consumer prices; by emphasizing the importance of protecting the

---

[101] On this notion see Odudu (n 17), ch 5; R Nazzini, 'Article 81 EC between Time Present and Time Past: A Normative Critique of "Restriction of Competition" in EU Law' (2006) 43 CMLRev 497, 505; B Robertson, 'What is a Restriction of Competition? The Implications of the CFI's Judgment in O2 Germany and the Rule of Reason' (2007) 28 ECLR 252, 255–257.

[102] See Guidelines on Art [101(3)] TFEU (n 25) paras 21–22. A number of commentators have discussed the rather nebulous approach to object restrictions. See A Jones, 'Left Behind by Modernisation? Restrictions by Object under Article 101(1)' (2010) 6 Euro CJ 649; S King, 'The Object Box: Law, Policy or Myth?' (2011) 7 Euro CJ 269; A Andreangeli, 'From Mobile Phones to Cattle: How the Court of Justice Is Reframing the Approach to Article 101 (Formerly 81 EC Treaty) of the EU Treaty' (2011) 34 W Comp 215; D Bailey, 'Restrictions of Competition by Object under Article 101 TFEU' (2012) 49 CMLRev 559.

[103] *T-Mobile* (n 67), paras 19–20.

[104] Ibid, paras 31, 36. See also Case C-286/13 P *Dole Food v Commission* (judgment of 19 March 2015), para 123.

[105] Ibid, para 38. *T-Mobile* (n 67), Opinion of AG Kokott, paras 57–60.

structure of the market it resorted to a formalistic approach to object restrictions. This formalistic approach reflects the ordoliberal tradition[106] and raises the question of how 'competition as such' is to be defined. Which is the relevant legal test that the courts should follow? It seems that the notions of the 'competitive process' and 'competition as such' are not straightforward, and can only be clarified with reference to a further objective.[107] Generally, everyone would agree that 'competition' is desirable. The further question, though, concerns the purpose for which it is desirable. Is it to promote efficiency, market integration, economic freedom, or some other value?[108]

In particular, in *T-Mobile* the ECJ approach seems to ultimately protect the economic interests of the dealers by outlawing outright a commercial agreement between mobile telephone operators. While it is true that the prohibition of Article 101(1) TFEU should not be narrowed down solely to behaviour having a direct influence on consumer prices, nonetheless the ECJ should reconsider its approach, especially in cases in which retail markets are involved and consumer harm is not evident.

On the other hand, the referring court in *T-Mobile* gave particular attention to the conditions of competition in the retail market; it specifically addressed the interests of end-users and rejected the formalism of examining only the reduction of inter-firm rivalry. This approach is interesting in the light of the ECJ judgment in *Allianz Hungária*,[109] where it stated that 'when determining that context, it is also appropriate to take into consideration the nature of the goods or services affected, as well as the real conditions of the functioning and structure of the market or markets in question'.[110] Arguably, a cursory examination of the market in question in *T-Mobile* would have allowed the practice to evade the object characterization.

If competition law analysis is to be imbued with the 'consumer interest' standard (narrow consumer welfare), then there is room to consider this in the assessment of the legal and economic context of the practice in alleged object cases. The GC approach in *GlaxoSmithKline* can be read in this light. In this case the GC reversed the earlier Commission decision and refused to accept that the GlaxoSmithKline dual pricing scheme constituted a restriction of competition by object.[111] It stated that:

---

[106] See text to nn 21–24.
[107] R Nazzini, 'Welfare Objective and Enforcement Standard in Competition Law' (2009) in A Ezrachi and U Bernitz (eds) *Private Labels, Brands and Competition Policy* (OUP 2009) 379, 387.
[108] Odudu (n 17) 2.
[109] Case C-32/11 *Allianz Hungária Biztosító Zrt. and Others v Gazdasági Versenyhivatal* [2013] 4 CMLR 25. For a criticism on this case see P Harrison, 'The Court of Justice's Judgment in *Allianz Hungária* is Wrong and Needs Correcting' (May 2013) *CPI Antitrust Chronicle* 1; C Graham, 'Methods for Determining Whether an Agreement Restricts Competition: Comment on *Allianz Hungária*' (2013) 38 ELRev 542. C I Nagy, 'The Distinction between Anti-competitive Object and Effect after Allianz: The End of Coherence in Competition Analysis?' (2013) 36 W Comp 541. See also Case C-67/13 P *Groupement des Cartes Bancaires v Commission* [2014] 5 CMLR 22, Opinion of AG Wahl, paras 50–52.
[110] *Allianz Hungária* (n 109), para 36. See also *Groupement des Cartes Bancaires* (n 109), para 53.
[111] However, it concluded that it had the effect of restricting competition. Case T-168/01 *GlaxoSmithKline Services* (n 67), para 190.

in effect, the objective assigned to [Article 101(1) TFEU]... is to prevent undertakings by restricting competition between themselves or third parties, from reducing the welfare of the final consumer of the products in question. Consequently, the application of Article [101(1) TFEU] to the present case cannot depend solely on the fact that the agreement in question is intended to limit parallel trade in medicines... but also requires an analysis designed to determine whether it has as its object or effect the... restriction... of competition, to the detriment of the final consumer... while it is accepted that an agreement intended to limit parallel trade must in principle be considered to have as its object the restriction of competition, that applies insofar as the agreement may be presumed to deprive final consumers of those advantages.[112]

In this case, the GC eschewed a formalistic treatment of the GlaxoSmithKline scheme, limiting parallel trade. In reaching that conclusion it took particular account of the specific conditions in the pharmaceutical industry, as well as the final consumers' interests.[113] Essentially, by viewing an increase in the welfare of final consumers as the aim of Article 101(1) TFEU,[114] the GC refused to accept that the GlaxoSmithKline scheme could be inferred to lead to a reduction in consumer welfare,[115] and thus to classify it as a restriction by object. Interestingly, the GC compares its analysis in this case with that adopted by the Court in the seminal *Consten and Grundig*,[116] suggesting that consumer welfare has been the guiding principle of EU competition law all along. In *Consten and Grundig*, the Court ruled that an absolute territorial protection constitutes a restriction by object; however, before reaching that conclusion, it undertook an 'abridged but real economic analysis' of this practice and its possible impact on the prices charged to final consumers.[117]

GlaxoSmithKline is important insofar as it makes a clear pronouncement of principle in favour of consumer welfare.[118] In this way, it reveals the potential ability of competition law to embrace and promote consumer interest, especially in markets in which the impact of anti-competitive practice on consumers is more evident. However, this decision was subsequently reversed by the ECJ, who treated this scheme as a restriction by object, without taking into account that it

---

[112] Case T-168/01 *GlaxoSmithKline Services* (n 67) paras 118–119, 121 (emphasis added).

[113] See P Rey and J Venit, 'Parallel Trade and Pharmaceuticals: A Policy in Search of Itself' (2004) 29 ELRev 153 for a very inclusive previous consideration of these conditions in the light of Case T-41/96 *Bayer AG v Commission* [2000] ECR II-3383.

[114] However, one should be cautious as to the meaning attributed to (final) consumers that includes both health insurance schemes and patients. See Case T-168/01 *GlaxoSmithKline Services* (n 67), 184–185.

[115] According to AG Trstenjak, this approach could not be applied in the *Beef Industry* case, given the absence of any statutory provisions that may prevent benefits from being passed on to consumers. Case C-209/07 *Competition Authority v Beef Industry* [2008] ECR I-8637, Opinion of AG Trstenjak, para 74.

[116] *Consten and Grundig* (n 30).

[117] Case T-168/01 *GlaxoSmithKline Services* (n 67), paras 120–121; *Consten and Grundig* (n 30) 343; V Korah, 'Judgment of the Court of First Instance in *GlaxoSmithKline*' (2007) 6 Comp Law 101, 104 stating that 'the judgment of the [GC] is an important reinterpretation of the [ECJ's] judgment in 1966, which I welcome'.

[118] A Howard, 'Object and Effect: What's in an Object?' (2009) 8 Comp Law 37, 42 arguing that 'the CFI has refocused the purpose of Article 81 EC within the scheme of the EC Treaty as a whole'.

was not likely to lead to a reduction in consumer welfare.[119] Thus, it adopted the same approach as the AG and the ECJ in the *T-Mobile* case, stating that:

Article [101 TFEU] aims to protect not only... but also *the structure of the market, and in so doing competition as such*... for a finding that an agreement has an anti competitive object, it is not necessary that final consumers be deprived of advantages of effective competition in terms of supply and price.[120]

Again, what is evident from this quote is the preference for the protection of competitive market structures over the consumer welfare aim. Despite the fact that they may at times yield the same outcomes, this is not the case here in the light of the factual circumstances in *GlaxoSmithKline*. In practical terms, classification of the GlaxoSmithKline scheme as a restriction by object makes it more difficult for the company to argue efficiencies under Article 101(3) TFEU, despite the fact that this is possible in theory.[121] Arguably, in this case the ECJ should have opted for the GC's approach and refrained from categorizing the conduct as a restriction by object. If a structural aim of Article 101 TFEU is adopted, namely protecting '*competition as such*', then a limit on parallel trade (despite the specific conditions in the pharmaceutical sector) falls under the object category. However, if consumer welfare is seen as the primary aim, in line with the Commission's policy pronouncements, then for the agreement to be labelled as restrictive of competition by object, it should at least be capable, from its content and the legal and economic context,[122] of reducing consumer welfare.

In addition, the focus of the GC on final consumers seems preferable in this case, despite the broader notion of consumers in competition law. This is explicable in the light of the nature of the product market concerned and its importance for end-users. In this case, the interests of intermediate customers (wholesalers) clashed with the interests of the final consumers. This fact was taken into account by the GC, who stated that:

In effect the wholesalers are economic agents operating at an intermediate stage of the value chain and may keep the advantage in terms of price which parallel trade may entail, *in which case the advantages will not be passed on to the final consumers*.[123]

Thus, given the conditions prevailing in the pharmaceutical industry, in this case parallel trade would benefit the intermediaries rather than the final consumers, a fact which the GC took into account in refusing to accept a restriction by object.

The assessment of object restrictions by its very nature entails a formalistic assessment. The latter should not preclude though a reorientation as to the aims of competition law and the resolution of conflicts between different aims. This can

---

[119] Case C-501/06P *GlaxoSmithKline Services* (n 67), paras 59–60.
[120] Ibid, para 63 (emphasis added).
[121] Case T-168/01 *GlaxoSmithKline Services* (n 67), para 233; *Consten and Grundig* (n 30) 342–343; *Matra Hachette* (n 51), para 85; Case T-374/94 *European Night Services v Commission* [1998] ECR II-3141, para 136; Guidelines on Art [101(3)] TFEU (n 25), para 46.
[122] Case T-168/01 *GlaxoSmithKline* (n 67), paras 110–111, 117–119.
[123] Ibid, para 122 (emphasis added).

take place in the assessment of the legal and economic context of an agreement and will permit consumer interest to trump the 'protection of competition' or 'market integration' aim in certain cases.

2. Effect restrictions and consumer interest

In effect cases there is more scope for a narrow consumer welfare approach. This is explicable in the light of the evaluation undertaken in these cases. In *O2 (Germany)*, the GC stated that:

> Such a method of analysis, as regards in particular the taking into account of the competition situation that would exist in the absence of the agreement, does not amount to carrying out an assessment of the pro- and anti-competitive effects of the agreement and thus to applying a rule of reason, which the Community judicature has not deemed to have its place under Article [101 TFEU]... The examination required... consists essentially in taking account of the impact of the agreement on existing and potential competition and the competition situation in the absence of the agreement, those two factors being intrinsically linked.[124]

The GC suggests that, under Article 101(1) TFEU, the analysis should address potential adverse effects on actual and potential competition (defined as possible negative effects on prices, output, innovation, or the variety or quality of goods and services),[125] an approach which is in line with the economic analysis of horizontal and vertical agreements.[126] Assessing the impact upon prices, output, innovation, and variety and quality of products echoes a consumer welfare economic approach and may allow for the evaluation of the interests of final consumers.

However, despite the economic approach to collusive practices, the notion attributed to the restriction of competition may still be influenced by the ideological undercurrent of EU competition law and allow room for other considerations not grounded on the economic analysis of anti-competitive effects. This is more likely to occur in relation to object restrictions. For example, in the context of vertical restraints the market integration objective has played a pivotal role in the development of the Commission's approach in the past. In early consumer guarantee cases,[127] while consumer interest was incidentally accommodated, the most important factor was market integration.[128] As the Commission concedes, the two are not necessarily in conflict since 'preservation of an open single market promotes an efficient allocation of resources throughout the Community for the benefit of consumers'.[129] However, the blank classification of restrictions to parallel trade as object restrictions, even in cases where no adverse effect on consumer welfare can be presumed,[130] suggests that there could be a conflict between the two and the latter is solved in favour of market integration.

---

[124] Case T-328/03 *O2 (Germany) v Commission* [2006] ECR II-1231, paras 69, 71.
[125] Guidelines on Art [101(3)] TFEU (n 25) para 24.
[126] See, for example, Guidelines on Horizontal Co-operation Agreements (n 87); Guidelines on Vertical Restraints [2010] (n 31).
[127] Case 31/85 *ETA Fabriques d'Ebauches v SA DK Investment and others* [1985] ECR 3933.
[128] J Goyder, 'Consumer Guarantees and Competition Issues' in J Lonbay (ed), *Enhancing the Legal Position of the European Consumer* (BIICL 1996) 80, 85 with references to the relevant case law.
[129] Guidelines on Art [101(3)] TFEU (n 25), para 13.
[130] See text to nn 111–123 in relation to the GlaxoSmithKline scheme.

b. Consumer interest in Article 101(3) TFEU

The bifurcated notion of Article 101 TFEU has sparked much debate on its application and the proper evaluation of pro and anti-competitive effects.[131] The Commission, relying on its practice and the CJEU case law, has provided clarity on this issue by stating that '[Article 101(3) TFEU] expressly acknowledges that restrictive agreements may generate objective economic benefits so as to outweigh the negative effects of the restriction of competition'.[132] Thus, Article 101(3) TFEU allows for the evaluation of pro-competitive effects, which are widely construed as including both productive and dynamic efficiencies as well as both cost and qualitative efficiencies.[133] According to Article 101(3) TFEU, a 'fair share' of the resulting efficiencies must accrue for consumers and the agreement must at least amount to a neutral effect upon the consumer affected directly or indirectly by the said agreement.[134]

Before the 'modernization' of EU competition law, the 'Braakman Report' suggested that the 'consumer passing on' condition should not have been understood literally, given the wide notion of the term 'consumer' in competition law, as well as the broad interpretation of 'benefit' in the CJEU case law.[135] It has generally been assumed in the application of the first condition of Article 101(3) TFEU that, as long as there are productive or dynamic efficiencies flowing from the agreement, these will generally be passed on to consumers.[136] Thus, this condition has been easily satisfied.[137]

Arguably, this is no longer the case since the adoption of an effects-based approach in the application of Article 101 TFEU.[138] Despite the fact that the Commission accepts that in cases in which the restrictive effects are limited, and efficiencies are substantial, it is not necessary to engage in a detailed analysis of this condition, provided that the other three conditions are met,[139] it does provide detailed economic guidance on the balancing of efficiencies with anti-competitive effects resulting from a restriction of competition under Article 101(1) TFEU.[140]

---

[131] See, for example, Nazzini (n 101); Odudu (n 17) 97–98; Townley (n 37) 177–178; See Case T-112/99 *Métropole télévision (M6) v Commission* [2001] ECR II-2459, para 74.

[132] Guidelines on Art [101(3)] TFEU (n 25), para 33; See also White Paper on Modernisation (n 29) para 57.

[133] Guidelines on Art [101(3)] TFEU (n 25), para 33, 50–72   [134] Ibid, para 85.

[135] Braakman Report (n 37), para 151; See *Philips/Osram* (Case IV/34.252) Commission Decision 94/986/EC [1994] OJ L378/37, 27; *EBU/Eurovision* (Case IV/32.150) Commission Decision 93/404/EEC [1993] OJ L179/23, 68; *Synthetic Fibres* (Case IV/30.810) Commission Decision 84/380/EEC [1984] OJ L207/17, 39; *BPCL/ICI* (Case IV/30.863) Commission Decision 84/387/EEC [1984] OJ L212/1, 36.

[136] Buttigieg (n 100) 70, 130; Howells and Weatherill (n 4) 534; B Suffrin, 'The Evolution of Article 81(3) of the EC Treaty' (2006) 51 AB 915, 933 arguing that 'in reality there is only one substantive condition, the first'; L Kjolbye, 'The New Commission Guidelines on the Application of Article 81(3): An Economic Approach to Article 81' (2004) 25 ECLR 566, 573, 575; Consumer Focus, 'Response to Vertical Restraints Block Exemption Regulation' (September 2009) <http://www.consumerfocus.org.uk/assets/1/files/2009/11/ConsumerFocusresponsetoconsultationonverticalrestraints.pdf> accessed 16 June 2014 in which it calls for increased attention from the Commission when this condition is evaluated.

[137] A Evans, 'European Competition Law and Consumers: The Article 85(3) Exemption' (1981) 2 ECLR 431, 431, 434.

[138] Kjolbye (n 136) 575.   [139] Guidelines on Art [101(3)] TFEU (n 25), para 90.

[140] Ibid, paras 92–104.

4.2.2 Consumer interest and Article 102 TFEU

a. Exploitative abuses

In Article 102 TFEU cases, consumer interest has only played a residual role, despite Article 102 TFEU being viewed by commentators, since its inception, as an instrument for combating only directly exploitative practices.[141] In the EU, it is now established case law that Article 102 TFEU catches both exploitative and exclusionary abuses.[142] This is in contrast with Section 2 of the Sherman Act, its US counterpart, which is not applicable to exploitative abuses, revealing more faith in the self-correcting potential of market mechanisms.[143] Exploitative abuses can take different forms, excessive pricing being the most common.[144]

Case law so far indicates that very few cases have been brought with regard to exploitative abuses, which can be partly attributed to the Commission's declared reluctance to act as price regulator, given the difficulties in calculating the excessiveness of the price.[145] So far, the Commission and the CJEU have been cautious

---

[141] R Joliet, *Monopolisation and Abuse of Dominant Position: A Comparative Study of the American and European Approaches to the Control of Economic Power* (Nijhoff 1970) 131, 249, 250; Akman (n 22), 296; see also H Schweitzer, 'The History, Interpretation and Underlying Principles of Section 2 Sherman Act and Article 82 EC' in CD Ehlermann and M Marquis (eds), *European Competition Law Annual 2007: a Reformed Approach to Article 82 EC* (Hart 2008) 119, 120 referring to the opposite opinion of Mestmäcker.

[142] *Continental Can* (n 38), para 26; *TeliaSonera* (n 57) para 24; *Post Danmark* (n 67), para 20; Guidance Paper (n 76) para 7.

[143] E Fox, 'Monopolization and Dominance in the United States and the European Community: Efficiency, Opportunity and Fairness' (1986) 61 Notre Dame L Rev 981, 993–994; *Verizon Communications Inc v Law Offices of Curtis V Trinko, LLP* 540 US 398, 407, 124 SCt 872 (2004); Questioning the self-correcting potential of exploitative abuses; A Ezrachi and D Gilo, 'Are Excessive Prices Really Self-Correcting?' (2008) 5 JCLE 249.

[144] On excessive pricing see *General Motors* (Case IV/28.851) Commission Decision 75/75/EEC [1975] OJ L29/14; on appeal Case 26/75 *General Motors Continental NV v Commission* [1975] ECR 1367, 12; *Chiquita* (Case IV/26.699) Commission Decision 76/353/EEC [1976] OJ L95/1; on appeal Case 27/76 *United Brands Company and United Brands Continental BV v Commission* [1978] ECR 207, paras 250–251; *British Leyland* (Case IV/30.615) Commission Decision 84/379/EEC [1984] OJ L207/11; on appeal Case 226/84 *British Leyland Plc v Commission* [1986] ECR 3263; *DSD* (Case COMP D3/34493) Commission Decision 2001/463 [2001] L166/1, para 111; on appeal T-151/01 *Der Grüne Punkt—Duales System Deutschland GmbH v Commission* [2001] ECR II-1607, para 121; *Deutsche Post* (Case COMP/C-1/36.915) Commission Decision 2001/892/EC [2001] OJ L331/40, paras 159–167. See P Akman, 'The Role of Exploitation in Abuse under Article 82 EC' in C Barnard and O Odudu (eds), *Cambridge Yearbook of European Legal Studies: Volume 11, 2008–2009* (Hart 2009) 165. In the UK, see *Napp Pharmaceuticals Holdings Ltd v Director General of Fair Trading* [2002] CAT 1, paras 353ff.

[145] Commission (EEC), Fifth Report on Competition Policy (Brussels, Luxembourg 1976) <http://ec.europa.eu/competition/publications/annual_report/ar_1975_en.pdf> accessed 16 June 2014, para 76; Commission (EC), XXIVth Report on Competition Policy 1994 (Brussels, Luxembourg 1995) <http://bookshop.europa.eu/is-bin/INTERSHOP.enfinity/WFS/EU-Bookshop-Site/en_GB/-/EUR/ViewPublication-Start?PublicationKey=CM9095283> accessed 16 June 2014, para 207; See M Motta and A de Streel, 'Excessive Prices and Margin Squeeze under EU Law' in CD Ehlermann and I Atanasiu (eds), *European Competition Law Annual 2003: What is an Abuse of a Dominant Position?* (Hart 2006) 91, 109 on these difficulties. See *Attheraces Ltd v The British Horseracing Board Ltd and BHB Enterprises plc* [2007] UKCLR 309, paras 6–7 on difficulties

in finding exploitative abuse and, in the majority of relevant cases, exclusionary abuse was also present.[146]

The Commission, however, appears prone to finding exploitative abuse under Article 102(c) TFEU in cases concerning final consumer interests. In *Football Cup 1998*, the Commission found discriminatory abuse in favour of French consumers although this did not affect the market structure. It expressly declared that:

> consumers' interests are protected by [Article 102], such protection being achieved either by prohibiting conduct by dominant undertakings which impairs free and undistorted competition or which is directly prejudicial to consumers.[147]

With regard to exploitative abuses, the finding of abuse is not based on the effects of the dominant undertaking's conduct on the market structure but, rather, on the impact of such conduct on consumers.[148] The EU approach to exploitative abuses is guided by a short-term consumer welfare rationale that could adversely impact on long-term consumer welfare and innovation.[149] This is very eloquently encapsulated in the following statement:

> If there are no high or insurmountable barriers to entry, it might well be that high prices are actually likely to be, on balance and with a longer-term perspective, good for consumers. There is much more for consumers to gain through increased competition than a mere decrease in prices: competition brings more choice, scope for differentiation in quality, innovation, etc.[150]

The approach to exploitative abuses has received widespread criticism by commentators, some of whom have called for limited application of Article 102 TFEU with regard to exploitative abuses[151] and others for a refined application, based

---

possibly encountered by UK courts in making pricing assessments. See also A Robertson, 'UK Competition Litigation: From Cinderella to Goldilocks?' (2010) 9 Comp Law 275, 284, who argues that the court addressed the issue of excessive pricing in a satisfactory manner.

[146] See, for example, *United Brands* (n 144) in which price discrimination, refusal to supply, and excessive pricing were addressed.

[147] *1998 Football World Cup* (Case IV/36.888) Commission Decision 2000/12/EC [2000] OJ L5/55, para 100. In the same vein Commission (EC), 'Commission Approves Ticketing Arrangements for Euro 2000' (Press Release, IP/00/591); Commission (EC), 'Commission Welcomes Improved Access to Tickets for the 2006 World Cup' (Press Release, IP/05/519); See also *Deutsche Post* (n 144) para 133.

[148] M Siragusa, 'The Application of Article 86 to the Pricing Policy of Dominant Companies: Discriminatory and Unfair Prices' (1979) 16 CMLRev 179, 187.

[149] R O'Donoghue and J Padilla, *The Law and Economics of Article 82 EC* (Hart 2006) 626.

[150] P Lowe, 'Consumer Welfare and Efficiency—New Guiding Principles of Competition Policy?' (Speech, 27 March 2007) <http://ec.europa.eu/competition/speeches/text/sp2007_02_en.pdf> accessed 14 June 2014.

[151] O'Donoghue and Padilla (n 149) 601, 602; E Paulis, 'Article 82 EC and Exploitative Conduct' in CD Ehlermann and M Marquis (eds), *European Competition Law Annual 2007: A Reformed Approach to Article 82 EC* (Hart 2008) 515; D Evans and J Padilla, 'Excessive Prices: Using Economics to Define Administrable Legal Rules' (2005) 1 JCLE 97, 99–100; Motta and de Streel (n 145). See also M Popofsky, 'Defining Exclusionary Conduct' (2006) 73 Antitrust LJ 435, 451 favouring the US per se legality approach to monopoly pricing. For a rich discussion see M Gal, 'Abuse of Dominance—Exploitative Abuses' in I Lianos and D Geradin (eds), *Handbook on European Competition Law* (Edward Elgar 2013) 385.

on first finding an effect on the market.¹⁵² The second approach is based on a two-step test: first finding an anti-competitive effect, and then consumer harm. This appears similar to the Commission's advocated approach towards exclusionary abuses.

Despite the justified calls for a cautionary approach to exploitative abuses, combating this type of abuse in certain cases, for example, in the light of entry barriers, is consistent with the wording of the Treaty and the case law, as well as with the Commission's pronouncements in favour of protecting consumer interests under the ambit of competition law. From a policy perspective, delivering concrete results to consumers plays an important role in winning their support and raising their interest in competition policy.

b. Exclusionary abuses

It was only after the seminal *Continental Can*¹⁵³ that the concept of exclusionary abuses came into play, as the second and most popular category of abuse, and this has been the dominant form of abuse in Article 102 TFEU jurisprudence ever since. The limited role of the consumer interest from the analysis undertaken can be partly attributed to the nature of exclusionary abuses, as 'practices detrimental to [consumers] through their impact on an effective competition structure'.¹⁵⁴ Final consumers are often a step too far from dominant firms' practices and their impact on the market.

The Commission attempted to gear the enforcement of Article 102 TFEU away from its former ordoliberal application towards a more economics-based approach.¹⁵⁵ It expressed its intention 'to ensure that dominant undertakings do not impair effective competition by foreclosing their competitors in an anti-competitive way, *thus having an adverse impact on consumer welfare*'. Thus, the Commission would focus on conduct leading to 'anti-competitive foreclosure', ie conduct that results in the exclusion of competitors *to the detriment of consumers* and would examine such foreclosure either at the intermediate level or the final consumer level, or both.¹⁵⁶ In cases where the intermediate users are actual or potential competitors of the dominant undertaking, the Commission would examine consumer harm further downstream.¹⁵⁷ However, the emphasis on retaining a competitive market structure remains deeply rooted in the enforcement of Article 102 TFEU, as the subsequent analysis reveals, and it may impede a more coherent examination of consumer interest despite the presence of some sparse elements of a nascent consumer welfare-oriented approach.

The prevailing opinion in the enforcement of Article 102 TFEU is that the protection of the competitive process safeguards consumer interest as well.¹⁵⁸ While it is true that economic freedom and consumer welfare might, at times, coincide,

---

[152] Akman (n 144) 176. [153] *Continental Can* (n 38). [154] Ibid, para 26.
[155] Discussion Paper (n 25); Guidance Paper (n 76). [156] Ibid, para 19.
[157] Ibid, n 15.
[158] P Marsden and P Whelan, '"Consumer Detriment" and its Application in EC and UK Competition Law' (2006) 27 ECLR 569, 576.

the fact that they are based on different normative values can also lead to different outcomes.¹⁵⁹ This is evident in *British Airways*, in which both the GC and the ECJ (in line with previous case law)¹⁶⁰ held that it was not necessary to examine the effects on consumers in order to find an abuse; it was sufficient that the conduct at issue had a restrictive effect on competition.¹⁶¹ Had the CJEU examined the effects of the abusive conduct on consumers and possible consumer detriment as a consequence, the outcome of this case might have been different.¹⁶²

Consumer interests have been taken into account in cases concerning refusal to supply an input protected under IP legislation.¹⁶³ This is due to the nature of these cases in the light of the test formulated in *Magill*.¹⁶⁴ According to this test, one of the conditions that need to be satisfied for a refusal to supply to be abusive is that it should prevent the emergence of *a new product* for which there is *potential consumer demand*.¹⁶⁵ This is consistent with AG Jacobs' dictum in *Oscar Bronner* that:

it is important not to lose sight of the fact that the primary purpose of [Article 102] is to prevent distortion of competition—and in particular to safeguard the interests of consumers—rather than to protect the position of particular competitors.¹⁶⁶

However, as *Microsoft* reveals, consumer interests, even where overtly addressed, do not play an important part in the analysis. Despite the fact that the GC, in this case, addressed potential instances of consumer harm (such as an impact on innovation and reduced consumer choice), once again, and in line with the Commission's decision,¹⁶⁷ the GC came to the conclusion that:

---

¹⁵⁹ L Lovdahl Gormsen, 'The Conflict Between Economic Freedom and Consumer Welfare in the Modernisation of Article 82 EC' (2007) 3 Euro CJ 329. Nazzini rejects consumer welfare as the aim of Article 102 TFEU. He argues that Article 102 TFEU jurisprudence pursues long-term social welfare whereas economic freedom and market integration are legal norms contributing to the attainment of this objective. R Nazzini, *The Foundations of European Union Competition Law* (OUP 2011) 4–5.
¹⁶⁰ *Continental Can* (n 38) 26.
¹⁶¹ Case T-219/99 *British Airways Plc v Commission* [2003] ECR II-5917, para 107. On rebates see E Rousseva, *Rethinking Exclusionary Abuses in EU Competition Law* (Hart 2010) 173–218.
¹⁶² P Akman, '"Consumer" versus "Customer": The Devil in the Detail' (2010) 37 JL & Soc 315, 334–337.
¹⁶³ Joined cases C-241/91 and 242/91P *RTE and ITP v Commission* [1995] ECR I-743 (*Magill*), paras 51–56; Case C-7/97 *Oscar Bronner v Mediaprint* [1998] ECR-I 7791, paras 39–41; Case C-418/01 *IMS Health GmbH and Co OHG v NDC Health GmbH and Co KG* [2004] ECR I-5039, paras 38, 52; *Microsoft* (n 67) [332]; Rousseva (n 161) 414–416 argues that the Guidance Paper makes 'consumer harm' a condition for ruling in all refusal to supply cases; Guidance Paper (n 76) paras 81, 86–88.
¹⁶⁴ *Magill* (n 163) paras 54–56.
¹⁶⁵ I Haracoglou, 'Competition Law, Consumer Policy and the Retail Sector: The Systems' Relation and the Effects of a Strengthened Consumer Protection Policy on Competition Law' (2007) 3 Comp L Rev <http://www.clasf.org/CompLRev/Issues/Vol3Issue2Art2Haracoglou.pdf> accessed 16 June 2014, 175, 202 argued that the decisive factor was the suppression of a new product, rather than the presence of consumer demand. See *Microsoft* (n 67), para 647 for a different and wider interpretation of the 'new product' requirement.
¹⁶⁶ *Oscar Bronner* (n 163), Opinion of AG Jacobs, para 58; See also Case T-184/01 *R IMS Health Inc v Commission* [2001] ECR II-3193, para 145.
¹⁶⁷ *Microsoft* (Case COMP/C-3/37.792) Microsoft Commission Decision of 24/3/2004, C(2004) 900 final, paras 93–708.

It is settled case law that Article [102 TFEU] covers not only practices that may prejudice consumers directly [exploitative abuses] but also those which indirectly prejudice them by impairing an effective competitive structure. In this case, Microsoft *impaired the effective competitive structure* on the work group server operating systems market *by acquiring a significant market share on that market*.[168]

The last part of the pronouncement above seems to condemn Microsoft only because of its market power, and thus embraces an ordoliberal rationale. In the light of this, it is questionable as to whether there is room for a more effects-based consumer-oriented approach in the application of Article 102 TFEU. AG Jacobs' Opinion in *Syfait* suggests that the answer to this may be positive. In this case, AG Jacobs argued that in the light of the specific conditions in the pharmaceutical industry 'it cannot be assumed that parallel trade would in fact benefit either the *ultimate consumers* of pharmaceutical products or the Member States, as primary purchasers of such products'.[169]

In his Opinion, AG Jacobs refrained from a formalistic application of Article 102 TFEU, and refused to accept that a refusal constitutes an abuse per se in the light of the dominant undertaking's intention to limit parallel trade.[170] Essentially, in this case (given the conditions pertaining in the pharmaceutical industry), AG Jacobs did not consider parallel trade to be beneficial to the consumer interest. In contrast, a limitation on parallel trade in this case would not amount to consumer harm. It could also have a positive impact on the firm's incentive to innovate.[171]

Regrettably, the ECJ did not issue a preliminary ruling in this case, since it did not consider the national body making the reference (the Greek Competition Commission) to be a court or tribunal.[172] It was only after a second preliminary reference that the ECJ expressed its opinion on this matter arguing that 'such an undertaking cannot base its arguments on the premise that the parallel exports which it seeks to limit are of only minimal benefit to the final consumer'.[173]

Reference to possible consumer detriment in the case of a margin squeeze abuse was made in *Deutsche Telekom*. According to the Court, conduct will be classified as an abusive margin squeeze:

If it has an exclusionary effect on competitors who are at least as efficient as the dominant undertaking itself by squeezing their margins and is capable of making market entry more difficult or impossible for those competitors, and thus of strengthening its dominant position on the market *to the detriment of consumers' interests*.[174]

---

[168] *Microsoft* (n 67), para 664 (emphasis added).
[169] *Syfait* (n 67), Opinion of AG Jacobs, para 100 (emphasis added).
[170] Ibid, para 69.
[171] Ibid, paras 89–91, 100. His analysis is consistent with the Commission's approach in its Guidance Paper. See Guidance Paper (n 76) paras 19–20, 31.
[172] *Syfait* (n 67), paras 37–38.
[173] Joined Cases C-468/06 to 478/06 *Sot Lelos kai Sia EE v GlaxoSmithKline AEVE* [2008] ECR I-7139, para 57.
[174] Case C-208/08P *Deutsche Telekom v Commission* [2010] ECR I-955, para 253. The Court also referred to consumer detriment when defining exclusionary abuse in *Post Danmark*. See *Post Danmark* (n 67) para 24.

In *Deutsche Telekom*, the ECJ placed the emphasis on the restriction of competition in the retail market in end-user access services and asserted that consumer detriment comprised a reduction in consumer choice coupled with the long-term prospect of having to pay higher prices.[175]

In *Post Danmark*, the ECJ discussed possible defences at the incumbent undertaking's disposal in order to escape the application of Article 102 TFEU, namely objective justifications and the efficiency defence. According to the ECJ, in relation to the latter 'it is for the dominant undertaking to show that the efficiency gains likely to result from the conduct under consideration counteract any likely negative effects on competition and consumer welfare in the affected markets'.[176] From the discussion of the efficiency defence, it may appear that Article 102 TFEU is enforced based on a consumer welfare rationale. However, this is not accurate, inasmuch as there is a mismatch between the Commission's burden of proving an abuse and the undertaking's burden in proving the efficiencies flowing therefrom. Inasmuch as the former is rather formalistic, it is futile to bring in the examination of effects a step ahead in the analysis.

Despite the Commission's overt efforts to reform Article 102 TFEU enforcement,[177] it seems that the EU courts are reluctant to steer away from the formalistic approach in the application of Article 102 TFEU and show an inconsistency in treating different forms of exclusionary abuses. On the one hand, recent margin squeeze and predation cases depict a more effects-based rationale and discuss the 'as efficient competitor test' suggested by the Commission's Guidance,[178] and on the other hand, the CJEU approach to rebates still shows signs of formalism.[179] Indicative of this is the CJEU approach in *Tomra*.[180] In *Tomra*, both the GC and the ECJ held that the Commission did not need to analyse the actual effects of exclusivity rebates on competition as long as it demonstrated that the

---

[175] Ibid, para 182, 258.
[176] *Post Danmark* (n 67) paras 41–42. The conditions for the successful invocation of the efficiency defence discussed by the Court reflect to a large extent the Guidance Paper (n 76), paras 30–31. See also *TeliaSonera* (n 57) para 76.
[177] With regard to the debate as to whether the Commission is acting within its competence see A Ezrachi, 'The European Commission Guidance on Article 82 EC—The Way in which Institutional Realities Limit the Potential for Reform' (2009) Oxford Legal Studies Research Paper No 27/2009 <http://ssrn.com/abstract=1463854> accessed 16 June 2014; L Lovdahl Gormsen, 'Why the European Commission's Enforcement Priorities on Article 82 EC Should Be Withdrawn' (2010) 31 ECLR 45. On whether the Commission has adopted a more economic approach to Article 102 TFEU see D Geradin, 'The Decision of the Commission of 13 May 2009 in the *Intel* Case: Where is the Foreclosure and Consumer Harm?' (2010) 1 JECLAP 112; P Marsden, 'Some Outstanding Issues from the European Commission's Guidance on Article 102 TFEU' in F Etro and I Kokkoris (eds), *Competition Law and the Enforcement of Article 102* (OUP 2010) 62–63.
[178] See text to n 174. See also *TeliaSonera* (n 57) paras 64–67; *Post Danmark* (n 67) para 25.
[179] On the CJEU's different approaches to rebates and other pricing practices see L Lovdahl Gormsen, 'Can Consumer Welfare Convincingly Be Said to Be an Objective of Article 102 When the Methodology Relies on an Inference of Effects?' in C Heide-Jorgensen and others (eds), *Aims and Values in Competition Law* (DJØF 2013) 183.
[180] Case T-155/06 *Tomra Systems and Others v Commission* [2010] ECR II-4361; On appeal case C-549/10P *Tomra Systems and Others v Commission* [2012] 4 CMLR 27.

conduct was capable of having such effect.¹⁸¹ This approach was re-affirmed by the GC in the much-awaited *Intel*.¹⁸²

A further point is that, in order for the Commission's policy initiative to succeed, the CJEU should adopt more explicitly the consumer welfare standard. After all, the CJEU 'is not formally bound by its own judgments' and 'has recognised the importance of adapting its case law in order to take account of changes that have taken place in other areas of the legal system or in the social context in which the rules apply'.¹⁸³ However, until the CJEU formally adopts a more effects-based approach, the Commission is still bound by its jurisprudence, not the other way around.¹⁸⁴

In addition, the differences between the Commission's and the CJEU's pronouncements allow room for confusion,¹⁸⁵ not only at the EU level, but also at national level as well,¹⁸⁶ since national courts are bound by European precedents and not the Commission's policy documents.¹⁸⁷ A more coherent theory of harm in EU jurisprudence will facilitate enforcement at the national level and, arguably, prompt consumers to bring follow-on actions before national courts. The current inconsistency in policy pronouncements and substantive enforcement of competition provisions unfortunately brings development two steps forward and one step back.

---

¹⁸¹ Case T-155/06 *Tomra* (n 180) paras 219, 288–290; Case C-549/10P *Tomra* (n 180), para 79.
¹⁸² Case T-286/09 *Intel v Commission* [2014] 5 CMLR 9, paras 80, 102–105, 143, 151–153. On this case see amongst others W Wils, 'The Judgment of the EU General Court in *Intel* and the So-called More Economic Approach to Abuse of Dominance' (2014) 37 W Comp 405; N Petit, 'Intel, Leveraging Rebates and the Goals of Article 102 TFEU' (2015) <http://papers.ssrn.com/sol3/papers.cfm?abstract_id=2567628> with further references.
¹⁸³ Joined Cases C-94/04 and C-202/04 *Federico Cipolla v Rosaria Fazari et al* [2006] ECR I-11421, Opinion of AG Maduro, paras 28–29.
¹⁸⁴ *British Airways* (n 161), Opinion of AG Kokott, para 28. See Case T-155/06 *Tomra* (n 180) para 219 pointing to the fact that 'the Commission, *even though the case-law does not require it*, also analysed, in the light of market conditions, the actual effects of the applicants' practices' (emphasis added). See also ibid, paras 287–289. Confirmed on appeal. Case C-549/10 P *Tomra* (n 180), para 79.
¹⁸⁵ See J Temple Lang, 'How Can the Problems of Exclusionary Abuses Under Article 102 TFEU be Resolved?' (2012) 37 ELRev 136, 141.
¹⁸⁶ A Ezrachi, 'The Commission's Guidance on Article 82 EC and the Effects Based Approach—Legal and Practical Challenges' in A Ezrachi (ed), *Article 82 EC: Reflections on its Recent Evolution* (Hart 2009) 51. See, for example, *National Grid plc v Gas and Electricity Markets Authority* [2009] CAT 21 for a national account in which the CAT rejected the claimant's argument that, because Article 102 TFEU aims at enhancing consumer welfare, the authority has to show that the alleged abusive conduct had a direct effect on consumers. See also *Burgess v OFT* [2005] CAT 25, para 344, 'Competition law is there in order to protect consumer choice, and to ensure that legitimate consumer needs and preferences are not thwarted by the actions of dominant firms, particularly for vulnerable classes of consumers'. In *The Competition Authority v O'Reagan and Others*, Irish Supreme Court [2007] IESC 22, the Irish Supreme Court declared that 'The entire aim and object of competition law is consumer welfare. Competitive markets must serve the consumer. That is their sole purpose. Competition law, as is often said, is about protecting competition not competitors, even if it is competitors who most frequently invoke it... Competition law does not outlaw economic power, only its abuse. Economic power may, and indeed should, be the reward of effective satisfaction of consumer needs'.
¹⁸⁷ However Nazzini (n 159) 521 argues that national courts should take into account the Commission's guidelines under Article 4(3) TEU (duty of cooperation).

5. Embracing 'Consumer Interest' in EU Competition Law

An adherence to the narrow consumer welfare standard and the formulation of a more coherent theory of consumer harm, through an economic analysis of the effects on the market, despite being complex and difficult to apply,[188] entails certain advantages. First, it is possible that over-enforcement of competition law will be avoided, thereby maintaining the functioning of competitive markets for the benefit of the consumer. At the same time, such an approach necessarily entails a higher burden of proof and, therefore, may lead to under-enforcement of competition law. However, if the preferred substantive standard of competition law enforcement is 'consumer welfare', the issue of under or over-enforcement of competition law is better addressed when regulating the burden of proof.[189] After all, difficulties in establishing a competition law violation should not caution against the adoption of a consumer welfare standard but, rather, act in favour of devising the necessary mechanisms that would render consumer welfare manageable and enforceable in practice.

Secondly, in procedural terms, the consumer welfare standard may trigger the increased involvement of consumers and consumer organizations in both private and public competition law enforcement. Such an approach towards consumer interest could potentially raise awareness among final consumers as the ultimate stakeholders in competition law and instigate a competition culture.

Since Articles 101 and 102 TFEU promote the same aim,[190] despite the different enforcement approaches, elevating consumer welfare as the principle aim and examining the impact on consumer interest in more detail could potentially bridge the differences in their application and align the substantive application of competition law with Commission rhetoric. However, the inconsistency between the rhetoric and EU competition law enforcement vividly points to the strong roots of the ordoliberal tradition and the market integration objective in EU competition law[191] that render very difficult attempts to redefine EU competition law goals. In addition, the controversies surrounding the meaning of consumer welfare, together with the occasional accommodation of public interest objectives in the analysis, further complicate the elevation of consumer welfare as the primary aim of EU competition law. But even if consumer welfare were to be elevated to become the primary aim, consumer interest forms only a narrow aspect of it. Thus, involving consumers in EU competition law enforcement could form an alternative route for increasing the relevance of consumer interest in competition law analysis.

---

[188] Rousseva (n 161) 342.
[189] For an interesting proposal see R Nazzini, 'The Wood Begun to Move: An Essay on Consumer Welfare, Evidence and Burden of Proof in Article 82 EC cases' (2006) 31 ELRev 518.
[190] *Continental Can* (n 38) 26.
[191] See text to nn 21–34.

If consumer participation in private competition law enforcement were to be enhanced through the adoption of appropriate procedural measures, then consumer interest would assume a more important role in competition analysis.[192] Enhanced consumer participation could not only allow competition policy to focus on consumer interest but, more importantly, it could also shift the current EU competition law enforcement standard towards a narrow consumer welfare approach.

In the past, procedural changes have influenced the substantive application of competition law.[193] The relationship between the introduction of Regulation 1/2003 and the shift towards a more economics-based approach in the application of Article 101 TFEU has been explored by Gerber. He argues that the Commission's success in introducing Regulation 1/2003 demonstrated that it would be easier for it to push forward with the adoption of a more economics-based approach towards competition law enforcement in the application of Article 101 TFEU.[194] Securing the necessary political support for Regulation 1/2003 provided the necessary impetus for the realization of the substantive reform.

Thus, it is arguable that, if the Commission's current initiative on the introduction of measures to facilitate private competition law enforcement and, more specifically, measures to facilitate consumer involvement succeed, this might signal an alteration in substantive competition law enforcement towards a real contemplation of the consumer interest.

To sum up, effective procedural measures supporting consumer involvement would allow the actual adoption of a consumer welfare standard since the Commission, having secured the necessary political will for the introduction of those measures, could appear more determined to go through with the substantive reform as well. Furthermore, consumer involvement could contribute to the actual identification of consumer harm in retail markets that in turn would influence the finding of a competition law violation. Increased consumer involvement can influence the substantive enforcement standard and vice versa; if the

---

[192] XXXth Report on Competition Policy (n 73) 7. See also Report on Competition Policy 2008 (n 94) para 368 which states that 'Consumer input is also an important asset in understanding markets, as consumers and their representatives are best placed to explain directly how they perceive the impact of a particular action'. See also ibid, 370; N Reich, 'Competition Law and the Consumer' in L Gormley (ed), *Current and Future Perspectives on EC Competition Law: A Tribute to Professor M. R. Mok* (Kluwer Law 1997) 126, 137; E Buttigieg, 'Consumer Interests under the EC's Competition Rules on Collusive Practices' [2005] EBLR 643, 664; Haracoglou (n 165) 196, 205; J Stuyck, 'EC Competition Law After Modernisation: More than Ever in the Interest of Consumers' (2005) 28 JCP 1, 16; A Asher, 'Enhancing the Standing of Competition Authorities with Consumers' (15 April 2004, ICN Conference, Korea).

[193] See S Calkins, 'Summary Judgment, Motion to Dismiss, and Other Examples of Equilibrating Tendencies in the Antitrust System' (1986) 74 Geo LJ 1065; W Kovacic, 'Private Participation in the Enforcement of Public Competition Laws' in M Andenas, M Hutchings, and P Whelan (eds), *Current Competition Law 2002* (BIICL 2003) 167; W Kovacic, 'The Intellectual DNA of Modern US Competition Law for Dominant Firm Conduct: The Chicago/Harvard Double Helix' [2007] Colum BLR 1, 63–64.

[194] D Gerber, 'Two Forms of Modernization in European Competition Law' (2008) 31 Fordham Int'l LJ 1235, 1257.

consumer interest is taken into account in competition law enforcement, more consumer involvement can be expected in the future.

6. Conclusion

The relationship between competition law and consumer law has been examined in this chapter, and consumer interest for the purposes of competition law analysis has been outlined. Further, it has been argued that the current overt movement towards the consumer welfare standard and the protection of consumer interest within the ambit of competition law in policy documents is not equally depicted in the substantive competition law analysis. This mismatch can have a negative impact not only on the protection of consumer interest but also on consistency in the application of EU competition law.

The analysis in this chapter calls for a more 'consumer-focused' application of competition law, which is by no means synonymous with a widening of the scope of competition law enforcement so as to embrace wider consumer considerations (such as safety issues[195] or unfair contract terms).[196] This falls under the ambit of consumer law. Instead, it argues for a more concrete adoption of the consumer welfare rationale in EU competition law jurisprudence, together with a detailed analysis of consumer interest in markets in which this is relevant.[197] Buttigieg argues that, if competition law provisions were to be enforced so as to further widen Union objectives, then such enforcement could also promote the interests of consumers.[198] The approach in this chapter is somewhat narrower. Not every consumer interest can be accommodated by competition law but, rather, only economic interests under the narrow notion of consumer welfare. In addition, the analysis herein does not adopt the view that competition law protection should only extend to final consumers. Rather, the point here is that, even though they are not the sole beneficiaries, they should be granted a more meaningful role in relation not only to substantive competition law enforcement but also (and more importantly) to procedural enforcement.

The analysis presented in this chapter has depicted an overall reluctance on the part of the EU courts to expressly address consumer interest, which can be attributed to the difficulties entailed in such an analysis, in terms of proving consumer harm as well as the deeply-embedded EU competition law objectives of market integration and economic freedom. However, the Commission has stressed, on numerous occasions, the importance of final consumers in relation to competition

---

[195] *Hilti* (n 41) paras 118–119; Guidance Paper (n 76), para 28.
[196] In the same vein C Osti, 'Interpreting Convergence: Where Antitrust Meets Consumer Law' (2009) 5 Euro CJ 377, 386. However, the distinction is not always a clear cut one: see Nebbia (n 59) 102; also Monti (n 60) 307–310.
[197] See, in a similar vein, S Waller, 'In Search of Economic Justice: Considering Competition and Consumer Protection Law' (2005) 36 Loyola U Chi LJ 631, 639.
[198] Buttigieg (n 100) 128.

Conclusion

law and policy. Thus, if aligning the Commission's rhetoric with substantive law application presents a complex task, which requires a careful and slow shift in the case law and the Commission's enforcement standard, then one needs to look at alternative paths towards increasing the importance of consumers' interest and role in competition law. This requires devising the necessary measures to allow the stakeholders themselves to assume a more active role in the enforcement of EU competition law.

3

Normative Justifications for Increased Consumer Involvement

1. Introduction

Two trends can be discerned in EU competition law over the last two decades. The first relates to the refocusing of its respective aims, calling for a more economics-based approach and pointing to 'consumer welfare' as the preferred standard in EU competition law analysis. This can be termed the substantive modernization of EU competition law enforcement.[1] The second trend can be termed procedural modernization and relates to alleviating the Commission of some of its enforcement burden as well as involving more actors in EU competition law enforcement (NCAs, national courts, and private parties).[2] Efforts to improve private EU competition law enforcement should be viewed as a further step in this direction.[3]

Since, as argued in Chapter 2, the substantive modernization has not yet fully succeeded, consumer participation in private competition law enforcement could be viewed as an alternative vehicle in bringing consumer interest into EU competition law analysis.[4] In Chapter 3 this option is addressed and normative

---

[1] See Chapter 2, text to nn 84–99.
[2] Council Regulation (EC) No 1/2003 on the Implementation of the Rules on Competition Laid Down in Articles 81 and 82 of the Treaty [2003] OJ L1/1. The Commission views Regulation 1/2003 as the 'keystone of the modernisation of the European Union's antitrust enforcement rules and procedures'. Commission (EC), 'Report on the Functioning of Regulation 1/2003' (Communication) COM(2009) 206 final, para 1.
[3] Commission (EC), 'Damages Actions for Breach of the EC Antitrust Rules' (Green Paper) COM(2005) 672 final (GP); Commission (EC), 'Damages Actions for Breach of the EC Antitrust Rules' (White Paper) COM(2008) 165 final (WP); Commission (EU), 'Proposal for a Directive of the European Parliament and of the Council on Certain Rules Governing Actions for Damages under National Law for Infringements of the Competition Law Provisions of the Member States and of the European Union' COM(2013) 404, 11 June 2013; Directive 2014/104/EU of the European Parliament and of the Council of 26 November 2014 on Certain Rules Governing Actions for Damages under National Law for Infringements of the Competition Law Provisions of the Member States and of the European Union [2014] OJ L349/1.
[4] Private enforcement is ascribed a narrow meaning encompassing only damages actions since, notwithstanding their contemporaneous character and the minimal consumer involvement therein, they have an additional compensatory function. In general, private enforcement can be defined as the invocation of competition law provisions in private litigation by private parties. See GP (n 3), para 1.1. It encompasses a variety of different tools, ranging from injunctive relief and the defensive use of competition law (Article 101(2) TFEU) to damages actions. In this book 'private

justifications for such participation are provided.[5] First and foremost, consumer damages claims could further the aims of private enforcement. In section 2, the principal aims of private competition law enforcement are identified by assessing EU jurisprudence and the Commission's policy documents. Despite the Commission's emphasis on the compensatory component of damages actions, EU jurisprudence suggests that increased attention should be given to their deterrent role. Together, compensation and deterrence are classified as the endemic/functional aims of damages actions (since they are endemic and pertain to the very function of competition law enforcement). If the choice and balance between the endemic/functional aims of damages actions is correct, this will further advance a range of ancillary benefits pertaining to the wider EU institutional framework. Section 3 discusses these benefits, which include primarily the enhancement of consumers' education and empowerment that will further contribute to the legitimization of EU competition policy (wider institutional benefits).

2. Endemic/Functional Aims of Private Competition Law Enforcement

2.1 Private enforcement of EU law

This section gives an overview of the debate on private enforcement of EU law before turning to examine private EU competition law enforcement in particular. The former analysis will put the competition law debate in context and will allow conclusions to be drawn regarding whether private EU competition law enforcement merits special attention. *Courage*[6] and *Manfredi*[7] specifically address the right to damages for competition law violations and form part of the Court's case law on the involvement of individuals in the enforcement of EU law before national courts.[8]

---

enforcement' and 'damages actions' are used interchangeably. See P Nebbia, 'Damages Actions for the Infringement of EC Competition Law: Compensation or Deterrence?' (2008) 33 ELRev 23 which points to a subtle difference in meaning.

[5] For a concise discussion see M Ioannidou, 'Enhancing Consumers' Role in EU Private Competition Law Enforcement: A Normative and Practical Approach' (2012) 8 Comp L Rev <http://www.clasf.org/CompLRev/Issues/CompLRevVol8Issue1.pdf> accessed 10 June 2014, 59, 65–69.

[6] Case C-453/99 *Courage Ltd v Bernard Crehan and Bernard Crehan v Courage Ltd and Others* [2001] ECR I-6297.

[7] Joined Cases C-295/04 to 298/04 *Vincenzo Manfredi and Others v Lloyd Adriatico Assicurazioni SpA and Others* [2006] ECR I-6619.

[8] Commission (EC), 'Annex to the Green Paper, Damages Actions for Breach of the EC Antitrust Rules', (Staff Working Paper) SEC(2005) 1732, 19 December 2005 (GP SWP), paras 19–20. See also J Temple Lang, 'The Principle of Effective Protection of Community Law Rights' in D O'Keeffe and R Bavasso (eds), *Judicial Review in European Union Law—Liber Amicorum in Honour of Lord Slynn of Hadley* (Kluwer Law International 2000) 235, 250, 273; H Smith, 'The Francovich Case: State Liability and the Individual's Right in Damages' (1992) 13 ECLR 129, 132; M Hoskins, 'Garden Cottage Revisited: The Availability of Damages in the National Courts for

In *Van Gend en Loos*, the ECJ acknowledged that EU law confers rights on individuals that arise not only when they are expressly granted but also as a derivative of clearly defined obligations imposed by the Treaty on individuals, Member States, and EU institutions.[9] It went on to state that:

the *vigilance of individuals* concerned to protect their rights amounts to an *effective supervision* in addition to the supervision entrusted by [Articles 258 and 259] to the diligence of the Commission and of the Member States…It follows…that [Article 30] must be interpreted as producing *direct effects* and creating *individual rights* which *national courts must safeguard*.[10]

The ECJ viewed private enforcement of EU law as complementary to the public enforcement avenues provided in the Treaty and suggested that individuals can become enforcement actors to the benefit of EU law.[11] According to the ECJ, certain EU norms have 'direct effect' and can be invoked before national courts provided that they confer rights upon individuals and are sufficiently clear, precise, and unconditional.[12] Thus, not only is EU law beneficial for individuals in the sense that it creates directly effective rights, it is also through the enforcement of those rights before the national courts that compliance with EU norms can be safeguarded.[13] Whether these rights have a substantive content or are merely restricted to an invocation entitlement depends on the nature of the Treaty provision at issue.[14]

However, the rights that individuals derive from directly effective EU norms have to be enforced before national courts according to national remedies and procedures,[15] since the Treaty was not intended to create new remedies.[16] This echoes the principle of national procedural autonomy[17] and the national courts'

Breach of the EEC Competition Rules' (1992) 13 ECLR 257, 259; Case C-128/92 *H J Banks & Co v British Coal Corporation* [1994] ECR I-1209, Opinion of AG van Gerven.

[9] Case 26/62 *NV Algemene Transport—en Expeditie Onderneming van Gend en Loos and Nederlandse Administratie der Belastingen* [1963] ECR 1, 12; See K Lenaerts, 'Constitutionalism and the Many Faces of Federalism' (1990) 38 AJCL 205, 209–210 for the importance of this judgment for the EU legal order.

[10] Ibid, 13 (emphasis added).

[11] P Craig, 'Once Upon a Time in the West: Direct Effect and the Federalization of EEC Law' (1992) OJLS 453, 455.

[12] *Van Gend en Loos* (n 9) 13. P Pescatore, 'The Doctrine of "Direct Effect": An Infant Disease of Community Law' (1983) 8 ELRev 155, 176–177. The direct effect of competition provisions has already been acknowledged in *BRT v SABAM*: Case 127/73 *Belgische Radio en Televisie and Société belge des auteurs, compositeurs et éditeurs v SV SABAM and NV Fonior 'BRT I'* [1974] ECR 51, paras 15–16.

[13] T Eilmansberger, 'The Relationship Between Rights and Remedies in EC Law: In Search of the Missing Link' (2004) 41 CMLRev 1199, 1205.

[14] Ibid, 1205–1206. Eilmansberger in this article attempts a classification of the relevant case law on the evolution of EU rights and remedies.

[15] Case 33/76 *Rewe v Landwirtschaftskammer fuer das Saarland* [1976] ECR 1989, para 5.

[16] Case 158/80 *Rewe Handelsgesellschaft Nord mbH and Rewe-Markt Steffen v Hauptzollamt Kiel* [1981] ECR-1805, para 44; Case C-432/05 *Unibet* [2007] ECR I-2271, para 40.

[17] For a critical appraisal of this principle see C Kakouris, 'Do the Member States Possess Judicial Procedural "Autonomy"?'(1997) 34 CMLRev 1389; see also M Ruffert, 'Rights and Remedies in European Community Law: A Comparative View' (1997) 34 CMLRev 307, 330. This term refers not only to procedural rules *stricto sensu*, but also to the wider set of rules for the enforcement of

obligation to enforce EU rights in line with the principle of equivalence and effectiveness.[18] At the same time, Member States have an obligation to provide remedies that are sufficient to safeguard effective judicial protection in the areas covered by EU law.[19]

The Court's case law has cast doubts on the existence of the principle of national procedural autonomy.[20] In *Factortame I*, the Court stressed the importance of the principle of effectiveness and required the national court to grant interim relief and set aside the national rule in question as it prevented EU rules 'from having full force'.[21] In *Francovich*, it expressly acknowledged that State liability for damages caused to individuals from a breach of EU law is inherent in the system of the Treaty.[22] It came to this conclusion by building on the *Van Gend en Loos* principle of directly effective Treaty rights and the national courts' obligation to safeguard them in accordance with the principle of sincere cooperation enshrined in Article 4(3) TEU.[23] The Court, with this formulation, caters for the 'full effectiveness of Community rules' and the 'protection of the rights which they grant'.[24] As AG Mischo observed, the formulation of State liability for damages as a matter of EU law also has the potential to act as an incentive for Member States to comply with their obligation,[25] thereby safeguarding the 'full effectiveness of Community

---

EU rights, either remedial or substantial. See A Komninos, 'Civil Antitrust Remedies Between Community and National Law' in C Barnard and O Odudu (eds) *The Outer Limits of European Union Law* (Hart 2009) 363, 372; P Haapaniemi, 'Procedural Autonomy: A Misnomer?' in L Ervo, M Graens, and A Jokela (eds), *Europeanization of Procedural Law and the New Challenges to the Fair Trial* (Europa Law Publishing 2009) 87, 94–95.

[18] *Rewe v Landwirtschaftskammer fuer das Saarland* (n 15), para 5; Case 45/76 *Comet v Produktschap voor Siergewassen* [1976] ECR 2043, para 13; Case 106/77 *Amministrazione delle Finanze dello Stato v Simmenthal* [1978] ECR 629, para 22; Case 199/82 *Administrazione delle Finanze dello Stato v SpA San Giorgio* [1983] ECR 3595, para 12.

[19] Article 19(1) TEU; On the significance of this provision see T Tridimas, *The General Principles of EU Law* (2nd edn, OUP 2006) 419–420; Also, Komninos (n 17) 375 comments that it is wrong to deduce from this provision that remedies are a matter of national law only.

[20] T Tridimas, 'Enforcing Community Rights in National Courts: Some Recent Developments' in D O'Keeffe and A Bavasso (eds), *Judicial Review in European Union Law—Liber Amicorum in Honour of Lord Slynn of Hadley* (Kluwer Law International 2000) 465; S Weatherill, 'Addressing Problems of Imbalanced Implementation in EC Law: Remedies in an Institutional Perspective' in C Kilpatrick (ed) *The Future of Remedies in Europe* (Hart 2000) 87, 99. Haapaniemi (n 17) 111–118.

[21] Case C-213/89 *R v Secretary of State for Transport, ex p Factortame Ltd* [1990] ECR I-2433, paras 20–21. On this case and the debate it generated regarding the relationship between EU law and the UK constitutional principle of parliamentary sovereignty see *R v Secretary of State for Transport, ex p Factortame Ltd* [1991] 1 AC 693 (HL); P Craig, 'Sovereignty of the United Kingdom Parliament after *Factortame*' (1991) 11 YEL 221; T Allan, 'Parliamentary Sovereignty: Law, Politics and Revolution' (1997) LQR 443; N Barber, 'The Afterlife of Parliamentary Sovereignty' (2011) 9 ICON 144.

[22] Joined Cases C-6/90 and 9/90 *Andrea Francovich and Others v Italian Republic* [1991] ECR I-5357, para 35. See also Joined Cases C-46/93 and 48/93 *Brasserie du Pêcheur SA v Federal Republic of Germany* [1996] ECR I-1029, paras 20, 22, 31–33. For case law paving the way to *Francovich* see Case 6/60 *Humblet* [1960] ECR 559, para 36; Case 60/75 *Carmine Antonio Russo v AIMA* [1976] ECR 45, para 9; *Simmenthal* (n 18), paras 22–23; *Factortame I* (n 21), paras 20–23. On the *Francovich* case, see P Craig, '*Francovich*, Remedies and the Scope of Damages Liability' (1993) 109 LQR 595.

[23] *Francovich* (n 22), paras 31–37.   [24] Ibid, paras 32–33.

[25] *Francovich* (n 22), Opinion of AG Mischo, para 92.

rules'. Thus, State liability under EU law is formulated so as to enlist the 'vigilance of individuals' for the enforcement of their rights and through this for the enforcement of EU law.[26]

The 'compliance role' ascribed to private litigation is particularly important in the field of competition law given that:

according to Article 3(1)(g) EC…[Article 101] constitutes a fundamental provision which is essential for the accomplishment of the tasks entrusted to the Community and, in particular, for the functioning of the internal market.[27]

Competition law provisions are attributed a public policy character.[28] They impose obligations on private parties, yet their aim is to safeguard the competitive process as a means of conferring benefits on consumers.[29] A competition law violation is established whenever certain conduct adversely impacts on the competition law aim, which serves the general interest. However, at the same time and depending on the nature of the competition law violation in each specific case, certain private interests are affected as well. This adds to the dual nature of competition provisions as laws for the protection of both private and public interests.[30] Through the protection of the rights of private parties before national

---

[26] For example, on the potential deterrent effect of private enforcement see Case 14/83 *Von Colson and Kamann v Land Nordrhein—Westfalen* [1984] ECR 1891, para 28; Case C-271/91 *Marshall v Southampton and South-West Hampshire Area Health Authority* [1993] ECR I-4367, para 24. On civil litigation's potential to strengthen compliance with quality standards, see also Case C-253/00 *Muñoz Cia SA and Superior Fruiticola Ltd and Redbridge Produce Marketing Ltd* [2002] ECR I-7289, paras 30–31. For a comment on this case see A Biondi, 'C-253/00 *Muñoz Cia SA and Superior Fruiticola Ltd and Redbridge Produce Marketing Ltd* [2002] ECR I-7289' (2003) 40 CMLRev 1241, 1246.

[27] Case C-126/97 *Eco Swiss China Time Ltd v Benetton International NV* [1999] ECR I-3055, para 36. For the potential changes to competition law and policy brought by the LT see R Lane, 'EC Competition Law Post Lisbon: A Matter of Protocol' in M Bulterman (ed), *Views of European Law from the Mountain: Liber Amicorum Piet Jan Slot* (Kluwer Law International 2009) 167; A Riley, 'The EU Reform Treaty and the Competition Protocol: Undermining EC Competition Law' (2007) 28 ECLR 703; R Barents, 'Constitutional Horse Trading: Some Comments on the Protocol on the Internal Market and Competition' in M Bulterman (ed), *Views of European Law from the Mountain: Liber Amicorum Piet Jan Slot* (Kluwer Law International 2009) 123; A Komninos, 'Continuity and Change in EU Competition Policy' (February 2010) CPI 1.

[28] *Eco Swiss* (n 27), paras 36–39; *Manfredi* (n 7), para 31; Case C-8/08 *T-Mobile Netherlands BV v Raad van Bestuur van de Nederlandse Mededingingsautoriteit* [2009] ECR I-4529, para 49. On the public policy character of competition law norms see L Gyselen, 'Comment from the Point of View of EU Competition Law' in J Wouters and J Stuyck (eds), *Principles of Proper Conduct for Supranational, State and Private Actors in the European Union: Towards a Ius Commune, Essays in Honour of Walter van Gerven* (Intersentia 2001) 135, 141–145. See also the GW SWP in which the Commission stresses the importance of private enforcement, in order to sustain the competitiveness of the European economy and the existence of open markets in the EU internal market. Thus, by linking damages actions to the promotion of these important public interest goals, the Commission seems to suggest that private litigation can also serve the public interest. GP SWP (n 8), paras 9–11, 52. This was also acknowledged by the Commission in Joined Cases T-22/02 and 23/02 *Sumitomo Chemicals v Commission* [2005] ECR II-4065, para 128.

[29] On the multiplicity of aims see Chapter 2, text to nn 20–61.

[30] M Freedland, 'The Evolving Approach to the Public/Private Distinction in English Law' in M Freedland and JB Auby (eds), *The Public Law/Private Law Divide* (Hart 2006) 93, 107 that views competition law as being 'indeterminate' between public and private law.

courts, the public element of competition law is reinforced. Thus, a court implementing those provisions will interpret them in the light of the public interest they seek to protect.[31]

2.2 Private enforcement of EU competition law: EU institutions' approach

Before the reinvigoration of the debate on private competition law enforcement, the Union institutions were cognizant of the potential application of EU competition law by national courts. In 1966, the Commission published a study on the situation regarding private enforcement of competition rules in the then six Member States. According to this study, private parties can have adequate recourse to national courts when damaged by a competition law violation.[32] In the Thirteenth Report on Competition Policy the Commission, for the first time, dedicated a separate section to the application of EU competition law by national courts, thereby acknowledging a widespread misconception regarding the Commission being the sole enforcer of competition law in the EU despite the national courts' potential to enforce competition norms as well.[33] It also stated that:

The machinery for enforcing competition law is thereby to some extent *decentralised*, the *availability of relief* more evenly distributed geographically and the place where *justice* can be obtained brought *closer* to the individuals seeking it... Scant use has yet been made of the possibility of actions for damages for breaches of the Community competition rules. There is a need to make all concerned more aware of this possibility. The Commission believes it desirable that the judicial enforcement of Articles 85 and 86 should also include the award of damages to injured parties because this would render *Community law more effective*.[34]

The above passage suggests that damages actions possess the potential to redress victims' harm, while at the same time bringing closer to the wider public the benefits of competition law enforcement and contributing to the effective enforcement of competition law. By quoting *BRT v SABAM*,[35] the Commission stresses the obligation of national courts to directly protect effective Treaty rights conferred

---

[31] Case C-360/09 *Pfleiderer AG v Bundeskartellamt* [2011] ECR I-5161, para 19.

[32] Commission (EEC), 'La Reparation des Consequences Dommageables d' une Violation des Articles 85 et 86 du Traite Instituant la CEE' (Brussels, 1966) *Série Concurrence* No 1, 5.

[33] It was timely for the Commission to explore the possibility of national courts' involvement some time after the enactment of Regulation 17/62, since this allowed time for the Union institutions to explore the implications of this Regulation and the Commission's exclusive competence to enforce Article 101(3) TFEU. Council (EEC) Regulation No 17: First Regulation Implementing Articles 85 and 86 of the Treaty [1962] OJ Spec Ed 87, Article 9(1).

[34] Commission (EC), Thirteenth Report on Competition Policy (Brussels, Luxembourg 1984) <http://bookshop.europa.eu/is-bin/INTERSHOP.enfinity/WFS/EU-Bookshop-Site/en_GB/-/EUR/ViewPublication-Start?PublicationKey=CB3883823> accessed 17 June 2014, paras 217–218 (emphasis added).

[35] *BRT I* (n 12).

on individuals.³⁶ At the same time, however, by referring to the 'decentralised [enforcement] machinery' it seems to suggest that damages actions possess additional merits other than delivering justice to affected individuals.³⁷ This was expressly stated two years later when the Commission accepted that:

the application by national courts would be in the interests of the proper functioning of the system of competition rules, which ultimately benefits all economic operators in Europe.³⁸

The Commission views private enforcement not only as a system for protecting individual rights but also as a wider instrument to secure the observance of EU competition norms. Despite emphasizing the former by pointing to the distinct functions of private and public enforcement, it nevertheless accepts its deterrent role as well.³⁹ After all, enlisting national courts as full-force enforcement authorities was one of the driving forces behind Regulation 1/2003.⁴⁰

The ECJ, in *Courage*,⁴¹ reiterated in a clearer manner the twin aims of private competition law enforcement, in line with the general approach to private enforcement of EU law and the Commission's pronouncements in relation to EU competition law in particular. In this case, Crehan (a publican) had signed two 20-year lease agreements with Intrepreneur Estates Ltd, which was co-owned by Courage (a brewery). The lease agreement contained an exclusive purchasing obligation for Crehan to obtain most of his beer supplies from Courage. Courage brought an action against Crehan before the English courts for the recovery of unpaid deliveries of beer. Crehan argued that the beer tie was contrary to

---

³⁶ Ibid. See also Case 37/79 *Marty v Estée Lauder* [1980] ECR 2481, para 13; Case C-234/89 *Stergios Delimitis v Henninger Braue AG* [1991] ECR I-935, para 45; Case C-242/95 *GT-Link AC v De Danske Statsbaner* [1997] ECR I-4349, para 57; Case C-282/95 P *Guerin Automobiles v Commission of the European Communities* [1997] ECR I-1503, para 39.

³⁷ This additional 'dissuasive effect' of damages actions was picked up by the ESC, which urged the Commission not to take measures that would induce excessive litigation: ESC, 'Opinion on the Thirteenth Report on Competition Policy' [1984] OJ C343/03, para 5; see also Commission (EC), Fourteenth Report on Competition Policy (Brussels, Luxembourg 1985) <http://bookshop.europa.eu/is-bin/INTERSHOP.enfinity/WFS/EU-Bookshop-Site/en_GB/-/EUR/ViewPublication-Start?PublicationKey=CB4184822> accessed 17 June 2014, para 47 where the Commission states that '[private enforcement] would allow the Commission's staff to deal more rapidly with particularly complicated cases'.

³⁸ Commission (EC), Fifteenth Report on Competition Policy (Brussels, Luxembourg 1986) <http://bookshop.europa.eu/is-bin/INTERSHOP.enfinity/WFS/EU-Bookshop-Site/en_GB/-/EUR/ViewPublication-Start?PublicationKey=CB4585430> accessed 17 June 2014, paras 38–39.

³⁹ Commission (EC), 'Notice on Cooperation between National Courts and the Commission in Applying Articles 85 and 86 of the EEC Treaty' [1993] OJ C39/6, paras 4, 16; Commission (EC), 'Notice on the Handling of Complaints by the Commission under Articles 81 and 82 of the EC Treaty' [2004] OJ C101/65, paras 1, 13; Commission (EC), 'Notice on the Cooperation between the Commission and the Courts of the EU Member States in the Application of Articles 81 and 82 EC' [2004] OJ C101/54, para 4.

⁴⁰ M Monti, 'Effective Private Enforcement of EC Antitrust Law' in CD Ehlermann and I Atanasiu (eds), *European Competition Law Annual 2001: Effective Private Enforcement of EC Antitrust Law* (Hart 2003) 3; J Sinclair, 'Damages in Private Antitrust Actions in Europe' (2002) 14 Loyola Consumer L Rev 547, 548.

⁴¹ *Courage* (n 6).

Article 101 TFEU and launched a counterclaim for damages suffered as a result.[42] The English Court of Appeal applied for a preliminary ruling and asked the Court whether the English *in pari delicto* rule, ie that a party to an illegal agreement cannot claim damages from the other party, thereby benefiting from its own misconduct, was contrary to the uniform application of EU law. In other words, could a party to an illegal agreement rely on Article 101 TFEU in order to claim damages as a result of his adherence to the prohibited clause, and should the English *in pari delicto* rule be disallowed as contrary to EU law? If yes, what circumstances should the national court take into consideration?[43]

The referring court pointed to the tension between the uniform application of Union law[44] and the principle of national procedural autonomy.[45] The issue was solved in favour of the uniform application of Union law, providing yet another example of the relativity of national procedural autonomy. The Court did not pronounce the existence of individual liability for infringement of competition law in an unequivocal way as it had in *Francovich* with regard to State liability, in which it stated that 'it is a principle of Community law that the Member States are obliged to make good loss and damage caused to individuals by breaches of Community law for which they can be held responsible'.[46] Nevertheless, if the Court's reasoning is cautiously followed, it could be suggested that it had actually arrived at the same conclusion. In *Courage,* the ECJ ruled, though not explicitly, on the existence of an EU right to damages for breaches of competition rules,[47] and alluded to its underlying aims.

---

[42] Ibid, paras 3–7. [43] Ibid, para 16.

[44] This being 'a fundamental requirement of the [Community] legal order': Joined cases C-143/88 and 92/89 *Zuckerfabrik AG v Hauptzollamt* [1991] ECR I-415, para 26.

[45] *Courage* (n 6), para 15.

[46] *Francovich* (n 22), para 37. *Courage* has been viewed as the extension of *Francovich* in the area of individual liability. The question of individual liability for breach of the competition law rules was first answered by AG van Gerven: *Banks* (n 8), Opinion of AG van Gerven, paras 36–45. AG van Gerven suggests that the principle of individual liability is inherent in the system of the Treaty in the same way as the principle of State liability. Ibid, paras 39–41, 45. This formulation was clearer than that of *Courage*.

[47] The majority of commentators accept that a Union right in damages exists; for example, see Komninos Assimakis, 'New Prospects for Private Enforcement of EC Competition Law: Courage v Crehan and the Community Right to Damages'(2002) 39 CMLRev 447; A Komninos, *EC Private Antitrust Enforcement—Decentralised Application of EC Competition Law by National Courts* (Hart 2008) 172–176; W van Gerven 'Harmonisation of Private Law: Do We Need It?' (2004) 41 CMLRev 505, 520; S Drake, 'Scope of Courage and the Principle of "Individual Liability" for Damages: Further Development of the Principle of Effective Judicial Protection by the Court of Justice' (2006) 31 ELRev 841, 849; N Reich, 'The "Courage" doctrine: Encouraging or Discouraging Violations for Antitrust Injuries?' (2005) 42 CMLRev 35, 38; N Dunne, 'The Role of Private Enforcement within EU Competition Law' (2014) (University of Cambridge Faculty of Law Research Paper No 36/2014) <http://papers.ssrn.com/sol3/papers.cfm?abstract_id=2457838> accessed 10 November 2014, 10–11; Contra C Miege, 'Modernisation and Enforcement Pluralism'—: The Role of Private Enforcement of Competition Law in the EU and the German Attempts in the 7th Amendment of the GWB' (2005) (Amsterdam Centre for Law and Economics, Workshop on Remedies and Sanctions in Competition Policy) 25–27; J Edelman and O Odudu, 'Compensatory Damages for Breach of Article 81' (2002) 27 ELRev 327, 336; O Odudu, 'Effective Remedies and Effective Incentives in Community Competition Law' (2006) 5 Comp Law 134, 141, fn 45; A Albors Llorens, 'The Ruling in *Courage v Crehan*: Judicial Activism or Consistent Approach?' (2002) 61 CLJ 38, 40–41; M Dougan, *National Remedies before the Court of Justice*

The Court began its reasoning by emphasizing the principles of supremacy and the direct effect of the EU legal order and the respective duties thereby imposed on national courts, as these were pronounced in the seminal *Costa v Enel*[48] and *Van Gend en Loos* cases, respectively.[49] It then reiterated *Eco Swiss* on the importance attributed to competition law provisions and *BRT v SABAM* on the directly effective nature of competition law provisions and the individual rights they create, which the national courts must safeguard.[50] After this three-step analysis based on the general principles of EU law and the nature of competition provisions, the Court concluded that:

any individual can rely on a breach of Article [101(1)] of the Treaty before a national court even where he is a party to a contract that is liable to restrict or distort competition within the meaning of that provision.[51]

Thus, the Court clarified the issue of who had standing, as a matter of principle, to invoke breach of competition provisions and suggested that as a matter of EU law standing is to be granted to any individual. Therefore, national laws denying standing to co-contractors (such as the English law at issue) will be contrary to EU law.[52] Note that AG Mischo also alluded to the possibility of consumers being potential claimants, as he stated that 'the individuals who can benefit from such protection are, of course, primarily third parties, that is to say consumers and competitors who are adversely affected by a prohibited agreement'.[53]

Defining the exact content and the beneficiaries of the individual rights under competition provisions is a complex task.[54] A formulation regarding the content of the right can be related to the obligation imposed by the same provisions.[55] In the case of an undertaking breaching its obligation not to engage in anti-competitive conduct, this will create rights for individuals following the *Van Gend en Loos* formulation. In this case, the right will be to undo the consequences of the anti-competitive breach. This was supported by AG Mischo in

---

(Hart 2004) 382–383; but see ibid, 386; See also Case T-395/94 *Atlantic Container Line v Commission* [2002] ECR II-875, para 414.

[48] Case 6/64 *Costa v ENEL* [1964] ECR 585.

[49] *Van Gend en Loos* (n 9); *Courage* (n 6), para 19. Note that in *Francovich* the Court began its reasoning in exactly the same way: *Francovich* (n 22), para 31.

[50] *Courage* (n 6), paras 20–23.   [51] *Courage* (n 6), para 24 (emphasis added).

[52] M Brkan, 'Procedural Aspects of Private Enforcement of EC Antitrust Law: Heading Toward New Reforms?' (2005) 28 W Comp 479, 494.

[53] See *Courage* (n 6), Opinion of AG Mischo, para 38.

[54] D Leczykiewicz, 'Private Party Liability in EU Law: In Search of the General Regime' in C Barnard and O Odudu (eds), *The Cambridge Yearbook of European Legal Studies—Volume 12, 2009-2010* (Hart 2010) 257, 278–279.

[55] See R Nazzini, 'Potency and Act of the Principle of Effectiveness: The Development of Competition Law Remedies and Procedures in Community Law' in C Barnard and O Odudu (eds), *The Outer Limits of the European Union* (Hart 2009) 401, 405 for a different approach. He views effective enforcement of Articles 101 and 102 TFEU as the legal basis of the right to damages. The content and function of the right to damages are formulated based on the principle of effectiveness. Eilmansberger criticizes this legal basis and instead argues in favour of the adoption of the 'protective scope' theory. Eilmansberger (n 13) 1241.

Courage, in which he observed that directly effective rights under Article 101 TFEU include 'the right, for individuals, to be protected from the harmful effects which an agreement which is automatically void may create'.[56]

Thus, if a competition law violation occurs, the primary obligation is breached giving rise to the derivative right, which can be protected through specific remedies before the national courts.[57] In *Courage*, the ECJ referred to 'the existence of such a right [in damages]'. Thus, the ECJ clarified the content of Union rights conferred on individuals by the directly effective competition provisions. The importance of *Courage* lies in the fact that the Court ruled that a private party can exercise this right to damages through an appropriate remedy that is not impeded by a national rule. Essentially, the Court ruled that the English *in pari delicto* rule (in its absolute form) should be set aside. This has the effect of giving co-contractors a remedy that is not available to them under English law.[58] The Court based its conclusion on the effective protection of individual rights and the effective enforcement of competition norms,[59] while here it is suggested that the deciding factor was the latter.[60]

In the formulation of the right to damages the principle of effectiveness has played a pivotal role. In *Courage*, the Court referred to the 'full effectiveness' of EU competition law rules and the 'protection of rights they confer on individuals'.[61] It further added that:

in particular, *the practical effect of the prohibition* laid down in [Article 101(1)] would be put at risk if it were not open to *any individual* to claim damages... Indeed, *the existence of such a right strengthens the working of the Community competition rules and discourages agreements or practices*, which are frequently covert, which are liable to restrict or distort competition. From that point of view, actions for damages before the national courts can make *a significant contribution to the maintenance of effective competition in the Community*.[62]

The practical effect of the competition law prohibitions is more important, especially given the fact that, in this very judgment, the Court pointed to the significance of those provisions for the accomplishment of the EU's objectives, the functioning of the internal market being underlined.[63] In the above quote, the

---

[56] *Courage* (n 6), Opinion of AG Mischo, para 37.

[57] For a detailed account of remedies in common law legal systems see R Zakrzewski, *Remedies Reclassified* (OUP 2005).

[58] Even if not expressly pronounced by the ECJ and despite the fact that the AG's reasoning in the case suggests that no new EU remedy was created: see *Courage* (n 6), Opinion of AG Mischo, para 47. To the contrary, the fact that *Courage* provided for a Union remedy regarding damages can also be supported by *Manfredi* (n 7), Opinion of AG Geelhoed, paras 52–57, 63.

[59] Unlike its AG and the ECJ in *Francovich* it did not refer to the principle of cooperation enshrined in [now] Article 4(3) TEU. See *Courage* (n 6), Opinion of AG Mischo, para 46; *Francovich* (n 22), para 36.

[60] See also Eilmansberger (n 13) 1226–1228. In the same vein see J Drexl, 'Competition Law as Part of the European Constitution' in A von Bogdandy and J Bast (eds), *Principles of European Constitutional Law* (2nd edn, Hart 2009) 659, 677–678.

[61] *Courage* (n 6), paras 25–26; cf *Francovich* (n 22), paras 32–33.

[62] *Courage* (n 6), paras 26–27 (emphasis added). [63] *Courage* (n 6), para 20.

Court endorses the deterrent effect of damages actions and their potential to act in the public interest.[64]

The ECJ approach in *Courage* was re-affirmed in *Manfredi*. In this case, consumers filed damages actions against insurance companies for damages flowing from an agreement that raised the price of insurance premiums following the agreement having been declared unlawful by the Italian NCA. The referring court asked the ECJ whether Article 101 TFEU (if applicable in this case) should be interpreted as allowing third parties with a relevant legal interest to claim damages when there is a causal connection between the prohibited practice and the harm. Furthermore, it addressed preliminary questions on limitation periods and punitive damages.[65]

As a new point the ECJ pronounced on the causality requirement and it stated that:

any individual can rely on the invalidity of an agreement or practice prohibited under that article and, where there is a *causal relationship* between the latter and the *harm* suffered, claim compensation for that harm.[66]

In adding causality as a condition of the right to damages, the ECJ again relied on the principle of effectiveness.[67] However, the Court did not refer to the potential of damages actions to contribute to the maintenance of effective competition in Europe, as it did in *Courage*.[68] Thus, one could conclude that the emphasis in *Manfredi* was on the effective protection of the right to damages rather than the effective enforcement of competition law. Nonetheless, this would have been a preliminary conclusion in that the ECJ stressed this element of damages actions in relation to the preliminary question on punitive damages, and actually linked it to the first reference to the principle of effectiveness in relation to the preliminary question on causation as a condition of the right to damages.[69]

Manfredi also discussed the possibility of granting punitive damages. The Court stated that damages actions can '[contribute] to the maintenance of effective competition in the Community'. Nonetheless, there is no obligation as a matter of EU law to award punitive damages.[70] Overall, *Manfredi* followed *Courage* on the point of the aims of damages actions and it was important for the additional reason that it concerned consumer damages actions, thereby pointing to their relevant deterrent function.

---

[64] Komninos (n 17), 382.   [65] *Manfredi* (n 7), paras 2, 20–21.
[66] Ibid, para 63 (emphasis added).   [67] Ibid, para 60.
[68] See text to n 62 above.   [69] *Manfredi* (n 7), paras 60, 90–91.
[70] The Directive on Damages Actions focuses on 'full compensation' that should not amount to overcompensation, either by means of punitive or multiple damages: Directive on Damages Actions (n 3), recital 12 and Article 3. In the UK, the CAT awarded exemplary damages in *2Travel Group PLC (in Liquidation) v Cardiff City Transport Services Ltd* [2012] CAT 19. In *Manfredi*, the Italian government argued that punitive damages were contrary to the Italian legal system (*Manfredi* (n 7), para 85); nonetheless, the referring court did award punitive damages: see Oxera, 'Quantifying Antitrust Damages: Towards Non-binding Guidance for Courts' (December 2009), Study prepared for the European Commission <http://ec.europa.eu/competition/antitrust/actionsdamages/quantification_study.pdf> accessed 26 July 2014, 94.

Since *Courage* and *Manfredi*, the Court has had ample opportunities to highlight the deterrent potential of damages actions and their respective potential to contribute to the effective enforcement of EU law. *Europese Gemeenschap v Otis NV and Others* concerned a follow-on claim brought by the Commission before the Belgian courts against elevator manufacturers that were fined by the Commission for their participation in the elevators cartel.[71] The defendants argued that if the Commission were allowed to bring a damages action against them, this would amount to a breach of the principle of judicial independence and equality of arms in the light of the Commission's role in the proceedings.[72] The ECJ rejected this argument by relying on *Courage* and *Manfredi* and reiterated that the EU principle of effectiveness would be jeopardized if it were not open to any individual to bring a damages action before national courts and stressed the potential of the right to damages to contribute to the maintenance of undistorted competition in the EU.[73] Article 47 of the Charter of Fundamental Rights of the EU does not preclude the Commission from bringing a damages action before national courts for losses sustained by EU institutions as a result of an agreement found by the Commission to be contrary to EU competition rules.[74]

In *Pfleiderer*, the Court was called to assess whether, in order to prepare their actions for damages, private parties should be granted access to the leniency file.[75] This issue is addressed in detail in Chapter 4 but here it is sufficient to say that in order to answer the preliminary reference question the Court reiterated the contribution of damages actions to the maintenance of effective competition in the EU.[76] In the subsequent *Donau Chemie AG*, the ECJ was asked whether a national provision, according to which third parties could only be granted access to documents for the purpose of filing a damages claim with the consent of all the parties in the proceedings and national courts could not weigh up the conflicting interests in order to grant access on a case-by-case basis, was contrary to

---

[71] Case C-199/11 *European Commission v Otis NV and Others* [2013] 4 CMLR 4.
[72] Ibid, para 24.   [73] Ibid, paras 40–43.
[74] Ibid, 77. On 24 November 2014 the Brussels Commercial Court subsequently dismissed the Commission claim for failing to prove the relevant damage and the causal link between the competition law infringement and the respective damage. See Stibbe, *Competition Law Newsletter December 2014* <http://www.stibbe.com/en/news/2014/december/competition-law-newsletter-december-2014> accessed 2 December 2014. The Commission has announced its intention to appeal. See A Maton, 'European Commission's Damages Litigation Illustrates Challenges in Domestic Regimes Pre-implementation of the Damages Directive' (Kluwer Competition Law Blog, 9 April 2015) <http://kluwercompetitionlawblog.com/2015/04/09/european-commissions-damages-litigation-illustrates-challenges-in-domestic-regimes-pre-implementation-of-the-damages-directive/#respond> accessed 10 April 2015.
[75] *Pfleiderer* (n 31).
[76] Ibid, para 29. See also Case T-344/08 *EnBW Energie Baden-Württemberg AG* [2012] 5 CMLR 4, paras 128, 148. On appeal Case C-365/12 P *Commission v EnBW Energie Baden-Württemberg AG* [2014] 4 CMLR 30, paras 104–108. The Court, on appeal, reversed the GC judgment placing the emphasis on 'the effective protection of the right to compensation' and stating that '[i]n the absence of any such necessity, the interest in obtaining compensation for the loss suffered as a result of a breach of Article [101 TFEU] cannot constitute an overriding public interest, within the meaning of Article 4(2) of Regulation No 1049/2001'. For more detail on this case, see Chapter 4, text to nn 145–153.

EU law.[77] The ECJ stressed the deterrent effect of the EU right to damages.[78] The procedural requirements for its exercise are determined by national law in accordance with the principle of equivalence and effectiveness.[79] However, in the light of *Pfleiderer*, national courts should be able to weigh up conflicting interests, namely the exercise of the right to compensation and the rights of the implicated undertakings as well as any adverse impact on incentives to cooperate with the competition authorities.[80] The ECJ assessed the possible impact of granting access to the leniency file in the course of private enforcement and the effectiveness of leniency programmes and made a bold statement in favour of the deterrent effect of damages actions:

as regards the public interest of having effective leniency programmes…it should be observed that, *given the importance of actions for damages brought before national courts in ensuring the maintenance of effective competition in the European Union*…the argument that there is a risk that access to evidence contained in a file in competition proceedings which is necessary as a basis for those actions may undermine the effectiveness of a leniency programme in which those documents were disclosed to the competent competition authority cannot justify a refusal to grant access to that evidence.[81]

In *CDC*, the GC made another clear statement in favour of the deterrent effect of damages actions when it stated that:

the leniency and co-operation programmes whose effectiveness the Commission is seeking to protect are not the only means of ensuring compliance with EU competition law. Actions for damages before the national courts can make a significant contribution to the maintenance of effective competition in the EU.[82]

In *Kone*, the ECJ was called to answer the question regarding whether a person can claim damages from cartel members for the loss caused by a non-party to the cartel that raised the prices of his or her products more than he or she would have done in the absence of the cartel (umbrella pricing).[83] The ECJ relied heavily on the principle of effectiveness and answered the question in the affirmative.[84] In particular, the ECJ stated that:

[i]t is true…that it is, in principle, for the domestic legal system of each Member State to lay down the detailed rules governing the application of the concept of the 'causal link'. However, it is clear from the case-law of the Court…that national legislation must ensure that European Union competition law is fully effective. Those rules must therefore specifically take into account *the objective pursued by Article 101 TFEU*, which aims to guarantee

---

[77] Case C-536/11 *Bundeswettbewerbsbehörde v Donau Chemie AG and Others* [2013] 5 CMLR 19, para 13.
[78] Ibid, para 23.   [79] Ibid, para 27.   [80] Ibid, paras 32–34.
[81] Ibid, para 46. Access to leniency documents has now been legislatively resolved in the Directive on Damages Actions. See Chapter 4, text to nn 169–170. The point made here is in relation to the Court stressing the deterrent potential of damages actions as opposed to their compensatory function.
[82] Case T-437/08 *CDC Hydrogen Peroxide v Commission* [2011] ECR II-8251, para 77.
[83] Case C-557/12 *Kone AG and Others v ÖBB Infrastruktur AG* [2014] 5 CMLR 5, para 17.
[84] Ibid, paras 34, 37.

effective and undistorted competition in the internal market, and, accordingly, prices set on the basis of free competition. In those circumstances, the Court has held... that national legislation must recognise the right of any individual to claim compensation for loss sustained.[85]

Thus, the ECJ appears to suggest that the right to damages is instrumental for guaranteeing free and undistorted competition in the internal market, ie contributing to the deterrence of competition law violations. To this end, even if Member States are free to set the rules governing the exercise of the right to damages before national courts,[86] such rules should not prevent the full effectiveness of competition rules. In *Kone*, the ECJ placed the emphasis on the effective enforcement of competition law rather than the effective judicial protection of litigants, thereby suggesting that damages actions primarily contribute to the former.[87]

Apart from the Court's jurisprudence highlighting the contribution of damages actions to the effective enforcement of EU competition law, the Commission has also highlighted this function on a number of occasions. In its Green Paper on Damages Actions, which spurred the policy debate on introducing EU measures in order to advance private competition law enforcement, the Commission, echoing a number of Commissioners' speeches at the time,[88] commented on the binary compensatory and deterrent function of damages actions.[89] In so doing, the Commission simply reiterated *Courage* and recognized compensation and deterrence as equally important goals of private enforcement.[90]

However, the Commission's rhetoric shifted in its subsequent White Paper on Damages Actions, in which it identified compensation as the first and foremost guiding principle for the proposed measures to improve the conditions for bringing

---

[85] Ibid, para 32.
[86] AG Kokott took a bolder stance than the Court, as she argued in her Opinion that national law determines the details rather than the existence of the right to damages and that the conditions of civil liability of cartel members for umbrella pricing are a matter of EU law. *Kone* (n 83), Opinion of AG Kokott, paras 23, 28.
[87] In the same vein, see *Kone* (n 83), Opinion of AG Kokott, para 30. On this case see N Dunne, 'It Never Rains but it Pours? Liability for "Umbrella Effects" under EU Competition Law in Kone' (2014) 51 CMLRev 1813.
[88] M Monti, 'Private Litigation as a Key Complement to Public Enforcement of Competition Rules and the First Conclusions on the Implementation of the New Merger Regulation' (Speech at IBA—8th Annual Competition Conference, Fiesole, 17 September 2004, SPEECH/04/403). In the same vein see also his successor N Kroes, 'Enhancing Actions for Damages for Breach of Competition Rules in Europe' (Speech at the Harvard Club, New York, 22 September 2005, SPEECH/05/553).
[89] GP (n 3), para 1.1; GP SWP (n 8), paras 4–6, 179–180.
[90] F Bulst, 'Of Arms and Armour—The European Commission's White Paper on Damages Actions for Breach of EC Antitrust Law' [2008] *Bucerius Law Journal* 81, 82. See C Hodges, 'Competition Enforcement, Regulation and Civil Justice: What is the Case?' (2006) 43 CMLRev 1381, 1382 in which he suggests that the Commission's approach towards private enforcement indicates its desire to use 'civil damages claims as an additional regulatory control in deterring breaches of competition law'; C Hodges, *Litigating Antitrust Claims in Europe: Proposals and Implications* (National Legal Centre for the Public Interest 2006) 3.

damages actions before the national courts.⁹¹ This shift can be attributed to the need for the proposed measures to be premised on a genuine European approach reflecting Member States' legal culture and tradition,⁹² since in the majority of Member States damages actions aim primarily at compensating the victim rather than deterring perpetrators.⁹³ The withdrawn Draft Damages Directive also reflected this approach.⁹⁴ On closer reading though, both the WP and the Draft Damages Directive seem to have adopted a functional approach towards private damages claims by enlisting private actors for the effective enforcement of competition law.⁹⁵ The Proposal for a Directive on Damages Actions has further shifted the focus from effective competition law enforcement, as one of the main aims of damages actions, to ensuring the effectiveness of the right to damages and optimizing the interaction between public and private competition law enforcement.⁹⁶ This has assuaged political opposition to the adoption of the Directive. However, it constitutes a retreat from the Court's bold approach to the effectiveness and deterrent effect of damages actions. However, the Directive does underline the public policy character of competition law provisions and the potential of damages actions to contribute to the effective enforcement of competition law in the EU.⁹⁷

⁹¹ WP (n 3), para 1.2; Commission (EC), 'Staff Working Paper accompanying the White Paper on Damages actions for breach of the EC antitrust rules' SEC(2008) 404, 2 April 2008 (WP SWP), paras 14–15.
⁹² WP SWP (n 91), para 16.
⁹³ See D Waelbroeck, D Slater, and G Even-Shoshan, 'Study on the Conditions of Claims for Damages in Case of Infringement of EC Competition Rules' (Comparative Report) (Ashurst Study) (31 August 2004) <http://ec.europa.eu/competition/antitrust/actionsdamages/comparative_report_clean_en.pdf> accessed 30 June 2014, 77; *Manfredi* (n 7), para 87 for the submissions of the Austrian government. See also Danish Ministry for Economic and Business Affairs, 'The Commission's Green Paper on Damages Actions for Breach of the EC Antitrust Rules' (19 April 2006); Secrétariat Général des Affaires Européennes, République Française, 'Note à la Commission Européenne'. For an account of the Dutch situation see J Kortmann, 'The Tort Law Industry' (2009) 17 ERPL 789, 799, 810. Essentially, this echoes the principle of corrective justice, which inflicts a rectification duty upon the tortfeasor and it can be contrasted with the prevailing economic analysis underlying common law. See J Coleman, 'The Practice of Corrective Justice' in D Owen (ed), *Philosophical Foundations of Tort Law* (Clarendon Press 1995) 54, 57, 66. On the principle of corrective justice and the importance of a 'bipolar relationship of liability' as an important feature of private law relations see E Weinrib, *The Idea of Private Law* (Harvard University Press 1995) 2, 56–83, 114–144; J Coleman, 'The Practice of Corrective Justice', 67. See also J Kortmann and C Swaak, 'The EC White Paper on Antitrust Damage Actions: Why the Member States are (Right to Be) Less than Enthusiastic' (2009) 30 ECLR 340, 341 which argues that 'in many European jurisdictions the instrumentalist view of tort law is a minority view'.
⁹⁴ Commission (EC), 'Proposal for a Council Directive Governing Actions for Damages for Infringements of Article 81 and 82 of the Treaty', Draft Damages Directive (Document withdrawn before publication—on file with the author), Explanatory Memorandum, para 1.1.
⁹⁵ For example, the proposal on opt-out collective actions (included in the WP and the Draft Damages Directive) supports the functional approach to private enforcement. Monti, in his Report on the single market, is also in favour of a functional approach to private enforcement. See M Monti, 'A New Strategy for the Single Market' (Report to the President of the European Commission, 9 May 2010), 102, 103.
⁹⁶ Proposal for a Directive on Damages Actions (n 3), para 1.2.
⁹⁷ Directive on Damages Actions (n 3), recitals 1, 3.

The above analysis indicates that there is an inconsistency between the Court's approach to private competition law enforcement and the aims identified by the Commission. The Court appears to emphasize the deterrent function of damages actions, whereas the Commission conceals the latter in an attempt to win Member States' support for its private enforcement initiative. Nonetheless, the Court jurisprudence indicates that damages actions can equally contribute to the effective enforcement of competition law and the deterrence of competition law violations while providing compensation for affected parties,[98] whereas emphasis is placed on the former function.

2.3 Scepticism as to the deterrent function of (follow-on) damages actions

Private damages actions carry different deterrence potential depending on whether they are brought as stand-alone or follow-on claims, ie claims that depend on a prior infringement decision by the Commission or an NCA.[99] From a pragmatic perspective, if private litigation levels were to increase in Europe, this would most probably concern follow-on rather than stand-alone actions,[100] which are seen as less beneficial in terms of deterrence since they freeride on public enforcement.[101]

Nevertheless, follow-on actions could still contribute to deterring competition law infringements. First, the distinction between stand-alone and follow-on actions is not as clear-cut as it first appears. One could distinguish between

---

[98] On the bifurcated functions of private competition law enforcement see W Wils, 'The Relationship Between Public Antitrust Enforcement and Private Actions for Damages' (2009) 32 W Comp 3, 5. For empirical evidence on the beneficial compensatory and deterrent effects of private enforcement see R Lande and JP Davis, 'Benefits From Private Antitrust Enforcement: An Analysis of Forty Cases' (2008) *University of San Francisco Law Review* 879; R Lande and JP Davis, 'Toward an Empirical and Theoretical Assessment of Private Antitrust Enforcement' (2013) University of San Francisco Law Research Paper No 2012-17 <http://papers.ssrn.com/sol3/papers.cfm?abstract_id=2132981> accessed 30 June 2014.

[99] For a definition see Komninos (n 47), 6–7.

[100] Cf W van Gerven, 'Private Enforcement of EC Competition Rules in the ECJ—*Courage v Crehan* and the Way Ahead' in J Basedow (ed), *Private Enforcement of EC Competition Law* (Kluwer Law International 2007) 19, 24; FW Bulst, 'Private Antitrust Enforcement at a Roundabout' (2006) 7 EBOR 725, 729. However, a quantitative analysis of the competition law litigation in different Member States suggests that the majority of relevant actions concern stand-alone claims. See B Rodger, 'The Empirical Data Part 1: Methodology, Case Law, Courts and Processes' in B Rodger (ed), *Competition Law, Comparative Private Enforcement and Collective Redress Across Europe* (Kluwer Law International 2014) 83, 110–116. This can be explained in the light of the nature of competition claims. For example, in Portugal, competition law was invoked as a defence or in the context of vertical agreements. See also V Brisimi and M Ioannidou, 'Stand-alone Damages Actions: Insights from Greece and Cyprus' (2013) 34 ECLR 654. In Italy, 75% of damages cases are stand-alone. See A Komninos, 'Private Enforcement in the EU with Emphasis on Damages Actions' in I Lianos and D Gerardin (eds), *Handbook on EU Competition Law: Enforcement and Procedure* (Edward Elgar 2013) 228, 247.

[101] M Harker and M Hviid, 'Competition Law Enforcement and Incentives for Revelation of Private Information' (2008) 31 W Comp 297; T Eilmansberger, 'The Green Paper on Damages Actions for Breach of the EC Antitrust Rules and Beyond: Reflections on the Utility and Feasibility of Stimulating Private Enforcement through Legislative Action' (2007) 44 CMLRev 431, 478.

follow-on actions in a technical sense, ie where a prior decision exists addressed to the defendants, and in a wider sense, ie where there are ongoing proceedings but no final decision or where the defendants are members of the same undertaking but not addressees of the infringement decision.[102] In *Nokia v AU Optronics and others*, Nokia brought a claim for damages against LCD manufacturers before the English High Court. At the same time there was an ongoing Commission investigation into LCD manufacturers, which resulted in the imposition of fines for larger LCDs. No fines were imposed on the smaller LCD manufacturers that were sued by Nokia before the High Court. Thus, Nokia's claim could be termed a 'hybrid' claim, since even though it could not benefit from a Commission's infringement decision Nokia developed its claim through disclosure in relevant US proceedings.[103] In this case, the Commission's investigation prompted Nokia to bring its hybrid claim and, in the absence of a Commission decision, Nokia developed its stand-alone claim. Sales J accepted a rather low threshold for pleading requirements and pointed to the tension between ensuring that claims are clearly pleaded to allow the defendant to answer and preserving justice by not preventing the claimant from bringing a meritorious case due to overly strict and demanding pleading rules.[104] The balance was struck 'by allowing a measure of generosity in favour of a claimant',[105] thereby indicating a preference for private enforcement that could potentially act as a disincentive to firms that are contemplating engaging in anti-competitive activities.

Another example of a hybrid claim comprising both a stand-alone and a follow-on element comes from *Toshiba Carrier v KME*.[106] In this case, the English Court of Appeal suggested that English subsidiaries of a cartel could not be sued as anchor defendants if they were not the addressees of the statement of objection and the parent company did not exercise decisive influence. Nonetheless, the court allowed the claim because it contained a stand-alone element.[107] Again, even though the infringement decision was not formally binding upon the national court, it triggered private litigation.

Second, there is a risk that reduced public enforcement can have a negative spill-over effect on follow-on claims. Regulating the interaction between public and private enforcement is the primary objective of the adopted Directive on Damages Actions[108]

---

[102] See B Rodger, 'Institutions and Mechanisms to Facilitate Private Enforcement' in B Rodger (ed), *Competition Law, Comparative Private Enforcement and Collective Redress Across Europe* (Kluwer Law International 2014) 23, 33.
[103] *Nokia AU Optronics and others* [2012] EWHC 731 (Ch), paras 20–25.
[104] Ibid, 62.
[105] Ibid, 67. See also *Toshiba Carrier UK Ltd v KME Yorkshire Ltd* [2012] EWCA Civ 1190, para 32.
[106] *Toshiba Carrier* (n 105).
[107] Ibid, paras 37–40. See also *Provimi Ltd v Aventis Animal Nutrition SA and others* [2003] 2 All ER 683, paras 31–32; *Cooper Tire and Rubber Company v Shell Chemicals UK* [2010] EWCA Civ 864, paras 43–44.
[108] Directive on Damages Actions (n 3), recital 6; Commission (EU), 'Damages Actions for Breach of the EU Antitrust Rules' (Impact Assessment Report) SWD (2013) 203 final, para 2.

and the interplay between damages actions and leniency programmes has been addressed therein.[109]

The possibility of facing follow-on damages actions can in itself deter undertakings from committing a competition law violation. Furthermore, the infringing undertaking might end up paying more in damages than in administrative fines.[110] For example, the Commission imposed fines totalling €388.128 million against seven undertakings for their participation in the hydrogen peroxide cartel.[111] CDC, a company purchasing claims on behalf of cartel victims brought damages claims against cartel participants in Germany and Finland and sought a total of €553 million plus interest.[112] So, if an undertaking (acting rationally)[113] engages in anti-competitive conduct only when the profits therefrom exceed the potential costs (comprising fines and damages) divided by the probability of detection, one can reasonably assume that if the potential costs increase,[114] then there is a greater deterrent effect on any potential anti-competitive conduct. Provided that the necessary procedural mechanisms are in place, the potential costs of a competition law violation (and thus deterrence) can rise significantly, given that 'victims of competition violations are foregoing not just millions but billions in compensation'.[115]

Finally, the assertion that follow-on actions do not contribute to the detection of competition law violations does not hold true in every case.[116] Follow-on actions

---

[109] Article 6(6) of the Directive on Damages Actions (n 3) on non-disclosure of leniency statements; Article 11(4) limiting the joint and several liability of the immunity applicant. The interplay between damages actions and public enforcement in follow-on litigation raises complex questions that remain unresolved in the Directive on Damages Actions, such as the calculation of the limitation period in follow-on actions when multiple infringers are involved and some appeal the decision and others not and the impact on leniency incentives. See P Akman, 'Period of Limitations in Follow-on Competition Cases: When Does a "Decision" Become Final?' (2014) 2 JAE 389. On the period of limitation and follow-on actions see *Deutsche Bahn AG and others v Morgan Crucible Company plc* [2014] UKSC 24.

[110] For an early US account see T Kauper and E Snyder, 'An Inquiry into the Efficiency of Private Antitrust Enforcement: Follow-on and Independently Initiated Actions Compared' (1986) Geo LJ 1163, 1222. M Block, FC Nold, and J Sidak, 'The Deterrent Effect of Antitrust Enforcement' (1981) 89 J Pol Econ 429, 444.

[111] *Hydrogen Peroxide and Perborate* (Case COMP/F/38.620) Commission Decision of 5 June 2006, C(2006) 1766 final.

[112] See <http://www.carteldamageclaims.com/portfolios/cdc-hydrogen-peroxide/>. In Finland, the case was settled on 19 May 2014 for a total amount of €18.5 million instead of the initially claimed €78 million. See <http://www.kemira.com/en/newsroom/whats-new/Pages/1786726_20140519073136.aspx>. See also E Waektare, 'Private Enforcement: Antitrust Damage Settlement between Claimant CDC and Hydrogen Peroxide Cartellist Kemira (Finland)' (2014) 5 JECLAP 701. Proceedings in Germany are pending following a preliminary question to the ECJ (Case C-352/13 *CDC Hydrogen Peroxide*).

[113] The rationality assumption is one of the basic principles of the Chicago School: see R Posner, 'The Chicago School of Antitrust Analysis' (1979) 127 U Pa L Rev 925.

[114] Here, increasing potential costs is taken to mean increasing the amount of damages. For reasons for not allowing fines to be raised beyond a certain standard see W Wils, *Efficiency and Justice in European Antitrust Enforcement* (Hart 2008) 62.

[115] See N Kroes, 'Consumers at the heart of EU Competition Policy' (2008) (Speech at BEUC, 22 April 2008, Speech 08/212).

[116] Kauper and Snyder (n 110) 1169.

can be attributed an indirect detection function in the following way: there is the possibility that private parties, in this case consumers or consumer organizations, are incentivized to alert the public authorities to a potential antitrust violation so that a decision in the course of public enforcement is adopted, thereby facilitating the subsequent damages actions.[117]

Another criticism often levied against private enforcement of competition law is based on its nature. Critics argue that because competition law is public law, private litigants are not in a position to achieve the policy goal of deterring competition law violations in order to protect competition in the market as a means of enhancing consumer welfare. Thus, it is probable that they deter legal actions as well (over-deterrence problem—Type I errors).[118] The fact that private parties usually act in their own self-interest entails the risk that they might engage in nuisance litigation.[119] Even if, in theory, there is a possibility of over-enforcement, the approach to private enforcement in EU law suggests that private individuals can act as agents for the public interest.[120] For example, when a consumer files a claim against an infringing undertaking, they do not seek to preserve the competitive process as a means of enhancing consumer welfare *in abstracto* but, rather, they are defending their own interests before a national court.[121] However, by so doing they may act in the public interest as well.[122]

---

[117] Jones argues that competition authorities proceedings most often take place because of private complaints. See C Jones, 'Into the Parallel Universe: Procedural Fairness in Private Litigation after the Damages Directive' (2014, 9th ASCOLA Conference Warsaw) <http://www.ascola-conference-2014.wz.uw.edu.pl/conference_papers/Jonesascola2014.pdf> accessed 22 July 2014.

[118] W Wils, 'Should Private Antitrust Enforcement Be Encouraged in Europe?' (2003) 26 W Comp 473, 482; Wils (n 114) 9; C Hodges, 'Competition Enforcement, Regulation and Civil Justice: What is the Case?' (2006) 43 CMLRev 1381, 1395; For the opposite view see OFT, 'Private Actions in Competition Law: Effective Redress for Consumers and Business' (Recommendations) (OFT 916resp, November 2007), para 2.3 where it is stated that when the OFT asked companies and their advisers for suggestions as to what could be done to improve compliance with competition law in the UK, the most frequent responses included encouraging private damages actions.

[119] W Baumol and J Ordover, 'Use of Antitrust to Subvert Competition' (1985) 28 JL & Econ 247, 248 where they point out that 'attempts to use the law as an instrument of subversion do not confine themselves to private lawsuits'; W Breit and K Elzinga, 'Private Antitrust Enforcement: The New Learning' (1985) 28 JL & Econ 405, 433; E Snyder and T Kauper, 'Misuse of the Antitrust Laws: The Competitor Plaintiff' (1991) 90 Mich L Rev 551; P McAfee, H Mialon, and S Mialon, 'Private Antitrust litigation: Procompetitive or Anticompetitive' (2005) Emory Law and Economics Research Paper No 05/18 <http://papers.ssrn.com/sol3/papers.cfm?abstract_id=784805> accessed 5 August 2014.

[120] See text to n 10. For a contrary opinion see BDI, 'Position—Commission White Paper on Damages Actions for Breach of the EC Antitrust Rules' <http://ec.europa.eu/competition/antitrust/actionsdamages/white_paper_comments/bdi_en.pdf> accessed 5 August 2014; CBI, 'Damages Actions for Breach of the EC Antitrust Rules—CBI Response to the Commission White Paper' <http://ec.europa.eu/competition/antitrust/actionsdamages/white_paper_comments/cbi_en.pdf> accessed 5 August 2014, 2.

[121] D Kelemen, 'Suing for Europe: Adversarial Legalism and European Governance' (2006) 39 *Comparative Political Studies* 101, 121 which argues that private parties can strengthen European policies.

[122] A fact accepted by the Commission: see WP SWP (n 91), para 313; See also OECD, 'Remedies Available to Private Parties under Competition Laws' (Report) COM/DAFFE/CLP/TD(2000)24/Final, para 3.

2.4 Ranking the endemic aims

Deterrence and compensation are termed endemic factors, since they pertain to the functions of competition law enforcement and are distilled from the Court's case law. The latter attributes equal weight to these goals, although in the light of the structure of the EU edifice and the direct effect of competition law provisions, a preference is granted to the deterrent function. This is further supported by the theory of optimal enforcement,[123] and the deterrence theory,[124] following which the optimal sanction shall exceed the gains resulting from the competition law violation divided by the probability of detection. Private litigation raises the financial stakes for undertakings that are contemplating engaging in anti-competitive conduct and could, thus, act as a disincentive for engaging in the said activity.

However, even if deterrence is granted priority over compensation, the latter should not be disregarded. The Court's jurisprudence, as well as the Commission's efforts, point to a delicate balancing exercise, reconciling the two aims if possible, rather than excluding one altogether. The right of private parties is derived from the Treaty and it cannot be excluded, as in the case of indirect purchasers in the US, for example, based on deterrence grounds only.[125] Proponents of the Chicago School approach have advanced arguments against the compensatory aim of private enforcement arguing that, from an economic perspective, it is excessively costly to identify the victims of antitrust violations and quantify their losses. The high costs involved in awarding compensation do not correspond to the value attributed to it by society—given the relatively low value of individual claims, especially when private actions are brought by consumers.[126] This approach cannot be accepted in a legal system that takes justice and fairness considerations into account, apart from economic arguments of efficiency and cost minimization. In the EU, the right to damages, as a right granted by EU law, should be effectively safeguarded.[127] This is also consistent with the right to a fair trial, which is guaranteed in the constitutions of individual Member States and by Article 6 ECHR as

---

[123] G Becker, 'Crime and Punishment: An Economic Approach' (1968) 76 J Pol Econ 169; G Becker and G Stigler, 'Law Enforcement, Malfeasance and Compensation of Enforcers' (1974) 3 J Legal Stud 1; W Landes and R Posner, 'The Private Enforcement of Law' (1975) 4 J Legal Stud 1; W Landes, 'Optimal Sanctions for Antitrust Violations' (1983) 50 U Chi L Rev 652, 656, 678. See also I Lianos, 'Competition Law Remedies in Europe—Which Limits for Remedial Discretion?' (2013) CLES Research Paper Series <https://www.ucl.ac.uk/cles/research-paper-series/index/edit/research-papers/cles-2-2013> accessed 17 August 2014, 29–30.

[124] See Wils (n 114) 56–58 which points to differences between the 'internalization approach' advocated by Becker and Landes (n 123) and the 'deterrence approach'.

[125] C Jones, *Private Enforcement of Antitrust Law in the EU, UK and USA* (OUP 1999) 186–187; M Brealy, 'Adopt *Perma Life*, but Follow *Hannover Shoe* to Illinois?' (2002) 1 Comp Law 127, 133; A Komninos, 'The Road to the Commission's White Paper for Damages Actions: Where We Came From' (2008) 4 CPI <https://www.competitionpolicyinternational.com/the-road-to-the-commissions-white-paper-for-damages-actions-where-we-came-from/> accessed 28 July 2014, 81, 101.

[126] W Schwartz, 'An Overview of the Economics of Antitrust Enforcement' (1980) 68 Geo LJ 1075, 1086; W Schwartz, *Private Enforcement of Antitrust Laws: An Economic Critique* (American Enterprise Institute for Public Policy Research 1981) 31, 32.

[127] Komninos (n 47) 10; C Jones, 'Private Antitrust Enforcement in Europe: A Policy Analysis and Reality Check' (2004) 27 W Comp 13, 14.

well as Article 47 of the Charter of Fundamental Rights of the European Union. This right incorporates the right to effective access to the courts.[128]

At the same time, compensation should not be viewed as an absolute goal; it should also be pursued in accordance with the proportionality principle.[129] In essence, this means that, in cases where the individual consumer does not view compensation as particularly important, the enforcement system should prioritize other aims without abandoning the compensatory aim completely. The compensatory function would yield to the deterrent function, and alternative forms for the provision of compensation could be devised. For example, cy-près mechanisms could be put in place.[130] This would allow the adoption of functional procedural mechanisms that would contribute to the deterrence of competition law infringements whilst also benefiting consumers and promoting wider policy goals.

3. Ancillary Institutional Benefits

3.1 Proliferation of information—contributing to consumer education and empowerment

In the consumer law field, increased attention is given to improving consumer education and empowerment, which in turn will raise consumer confidence in cross-border shopping.[131] The role of consumers exerts a vital influence in any given market.[132] '[J]ust as competition is good for consumers, enhancing the power of consumer choice is good for competition.'[133] Indeed, the power of consumer choice can be improved through regulatory instruments under consumer protection law.[134] This section builds on the interplay between competition and consumer law and argues that more active consumer involvement in private

---

[128] See EESC (EC), 'Defining the Collective Actions System and Its Role in the Context of Community Consumer Law' (Opinion) [2008] OJ C162/1, 3, 14.
[129] C Hodges, *The Reform of Class and Representative Actions in European Legal Systems* (Hart 2008) 188.
[130] Cf European Justice Forum, 'Comments on the Commission White Paper' <http://ec.europa.eu/competition/antitrust/actionsdamages/white_paper_comments/eurjfor_en.pdf> accessed 5 August 2014, para 1; D Shapiro, 'Consumer Class Actions Made Easy' (2008) 7 Comp Law 203, 207.
[131] Commission (EC), 'Consumer Policy Strategy 2002–2006' (Communication) COM(2002) 208 final, OJ [2002] C137/02, para 3.3.2.2; Commission (EC), 'EU Consumer Policy Strategy 2007–2013' (Communication) COM(2007) 99 final, 8, 11; Regulation (EU) No 254/2014 of the European Parliament and of the Council of 26 February 2014 on a Multiannual Consumer Programme for the Years 2014–20 and Repealing Decision No 1926/2006/EC [2014] OJ L84/42, Article 2, Article 3(1)(b). For a UK account see DTI, 'Extending Competitive Markets: Empowered Consumers, Successful Business' (June 2005), para 5.
[132] M Waterson, 'The Role of Consumers in Competition and Competition Policy' (2001) Warwick Economic Research Papers No 607 <http://www2.warwick.ac.uk/fac/soc/economics/research/workingpapers/publications/twerp607.pdf> accessed 5 August 2014.
[133] J Vickers, 'Healthy Competition and its Consumer Wins' (2002) 12 CP Rev 142, 146.
[134] See to that end mandatory information disclosure and harmonized rules to protect consumers' health and safety: Consumer Policy Strategy 2002–2006 (n 131), para 2.

competition law enforcement can in turn raise consumer awareness and improve the conscious exercise of consumer choice. It can, thus, be seen as an alternative form of information proliferation and consumer education, which in turn will increase literacy and consumer choice as a spur to competitiveness.[135]

Information asymmetries constitute a frequently identified market failure on the demand side.[136] Consumers fail to exercise their right to choose according to their needs due to a lack of necessary information. Thus, the provision of information is a common regulatory approach in the field of consumer law.[137] A further related question is how much information is actually enough, since recent studies suggest that the consumer cannot always process the information in an effective way, thus creating further market problems.[138] Getting consumers more actively involved in private competition law enforcement will result in an increased information flow without the need to adopt specific measures for information disclosure.

Imagine the following situation: a consumer organization A brings an action for damages against two retailers, B and C (both large toy outlets) following a competition authority's decision. A claims that because of the price-fixing agreement between B and C regarding the price of a popular item, consumers were damaged by x amount. The court rules in favour of A. This judgment (with the publicity that it could be expected to receive) could signal to consumers that they should engage in price comparisons. At the same time, it would allude to the possibility of getting involved in competition law enforcement. In turn, the availability of this participatory right could prompt consumers to process the available information responsibly and be more careful when exercising their right to choose.[139]

3.2 Legitimization of EU policies

Competition policy lacks the necessary social support due to the fact that consumers' voices are rarely heard in competition policy.[140] Further procedural measures allowing for active consumer involvement in private competition law enforcement possess the potential to bring EU citizens in their capacity as consumers closer to EU competition policy, and act as an alternative form of control in the

---

[135] See Ioannidou (n 5) 68.
[136] K Cseres, 'What Has Competition Done for Consumers in Liberalised Markets?' (2008) 4 Comp L Rev <http://www.clasf.org/CompLRev/Issues/Vol4Iss2Art1Cseres.pdf> accessed 5 August 2014, 77.
[137] Commission (EC), 'Proposal for a Directive of the European Parliament and of the Council on Consumer Rights' COM(2008) 614 final, 8 October 2008.
[138] Cseres (n 136) 91 with further references. G Howells, 'The Potential and Limits of Consumer Empowerment by Information' (2005) 32 JL & Soc 349, 356–362.
[139] See Commission (EU), 'Consumer Empowerment in the EU' (Staff Working Paper) SEC(2011) 469 final, para 3 on consumer empowerment depending on accessible means of redress. However, this document addresses consumer empowerment only as a consumer law matter.
[140] O Dayagi-Epstein, 'Furnishing Consumers with a Voice in Competition Policy' (2005) <http://www.luc.edu/media/lucedu/law/centers/antitrust/pdfs/publications/workingpapers/dayagi_epstein_consumers_voice.pdf> accessed 5 August 2014.

Commission and NCAs' decision-making. Increased consumer involvement could potentially bridge the gap between EU competition policy and its addressees and it should be seen in the light of two initiatives in the EU: the first concerns efforts to improve European governance and the second concerns efforts to promote private enforcement of EU law.

The first initiative concerning European governance 'proposes opening up the policymaking process to get more people and organisations involved in shaping and delivering EU policy'.[141] One of the proposals for change concerns the involvement of civil society.[142] This is a form of *ex ante* participation. For example, consumers, either on their own or through their respective organizations as actors of civil society, can provide comments in an open debate prior to the adoption of any concrete legislative measure or policy decision.[143]

Ex ante participation is important for our purposes since it allows an interesting analogy to be made. In the field of *ex ante* participation, new modes of governance have emerged (ranging from framework directives, the Open Method of Coordination, and other soft law instruments),[144] which complement the traditional 'command and control' type of regulation adopted in the past.[145] The participation of interested stakeholders in the legislative process constitutes one of the key characteristics of these emerging forms of governance in the EU.[146] The element of involvement as a desideratum is the same in both *ex ante* and *ex post* enforcement procedures and can contribute towards increased openness and accountability.

The second effort concerns a decided shift from the administrative-led enforcement of EU law to a model where affected actors should assume a more active role. Note, for example, the initiatives in the consumer field,[147] the Environmental

---

[141] Commission (EC), 'European Governance' (White Paper) COM(2001) 428 final (Governance White Paper), Executive Summary 2. The Governance White Paper defines 'governance' as the rules, processes, and behaviour that affect the way in which powers are exercised at European level, particularly with regard to openness, participation, accountability, effectiveness, and coherence. Ibid, n 1. See H Hartnell, 'EUstitia: Institutionalising Justice in the European Union' (2002) 23 Nw J Int'l L &Bus 65, 128 which points to the different meanings of 'governance'.

[142] Governance White Paper (n 141) 14. See also Commission (EU), 'Single Market Act—Twelve Levers to Boost Growth and Strengthen Confidence' (Communication) COM(2011) 206 final, 20; K Armstrong, 'Rediscovering Civil Society: The European Union and the White Paper on Governance' (2002) 8 ELJ 102 for a critical account of the notion of civil society in the Governance White Paper. On the notion of civil society see also S Smismans, 'Civil Society and European Governance: from Concepts to Research Agenda', in S Smismans (ed), *Civil Society and Legitimate European Governance* (Edward Elgar 2006) 3.

[143] See Articles 10(3) and 11 TEU; BEUC, 'Response to the White Paper on Governance' (28/03/2002, BEUC/156/02).

[144] For a criticism of these new forms of governance see T Idema and D Kelemen, 'New Modes of Governance, the Open Method of Co-ordination and Other Fashionable Red Herring' (2006) 7 *Perspectives on European Politics and Society* 108.

[145] F Cafaggi and H Muir-Watt, 'Introduction' in F Cafaggi and H Muir-Watt (eds), *Making European Private Law: Governance Design* (Edward Elgar 2008) 7; G de Burca and J Scott, 'Introduction: New Governance, Law and Constitutionalism' in G de Burca and J Scott (eds), *Law and New Governance in the EU and US* (Hart 2006).

[146] De Burca and Scott (n 145) 3.

[147] See, for example, Directive 2013/11/EU on Alternative Dispute Resolution for Consumer Disputes and Amending Regulation (EC) 2006/2004 and Directive 2009/22/EC [2013] L 165/63;

Liability Directive,[148] and, most importantly for the subject matter of this book, the private enforcement initiative in the field of competition law.[149] The increased employment of litigious *ex post* enforcement methods reveals the advent of the 'adversarial legalism' movement in Europe.[150]

Adversarial legalism is identified as the dominant regulatory style in the US. One of its main characteristics is the increased role of adversarial procedures in solving disputes.[151] Member States' legal cultures cannot support the rise of litigation, as is the case in the US.[152] But this does not detract from the fact that this tendency is indeed present and can assume an ancillary role, as the efforts to enhance access to justice, grant a more active role to national judiciaries, and expand EU rights reveal.[153] This is particularly true in the field of competition law since *Courage* and *Manfredi* and the changes to the enforcement system brought by Regulation 1/2003.

Promoting consumer damages claims in EU competition law can be located in the juncture between the two tendencies identified above. It brings the beneficial element of the participation of interested stakeholders into a changing landscape of enforcement and can increase the legitimacy of competition policy.[154] Scharpf distinguishes between input and output legitimacy, the former reflecting authentic preferences of citizens and the latter catering for effective outcomes.[155] Consumer participation in private competition law enforcement, inasmuch as it enhances effective enforcement of EU competition law, can account for better

---

Regulation (EU) No 524/2013 on online dispute resolution for consumer disputes and amending Regulation (EC) No 2006/2004 and Directive 2009/22/EC (Regulation on Consumer ODR) [2013] L165/1.

[148] Council Directive 2004/35/EC of 21 April 2004 on environmental liability with regard to the prevention and remedying of environmental damage [2004] OJ L143/56.

[149] GP (n 3); WP (n 3); Directive on Damages Actions (n 3).

[150] D Kelemen, 'Americanisation of European Law? Adversarial Legalism à la européenne' (2008) 7 *European Political Science* 32 in which the author examines whether the adversarial legalism approach can be transposed to the EU.

[151] R Kagan, *Adversarial Legalism: The American Way of Law* (Harvard University Press 2001) 7–8.

[152] R Kagan, 'American and European Ways of Law: Six Entrenched Differences' in V Gessner and D Nelken (eds), *European Ways of Law: Towards a European Sociology of Law* (Hart 2007) 41, 57.

[153] These three variables are identified by Kelemen as evidence of the advent of adversarial legalism in the EU: Kelemen (n 121) 103.

[154] See A Estella de Noriega, *The EU Principle of Subsidiarity and its Critique* (OUP 2002) 37–53 on the concept of legitimacy.

[155] See F Scharpf, 'Economic Integration, Democracy and the Welfare State' (1997) JEPP 18, 19. Scharpf places increased emphasis on output legitimacy. In the same vein see A Menon and S Weatherill, 'Legitimacy, Accountability, and Delegation in the European Union' in Arnull and Wincott (eds), *Accountability and Legitimacy in the European Union* (OUP 2002) 113. See also Wincott, 'The Governance White Paper, the Commission and the Search for Legitimacy' in A Arnull and D Wincott (eds), *Accountability and Legitimacy in the European Union* (OUP 2002) 379, 380 which states that 'legitimacy might be improved if the peoples of Europe were better served by and/or more fully involved in the Union'. To the contrary, Craig underlines the importance of input legitimacy as well. See P Craig, 'Integration, Democracy and Legitimacy' in P Craig and G de Burca (eds), *The Evolution of EU Law* (2nd edn, OUP 2011) 13, 39–40.

output legitimacy. At the same time, it improves input legitimacy since it provides an avenue for affected consumers to get involved in the enforcement of EU competition law.

Competition officials have welcomed the initiative on private competition law enforcement, stressing that '[i]n difficult times for the Union, such a development in terms of democratisation and the connection between its law and its citizens is only to be welcome'.[156] European consumers, as market actors, enjoy market rights, whereas European citizens enjoy not only market rights but also political and social rights.[157] Consumer involvement in private competition law enforcement aims at protecting the market rights of consumers and, more specifically, rights derived from competition law. At the same time, though, it reinforces the element of citizen participation.[158]

Allowing consumers to get involved in the enforcement of competition law could potentially raise their trust in market forces.[159] This is even more important if one considers the consumer protection model adopted in the EU. The emphasis is on market-oriented outcomes (trust in competition) accompanied by a modest adoption of consumer regulation.[160] So, insofar as the individual is ascribed a more responsible role,[161] the necessary tools should be put in place for this role to be effectively exercised.

This has become even more important since the adoption of the LT and the symbolic shifting of the objective of undistorted competition from the first Treaty provisions to a protocol. Even if this does not change the application of EU competition law, it reveals a certain scepticism towards EU competition policy. So, now it may be more imperative for European citizens to realize the advantages that derive from competition law enforcement. Arguably, the best way forward is for the actual beneficiaries to be more involved in the enforcement process by devising the appropriate mechanisms to enable them to do so. This is also in line

---

[156] Foreword by Emil Paulis in D Ashton and D Henry, *Competition Damages Actions in the EU—Law and Practice* (Edward Elgar 2013). For a distinction between the citizen's role and the consumer's role see M Hesselink, 'European Contract Law: A Matter of Consumer Protection, Citizenship or Justice?' in S Grundmann (ed), *Constitutional Values and European Contract Law* (Kluwer Law International 2008) 241, 248, 262–264. On concepts of citizenship see J Davies, *The European Consumer Citizen in Law and Policy* (Palgrave Macmillan 2011) 78–87. On EU citizenship evolving from market citizenship see MP Maduro, 'Europe's Social Self: "The Sickness Unto Death"' in J Shaw (ed), *Social Law and Policy in an Evolving European Union* (Hart 2000) 325, 332–340. See also M Everson, 'The Legacy of the Market Citizen' in J Shaw and G More (eds), *New Legal Dynamics of European Union* (Clarendon Press 1995) 73; NN Shuibhne, 'The Resilience of EU Market Citizenship' (2010) 47 CMLRev 1597.

[157] W van Gerven, *The European Union. A Polity of States and People* (Hart 2005) 200.

[158] This participation element can be seen as an aspect of the 'consumer citizen'. On this term see Davies (n 156) 90.

[159] B Van Rompuy, 'How to Preserve Trust in Anti-Trust' (*EUbusiness*, 8 October 2009) <http://www.eubusiness.com/Members/bvrompuy/competition-day> accessed 30 June 2014.

[160] K Cseres, *Competition Law and Consumer Protection* (Kluwer Law International 2005) 3, 202.

[161] M Arkenstette, 'Reorientation in Consumer Policy—Challenges and Prospects from the Perspective of Practical Consumer Advice Work' (2005) 28 JCP 361, 368.

with the changes introduced by the LT in order to enhance citizens' participation and the EU's democratic legitimacy.[162]

4. Conclusion

This chapter discussed the two main functions of consumer claims in the field of competition law (as a sub-category of damages claims) according to the Court's jurisprudence and the Commission's policy initiative on private competition law enforcement that comprise deterrence and compensation. In identifying the primary function the Court favours the effective enforcement of EU competition law norms over the effective protection of individual rights. To the contrary, the Commission places considerable emphasis on the compensatory rationale of damages actions, departing from the CJEU's approach. The primary aim attributed by the Commission to damages actions is important, since it impacts on the form of the proposed measures. Procedural and remedial measures should be structured in accordance with the aim of the EU right to damages, as pronounced by the CJEU. As AG Tesauro noted, 'Member States' autonomy with regard to judicial remedies for the infringement of rights conferred by Community provisions is firmly tied to the result sought by Community law'.[163] The same goes for the Commission's discretion with regard to proposed measures for the enforcement of EU rights emanating directly from effective Treaty provisions. This is not to suggest that the proposals in the Directive on Damages Actions are inconsistent with the primary aim of the right to damages but, rather, to underline that the Commission should have taken a bolder stance in the light of the deterrence aim, as will be discussed in more detail in subsequent chapters. This could have made consumer claims instrumental in maintaining effective competition in the EU.

Apart from the instrumental role of consumer damages claims, if structured correctly, they can account for two very important ancillary benefits. First, they can act as an information mechanism raising consumer awareness and empowerment and second they can add a modicum of legitimacy to EU competition policy.

---

[162] See, for example, Article 11(4) TEU which introduces the European Citizens' Initiative.
[163] *Brasserie du Pêcheur* (n 22), Opinion of AG Tesauro, para 47.

PART B

PRACTICAL APPROACH TO CONSUMER PARTICIPATION

4

Improving Consumers' Role

'Standing' and 'Access to Evidence'

1. Introduction

The analysis so far has provided the theoretical background justifying increased consumer involvement in EU private competition law enforcement. It has shown reluctance on the part of the Union institutions to endorse consumer interest and adopt a narrow consumer welfare approach in the substantive application of competition law, thereby revealing a mismatch between policy pronouncements and actual practice. Given the complexity of changing the enforcement standard, more active consumer involvement in private competition law enforcement is seen as an alternative in bringing consumer interest to the fore in a way that can actually influence competition law and policy. Effective measures, based primarily on the deterrence principle, should be adopted in this field, since this would permit consumer involvement, which would bring a number of additional tangible benefits.

The analysis in this chapter undertakes a forward-looking approach and develops a practical framework in order to enhance consumer involvement in private competition law enforcement. It first alludes to the intrinsic characteristics of consumer claims, in a bid to justify why consumer claims warrant a different treatment to claims from customers and competitors (section 2). Following the normative discussion, proposals focusing on pass-on and access to evidence are discussed in the light of the proposals in the EU Directive on Damages Actions. In Chapter 5 the more acute problems encountered by consumer claims are examined.

2. Characteristics of Consumer Claims: Justifying a More 'Enabling' Approach

Obstacles to private damages actions, as identified by the Commission in its effort to increase private enforcement, encompass a wide range of issues; some of these are substantive and others are procedural. They include, amongst other points: (1) indirect purchasers' standing; (2) the availability of the passing-on defence; (3) access to evidence; (4) collective action mechanisms; and, (5) costs of actions,[1] which appear to be particularly severe for minor consumer claims. These obstacles are likely to be encountered by every consumer claim with varying degrees of severity depending on the amount of the claim and whether the claim is of the stand-alone or follow-on type. The following analysis addresses the intrinsic characteristics of consumer claims and provides a further pragmatic argument in favour of adopting procedural measures to advance deterrence against competition law violations.

Long before the debate on the private enforcement of competition law, the Commission alluded to the possibility of consumers seeking application of the competition rules in national courts.[2] Consumer claims should be distinguished from competitors' and customers' claims in light of the nature of the claimant being the weaker party in the transaction, as well as the nature of the claim itself, the latter usually being of a very low value.[3] First, it is unlikely that consumers will identify a competition law infringement given their often-covert nature (the 'information inadequacy' or 'information asymmetry' problem),[4] as well as actual consumer ignorance concerning competition law matters.[5]

---

[1] Commission (EC), 'Staff Working Paper accompanying the White Paper on Damages Actions for Breach of the EC Antitrust Rules' SEC(2008) 404, 2 April 2008 (WP SWP), paras 7–11; Commission (EU), 'Staff Working Document—Impact Assessment Report—Damages Actions for Breach of the EU Antitrust Rules' COM(2013) 404 final (IAR) para 38. The OFT has identified the same obstacles in the UK regarding consumer and SMEs claims: see OFT, 'Private Actions in Competition Law: Effective Redress for Consumers and Businesses' (Discussion Paper, April 2007) (OFT 916), paras 1.2, 2.12, 3.1–3.10; BIS, 'Private Actions in Competition Law: A Consultation and Options for Reform' (April 2012), paras 3.12–3.14.

[2] Commission (EC), Sixteenth Report on Competition Policy (Brussels, Luxembourg 1987) <http://bookshop.europa.eu/is-bin/INTERSHOP.enfinity/WFS/EU-Bookshop-Site/en_GB/-/EUR/ViewPublication-Start?PublicationKey=CB4886060> accessed 3 July 2014, para 11; Commission (EC), XXIIIrd Report on Competition Policy 1993 (Brussels, Luxembourg 1994) <http://bookshop.europa.eu/is-bin/INTERSHOP.enfinity/WFS/EU-Bookshop-Site/en_GB/-/EUR/ViewPublication-Start?PublicationKey=CM8294650> accessed 3 July 2014, para 228.

[3] S Peyer, 'Myths and Untold Stories—Private Antitrust Enforcement in Germany' (2010) UEA CCP Working Paper 10–12 <http://papers.ssrn.com/sol3/papers.cfm?abstract_id=1672695> accessed 3 July 2014, 40–41 provides empirical data for the very limited consumer participation in Germany and compares it to the frequent involvement of customers and competitors. For a detailed account of the situation in different Member States and the very limited involvement of consumers see B Rodger, 'Collective Redress Mechanisms and Consumer Case Law' in B Rodger (ed), *Competition Law Comparative Private Enforcement and Collective Redress Across Europe* (Kluwer 2014) 157, 162–163. See SC Salop and LJ White, 'Economic Analysis of Private Antitrust Litigation' (1986) 74 Geo LJ 1001, 1005 for a US account.

[4] R van den Bergh and L Visscher, 'The Preventive Function of Collective Actions for Damages in Consumer Law' (2008) 1 Erasmus L Rev 55, 13; A Renda, J Peysner, A Riley, B Rodger, and others, 'Making Antitrust Damages Actions More Effective in the EU: Welfare Impact and Potential Scenarios' (Report for the European Commission) (December 2007) <http://ec.europa.eu/competition/antitrust/actionsdamages/files_white_paper/impact_study.pdf> accessed 3 July 2014 (External Impact Study) 28.

[5] Consumers' unfamiliarity with competition law issues is evident in two studies concerning criminal sanctions against cartels in which the vast majority of consumers did not perceive cartel conduct as similar to theft. See A Stephan, 'Survey of Public Attitudes to Price Fixing and Cartel Enforcement in Britain' (2008) 5 Comp L Rev 123, 136–137; V Brisimi and M Ioannidou, 'Criminalising Cartels in Greece: A Tale of Hasty Developments and Shaky Grounds' (2011) 34 W Comp 157.

The 'information asymmetry' problem is more acute for consumer claims rather than for competitors' or customers' claims.[6] Consumer claims will usually concern damages arising from cartel agreements, whereas competitors' and customers' claims will run to significant amounts and concern abusive exclusionary practices or anti-competitive vertical restraints. In the latter cases, the claimants are more incentivized to pursue the claim and are in possession of more factual information, sometimes more than the Commission or NCAs themselves.[7]

Second, individual consumers' damages are often too insignificant to act as an incentive for them to bring damages actions.[8] The low value of their claims does not justify the litigation costs,[9] and creates the so-called 'rational apathy' problem, where injured individuals lack the incentive to claim an otherwise very large aggregate damage.[10] The 'rational apathy' problem is aggravated in situations where the infringer intentionally inflicts widespread damage,[11] which is precisely what happens in cartel cases. This problem is relevant and can be observed in relation to consumer claims of a certain value that can be litigated individually or through an aggregation mechanism.[12] For example, the Commission WP stated that:

individual consumers, but also small businesses, especially those who have suffered scattered and relatively low damage, are often deterred from bringing an individual action for

---

[6] Here, the term 'information asymmetry' does not indicate market failures on the demand side, but rather the fact that, in competition cases, the defendant (or third parties) will be in possession of important evidence and information which is not readily accessible to the claimant. See, for example, Commission (EC), 'Accompanying Document to the White Paper on Damages Actions for Breach of the EC Antitrust Rules—Impact Assessment' SEC(2008) 405, para 52; Commission (EC), 'Proposal for a Council Directive Governing Actions for Damages for Infringements of Article 81 and 82 of the Treaty' (Draft Damages Directive) (document withdrawn before publication—on file with the author), Explanatory Memorandum, para 4.3.

[7] On the revelation of private information as a boost to competition law enforcement see M Harker and M Hviid, 'Competition Law Enforcement and Incentives for Revelation of Private Information' (2008) 31 W Comp 297. See also T Reher and A Sanchez Graells, 'The Commission's Green Paper on Damages Actions for Breach of Competition Rules' [2007] *European Antitrust Review* 42, 43, which points to the fact that problems of access to evidence arise in cases of horizontal agreements.

[8] Commission (EC), 'Annex to the Green Paper, Damages Actions for Breach of the EC Antitrust Rules', (Staff Working Paper) SEC(2005) 1732, 19 December 2005 (GP SWP), para 188; WP SWP (n 1), para 39.

[9] WM Landes and RA Posner, 'The Private Enforcement of Law' (1975) 4 J Legal Stud 1, 33.

[10] HB Schaefer, 'The Bundling of Similar Interests in Litigation. The Incentives for Class Actions and Legal Actions Taken by Associations' (2000) 9 Eur JL & Econ 183, 185; van den Bergh and Visscher (n 4) 14; R van den Bergh, 'Private Enforcement of European Competition Law and the Persisting Collective Action Problem' (2013) 20 *Maastricht Journal of European and Comparative Law* 12, 14, 20–23.

[11] Schaefer (n 10) 185.

[12] In a study conducted for DG SANCO Member States' national reporters were asked to estimate the threshold for claims (in Euros) under which a rational consumer would refrain from seeking individual redress through ordinary court procedures. See Civic Consulting, 'Evaluation of the Effectiveness and Efficiency of Collective Redress Mechanisms in the European Union' (26 August 2008) (Report prepared for DG SANCO) (Civic Consulting Study) and also National Reports Submitted under this project (Civic Consulting National Reports) <http://ec.europa.eu/consumers/redress_cons/collective_redress_en.htm> accessed 3 July 2014, question [1.7.1]. In this study, the national reporters were asked to estimate the threshold for a rational consumer to seek individual redress before the courts. The lowest threshold was estimated in Germany, where it was between €50 and €250. Other national reports suggest that consumers would be reluctant to engage in litigation even for larger claims. The Commission Staff Working Paper on Consumer Empowerment supports this. Based on a survey on 55,000 consumers, the Commission concluded that the threshold for

damages by the costs, delays, uncertainties, risks and burdens involved. As a result many of the victims remain uncompensated.[13]

However, consumer damage from competition law violation is usually of such a minimal value that actions can only be brought collectively.[14] In this case, collective actions are not only a procedural device that permits the bundling of small, scattered claims so as to create economies of scale in litigation,[15] they can also be viewed as a regulatory vehicle, which, through the enforcement of consumers' rights, enhances compliance with competition law provisions. Instances of individual consumer claims cannot be excluded, although these would appear to be rare due to the intrinsic characteristics of consumer claims.[16] The 'Italian motor vehicle insurance companies cartel' provides an example of individual consumer claims for competition law violations since it gave rise to a number of consumer actions brought by individual consumers.[17] It prompted *Manfredi*,[18] in which the ECJ had a second opportunity (after *Courage*)[19] to rule on questions of private enforcement in the context of competition law. In this case the Italian small claims court awarded Mr Manfredi damages (approximately €890) and legal costs (approximately €500),[20] indicating that, in this case, the amount of individual consumer damage was high

---

losses for which consumers are willing to go to court is €1,000. See Commission (EU), 'Consumer Empowerment in the EU' (Staff Working Paper) SEC(2011) 469 final, paras 5, 11.

[13] Commission (EC), 'Damages Actions for Breach of the EC Antitrust Rules' (White Paper) COM(2008) 165 final (WP), para 2.1. The latter procedure is defined in the withdrawn Draft Damages Directive as a group action, and the way it is framed resembles joinder procedures, rather than actual workable group actions in which a large number of victims are involved. See Draft Damages Directive (n 6), Article 5.

[14] For an attempt to distinguish between different types of claims see M Ioannidou, 'Enhancing Consumers' Role in EU Private Competition Law Enforcement: A Normative and Practical Approach' (2012) 8 Comp L Rev <http://www.clasf.org/CompLRev/Issues/CompLRevVol8Issue1.pdf> accessed 10 June 2014, 59, 69–71.

[15] Van den Bergh and Visscher (n 4) 18; T Eisenberg and G Miller, 'The Role of Opt-Outs and Objectors in Class Action Litigation: Theoretical and Empirical Issues' (2004) NYU Law and Economics Research Paper No 04/004 <http://papers.ssrn.com/sol3/papers.cfm?abstract_id=528146> accessed 29 January 2012, 1.

[16] A detailed study on private competition law enforcement in different Member States reported more individual than collective consumer cases. However, this could be attributed to the lack of appropriate collective action mechanisms. Rodger (n 3) ibid.

[17] External Impact Study (n 4) 40; R Incardona and C Poncibo, 'The Corte di Cassazione takes "Courage". A Recent Ruling Opens Limited Rights for Consumers in Competition Cases' (2005) 26 ECLR 445, 446–447. M Carpagnano, 'Private Enforcement of Competition Law Arrives in Italy: Analysis of the Judgment of the European Court of Justice in Joined Cases C-295–289/04 Manfredi' (2006) 3 Comp L Rev <http://www.clasf.org/CompLRev/Issues/Vol3Issue1Art3Carpagnano.pdf> accessed 3 July 2014, 47, 53–55. Note that, at the time, consumers in Italy were denied standing, an unfortunate situation that was reversed by the *Unipol* judgment of the Italian Supreme Court (Corte di Cassazione, Decision No 2207/2005); Incardona and Poncibo (ibid).

[18] Joined Cases C-295/04 to 298/04 *Vincenzo Manfredi and Others v Lloyd Adriatico Assicurazioni SpA and Others* [2006] ECR I-6619 (*Manfredi*).

[19] Case C-453/99 *Courage Ltd v Bernard Crehan and Bernard Crehan v Courage Ltd and Others* [2001] ECR I-6297 (*Courage*).

[20] P Nebbia, 'So What Happened to Mr Manfredi? The Italian Decision Following the Ruling of the European Court of Justice' (2007) 28 ECLR 591 with further reference to Sentenza del Giudice

enough to incentivize consumers to engage in litigation. However, since the majority of consumer claims will be of minimal value, where the judicial costs exceed the value of the claim, these call for special procedural and aggregation mechanisms that advance deterrence and perform an instrumental role in the competition law enforcement system.

3. Consumer Standing and Passing-on

The analysis in this section deals with the issue of consumer standing to raise competition law claims, the standing of indirect purchasers, as consumers often will be, and the directly linked issue of the passing-on defence. In damages actions, passing-on can be invoked by the defendant arguing that the claimant is not entitled to compensation, as the overcharge[21] has been passed on to customers further down the supply chain and, therefore, no damage has been sustained (defensive passing-on). If the indirect purchaser was the one harmed by the anti-competitive conduct, his standing to sue the infringer should be recognized (offensive passing-on).

Depending on the industry, the supply chain may have many different levels before the product reaches the final consumer. In this case, different intermediate producers qualify as indirect purchasers and can potentially bring damages actions against the infringer.[22] Pass-on of the overcharge is relevant for consumer claims, since consumers are more likely to claim damages resulting from cartel overcharges or abusive excessive pricing as opposed to competitors claiming damages from abusive exclusionary conduct. However, consumer claims are distinguished by the fact that the passing-on defence cannot be raised against them, since consumers are last in the supply chain, and so, by definition, cannot pass on the overcharge any further.

This section first addresses the theoretical debate on indirect purchasers' standing and the passing-on defence as depicted in the approach of the Supreme Court of the United States (SCOTUS) before moving on to discuss the EU approach

---

di Pace di Bitonto No 172/2003, *Manfredi c Lloyd Adriatico*; see Oxera, 'Quantifying Antitrust Damages: Towards Non-binding Guidance for Courts' (December 2009), Study prepared for the European Commission <http://ec.europa.eu/competition/antitrust/actionsdamages/quantification_study.pdf> accessed 3 July 2014, 94.

[21] Defined as the difference between the price that would have existed in the absence of the violation and the price actually paid after the competition law violation. See Directive 2014/104/EU of the European Parliament and of the Council of 26 November 2014 on Certain Rules Governing Actions for Damages under National Law for Infringements of the Competition Law Provisions of the Member States and of the European Union [2014] OJ L349/1 (Directive on Damages Actions), Article 2(20). Maier Rigaux argues that the term 'mark up' is more accurate to describe this situation, as overcharge signifies the multiplication of the price difference (mark up) by the quantity purchased. See F Maier-Rigaud, 'Towards a European Directive on Damages Actions' (2014) 10 JCLE 341, 344.

[22] Oxera Study (n 20), para 2.3 for an illustrative presentation of the parties who are potentially harmed.

to consumer standing and passing-on, as pronounced by the CJEU. Then, the EU legislative solution on the issue of passing-on is presented and assessed in the light of the US experience, EU jurisprudence, and the Member States' practice and experience, in order to determine whether this proposal will, in fact, facilitate consumer claims.

3.1 A theoretical account: SCOTUS approach

The rather controversial US solution to the passing-on problem,[23] as shaped by the US Supreme Court in its landmark rulings *Hanover Shoe*[24] and *Illinois Brick*,[25] is relevant in the EU context to the extent that it highlights the controversy and the difficult policy choices involved in solving the passing-on issue.

In *Hanover Shoe*, the defendant raised the passing-on defence and argued that the claimant had suffered no damage since the illegal overcharge had been further passed on to the claimants' customers by the claimant charging a higher price on the goods sold to them.[26] The US Supreme Court rejected this argument based on the following considerations:

a. the claimant's right to damages should not be compromised by its own efforts to maintain its profit level;[27]

b. 'insurmountable difficulties' in establishing the passing-on defence complicating the already complex antitrust proceedings (efficiency argument);[28] and

c. the existence of the passing-on defence would deter efficient claimants from bringing damages actions, leaving this task to the ultimate consumers, who would be reluctant to initiate damages actions since they suffer very low damages. Effectively this would result in a dearth of antitrust damages claims, compromising the deterrent effect of such actions (effectiveness argument).[29]

The passing-on defence is irrelevant for consumer damages claims, since consumers are, in any case, the last ring in the supply chain. However, *Hanover Shoe* is important in that it directly influenced SCOTUS' ruling on indirect purchaser

---

[23] Indicative of the controversy surrounding passing-on are two seminal papers on this issue published in the aftermath of the above decisions. See WM Landes and RA Posner, 'Should Indirect Purchasers Have Standing to Sue under the Antitrust Laws? An Economic Analysis of the Rule of Illinois Brick' (1979) 46 U Chi L Rev 602; RG Harris and LA Sullivan, 'Passing on the Monopoly Overcharge: A Comprehensive Policy Analysis' (1979) 128 U Pa L Rev 269; Also WM Landes and RA Posner, 'The Economics of Passing on: A Reply to Harris and Sullivan' (1980) 128 U Pa L Rev 1274; RG Harris and LA Sullivan, 'Passing on the Monopoly Overcharge: A Response to Landes and Posner' (1980) 128 U Pa L Rev 1280.
[24] *Hanover Shoe, Inc v United Shoe Machinery Corp* 392 US 481, 88 SCt 2224 (1968).
[25] *Illinois Brick Co v Illinois*, 431 US 720, 97 SCt 2061 (1977).
[26] *Hanover Shoe* (n 24) paras 488, 491–492.   [27] Ibid, para 489.
[28] Ibid, para 493.   [29] Ibid, para 494.

standing.[30] In *Illinois Brick*, the US Supreme Court stated that whatever the rule on passing-on, it should apply equally to plaintiffs and defendants. Thus, it had the choice to either overrule *Hanover Shoe* or deny standing to indirect purchasers.[31] Essentially, the US Supreme Court reiterated the effectiveness and efficiency arguments advanced in *Hanover Shoe* and refused to grant standing to indirect purchasers (except in certain limited situations).[32] In addition, the US Supreme Court reached this conclusion because it feared that, if only offensive passing-on were allowed, this could result in multiple liability for the defendants.[33] The denial of standing to indirect purchasers confines the role of final consumers in federal antitrust litigation to a minimum level.

States have reacted to the US Supreme Court rulings on passing-on, probably for political reasons,[34] by either enacting 'Illinois Brick Repealer Statutes' or through court judgments which effectively allow standing for indirect purchasers at the state level.[35] In *California v ARC America Corp*,[36] the US Supreme Court held that those state laws were not pre-empted by federal competition law. The current position of US law with regard to passing-on results in multiple claims being brought in state and federal courts that complicate class certification and case consolidation.[37] The Antitrust Modernization Commission (AMC) tried to address this problem and proposed a reversal of the current status quo through legislative action.[38]

---

[30] The following quotation from Justice Blackmun, dissenting, is illustrative in that regard: 'plaintiffs-respondents...are the victims of an unhappy chronology. If (*Hanover Shoe*) had not preceded this case, and were it not "on the books," I am positive that the Court today would be affirming, perhaps unanimously, the judgment of the Court of Appeals (which granted standing to indirect purchasers)'. See *Illinois Brick* (n 25), para 765.
[31] *Illinois Brick* (n 25), paras 728–729; However, Justice Brennan in his dissenting opinion (endorsed by two other Justices) argued in favour of treating offensive and defensive passing-on differently. See *Illinois Brick* (n 25), para 753.
[32] *Illinois Brick* (n 25), para 736.   [33] *Illinois Brick* (n 25), paras 731–732.
[34] F Cengiz, 'Passing-on Defence and Indirect Purchasers Standing in Actions for Damages against the Violations of Competition Law: What Can the EC Learn from the US' (2007) UEA CCP Working Paper No 07/21 <http://papers.ssrn.com/sol3/papers.cfm?abstract_id=1038521> accessed 4 July 2014, 19.
[35] For the situation in the US see AMC, 'Report and Recommendations' (April 2007) <http://govinfo.library.unt.edu/amc/report_recommendation/amc_final_report.pdf> accessed 4 July 2014, 266, 268–269; F Cengiz, 'Antitrust Damages Actions: Lessons from American Indirect Purchasers' Litigation' (2010) 59 ICLQ 39, 47–51; KJ O'Connor, 'Is the Illinois Brick Wall Crumbling?' (2001) 15 Antitrust LJ 34, 35; R Folsom, 'Indirect Purchasers: State Antitrust Remedies and Roadblocks' (2005) 50 AB 181; DR Karon, '"Your Honor, Tear Down that Illinois Brick Wall!" The National Movement towards Indirect Purchaser Antitrust Standing and Consumer Justice' (2004) 30 Wm Mitchell L Rev 1351–1402. On the various different types of Illinois Brick Repealer Statutes see R Lande, 'New Options for State Indirect Purchaser Litigation: Protecting the Real Victims of Antitrust Violations' (2010) 61 Alabama L Rev 447, 451–465.
[36] *California v ARC America Corp* 490 US 93,109 SCt 1661 (1989).
[37] See WH Page, 'The Limits of State Indirect Purchaser Suits: Class Certification in the Shadow of Illinois Brick' (1999) 67 Antitrust LJ 1 on class certification problems; WH Page, 'Class Certification in the Microsoft Indirect Purchaser Litigation' (2005) 1 J Comp L & Econ 303. CAFA 2005 (Class Action Fairness Act, Pub L 109-2—18 Feb 2005) tried to address concerns of case consolidation. See 28 USC para 1332(d)(2).
[38] AMC Report (n 35) 267. For a critical account of this proposal see WH Page, 'Class Interpleader: The Antitrust Modernization Commission's Recommendation to Overrule Illinois Brick' (2008) 53 *Antitrust Bulletin* 725.

States' reaction towards the approach of passing-on at federal level provides a first indication that the federal approach is rather problematic. Criticism may be raised at two levels, such that this approach cannot be accommodated in the EU context. First, from a legal perspective, the rejection of the compensatory function of damages actions cannot be accepted, in particular given the Commission's emphasis on compensation in the context of private enforcement.[39] *Illinois Brick* denied many injured parties the right to claim compensation, as, arguably, the overcharge is likely to be passed on to the next levels of the supply chain and ultimately to the final consumer.[40] In the modern economic world in which transactions consist of multilevel supply chains, *Illinois Brick* raises serious justice considerations. The only parties entitled to compensation, ie the direct purchasers, would most probably not have suffered any harm, whereas many injured parties at different levels remain uncompensated.[41] The same holds true for final consumers. Denying redress to consumers is very difficult to justify politically, especially in Europe, where competition authorities have repeatedly stressed that competition law aims at protecting consumer interest.[42]

Second, it is questionable from an economic perspective, whether it sufficiently promotes the deterrent function and reduces the social costs of litigation, especially if one takes into account the unlevel playing field between the federal level and the state level. Even if deterrence were to be recognized as the primary objective, the economic and legal literature has contested whether the *Illinois Brick* approach better serves this aim.[43] It has challenged the idea that direct purchasers are the most efficient plaintiffs since they might be reluctant to sue their suppliers so as not to disrupt their ongoing contractual relationships.[44] In

---

[39] Arguably the rejection of the compensatory component cannot be accommodated in the US either, since the Clayton Act embraces both a compensatory and a deterrence rationale. See BD Richman and CR Murray, 'Rebuilding Illinois Brick: A Functionalist Approach to the Indirect Purchaser Rule' (2007) Duke Law School Legal Studies Paper No 155 <http://ssrn.com/abstract=978968> accessed 4 July 2014, 24; *Illinois Brick* (n 25) (Justice Brennan Dissenting Opinion), para 748.

[40] *Illinois Brick* (n 25) (Justice Brennan Dissenting Opinion), para 749; F Bulst, 'Private Antitrust Enforcement at a Roundabout' (2006) 7 EBOR 725, 734 with further references to Harris and Sullivan (n 23) 321ff and 337ff; cf Joined Cases C-204/00 P, C-205/00 P, C-211/00 P, C-213/00 P, C-217/00 P, and C-219/00 P *Aalborg Portland and Others v Commission of the European Communities* [2004] ECR I-123, para 53.

[41] Richman and Murray (n 39) 26 where they argue that the *Illinois Brick* trade off between compensation and deterrence cannot be accepted in the modern globalized economy; contra I Gubbay and A Maton, 'Private Enforcement Claims—Are They a Risk for Consumers and Businesses?' (2009) 8 (1) CLI 8, 9 where they argue that the fact that businesses in a typical cartel pass on the overcharge to the next levels of the chain until the final consumer exists in 'an economic fairyland'.

[42] See Chapter 2, text to nn 84–99. In fact, this option was never contemplated by the Commission, not even under the proposal of excluding the standing of indirect purchasers (Option 22 in the GP). See GP SWP (n 8), para 183.

[43] See, for example, LJ Basso and RT Ross, 'Measuring the True Harm from Price Fixing to Both Direct and Indirect Purchasers' (Draft, January 2008) <http://strategy.sauder.ubc.ca/ross/MeasuringtheTrueHarmfromPriceFixing.pdf> accessed 4 July 2014; M Hellwig, 'Private Damages Claims and the Passing-on Defence in Horizontal Price-Fixing Cases—An Economist's Perspective' in J Basedow (ed), *Private Enforcement of EC Competition Law* (Kluwer Law International 2007) 121. See also OECD, 'Private Remedies' (2009) *OECD Journal: Competition Law and Policy* 7, 16.

[44] Harris and Sullivan (n 23) 352; H Hovenkamp, 'Book Review—The Rationalisation of Antitrust' (2003) 116 Harv L Rev 917, 942, in which he cites the *Microsoft* litigation example where

addition, antitrust violators might grant direct purchasers a share of the cartel profits in return for their inertia in commencing proceedings.[45] Furthermore, it is true that calculating the amount of the overcharge is complex, but it is possible to calculate it by employing certain economic models and by taking into account certain market characteristics.[46] In addition, the fact that this calculation entails a detailed economic analysis is no different from other concepts in competition law, such as defining the relevant market and assessing market power.[47]

To sum up, it can be said that, in the US, the balancing of the conflicting considerations regarding passing-on has not resulted in a satisfactory solution. the US Supreme Court erred in favour of deterrence and restricted the role of consumers in private antitrust litigation. This might be due to the nature of the US private enforcement system. However, in the EU context, the approach to passing-on is different.

3.2 The European Court's approach

3.2.1 Consumer standing

Consumer standing to bring competition law claims is relevant not only to the question of allowing indirect purchaser standing but also to the broader matter of principle, regarding whether consumers, irrespective of their situation as direct or indirect purchasers, can act as claimants under competition law. This is because, in some Member States, claimants have had to fall under the protective scope of competition law in order to bring damages claims.[48]

---

direct purchasers were reluctant to bring claims against Microsoft; a point also accepted by the Supreme Court in *Illinois Brick* (n 25), para 746.

[45] MP Schinkel, J Tuinstra, and J Rueggeberg, 'Illinois Walls: How Barring Indirect Purchaser Suits Facilitates Collusion' (2008) 39 *The RAND Journal of Economics* 683 with examples of recent US cases that indicate symptoms of 'Illinois Walls'.

[46] Harris and Sullivan (n 23) 269, 272–273; See Oxera Study (n 20), para 4.4. Commission (EU), 'Staff Working Document—Practical Guide—Quantifying Harm in Actions for Damages Based on Breaches of Article 101 or 102 of the Treaty on the Functioning of the European Union' SWD (2013) (205) (Strasbourg, 11 June 2013) (Quantification Guide), paras 166–71.

[47] Richman and Murray (n 39) 34.

[48] For example, in Germany, prior to the 7th amendment of the German Act Against Restraints of Competition (new Article 33(3) GWB), only persons falling within the protective scope of competition law could bring damages claims. See U Boege and K Ost, 'Up and Running, or Is It? Private Enforcement—The Situation in Germany and Policy Perspectives' (2006) 27 ECLR 197, 199; A Klees, 'Breaking the Habits: The German Competition Law after the 7th Amendment to the Act Against Restraints of Competition (GWB)' (2006) 7 *German LJ* 399, 416; see also Komninos, *EC Private Antitrust Enforcement—Decentralised Application of EC Competition Law by National Courts* (Hart 2008) 189 with references to relevant German case law. In Italy, consumers were seen as falling outside the protective scope of competition law and were, therefore, excluded from bringing competition law claims. See Nebbia (n 20) 592 with reference to *Unipol*, Decision No 2207/2005 reversing this approach. See also Incardona and Poncibo (n 17) 445; C Tesauro and D Ruggiero, 'Private Damage Actions Related to European Competition Law in Italy' (2010) JECLAP 514, 517. Similarly, prior to the latest competition law amendments, consumers could not bring claims for competition law violations in Finland and Sweden. See Rodger (n 3) 168, 186.

Essentially, the issue of standing has been resolved by the Court.[49] Following *Courage* and *Manfredi*, the controversy as to whether consumers enjoy a right to damages under competition law, and whether they have standing to raise a competition law claim, has been resolved. According to *Courage* any individual can rely on a breach of competition provisions. AG Mischo, in this case, was even more specific by stating that the parties that can primarily benefit from such protection are competitors and consumers.[50]

In *Manfredi*, the Court went a step further by elaborating on the conditions of the right to damages, these being violations of competition provisions, harm and causation between the violation, and the respective harm. Thus, if there is a violation of competition provisions, any individual, irrespective of whether they are a direct or indirect purchaser, that can prove his/her harm and a causal connection between the harm and the competition law violations, has a right to raise a damages claim.[51] *Manfredi* is important for consumers' right to damages for competition law violations given that the preliminary ruling came as a result of consumer claims raised before the Italian courts.

The Court's pronouncements on standing and the right to damages have been summarized in Article 3(1) of the Directive on Damages Actions, which states that 'Member States shall ensure that any natural or legal person who has suffered harm caused by an infringement of competition law is able to claim and to obtain full compensation for that harm'.

3.2.2 Passing-on defence

No similar *acquis communautaire* exists on the issue of the passing-on defence in competition law. However, as the GP SWP suggests, some insights can be drawn from the Court's unjust enrichment cases on non-contractual liability of EU institutions and on Member States' liability for illegally levied taxes.[52] This line of case law could potentially shed some light on the passing-on defence problem in competition law cases. However, the latter are usually more complex in the light of the wider cartel effects globally.[53]

---

[49] See WP SWP (n 1), paras 33–37; cf Boege and Ost (n 48) 201 in which they argue that, as *Courage* did not concern an indirect purchasers' claim, it did not provide a definite answer to the question of indirect purchasers' standing. For a thorough discussion, and an argument regarding the unresolved nature of this issue, calling for a resolution at Union level, see V Milutinović, *The 'Right to Damages' under EU Competition Law: from Courage v. Crehan to the White Paper and Beyond* (Kluwer Law International 2010) ch 10. Milutinović points to the same wording of Section 4 of the Clayton Act regarding the 'any individual' formulation and the different solution formulated by SCOTUS. Ibid, 218.

[50] *Courage* (n 19), Opinion of AG Mischo, para 38. On *Courage* see Chapter 3, nn 41–64.

[51] On *Manfredi* see Chapter 3, nn 65–70.

[52] GP SWP (n 8), para 165. See reference to this case law in *Courage* (n 19), para 30; *Manfredi* (n 18), para 94. For a detailed discussion of this case law see D Ashton and D Henry, *Competition Damages Actions in the EU* (Edward Elgar 2013) paras 3.037–3.063.

[53] GP SWP (n 8), para 167.

In *San Giorgio*, the Court held that a Member State should, in principle, repay the charges levied contrary to EU law.[54] While it is not contrary to EU law to resist the repayment of such charges, when this would result in the unjust enrichment of the recipients,[55] EU law precludes any presumption or rule of evidence that shifts the burden of proving that the charges have not been passed on to the trader concerned.[56]

In *Comateb*, the ECJ accepted that:

> the trader may have suffered damage as a result of the very fact that he has passed on the charge...because the increase in the price of the product brought about by passing on the charge has led to a decrease in sales...In such circumstances the trader may justly claim that, although the charge has been passed on to the purchaser, the inclusion of that charge in the cost price has, by increasing the price of the goods and reducing sales, caused him damage, which excludes, in whole or in part, any unjust enrichment.[57]

In *Weber's Wine*, the ECJ maintained that:

> as that exception [from the obligation to make a repayment] is a restriction on a subjective right derived from the Community legal order, it must be interpreted restrictively, taking account in particular of the fact that passing on a charge to the consumer does not necessarily neutralise the economic effects of the tax on the taxable person,[58]

and concluded that:

> the rules of Community law...are to be interpreted as meaning that they preclude national rules which refuse...repayment of a charge incompatible with Community law on the sole ground that the charge was passed on to third parties, without requiring that the degree of unjust enrichment that repayment of the charge would entail for the trader be established.[59]

According to the Court, the passing-on of charges does not necessarily amount to unjust enrichment. Passing-on can be viewed as a necessary, but not the sole, condition for unjust enrichment. Thus, the Court accepts the passing-on defence as long as the passing-on of the overcharge has not resulted in any reduction in sales. The Commission, after reviewing the relevant case law, concluded that no passing-on defence existed as a matter of EU law. Only an unjust enrichment

---

[54] Case 199/82 *Administrazione delle Finanze dello Stato v SpA San Giorgio* [1983] ECR 3595, para 12; cf Joined Cases C-441/98 and 442/98 *Kapniki Mikhailidis AE v Idryma Koinonikon Asfaliseon* [2000] ECR I-7145, para 30.
[55] *San Giorgio* (n 54), para 13; *Kapniki Mikhailidis* (n 54), para 31; Case 68/79 *Hans Just v Danish Ministry for Fiscal Affairs* [1980] ECR 501, para 26.
[56] *San Giorgio* (n 54), para 14; *Kapniki Mikhailidis* (n 54), paras 36–37, 42.
[57] Joined Cases C-192/95 to 218/95 *Société Comateb and others v Directeur Général des Douanes et Droits Indirects* [1997] ECR I-165, paras 31–32.
[58] Case C-147/01 *Weber's Wine World Handels-GmbH v Abgabenberufungskommission Wien* [2003] ECR I-11365, para 95.
[59] Ibid, para 102.

defence, which requires proof of passing-on and proof of no reduction in sales or other reduction in income, exists.⁶⁰

If the gist of this case law is applied in the context of competition law, this means that, in order for the claimant not to be unjustly enriched, the defendant would have to prove that the overcharge has been passed further down the production chain and that no other reduction in income (due to, for example, a reduction in sales) has been sustained. The Court's approach to passing-on is enshrined in the preamble of the Directive on Damages Actions, which expressly states that when passing-on the overcharge results in reduced sales, the right to compensation for such loss of profit remains unaffected,⁶¹ as well as Article 12(3), which provides that the rules on passing-on 'shall be without prejudice to the right of an injured party to claim and obtain compensation for loss of profits due to a full or partial passing-on of the overcharge'. Furthermore, this is reflected in bolder terms in the Commission's guide to the quantification of damages, since the Commission expressly links the passing-on effect with the relevant reduction in sales (volume effect).⁶²

3.3 Legislative solution

The Commission has proposed, in line with the Court's case law and the Member States' approach, the recognition of standing for any individual, which includes indirect purchasers.⁶³ This is now incorporated in the Directive on Damages Actions, which recognizes the right to full compensation for any natural or legal person suffering harm caused by a competition law infringement (Article 3, para 1). Article 12(1) explicitly recognizes standing for direct and indirect purchasers in order to 'ensure the full effectiveness of the right to full compensation'. The emphasis is on the right to compensation, although the reference to the full effectiveness of this right may imply that its exercise could also contribute to the effectiveness of EU competition rules. This is because in the Court's case law on private enforcement of EU competition law, the Court consistently referred to the full

---

⁶⁰ GP SWP (n 8), para 173; See T van Dijk and F Verboven, 'Cartel Damages Claims and the Passing-on Defence' (2007) CEPR Discussion Paper No DP6329 <http://papers.ssrn.com/sol3/papers.cfm?abstract_id=1136655> accessed 30 January 2015, 5 where they call this unjust enrichment defence an adjusted version of the passing-on defence, which also takes into account the 'output effect' following the passing-on. They attempt to show how this 'adjusted passing-on defence' operates in a variety of competitive circumstances.

⁶¹ Directive on Damages Actions (n 21), recital 40.

⁶² Quantification Guide (n 46) para 163. For guidance in quantifying the volume effect, see ibid, paras 175–79.

⁶³ WP (n 13), para 2.1; Draft Damages Directive (n 6), Article 4(1); on the four proposals initially put forward see Commission (EC), 'Damages Actions for Breach of the EC Antitrust Rules' (Green Paper) COM(2005) 672 final (GP), para 2.4. All Member States recognize, in principle, standing for indirect purchasers. See V Milutinović, 'Private Enforcement' in G Amato and CD Ehlermann (eds), *EC Competition Law—A Critical Assessment* (Hart 2007) 725, 730–735 on the issue of standing; Komninos (n 48) 190; M Brkan, 'Procedural Aspects of Private Enforcement of EC Antitrust Law: Heading Toward New Reforms?' (2005) 28 W Comp 479, 490.

effectiveness of EU law, rather than the full effectiveness of the substantive EU law right.[64]

Apart from recognizing indirect purchaser standing, the Commission took due account of the difficulties faced by indirect purchasers in quantifying their harm. Notwithstanding the strong opposition from businesses,[65] the Commission chose to alleviate the indirect purchasers' burden of proof by proposing the adoption of a rebuttable presumption regarding the passing-on of overcharges to the level of the indirect purchasers.[66] This is now incorporated in Article 14 of the Directive on Damages Actions. Article 14(1) begins with a statement of principle, namely that commercial practice suggests that price increases are passed on down the supply chain and that the burden of proving the respective pass-on rests with the claimant. However, Article 14(2) reverses this approach and introduces a rebuttable presumption in favour of the claimant. In particular, the indirect purchaser shall be deemed to have proven passing-on of the overcharges to his level as long as he fulfils three conditions: first, he needs to prove a competition law infringement by the defendant; second, he must prove that the infringement resulted in an overcharge at the direct purchasers' level; and third, he must prove that the claimant purchased goods or services that were the subject of the competition law infringement (or contained the latter).[67] Article 14(2) does not apply where the defendant 'can demonstrate credibly to the satisfaction of the court that the overcharge was not, or not entirely, passed on to the indirect purchaser'.[68]

The Commission Quantification Guidance can aid defendants in rebutting the passing-on presumption.[69] First of all, the Guidance points to two different approaches in relation to proving the pass-on of the overcharge. It states that the indirect customer can either (a) prove the initial overcharge and that the latter was passed on to his level; or (b) merely quantify his overcharge (without proving the pass-on rate) by employing a comparator-based approach, ie the price actually paid and the hypothetical price in a non-infringement scenario.[70] The Guidance

---

[64] See Chapter 3 text to n 61.
[65] See, for example, EuroCommerce, 'White Paper on Damages Actions for Breach of EC Antitrust Rules—EuroCommerce Response' (July 2008) 7–8; SEV (Hellenic Federation of Enterprises), 'Comments on the WP' 2; AmCham, 'Comments on the European Commission's White Paper on Damages Actions for Breach of the EC Antitrust Rules' (7 July 2008) 7; BDI, 'Position—Commission White Paper on Damages Actions for Breach of the EC Antitrust Rules', 19-10.
[66] WP (n 13), para 2.6; Draft Damages Directive (n 6), Article 11(2).
[67] Article 14(2) of the Directive on Damages Actions (n 21). As the Commission recognizes, the presumption of the overcharge being passed on is an important, although very limited, alleviation of the claimant's burden of proof. See G Cumming and M Freudenthal, *Civil Procedure in EU Competition Cases before the English and Dutch Courts* (Kluwer 2010) 107–108, who drew a distinction between the evidential burden of proof of having suffered damage, which falls on the indirect purchaser, and the legal burden of disproving this damage, which falls on the defendant.
[68] Ibid.
[69] Quantification Guide (n 46) paras 165–71. The Commission will also issue Guidelines for national courts on how to estimate the overcharge that was passed on to the indirect purchaser. Article 16 of the Directive on Damages Actions (n 21).
[70] Ibid, paras 166–67.

refers to the indirect customer having to prove the pass-on, which is misleading in the light of the rebuttable presumption introduced by the Directive that shifts the burden of proving pass-on to the defendant. Thus, it is the defendant rather than the indirect purchaser that will employ the above techniques to prove that no pass-on took place.

Quantifying the pass-on rate is complex and dependent on market characteristics and conditions.[71] The Guidance identifies situations where pass-on is unlikely. For example, where the direct purchasers use the cartelized product to compete in the downstream market, they will, in all likelihood, not be able to pass-on the overcharge if their competitors in the downstream market are not subjected to the same overcharge because, for instance, they buy the product elsewhere, not from the cartel members.[72] When all competitors are subjected to the same overcharge, however, pass-on is likely. The extent of pass-on depends on the prevailing conditions in the downstream market; if the latter is perfectly competitive, then the expected rate of pass-on is 100%. The cost structure; the demand faced by the direct customer; the price elasticity of demand; the variation of marginal cost with output reductions; the impact of the infringement on different types of costs; and the duration of the infringement are some of the factors identified in the Guidance as determinants of the pass-on rate.[73]

Thus, it appears that the issue of passing-on has been resolved in favour of indirect purchasers. Although the passing-on defence is available to infringers (Article 13), indirect purchasers benefit from a rebuttable presumption, ie they do not have to prove passing-on themselves, whereas the defendants do. This may provide an impetus for consumer damages claims, since it reduces the claimant's burden of proof to some, albeit a limited, extent. However, situations of multiple liability need to be accounted for.[74] The Commission accepted that adducing proof of pass-on is equally difficult for both the claimant and the defendant and that it is fairer for the infringer to bear the risks of its illegal act.[75] In order to prevent situations of multiple liability, Article 15(1) of the Directive on Damages Actions requires national courts to take into account related claims for the same competition law infringement raised by claimants from different levels of the supply chain, any relevant judgments following such actions, and relevant information in the public domain from public enforcement cases. Article 15(2) further clarifies that this is without prejudice to Article 30 of Regulation 1250/2012 (Revised Brussels I Regulation) on the treatment of related actions before courts in different Member States.[76] It has been observed by commentators that the Brussels I Regulation may not prevent situations of multiple liability and therefore an EU-wide coordination mechanism for competition law claims may need to be

---

[71] Ibid, para 168.   [72] Ibid, para 169.   [73] Ibid, paras 170–71.
[74] JS Kortmann and CR Swaak, 'The EC White Paper on Damages Actions: Why the Member States are (Right to Be) Less than Enthusiastic' (2009) 30 ECLR 340, 345–346.
[75] WP SWP (n 1), para 218; IAR (n 1) paras 156–57.
[76] Regulation (EU) No 1250/2012 on Jurisdiction and the Recognition and Enforcement of Judgments in Civil and Commercial Matters (recast) [2012] OJ L351/1.

devised.[77] The Directive did not go this far; however, Article 15(1) can be read in this light.

To sum up, the proposal of the rebuttable presumption offers yet another example of the deterrence principle as the main guiding principle for the Commission's efforts in private enforcement, but at the same time it is in line with the compensatory nature of damages in most Member States.[78] The legislative resolution of passing-on is further beneficial as it harmonizes a procedural matter that has been dealt with differently in different Member States. The Commission acknowledges that the majority of Member States do not legislate on the issue of passing-on and equally that there is no case law on the matter.[79] However, passing-on has been explicitly accepted by some national courts in Europe,[80] although with varying approaches as to the burden of proof.[81] The issue has now been resolved at EU level. The Directive on Damages Actions provides for both defensive and offensive passing-on with the reversal of the burden of proof in favour of indirect purchasers. This reveals an attempt to reconcile different approaches to private enforcement in the EU.

---

[77] R O'Donoghue, 'Europe's Long March Towards Antitrust Damages Actions' (April 2011) *CPI Antitrust Chronicle* 2, 7; Cengiz (n 35) 56–63, where she argues that the EU can benefit from the US experience, not in terms of a substantive approach to the passing-on problem, but in order to devise the appropriate procedural mechanisms. See also R Nazzini and A Nikpay, 'Private Actions in EC Competition Law' (2008) 4 CPI 107, 133.

[78] D Waelbroeck, D Slater, and G Even-Shoshan, 'Study on the Conditions of Claims for Damages in Case of Infringement of EC Competition Rules' (Comparative Report) (Ashurst Study) (31 August 2004) <http://ec.europa.eu/competition/antitrust/actionsdamages/comparative_report_clean_en.pdf> accessed 4 July 2014, 48, 84.

[79] IAR (n 1) paras 41, 158. See also BIS, 'Private Actions in Competition Law: A Consultation on Options for Reform—Government Response' (January 2013), paras 4.38–4.39. The UK proposals did not introduce a legislative solution on passing-on as, according to the government's response, general principles of tort law allow the passing-on defence.

[80] In regard to the complex situation in Germany see N Reich, 'The "Courage" Doctrine: Encouraging or Discouraging Violations for Antitrust Injuries?' (2005) 42 CMLRev 35, 42; W Wurmnest, 'A New Era for Private Antitrust Litigation in Germany? A Critical Appraisal of the Modernized Law against Restraints of Competition' (2005) 6 *German LJ* 1173, 1184; C Cook, 'Private Enforcement of EU Competition Law in Member State Courts: Experience to Date and the Path Ahead' (2008) 4 CPI 3, 59. The judgment of the German Supreme Court for Civil Matters of 28 June 2011, KZR 75/10 allowed both the standing of indirect purchasers and the passing-on defence and ended the previous controversy on these issues (Carbonless paper cartel). See External Impact Study (n 4), fn 680 regarding the situation in Italy; see Oxera Study (n 20) 119–120; see Y Utzschneider and H Parmentier, 'The New Frontiers of Antitrust: Damages Actions by Indirect Purchasers and the Passing-On Defence in France and California' (2011) 32 ECLR 266, 267–268 for the situation in France; see *Devenish Nutrition Ltd v Sanofi-Aventis SA (France)* [2008] EWCA Civ 1086, [2009] 3 All ER 27 for the situation in the UK; A Murray, 'Collective Cartel Damages Claims—Practical Financial Considerations for Businesses Bringing an Action in the English High Court' (2008) 7 (12) CLI 14 in which he draws attention to *Devenish Nutrition* where the Court of Appeal stated that the English courts will compensate losses suffered, wherever they fall. For the situation in Spain see F Cachafeiro, 'Damages Claims for Breach of Competition Law in Spain' (2014) <http://papers.ssrn.com/sol3/papers.cfm?abstract_id=2456964> accessed 8 July 2014 17–18; F Marco, 'Damages' Claims in the Spanish Sugar Cartel' (Working Paper IE Law School AJ8-213-I) (2014) <http://papers.ssrn.com/sol3/papers.cfm?abstract_id=2514239> accessed 11 December 2014 19–23.

[81] IAR (n 1), para 41.

90   *Consumers' Standing and Access to Evidence*

4. Access to Evidence

Access to evidence has been identified as one of the main obstacles for competition damages claims.[82] In this section the problems associated with access to evidence are specifically addressed in the context of consumer claims,[83] and questions as to whether specific measures should be adopted are raised in the light of the distinguishing characteristics of consumer claims.

4.1 Disclosure of evidence: Promoting stand-alone consumer claims

Discovery procedures of the US type are alien to continental legal systems and were never seriously contemplated in the EU.[84] This does not preclude the adoption of discovery procedures of a different type, provided that certain safeguards important for continental law legal systems are retained. Procedural rules are sometimes the product of historical circumstances and can therefore be attributed to chance rather than reason. Thus, 'mere divergence' (discovery rules falling under this category), as opposed to systemic differences, is prone to harmonization. [85] In that regard, the UK system can serve as a useful example of a jurisdiction bridging the US approach with the continental approach.[86] The UK system provides for court-supervised pre-action disclosure, provided that the application is supported by evidence and is not merely speculative.[87] The UK courts have applied the conditions for pre-action disclosure cautiously,[88] thereby preventing 'fishing expeditions'.[89]

---

[82] GP SWP (n 8), para 54; WP SWP (n 1), para 67; Ashurst Study (n 78) 11; External Impact Study (n 4) 345.

[83] The difficulties in obtaining disclosure orders have also been highlighted by consumer associations. See IAR (n 1), para 12.

[84] See V Stuerner, 'Duties of Disclosure and Burden of Proof in the Private Enforcement of European Competition Law' in J Basedow (ed), *Private Enforcement of EC Competition Law* (Kluwer Law International 2007) 163, 170–173 for a comparison of the two systems; see National Commission Staff Papers, 'Scope of Discovery' (1979) 48 Antitrust LJ 1063 on the US system; ED Cavanagh, 'Pleading Rules in Antitrust Cases: A Return to Fact Pleading' (2002) 21 Rev Litigation 1; see *Bell Atlantic Corp et al v Twombly et al* 550 US 127 SCt 1955, 1965 (2007) on introducing limitations to discovery in antitrust cases; see ED Cavanagh, 'Twombly, the Federal Rules of Civil Procedure and the Courts' (2008) 82 St John's L Rev 877 for a comment. See also O Odudu, 'Developing Private Enforcement in the EU: Lessons for the Roberts Court' (2008) 53 Antitrust Bulletin 873, 877–878; R Epstein, 'Of Pleading and Discovery: Reflections on Twombly and Iqbal with Special Reference to Antitrust' [2011] U Ill L Rev 187.

[85] K Kerameus, 'Political Integration and Procedural Convergence in the European Union' (1997) 45 Am J Comp L 919, 928, 930.

[86] See M Brealey and N Green (eds), *Competition Litigation: UK Practice and Procedure* (OUP 2010) 219 for an account of the UK system.

[87] CPR 31.16.

[88] *Black v Sumitomo* [2001] EWCA Civ 1819, para 95; *Trouw UK Ltd v Mitsui & Co (UK) plc* [2007] EWHC 863 (Comm), paras 43–44; *Hutchison 3G UK Ltd v O2 Ltd and others* [2008] EWHC 55 (Comm), paras 51, 58, 63.

[89] Brealey and Green (n 86) 221, 222. See also C Brown and D Ryan, 'The Judicial Application of European Competition Law' (FIDE Congress Madrid, 2010) <http://www.ukael.org/associates_21_2528442727.pdf> accessed 9 July 2014, paras 16.3–16.5.

The Directive on Damages Actions has struck a sensible balance between the adoption of wide—US type—discovery rules and a more modest adoption of disclosure mechanisms that nonetheless are more advanced than those existing in many Member States. This has dispelled three main concerns relevant to wide discovery rules: first, the strategic use of discovery rules to gain access to competitors' business secrets.[90] This risk is less present in consumer claims than in customers' and competitors' claims. Second, another justified concern regarding discovery procedures is their impact on the defendants' due process rights in Member States that provide for criminal enforcement of competition law.[91] *Orkem* established a limited right against self-incrimination in administrative procedures. The undertaking being investigated cannot be compelled to answer questions that involve admission of the infringement;[92] however, this does not apply in relation to factual questions or requests to provide documents.[93] The Court held that this limited right against self-incrimination does not apply in national civil proceedings, since evidence obtained in the course of those proceedings cannot be used in administrative proceedings for the establishment of the violation.[94] Thus, in order for discovery procedures not to jeopardize the defendant's due process rights, Member States may provide that evidence obtained in the course of civil proceedings cannot be used in subsequent criminal proceedings.[95] Alternatively, the limited right against self-incrimination in administrative proceedings could be extended to civil proceedings as well.

Third, the cost of discovery could militate against the introduction of relevant procedures. The potential cost of discovery should be weighed against the inability to raise stand-alone competition claims. Carefully structured discovery rules and active case management by courts could prevent abuses of discovery rules.[96]

The above considerations have informed the provisions on disclosure of evidence in the Directive on Damages Actions. Article 5 provides the general rule on disclosure of evidence. Article 5(1) stipulates that national courts shall order the disclosure of relevant evidence that is under the control of the defendant or

---

[90] GP SWP (n 8), para 57; W Wils, 'The Relationship Between Public Antitrust Enforcement and Private Actions for Damages' (2009) 32 W Comp 3, 8.

[91] A Sanchez Graells, 'Discovery, Confidentiality and Disclosure of Evidence' (2006) IE Working Papers Derecho WPED06-05 <http://papers.ssrn.com/sol3/papers.cfm?abstract_id=952504> accessed 9 July 2014, 12; F Jacobs and T Deisenhofer, 'Procedural Aspects of the Effective Private Enforcement of EC Competition Rules: A Community Perspective' in CD Ehlermann and I Atanasiu (eds), *European Competition Law Annual 2001: Effective Private Enforcement of EC Antitrust Law* (Hart 2003) 188, 205.

[92] Case 374/87, *Orkem v Commission* (1989) ECR 3283, para 35; Case C-301/04 P *Commission v SGL Carbon AG* [2006] ECR I-5915, paras 40–45; Council Regulation (EC) 1/2003 on the Implementation of the Rules on Competition Laid Down in Articles 81 and 82 of the Treaty [2003] OJ L1/1 (Regulation 1/2003), recital 23.

[93] Case T-112/98, *Mannesmannröhren-Werke AG v Commission* (2001) ECR II-729, para 78.

[94] Case C-60/92 *Otto BV v Postbank NV* [1993] ECR I-5683, paras 17, 20.

[95] Article 7(3) of the Directive on Damages Actions (n 21) now provides that 'Member States shall ensure that evidence which is obtained by a natural or legal person solely through access to the file of a competition authority and which does not fall under paragraphs 1 or 2, *can be used in an action for damages only by that person*' (emphasis added).

[96] OECD (n 43) 15.

a third party[97] provided that the claimant has 'presented a *reasoned justification* containing *reasonably available facts and evidence* sufficient to support the plausibility of its claims for damages' (emphasis added). This rule applies equally to requests of disclosure by the defendant. According to Article 5(2) the disclosure concerns 'specified pieces of evidence or relevant categories of evidence'. Thus, the disclosure depends on fact pleading and concerns not only specified evidence but also, more broadly, categories of evidence.

The Directive clarifies the fact pleading requirement, namely that the claimant has to present a plausible claim supported by facts that he suffered harm caused by the defendant.[98] Furthermore, if the disclosure order sought refers to categories of evidence, then the latter should be defined as precisely and narrowly as possible and be identified by reference to their common features, containing, for example, the nature, object, and content of documents and the time they were drafted.[99] As will be discussed below this is a high threshold for consumer claims.

Article 5(3) strengthens the courts' role in the disclosure of evidence. Effectively, the court should perform a proportionality assessment and weigh the legitimate interests of all of the implicated parties when assessing the disclosure request. In particular, the court shall take into account: (a) the available facts and evidence supporting the claim; (b) the requested scope and cost of disclosure (especially in relation to third parties) in a bid to prevent a general non-specific search for information that is unlikely to be of relevance to the implicated parties (fishing expeditions);[100] and (c) any confidential information contained in the requested evidence (especially pertaining to third parties), and it shall take steps to prevent the disclosure of such information. In the light of the case law,[101] Article 5(5) clarifies that the interest of undertakings to avoid damages actions is not an interest that warrants protection. Despite Article 5(3)(c), Article 5(4) allows national courts to disclose evidence containing confidential information if they believe that it is relevant for the damages action, provided that they protect such information. Measures for the protection of confidential information include, for example, the reduction of sensitive information, conducting hearings in camera, restricting the number of persons allowed access to information, and producing non-confidential summaries of the relevant information.[102] The Directive underlines the importance of the right to damages since it explicitly allows the disclosure of confidential information provided that reasonable steps are taken for its protection.

When ordering disclosure of evidence, national courts should 'give full effect to applicable legal professional privilege under EU or national law' and should also

---

[97] 'Third parties' include public authorities. See Directive on Damages Actions (n 21), recital 15.
[98] Ibid, recital 16.
[99] Ibid. This essentially reflects previous Commission proposals that required that 'sufficient specification is made of the precise categories of evidence to be disclosed'. For previous proposals see Draft Damages Directive (n 6), Article 8; WP (n 13), para 2.2.
[100] Fishing expedition refers to a strategy of obtaining information from the alleged infringer in an unfocused manner with the hope of finding some evidence that could possibly support a damages claim. WP SWP (n 1), para 70.
[101] Case T-437/08 *CDC Hydrogen Peroxide v Commission* [2011] ECR II-8251, para 49.
[102] Directive on Damages Actions (n 21), recital 18.

respect the right to be heard of the party against which the disclosure is ordered (Article 5(6) and (7)). Finally, Article 5 introduces minimum harmonization rules, since Member States remain free to introduce wider disclosure rules (Article 5(8)).

The rules on disclosure of evidence in the Directive on Damages Actions are similar to previous Commission proposals, except that they appear wider since they no longer include the claimant's inability to assert the relevant evidence, despite applying all efforts reasonably expected, as a specific requirement for granting a disclosure order.[103] The adopted rules on evidence disclosure are more advanced than the civil procedure rules in some Member States, in which disclosure concerns not the category of documents but, rather, specific documents.[104] Nonetheless, they may fall short of being capable of facilitating stand-alone consumer claims.

In particular, these rules fail to take account of the fact that competition law infringements of the cartel type are secret in nature, as the vast bulk of evidence remains under the control of the competition law violators.[105] The proposed harmonized disclosure rules seem to be operational only in follow-on claims, since the fact pleading requirement, together with the specification condition, will be very difficult to satisfy in stand-alone claims.[106]

In order to promote stand-alone consumer claims wider disclosure rules should be introduced.[107] This is because consumer claims would usually concern damages flowing from cartel agreements, which by definition are covert and the relevant incriminating evidence remains with the infringer. So, in the case of consumer damages claims in the context of competition law, civil procedure rules could provide that the court could order the defendant to grant access to the relevant evidence, provided that: (i) the claimant has presented a plausible claim concerning the existence of a cartel; (ii) the disclosure concerns broadly-defined categories of documents; and (iii) the relevant material gathered under the disclosure order is used strictly for the purposes of private litigation. Another proposal is the introduction of a general pre-action disclosure rule under strict conditions. The disclosure order should be granted only exceptionally, in cases of insurmountable 'information asymmetry' between the parties.[108]

The second proposal is more prone to abuse, since it is applicable to all competition law claims (not just consumer claims), and could also potentially contribute to greater legal uncertainty.[109] Therefore, the first option is to be preferred. The

---

[103] For previous proposals see Draft Damages Directive (n 6), Article 8; WP (n 13), para 2.2.
[104] See External Impact Study (n 4) 349 for a list of these countries.
[105] C Jones, 'Exporting Antitrust Courtrooms to the World: Private Enforcement in a Global Market' (2004) 16 Loy Con L Rev 409, 428.
[106] See External Impact Study (n 4) 349.
[107] See A Sarra and A Marra, 'Are Monetary Incentives Enough to Boost Actions for Damages in the European Union? On the Relevance of Incompleteness of Laws and Evidentiary Requirements' (2008) 31 W Comp 369 for a similar opinion advocating the introduction of mandatory discovery.
[108] The Directive on Damages Actions (n 21) acknowledges that information asymmetry is a characteristic of competition law litigation. Ibid, recital 15.
[109] In a similar vein see External Impact Study (n 4) 262, but regarding the introduction of a fee-shifting rule, where arguably leaving it up to the judge's discretion to invoke it, provided that

first option could be introduced as an exception to the general proposal on disclosure based on fact pleading and strict judicial supervision in order to address 'information asymmetry' in consumer damages claims. Essentially, to a large extent, it is similar to the Commission's proposal but it could be more workable for consumer claims because it dispenses with the 'relevant categories of evidence' requirement.[110] In addition, it is consistent with the Commission Recommendation on collective redress, which rejects 'intrusive pre-trial discovery procedures'[111] and indicates that possibly consumer claims for competition law violations warrant a different treatment to that of other collective claims.

4.2 Promoting follow-on consumer claims— preserving the effectiveness of public enforcement

Access to competition authorities' files for the purposes of bringing actions for damages is a thorny issue in the light of its potential to raise negative repercussions for public competition law enforcement. In a growing string of cases, private claimants have sought access to the Commission's and NCAs' files. Access to the Commission's file falls under the scope of Regulation 1049/2001,[112] whereas access to NCAs' files is regulated by national procedural rules. The EU courts have had opportunities to assess the consistency of the latter rules with EU law (*Pfleiderer* and *Donau Chemie*) as well as to circumscribe the Commission's discretion to deny access to its file under the exemptions in Regulation 1049/2001 (*Lombard* and *EnBW*).[113] The legislative resolution regarding access to files in the Directive on Damages Actions has harmonized the national rules on access to documents before national courts and put an end to diverse national approaches.[114] However, it does not affect the application of Regulation 1049/2001. Nonetheless, it may lead to a similar interpretation and application of Regulation 1049/2001. Thus,

---

it is warranted by the plaintiff's resources and the risks of litigation, can prove conducive to greater legal uncertainty.

[110] See text to n 97.

[111] Commission (EU), 'Recommendation of 11 June 2013 on common principles for injunctive and compensatory collective redress mechanisms in the Member States concerning violations of rights granted under Union Law' [2013] OJ L201/60, recital 15.

[112] Council Regulation 1049/2001 Regarding Public Access to European Parliament, Council and Commission Documents [2001] OJ L145/43 (Regulation 1049/2001).

[113] See Case C-360/09 *Pfleiderer AG v Bundeskartellamt* [2011] ECR I-5161; Case T-344/08 *EnBW Energie Baden-Württemberg AG* [2012] 5 CMLR 4. On appeal Case C-365/12 P *Commission v EnBW Energie Baden-Württemberg AG* [2014] 4 CMLR 30; Case C-536/11 *Bundeswettbewerbsbehörde v Donau Chemie AG and Others* [2013] 5 CMLR 19. Case T-2/03 *Verein für Konsumenteninformation v Commission* (2005) ECR II-1121 (*Lombard*). Discussing access to competition authorities' files and arguing that recent case law and Commission practice show signs of favouring public enforcement over follow-on actions, see S Peyer, 'Access to Competition Authorities' Files in Private Antitrust Litigation' (2015) 3 *JAE* 58.

[114] See Amtsgericht Bonn, decision of 18 January 2012, case No 51 Gs 53/09 (*Pfleiderer II*) (January 2012); Oberlandesgericht Düsseldorf, decision of 22 August 2012, case No B-4 Kart 5/11 (OWi) (*Coffee Roaster*) (August 2012) in Germany. For the situation in the UK see *National Grid Electricity Transmission Plc v ABB Ltd* [2012] EWHC 869 (Ch) (*National Grid II*) (April 2012).

it should be seen as a welcome development. The adoption of the Directive on Damages Actions has prompted the Commission to plan a revision of Regulation 773/2004[115] and the notices on access to the file, leniency, settlements, and cooperation with national courts,[116] in order to align the rules on access to the Commission's file with the harmonized rules on access to NCAs' files.[117]

4.2.1 Access to Commission file

No specific provisions exist with regard to regulating access to the Commission's documents for third parties in competition cases. EU citizens have a right of access under Article 15(3) TFEU (formerly 255 TEC), Regulation 1049/01, and Article 42 of the Charter of Fundamental Rights of the EU.[118] This right has the purpose of enhancing the transparency and accountability of the Union institutions.[119] Thus, an interesting analogy can be drawn between this right and greater consumer involvement in private competition law enforcement, since both constitute mechanisms that possess the potential to increase transparency in the Union. This analogy is also supported by the simultaneous attempts by the Commission to revise Regulation 1049/2001[120] and enhance private competition law enforcement.

---

[115] Commission Regulation 773/2004 relating to the Conduct of Proceedings by the Commission Pursuant to Articles 81 and 82 of the EC Treaty [2004] OJ L123/18.

[116] Commission (EC), Notice on the Rules for Access to the Commission File [2005] C325/7 (Notice on Access to the Commission File); Commission (EU), 'Notice on Immunity from Fines and Reduction of Fines in Cartel Cases' [2006] OJ C298/17 (Leniency Notice); Commission (EU), 'Commission Notice on the Conduct of Settlement Procedures in View of the Adoption of Decision Pursuant to Article 7 and Article 23 of Council Regulation (EC) No 1/2003 in Cartel Cases' [2008] OJ C167/1; Commission (EC) 'Notice on the Cooperation between the Commission and the Courts of the EU Member States in the Application of Articles 81 and 82 EC' [2004] OJ C101/54.

[117] See Commission (EU), 'Consultation on Proposed Modifications to Regulation 773/2004 and the Notices on Access to the File, Leniency, Settlements and Cooperation with National Courts' <http://ec.europa.eu/competition/consultations/2014_regulation_773_2004/index_en.html> accessed 20 December 2014. Consultation period extends from 17 December 2014 to 25 March 2015.

[118] Regulation 1049/2001 (n 112). Commission (EC), 'Detailed Rules for the Application of Regulation (EC) No 1049/2001 of the European Parliament and of the Council Regarding Public Access to European Parliament, Council and Commission Documents' (Decision) [2001] OJ L345/94. See Regulation 1/2003 (n 92), Articles 27 and 28; Regulation 773/2004 (n 115), Articles 15 and 16; Notice on Access to the Commission File (n 116), paras 1–3, 7. These concern ongoing procedures and are specific to the rights of defence for the incumbent undertakings. On the relationship between Regulations 1/2003 and 773/2004 and Regulation 1049/2001 see Case C-365/12 P *Commission v EnBW Energie Baden-Württemberg AG* (n 113) paras 83–84; See also S Bartelt, 'Case T-2/03 *VKI v Commission*' (2006) 43 CMLRev 191, 197, 205.

[119] Regulation 1049/2001 (n 112), recitals 1–4. See also the Commission linking the current revision of Regulation 1049/2001 with the 'European Transparency Initiative' in Commission (EC), 'Proposal for a Regulation of the European Parliament and of the Council Regarding Public Access to European Parliament, Council and Commission Documents' COM(2008) 229 final (Proposal Amending Regulation 1049/2001), para 1.2.

[120] For the relevant documentation see Statewatch Observatory: The Regulation on Access to EU Documents: 2008–ongoing <http://www.statewatch.org/foi/observatory-access-reg-2008-2009.htm> accessed 7 May 2015.

The right of access to Commission documents is not unconditional, but subject to limitations on the grounds of public or private interest.[121] Article 4(2) relates to access to the Commission's file in competition law proceedings and provides that:

The institutions shall refuse access to a document where disclosure would undermine the protection of:
— *commercial interests* of a natural or legal person, including intellectual property,
— court proceedings and legal advice,
— the *purpose of inspections*, investigations and audits,
unless there is an overriding public interest in disclosure.

The Commission may also refuse access to its internal documents if this would jeopardize its decision-making process (Article 4(3)). These limitations should be interpreted restrictively so as not to defeat the purpose of Regulation 1049/2001.[122] The Commission has applied the Article 4(2) limitations in a liberal manner in order to refuse access to its file in competition proceedings. This is explicable in the light of the view expressed by the Commission that Regulation 1049/2001 'normally does not constitute an appropriate legal basis for obtaining access to evidence for the purposes of pursuing private damages actions'.[123] However, nothing in the Regulation suggests that such an exception is permissible, especially in the light of the recognized Treaty right of access to documents of the Union institutions. The fact that the Commission would have to carry out a balancing exercise between the protection of commercially sensitive information or the purpose of its investigation and the said right does not lead to the exclusion of this right altogether in the field of damages actions for competition law violations.[124] This balancing exercise has been reviewed by the European Courts, which has led to conflicting outcomes. However, the most recent case law suggests that the right of access to the Commission's file for the purpose of raising damages actions is rather limited.[125]

---

[121] Article 15(3) TFEU; Regulation 1049/2001 (n 112), Article 4; ME De Leeuw, 'The Regulation on Public Access to European Parliament, Council and Commission Documents in the European Union: Are Citizens Better Off?' (2003) 28 ELRev 324, 333.
[122] Joined Cases T-391/03 and T-70/04 *Franchet and Byk v Commission* [2006] ECR II-2023, para 84; Case T-516/11 *Mastercard v Commission* (judgment of 9 September 2014), para 47.
[123] WP SWP (n 1), para 104. Wils argued that a specific access regime for claimants should be created under Regulation 1/2003. See Wils (n 90) 18.
[124] See Decision of the European Ombudsman closing his inquiry into complaint 3699/2006/ELB against the European Commission (Ombudsman decision on 3699/2006), paras 53, 92 which points out that 'the existence of privileged access rights under specific regulations does not exclude the possibility to request access under Regulation 1049/2001' with reference to Case T-403/05 *My Travel v Commission* [2008] ECR II-2027, para 89.
[125] See *Lombard* (n 113). On access to the statement of contents of the case file in a cartel case see *CDC* (n 101); Case C-365/12 P *Commission v EnBW Energie Baden-Württemberg AG* (n 113). On access to documents in state aid cases see Case C-139/07 P *Commission v Technische Glaswerke Ilmenau GmbH* [2010] ECR I-5885. On access to documents in merger cases see *My Travel v Commission* (n 124) and on appeal Case C-506/08 P *Kingdom of Sweden v Commission and My Travel Group* [2011] ECR I-6237; Case T-237/05 *Éditions Jacob v Commission* [2010] ECR II-2245 and on appeal Case C-404/10 P *Commission v Éditions Odile SAS* [2012] 5 CMLR 8; Case T-111/07 *Agrofert v Commission* [2011] 4 CMLR 6 and on appeal Case C-477/10 P *Commission v Agrofert*

In *Lombard*, following the Commission's decision to fine Austrian banks for their participation in a cartel agreement,[126] VKI, an Austrian consumer organization, sought to claim damages on behalf of Austrian consumers. In order to substantiate its claim, it invoked the right of access to documents and sought access to the Commission's file, claiming that:

in order to secure damages for the consumers on whose behalf it was acting, it had to be able to put forward *specific claims* regarding both the *illegality of* BAWAG's *conduct under competition law* and the *effects of that conduct*. To that end, consultation of the Lombard Club file would have been a significant, or even indispensable, help to it.[127]

The Commission rejected VKI's request. Its decision in this case is important as it demonstrates an inconsistency between the Commission's pronouncements on the potential of competition law to protect consumers' interests and the actual practice of the Commission, and furthermore, because it depicts the evidentiary difficulties faced by consumer organizations in follow-on actions, even if the Commission's decision on a competition law violation is binding upon civil courts.[128] The Commission, in this case, failed to take account of the fact that the request for access to its file was submitted by a consumer organization. It refused access by invoking the exceptions in Regulation 1049/2001 and emphasizing the workload that acceding to this request would have entailed.[129]

The GC annulled the Commission's decision, offering a narrower interpretation of the exceptional conditions for refusing access to the Commission's documents. The GC stated that, in principle, the Commission must undertake a concrete individual examination of each document requested in order to refuse disclosure,[130] and identified as exceptions certain limited situations where such a concrete and individual examination was not warranted.[131] The Commission relied on Article 4(2) of Regulation 1049/2001 (third indent) and argued that disclosure in this case would jeopardize the purpose of inspections, as despite the

---

[2012] 5 CMLR 9. On these cases see G Goddin, 'Recent Judgments Regarding Transparency and Access to Documents in the Field of Competition Law: Where does the Court of Justice of the EU Strike the Balance?' (2011) 2 JECLAP 10; P Leino, 'Just a Little Sunshine in the Rain: The 2010 Case Law of the European Court of Justice on Access to Documents' (2011) 48 CMLRev 1215.

[126] *Lombard Club* (Case COMP 36.571/D-1) Commission Decision 2004/138/EC [2004] OJ L56/1.

[127] *Lombard* (n 113), para 9 (emphasis added).

[128] Commission decisions are binding upon civil courts according to Article 16(1) of Regulation 1/2003. On the binding effect of NCAs' decisions see Article 9 of the Directive on Damages Actions (n 21). Article 9(2) provides that a final NCA decision presented before a court in another Member State provides prima facie evidence of the infringement as opposed to previous Commission proposals suggesting that final NCA decisions should serve as irrebuttable proof of the infringement. On previous proposals see WP (n 13), para 2.3; Draft Damages Directive (n 6), Article 13. Komninos was critical of the previous approach as it risked undermining private enforcement: Komninos (n 48) 229–230.

[129] *Lombard* (n 113) paras 18, 20. The Commission reiterated the problem of the substantial administrative burden entailed in applications of this type in Commission (EU), 'Report on the Application in 2009 of Regulation No 1049/2001 Regarding Public Access to European Parliament, Council and Commission Documents' COM(2010) 351 final, para 8.1.

[130] Ibid, paras 72, 74.

[131] Ibid, paras 75, 77.

adoption of the Commission's decision, the latter was challenged before the GC. Furthermore, a number of documents were provided voluntarily by the parties during the course of the proceedings and also during the leniency proceedings. Disclosing these documents would deter undertakings from cooperating with the Commission and would be detrimental to inspections and investigations in future cases.[132] The GC held that the Commission should not have refused disclosure without first undertaking a concrete and individual examination of the individual documents.[133] The GC acknowledged, however, that in light of Article 6(3) of Regulation 1049/2001 and the principle of good administration, the Commission may not perform a concrete and individual examination in exceptional cases where this would amount to an unreasonable amount of administrative work.[134]

In *CDC*, following the Commission's decision on the hydrogen peroxide cartel, CDC, a company representing undertakings damaged by the cartel, sought to bring follow-on claims and requested access to the statement of contents in the Commission's files. The Commission at first refused to disclose the statement of contents and then disclosed only the non-confidential version by invoking the protection of commercial interests of the undertakings concerned and the purpose of the investigations (Article 4(2), first and third indents).[135] The GC clarified that commercial interests are different from 'business interests' in the Notice on Access to the Commission File.[136] Commercial interests do not include any information about a company and its business relations since this would frustrate the principle of giving the public the widest possible access to documents.[137] Thus, a statement of contents with mere references to the Commission's documents but not containing specific information, for example, on prices and business dealings, does not constitute commercial interest and, while it may help the claimant identify certain documents, it is for the national court to decide whether such a disclosure will be granted.[138] Most importantly, the interest of a cartel participant to avoid damages actions does not count as a commercial interest worthy of protection.[139]

The GC further stated that in relation to Article 4(2), third indent, the aim is to protect the purpose of the investigation and not the investigation as such, the purpose being to determine a competition law infringement and penalize the implicated companies,[140] not, as the Commission argued, to protect generally the purposes of its cartel policy and the effectiveness of its leniency programme.[141] The investigation is completed once the Commission adopts its decision irrespective of any pending actions for annulment.[142]

---

[132] Ibid, para 81.
[133] Ibid, para 82. The GC reached the same conclusion in relation to the other exceptions invoked by the Commission (namely, protection of commercial interests, protection of court proceedings, and the protection of privacy and the integrity of the individual) according to Article 4(2), first and second indents and Article 4(1)(b) of Regulation 1049/2001. Ibid, para 89.
[134] Ibid, paras 101–103, 107, 112.   [135] *CDC* (n 101), paras 6, 9.
[136] Ibid, paras 42–43.   [137] Ibid, para 44.   [138] Ibid, paras 45, 48.
[139] Ibid, para 49.   [140] Ibid, para 59.   [141] Ibid, paras 68–70.
[142] Ibid, paras 62, 64.

Despite its pro-claimant stance in *CDC*, the GC adopted a different stance in *Netherlands v Commission*,[143] aligning its approach with earlier Court rulings limiting access to the Commission's file in state aid and merger cases.[144] This approach was recently reaffirmed by the Court in *EnBW*, which set aside the GC judgment[145] and also adopted a different—wider—approach than the GC in *CDC* and *Lombard*. In so doing, the Court has widened the Commission's discretion to refuse access to certain categories of documents in the light of the exceptions contained in Article 4(2) of Regulation 1049/2001.[146] In particular, following *EnBW*, the Commission does not have to undertake a concrete examination of the documents requested, contrary to the GC judgment in *Lombard*. In addition, contrary to *CDC*, the Commission may refuse access to its documents, for the purpose of its investigation, until the Commission's decision becomes final, ie it is no longer subject to appeal.

The Court interpreted Regulation 1049/2001 in the light of the specific rules on access to documents in EU competition law[147] and held that:

> for the purposes of the application of the exceptions provided for in the first and third indents of Article 4(2) of Regulation No 1049/2001, the Commission is entitled to presume, *without carrying out a specific, individual examination of each of the documents* in a file relating to a proceeding under Article [101 TFEU], that disclosure of such documents will, in principle, undermine the protection of the commercial interests of the undertakings involved in such a proceeding and the protection of the purpose of the investigations relating to the proceeding.[148] (emphasis added)

Nonetheless, the general presumption against disclosure is rebuttable by demonstrating that the disclosure of a specific document is not covered by the presumption or that there is an overriding public interest in the disclosure. This does not mean, however, that the Commission has to examine individually all of the documents requested since that would deprive the general presumption of its effect.[149] *EnBW* reverses the burden of proof in favour of the Commission inasmuch as it allows the Commission to refuse a general request for access and it falls upon the party making the request to rebut this presumption in relation to specific documents. In *EnBW*, the relevant documents were classified into six broad categories, namely:

(1) documents provided in connection with an immunity or leniency application (category 1);
(2) requests for information and the respective parties' replies (category 2);

---

[143] Case T-380/08 *Netherlands v Commission* (judgment of 13 September 2013).
[144] Ibid, paras 35–37.
[145] Case T-344/08 *EnBW Energie Baden-Württemberg AG* (n 113).
[146] Case C-365/12 P *Commission v EnBW Energie Baden-Württemberg AG* (n 113).
[147] See Regulation 1/2003 (n 92), Articles 27 and 28; Commission Regulation 773/2004 Relating to the Conduct of Proceedings by the Commission Pursuant to Articles 81 and 82 of the EC Treaty [2004] OJ L123/18, Articles 15 and 16.
[148] Case C-365/12 P *Commission v EnBW Energie Baden-Württemberg AG* (n 113) para 93.
[149] Ibid, paras 100–101.

(3) documents obtained during inspections (category 3);
(4) the statements of objections and the respective parties' replies (category 4); and
(5) internal documents, comprising:
   (a) documents relating to the facts (background notes, correspondence with other competition authorities, and internal consultations with other Commission departments) (category 5(a)); and
   (b) procedural documents such as inspection warrants and inspection reports (category 5(b)).[150]

The above categories benefit from a rebuttable presumption of non-disclosure and cover the majority of documents in the Commission file. Furthermore, the Court, contrary to the GC in *CDC*, held that investigations can be regarded as completed only when the Commission decision becomes final.[151] The broader definition given to the 'purposes of the investigation' may afford the Commission carte blanche to reject the disclosure of documents. Thus, this judgment substantially restricted the right of access to the Commission file for the purpose of follow-on damages claims.

EnBW can be criticized for curtailing the right to damages for competition law violations. The Court stated that:

[i]n order to ensure effective protection of the right to compensation enjoyed by a claimant, there is no need for every document relating to a proceeding under Article [101 TFEU] to be disclosed to that claimant on the ground that that party is intending to bring an action for damages, as it is highly unlikely that the action for damages will need to be based on all the evidence in the file relating to that proceeding... the interest in obtaining compensation for the loss suffered as a result of a breach of Article 81 EC cannot constitute an overriding public interest, within the meaning of Article 4(2) of Regulation No 1049/2001.[152]

The claimant has to rebut the presumption of non-disclosure and must establish that it is necessary to be granted access to specific documents in the Commission file.[153] In principle, the Court does not deny that the right to compensation may constitute an overriding public interest for disclosing certain documents,[154] but by raising the threshold for the claimant it renders it void of any practical significance.

The more recent addition to the EU case law on access to documents in the Commission file in cartel cases that allows room—albeit very limited—for a more claimant-friendly approach is *Schenker*,[155] which followed on from the Commission decision involving the air freight cartel.[156] Schenker requested access to the Commission file, or alternatively to the full Commission decision, or

---

[150] Ibid, para 16.   [151] Ibid, para 99.   [152] Ibid, 106–108.   [153] Ibid.
[154] See also Ombudsman decision on 3699/2006 (n 124), paras 97–98.
[155] Case T-534/11 *Schenker AG v European Commission* (judgment of 7 October 2014) (in Greek).
[156] Commission decision of 9 November 2010, Case COMP/39258–Airfreight (published on 8 May 2015).

Access to Evidence 101

alternatively to the redacted non-confidential version of the latter.[157] In relation to access to the Commission file, the GC, in line with previous case law, accepted that the Commission may refuse disclosure based on general presumptions applicable to certain categories of documents for the protection of the undertakings' commercial interests and the purposes of the investigation.[158] The claimant here failed to rebut this presumption by claiming public interest considerations linked to the bringing of damages claims before national courts.[159]

However, in relation to granting access to the non-confidential version of the decision, the GC stated that the Commission cannot refuse the disclosure of a document that it has an obligation to publish under Regulation 1/2003 and that the Commission cannot refuse the disclosure of the non-confidential version of its decision in relation to any parts for which the addressees have not requested confidential treatment.[160] This judgment should be read in light of *Emerald Supplies*, where the English High Court criticized the Commission for an unreasonable delay in publishing the non-confidential version of its decision involving the air freight cartel and subsequently ordered disclosure of a redacted version to members of a confidentiality ring.[161]

4.2.2 Access to the Competition Authority's file— Disclosure before national courts

In *Pfleiderer*,[162] the Court had its first opportunity to pronounce on the potential disclosure of leniency material. *Pfleiderer* concerned a preliminary reference question as to whether the German NCA should grant access to documents submitted by a leniency applicant for the purpose of suing the members of the (decor paper) cartel. The Court highlighted that there are no common EU rules on the right of access to documents submitted in the course of national leniency proceedings to an NCA and the matter should be solved according to national procedural rules. National rules on access to documents, while within the ambit of Member State competence, should be exercised in line with the principles of equivalence and effectiveness.[163] Whereas the Court accepted that leniency programmes contribute towards the effective application of competition law and that access to leniency material may adversely affect their dissuasive effect, it also underlined the existence of the right to damages and its contribution to the effective maintenance of competition in the EU. Based on these observations, the Court invited national courts to weigh up the conflicting interests, namely the effectiveness of leniency

---

[157] Ibid, paras 1, 27.   [158] Ibid, paras 57–58.   [159] Ibid, paras 96–97.
[160] Ibid, paras 115–117, 137–138. On publishing a non-confidential version of the Commission decision and the information that can be contained therein see Case T-345/12 *AKZO Nobel v Commission* [2015] 4 CMLR 12, paras 88–91. The GC stated that 'it is for the Commission alone to balance, in the circumstances of the case at hand, the effectiveness of the leniency programme, on the one hand, and the interest of the public and of economic operators in knowing the content of its decision and taking action in order to protect their rights, on the other'.
[161] On this case see text to n 171.   [162] *Pfleiderer* (n 113).
[163] Ibid, paras 20–24.

programmes and the effective exercise of the right to damages, before they grant access to the leniency file on a case-by-case basis.[164] *Pfleiderer*, while carefully balanced, did not provide any guidance as to how national courts should perform the respective balancing exercise.[165] AG Mazák, on the other hand, and in the light of the Commission's submissions in this case, drew a distinction between corporate statements and pre-existing documents and argued in favour of non-disclosure of the former category.[166]

Pfleiderer was reaffirmed in *Donau Chemie*, where the Court held that a national rule making access to documents, including documents submitted in the context of leniency proceedings, conditional upon the consent of all of the parties in the proceedings, without allowing national courts to decide this on a case-by-case basis, is contrary to the principle of effectiveness as it renders the exercise of the right to damages excessively difficult.[167]

Pfleiderer resulted in inconsistent judgments before national courts. In *Pfleiderer II*, the German court (Amtgerichts Bonn) refused to grant access to the material submitted in the context of leniency proceedings, whereas in *National Grid*, the English High Court granted limited access to leniency material.[168] Article 6(6) of the Directive on Damages Actions puts an end to the controversy in relation to leniency statements and settlement submissions, effectively reflecting the Commission's view on *Pfleiderer*, and submitting that access to corporate statements should not be granted, while access to the rest of the documents should be assessed on a case-by-case basis.[169]

In particular, Article 6 of the Directive on Damages Actions harmonizes the rules on disclosure of evidence included in the file of a competition authority. As a general rule, national courts shall review the proportionality of the disclosure request in accordance with the criteria in Article 5(3) and in addition take into account: (a) the specificity of the request in relation to the 'nature, object or content of documents' submitted in the file of the competition authority; (b) whether the request is related to a damages action; and (c) specific requirements pertaining to safeguarding the effectiveness of public competition law enforcement (Article 6(4)).

In relation to the third requirement described above, the Directive formulates two separate categories of documents that may be deemed inadmissible in private damages actions. The first, 'black list', refers to leniency statements and settlement submissions that are always inadmissible (Article 6(6) in conjunction with Article 7(1))

---

[164] Ibid, paras 26–32.   [165] Ashton and Henry (n 52), para 4.030.
[166] *Pfleiderer* (n 113), Opinion of AG Mazák, paras 43–44, 47.
[167] *Donau Chemie* (n 113), paras 34, 39, 43, 49.
[168] *National Grid II* (n 114). *Pfleiderer II* (n 114).
[169] *Pfleiderer* (n 113), Opinion of AG Mazák, para 17. See also Commission submissions before the English High Court in *National Grid Electricity Transmissions v ABB* [2011] EWHC 1717 (Ch) (*National Grid I*), para 16. See also ECN, 'Protection of Leniency Material in the Context of Civil Damages Actions' (Resolution of the Meeting of Heads of the European Competition Authorities of 23 May 2012) <http://ec.europa.eu/competition/ecn/leniency_material_protection_en.pdf> accessed 20 September 2014.

and the second, 'grey list', contains information prepared specifically for the proceedings of a competition authority, information prepared by the competition authority and sent to the parties in the course of proceedings, and withdrawn settlement submissions that are deemed either inadmissible or inadmissible until the proceedings are closed by decision or otherwise (Article 6(5) in conjunction with Article 7(2)). Other information obtained by a person through access to a competition authority's file can be used in an action for damages only by that person (Article 7(3)). Article 7(2) in conjunction with Article 6(5) of the Directive on Damages Actions clarifies that documents prepared in the course of the proceedings are only inadmissible until the adoption of the decision. This reflects the balance between protecting the purposes of the investigation and the right to access to the file for the purposes of private litigation.[170] However, this does not suggest that these documents can be disclosed in any event after the adoption of the decision.

Emerald Supplies concerned a request for disclosure of the non-confidential version of a Commission decision. This case can be distinguished from *Pfleiderer* and *Donau Chemie* in that, in the latter cases, the claimants sought access to the NCA file, while in *Emerald Supplies* the national court was called to assess whether the Commission decision should be disclosed. In *Emerald Supplies*, the applicants requested the English High Court to review the lawfulness of the redactions made by British Airways and other airlines to the Commission decision involving the air freight cartel.[171] The Commission decision was issued on 9 November 2010 and has been made public almost 5 years later.[172] British Airways as an addressee of the Decision had a copy of it. Since the Commission has been unable to redact and publish its decision, even after four years, the applicants sought disclosure directly from British Airways. The applicants were not content with the redacted version and therefore asked the English High Court to review the appropriateness and lawfulness of the redaction.

From the facts briefly described above, *Emerald Supplies* is an interesting case that elucidates the complex interplay between requests for access to documents and the role of national courts. It also alludes to the interplay between public and private competition law enforcement and the delicate balancing required in order to grant access to documents for the purposes of follow-on damages actions without jeopardizing the functioning of the Commission leniency programme.

In *Emerald Supplies*, three issues were raised to oppose disclosure, namely redaction of leniency material, redaction of information that may breach the presumption of innocence of other airlines, non-addressees of the decision

---

[170] This is also reflected in other Commission policy documents. See Leniency Notice (n 116), para 33; Notice on Settlements (n 116), para 39. There have been proposals to widen the 'black list'. See ELI, 'Statement of the European Law Institute on Collective Redress and Competition Damages Claims' (2014) <http://www.europeanlawinstitute.eu/fileadmin/user_upload/p_eli/Projects/S-5-2014_Statement_on_Collective_Redress_and_Competition_Damages_Claims.pdf> accessed 10 April 2015, 72.
[171] *Emerald Supplies Ltd v British Airways Plc* [2014] EWHC 3513 (Ch) para 1.
[172] See text to n 156.

104 *Consumers' Standing and Access to Evidence*

(*Pergan* principle),[173] and redaction of materials pertaining to legal professional privilege.[174] Peter Smith J ordered the disclosure of the Commission decision to a confidentiality ring comprising the parties to this case, redacted only in relation to the leniency material and material pertaining to legal profession privilege, in order to put them on an equal basis within the litigation. [175]

5. Conclusion

The analysis presented in this chapter has pointed to the intrinsic characteristics of consumer claims that may justify more enabling procedural rules. The focus is on measures enhancing consumer participation in private competition law enforcement, and consumer standing, passing-on considerations, and access to evidence problems have been addressed.

With regard to passing-on, the Directive on Damages Actions has provided an overall satisfactory solution, since the introduction of a rebuttable presumption in favour of indirect purchasers reveals a deterrence rationale and is capable of incentivizing consumers in competition litigation. However, as far as access to evidence is concerned, the adopted rules seem unlikely to increase consumer involvement. It has been suggested that the disclosure mechanisms in the Directive on Damages Actions are unlikely to actually promote stand-alone consumer damages claims. Since there are important underlying policy justifications for promoting these types of claims at a normative level, the Commission should introduce specific 'disclosure' rules for consumer claims. Arguably, though, gaining political support for a proposal of this type does not appear to be a realistic possibility. The second best option for the Commission would be to devise appropriate mechanisms to facilitate consumer access to Commission and NCA documents so as to boost follow-on consumer claims.

On access to documents in the competition authorities' files, the adopted rules regarding the non-disclosure of corporate statements submitted in the course of leniency applications is in line with the Court's approach in *Pfleiderer* and *Donau Chemie*, as it balances the conflicting interests of preserving the effectiveness of leniency programmes and private enforcement and is relatively

---

[173] The decision contained information relevant to the potential implication in the cartel of airlines which were not addressees of the Commission decision. The respondent airlines argued that following *Pergan* such material should not be disclosed: *Emerald Supplies* (n 171), paras 86–91, 97. See Case T-474/04 *Pergan Hilfsstoffe v Commission* [2007] ECR II-4225.

[174] *Emerald Supplies* (n 171), para 62.

[175] *Emerald Supplies* (n 171), paras 56–57, 83, 98, 102–3, 106–9. In a similar vein see Commission (EU), 'Interchange Fee Litigation before the Judiciary of England and Wales: Wm. Morrison Supermarkets plc and Others v MasterCard Incorporated and Others (Claim Nos 2012/699; 2012/1305–1311)' (Commission Opinion) C(2014) 3066 final, paras 19–20. See also A Howard, 'Disclosure of Infringement Decisions in Competition Damages Proceedings: How the UK Courts Are Leading the Way Ahead of the Damages Directive' (2015) 6 JECLAP 256.

Conclusion

modest.[176] This proposal may act as an impediment to consumer claims. However, on balance it is necessary to preserve the integrity of national leniency programmes.[177] It is also in line with the Court's approach in *EnBW*. At a normative level it could be argued that, corporate statements aside (these being narrowly construed), the Commission should provide access to its file, especially when these requests are raised by consumer organizations acting in the consumer interest. In the light of *EnBW*, the Commission is unlikely to adopt such an approach.[178] This is deplorable since it can lead to double standards when requesting access to NCAs' and the Commission's files. For example, national courts may order the disclosure of 'grey list' documents in the NCA file after the NCA has closed its proceedings by adopting a decision or otherwise (Article 6(5)). However, unlike *EnBW*, the Directive on Damages Actions stipulates that the decision does not have to be final as according to recital 25 it suffices that the NCA adopts a decision. Further, as suggested by *Emerald Supplies*, it appears that national courts are prone to encourage private litigation and allow access to certain documents, whereas the Commission, by taking a long time to redact its decision, appears to be more inclined to safeguard the interests of cartel participants. Recently, in *AKZO*, the Commission has struck a sensible balance between the interests of cartel participants and potential private litigation.[179]

Insofar as the Commission's practice and its proposal for reviewing Regulation 1049/2001 do not seem to pay adequate attention to providing access to documents to consumer organizations, additional measures should be put in place,[180] for example, a provision akin to the one in Regulation 1367/2006 stating that 'the grounds for refusal as regards access to [Commission information] should be interpreted in a restrictive way, taking into account the public interest served by disclosure'.[181] The public interest in increasing consumer participation in private competition law enforcement should be considered, thereby tipping the balance in favour of granting, rather than denying, access to documents.

---

[176] For an opposite view see C Kersting, 'Removing the Tension between Public and Private Enforcement: Disclosure and Privileges for Successful Leniency Applicants' (2014) 5 JECLAP 2.

[177] R Nazzini, 'Potency and Act of the Principle of Effectiveness: The Development of Competition Law Remedies and Procedures in Community Law' in C Barnard and O Odudu (eds), *The Outer Limits of the European Union* (Hart 2009) 401, 404, 429–433.

[178] However, the Commission has opted for a more permissive approach in *AKZO*. See *AKZO* (n 160) paras 80–90.

[179] Ibid.

[180] See also EP, 'Non-legislative Resolution on the White Paper on Damages Actions' (2008/2154(INI)), para 13, that '[calls] for the Commission to be required to allow victims of competition infringements access to the necessary information for exercising damages actions and [stresses] that Regulation (EC) No 1049/2001 defines a right of access to documents of the institutions. The Commission must interpret this regulation accordingly, or propose an amendment thereof'.

[181] Council Regulation No 1367/2006 on the Application of the Provisions of the Aarhus Convention [2006] L263/13, recital 15 and Article 6(1).

Interestingly, a recurrent observation in trying to formulate measures to promote consumer damages actions in the competition field relates to the distinguishing characteristics of consumer claims as opposed to customers' and competitors' claims. Due to these characteristics, specific measures regarding passing-on and access to evidence may need to be adopted, potentially signalling the need to treat consumer claims differently, or even undertake a separate policy initiative, as opposed to generally boosting the private enforcement of EU competition law. This is more evident in the examination in Chapter 5 of the adequate collective action mechanisms in the competition field.

5
Improving Consumers' Role
Collective Actions

1. Introduction

The analysis in this chapter discusses and develops a collective redress mechanism for addressing consumer claims for competition law violations. First, a terminological clarification is warranted. The Commission employs the term 'collective redress mechanism' to include both collective/group and representative actions.[1] Group actions are initiated by a member of the group (eg US class actions), whereas representative actions are initiated by a representative organization, for example, a consumer organization.[2] In its Recommendation the Commission defines collective redress as covering both injunctive and compensatory collective redress.[3] This chapter focuses on compensatory collective redress and the terms 'collective action' and 'collective redress' are used interchangeably as generic terms comprising both representative and group actions.

This chapter undertakes first a historical analysis of the approaches towards collective redress at EU level (section 2). This historical account of policy efforts to improve collective redress mechanisms points towards a distinct treatment of consumer claims in competition law. This analysis serves as the springboard for the argument advanced in section 3, namely that the function of the collective action mechanism in competition law should be different, and thereby questions the Commission's modest Recommendation encompassing the common principles underpinning all areas of collective redress policy (injunctive and compensatory).[4]

---

[1] See Commission (EU), 'Staff Working Paper Accompanying the White Paper on Damages Actions for Breach of the EC Antitrust Rules' COM(2008) 165 final (WP SWP) paras 40–41.

[2] Ibid, paras 49 and 59. On the various different terms see Parliament (EU), *Collective Redress in Antitrust* (2012) 8–9.

[3] Commission (EU), 'Recommendation of 11 June 2013 on Common Principles for Injunctive and Compensatory Collective Redress Mechanisms in the Member States Concerning Violations of Rights Granted under Union Law' [2013] OJ L201/60, para 3(a).

[4] See Commission Recommendation (n 3); J Almunia, 'Common Standards for Group Claims Across the EU' (Speech at the School of Law, University of Valladolid, Speech 10/554); Commission (EU), 'Public Consultation: Towards a Coherent European Approach to Collective Redress' (Staff Working Document) SEC(2011) 173 final, 4 February 2011 (Public Consultation), para 15.

In section 3, additional normative justifications are offered in support of the adoption of specific collective action mechanisms for consumer claims in competition law. A distinction needs to be drawn between three main types of aggregation mechanisms, namely those that improve procedural efficiency; those that alter the claimants' incentives to bring an action; and those that permit the raising of a claim that would have not been brought otherwise.[5] Effectively, collective actions for low value consumer claims, in the light of their specificities,[6] fall into the third category and should be structured based on the deterrence principle. The compensatory potential of collective actions is not eschewed in so doing. Nonetheless, it is argued that this cannot be the prevailing rationale given that minimal consumer claims form the vast majority of the respective claims in the competition law field. The argument for devising different mechanisms is based on the interpretation of the 'access to justice' goal and the distinction between the aggregation of individual consumer interests, on the one hand, and the collective consumer interest, on the other.

Following the justification of the necessity for different collective action mechanisms in the field of competition law, the analysis in section 4 discusses the necessary structural characteristics of effective consumer collective action mechanisms by reference to the federal US model. Section 5 explores whether the collective redress systems available in different Member States demonstrate these structural characteristics. The chosen thematic approach (as opposed to a detailed jurisdictional approach) better elucidates the lack of collective action mechanisms capable of addressing minimal consumer claims for competition law violations. A collective action framework that would promote consumer claims while paying due respect to EU legal culture and Member States' individual traditions is presented in section 6. In building this framework, the EU approach towards collective actions to date is explored and contrasted with the desired structural characteristics/themes.

2. EU Developments on Collective Redress: A Historical Account

Improving consumer collective redress has been an aspiration in EU consumer policy for quite some time now.[7] This aim appeared later in the competition policy

---

[5] Calabresi points to the difference between two types of collective actions, namely the distinction between the 'lawyer-driven representative type of class action, where someone assembles the group of people who otherwise would not have done anything, and the aggregation type of class action...combining suits that would have been there anyway but may be brought a lot more cheaply by aggregation'. See G Calabresi, 'Class Actions in the US Experience: The Legal Perspective' in J Backhaus, A Cassone, and G Ramello (eds), *The Law and Economics of Class Actions in Europe—Lessons from America* (Edward Elgar 2012) 10, 11.

[6] See Chapter 4, text to nn 1–20.

[7] Commission (EEC), 'Consumer Redress' (Memorandum) COM(1984) 629 final (Consumer Redress Memorandum); Commission (EC), 'Consumer Policy Action Plan 1999–2001'

field and can be associated with the shift in policy aims, the efforts to promote private competition law enforcement, and the increased attention given to the consumer interest.

Initially, the approach to collective redress was distinct for competition and consumer law. The Green Paper on Consumer Collective Redress did not address collective redress procedures for victims of competition law infringements in the light of the specific nature of competition law.[8] In that paper, the Commission put forward four possible options[9] but failed to clearly articulate its objectives, since, while the paper apparently sought to improve the conditions for consumers to obtain redress and compensation,[10] it also discussed collective mechanisms that could primarily enhance deterrence. For example, one of the proposals discussed the possible introduction of a skimming-off procedure that would effectively benefit consumers by deterring future illegal behaviour.[11] The paper also covered opt-out collective actions, although it did not allude specifically to their potential to deter illegal activity.[12] The first step for putting in place effective collective redress procedures should have been to explicitly recognize their aims, respective functions, and the complex aspects of the problem they seek to tackle.[13] Regrettably the Commission has not done this either in the competition or the consumer field.

In the competition field, however, the Green Paper, the White Paper, and the withdrawn Draft Damages Directive all contained concrete proposals for consumer collective redress. The Green Paper discussed the introduction of a

---

(Communication) COM(1998) 696 final, 18; Commission (EC), 'Green Paper—Liability for Defective Products' (Green Paper) COM(1999) 396 final, 31–33. Commission (EC), 'Green Paper on Consumer Collective Redress' (Green Paper) COM(2008) 794 final, 27 November 2008 (Green Paper on Consumer Collective Redress). Commission (EEC), 'Three Year Action Plan of Consumer Policy in the EEC (1990–1992)' COM(1990) 98 final; P. Sutherland, 'Internal Market after 2002: Meeting the Challenge' (Sutherland Report) SEC(92) 2044, 10; Commission (EC), 'Consumer Policy Strategy 2002–2006' (Communication) COM(2002) 208 final, para 3.2.3; Commission (EC), 'Consumer Policy Strategy 2007–2013' (Communication) COM(2007) 99 final, para 5.3.

[8] Green Paper on Consumer Collective Redress (n 7) para 5.

[9] Green Paper on Consumer Collective Redress (n 7), paras 13–14, 19–60. The subsequent Commission consultation paper included a fifth option. See Commission (EC), 'Follow-up to the Green Paper on Consumer Collective Redress' <http://ec.europa.eu/consumers/redress_cons/docs/consultation_paper2009.pdf> accessed 11 July 2014 (Follow-up to the Green Paper on Consumer Collective Redress), paras 60–64. See also 'Overview of the Results of the Consultation on Consumer Collective Redress' <http://ec.europa.eu/consumers/redress_cons/docs/overview_results_coll_redress_en.pdf> accessed 11 July 2014.

[10] Green Paper on Consumer Collective Redress (n 7), para 19.

[11] Green Paper on Consumer Collective Redress (n 7), para 45. Follow-up to the Green Paper on Consumer Collective Redress (n 9), para 40.

[12] Green Paper on Consumer Collective Redress (n 7), paras 56–57. The same is true for the EESC but there is a preference for opting in. See EESC, 'Opinion on the Green Paper on Consumer Collective Redress' [2010] OJ C128/97, paras 5.1.2, 5.2.3; EESC, 'Opinion on Defining the Collective Action System and Its Role in the Context of Community Consumer Law' [2008] OJ C162/1, para 7.2; R Mulheron, 'The Case for an Opt-out Class Action for European Member States: A Legal and Empirical Analysis' (2009) 15 Colum J Eur L 409, 451.

[13] See S Gibbons, 'Group Litigation, Class Actions and Lord Woolf's Three Objectives—A Critical Analysis' [2008] CJQ 208, 241–242, for a similar criticism of UK policymakers.

cause of action brought by consumer organizations in order to defend consumer interests,[14] while the White Paper and the withdrawn Draft Damages Directive contained more specific proposals, namely representative actions brought by qualified entities such as consumer organizations on behalf of identified or, in certain limited cases, identifiable victims as well as opt-in group actions.[15] The latter proposals were supported by consumer representatives while they received negative reactions amongst the business community, which criticized the Commission's different approaches in the consumer and competition law fields and called for a consistent approach.[16] The European Parliament was also in favour of a horizontal approach,[17] while acknowledging the specificities of competition law claims, given the binding effect of NCAs' decisions and the interplay between follow-on actions and leniency.[18]

Thus, following the initial distinct approach, the Commission shifted the focus of the debate and announced the initiation of a public consultation on the common legal principles that should guide any future proposals on EU collective redress procedures.[19] The principles identified in the public consultation stressed the need for effective and efficient redress and effective enforcement and emphasized the role of representative organizations and the need to avoid abusive litigation.[20]

The public consultation led to the adoption of the Commission Recommendation on collective redress, which was accompanied by a Commission Communication advocating a horizontal approach.[21] The specificities of competition claims are addressed in the Directive on Damages Actions, which, together with the Recommendation, are seen by the Commission as a package representing a balanced approach.[22] The former addresses the specificities identified in relation to competition claims, but fails to address the particularities of minimal consumer

---

[14] Commission (EC), 'Damages Actions for Breach of the EC Antitrust Rules' (Green Paper) COM(2005) 672 final, option 25.
[15] Commission (EC), 'Damages Actions for Breach of the EC Antitrust Rules' (White Paper) COM(2008) 165 final, part 2.1; Commission (EC), 'Proposal for a Council Directive Governing Actions for Damages for Infringements of Article 81 and 82 of the Treaty'; Draft Damages Directive (Document withdrawn before publication—on file with the author), Articles 5–6.
[16] Public Consultation (n 4) para 11.
[17] EP, 'Resolution of 26 March 2009 on the White Paper on Damages Actions for Breach of the EC Antitrust Rules' (2008/2154(INI)) (Committee on Economic and Monetary Affairs, Rapporteur: Klaus-Heiner Lehne), paras 3–6.
[18] Ibid; EP, Resolution on 'Towards a Coherent European Approach to Collective Redress' (2011/2089(INI)) (2 February 2012), paras 6, 21, 28.
[19] Commission (EU), 'Commission Work Programme 2010' (Communication) COM(2010) 135 final, 8; Commission (EU), 'Commission Work Programme 2011' (Communication) COM(2010) 623 final, 8. See also V Reding, J Almunia, and J Dalli, 'Towards a Coherent European Approach to Collective Redress: Next Steps' (Joint Information Note) SEC(2010) 1192.
[20] Public Consultation (n 4) para 15.
[21] Commission Recommendation (n 3); Commission (EU), 'Towards a European Horizontal Framework for Collective Redress' (Communication) COM(2013) 401 final, 3–4.
[22] Ibid. Directive 2014/104/EU of the European Parliament and of the Council of 26 November 2014 on Certain Rules Governing Actions for Damages under National Law for Infringements of the Competition Law Provisions of the Member States and of the European Union [2014] OJ L349/1.

claims in competition law. Thus, it is regrettable that the Directive on Damages Actions does not address consumer collective redress.[23]

A coherent approach to collective redress and the identification of common principles[24] can be seen as a welcome development. However, this approach is flawed both procedurally and substantively. From a procedural perspective, the Recommendation is not binding upon the Member States (Article 288 TFEU) and, while it contains certain common principles, it is likely that it will only complicate the already diverse landscape of collective redress in different Member States. From a substantive perspective, distinctive characteristics of specific EU law fields, such as EU competition law, require a different approach.[25] The principles discussed are not likely to contribute to the effective enforcement of EU law and the effective protection of EU rights.

The Commission should nonetheless be praised for pronouncing on common principles on such a complex matter at national level. The possible next steps could be the discussion of the specificities and the relevant adjustment of these principles, when necessary, in specific EU law fields. Instead of denouncing the policy discussions to date for the introduction of collective redress mechanisms in competition law, the Commission should instead build on these discussions and steer the debate towards more appropriate proposals in the competition law field. In the light of the evaluation of the Recommendation's implementation in different Member States four years after its adoption,[26] this appears to be a plausible way forward. Nevertheless, the Recommendation constitutes a missed opportunity to propose effective collective procedures for low value consumer claims in competition law.

3. Demarcating Collective Action Mechanisms in the Field of Competition Law

3.1 Individual v collective consumer interest

The analysis in this section builds on the distinction between the aggregation of individual consumer interests and the collective consumer interest.[27] The collective

---

[23] In this vein see Opinion of the European Economic and Social Committee on the 'Proposal for a Directive of the European Parliament and of the Council on Certain Rules Governing Actions for Damages under National Law for Infringements of the Competition Law Provisions of the Member States and of the European Union' [2014] OJ C67/83, para 1.2.9.

[24] Public Consultation (n 4), para 30. Communication on Collective Redress (n 21) 3.

[25] Certain Member States, like the UK and Sweden, are in favour of the adoption of specific rules in the field of competition. See Communication on Collective Redress (n 21) 6. See also DP Tzakas, 'Collective Redress in the Field of EU Competition Law: The Need for an EU Remedy and the Impact of the Recent Commission Recommendation' (2014) 41 *Legal Issues of Economic Integration* 225, 235. Advocating a sectoral approach in competition law, see Parliament Study (n 2) 63. On the field of environmental law and its respective specificities see M Eliantonio, 'Collective Redress in Environmental Matters in the EU: A Role Model or a "Problem Child"?' (2014) 41 *Legal Issues of Economic Integration* 257, 259–60.

[26] Commission Recommendation (n 3), recital 26 and paras 38–41; Communication on Collective Redress (n 21) 16.

[27] See M Cappelletti and B Garth, 'Access to Justice: The Worldwide Movement to Make Rights More Effective—A General Report' in M Cappelletti and B Garth (eds), *Access to Justice—a World*

consumer interest is protected by other EU law measures.[28] It is submitted that collective actions for low value consumer claims serve individual consumer interests, but, principally, the function of those mechanisms promotes the collective consumer interest and this should be reflected in the structure of the mechanisms adopted.

Collective consumer interests are not uniformly defined in these EU measures, since they are either perceived as 'interests which do not include the cumulation of interests of individuals who have been harmed by an infringement. This is without prejudice to individual actions brought by individuals who have been harmed by an infringement'[29] or as 'the interests of a number of consumers that have been harmed or are likely to be harmed by an infringement'.[30] Arguably, these approaches to collective consumer interests appear contradictory, but can be reconciled. Collective actions for low value consumer claims in competition law should serve primarily the collective consumer interest since, even if they are capable of bringing redress to affected consumers, thereby promoting individual interests, in light of the low value of consumer claims and their inertia to claim their individual damages, the benefits accrue to the affected group rather to affected individuals. Thus, they promote the collective consumer interest, which is broader than the sum of its parts.

Individual consumer interests are served when consumers receive compensation for damage sustained due to a competition law violation. On the other hand, the collective consumer interest is akin to the general consumer interest and should be distinguished from the sum of its parts, ie individual consumer interests.[31] Even if not every affected consumer receives compensation, collective actions for competition law violations may promote collective consumer interest in two distinct ways. First, by increasing the deterrence against competition law

---

Survey (Sijthoff 1981) 53 on the distinction between diffuse/collective interests and individual interests; A Gidi, 'The Class Action Code: A Model for Civil Law Countries' (2005) 23 Ariz J Intl & Comp L 37, 38; A Gidi, 'Class Actions in Brazil—A Model for Civil Law Countries' (2003) 51 Am J Comp L 311, 350 for an interesting distinction between 'transindividual' (ie rights belonging to the class as a whole) and 'individual' rights (ie rights belonging to individual members of the class) corresponding to the three types of group rights (diffuse, collective, and homogeneous individual) according to the Brazilian Consumer Code. See U Reifner and M Volkmer, 'Neue Formen der Verbraucherrechtsberatung' cited in N Reich, 'Diverse Approaches to Consumer Protection Philosophy' (1992) 14 JCP 257, 279 for an idea relating to the potential of the collective consumer interest to avoid organizational problems in the consumer movement. In the same vein see E Kocher, 'Collective Rights and Collective Goods: Enforcement as Collective Interest' in J Steele and WH van Boom, *Mass Justice: Challenges of Representation and Distribution* (Edward Elgar 2011) 118, 127.

[28] See Council Directive 98/27 EC on Injunctions for the Protection of Consumers' Interests [1998] OJ L166/51, Article 1; Council Directive 2009/22/EC on Injunctions for the Protection of Consumers' Interests (codified version) [2009] OJ L110/30, Article 1 (Injunctions Directive); Council Regulation (EC) 2006/2004 on Cooperation between National Authorities Responsible for the Enforcement of Consumer Protection Laws (Regulation on Consumer Protection Cooperation) [2004] OJ 2004 L364/1, Articles 1 and 2(4).

[29] Injunctions Directive (n 28), recital 3.

[30] Regulation on Consumer Protection Cooperation (n 28), Article 3(k).

[31] Injunctions Directive (n 28), recital 3; The Study Centre for Consumer Law—Centre for European Economic Law, Katholieke Universiteit Leuven, 'An Analysis and Evaluation of Alternative

violations and thereby contributing to the maintenance of competitive markets and, second, by providing for moral satisfaction that the perpetrator has been stripped of its illicit gains.

A comparative argument to support the fact that collective actions for low value consumer claims promote mainly the collective consumer interest, without disregarding individual consumer interests, can be drawn from the US system. In the US system consumer class actions, as the prime example of small claims class actions, are distinguished from other types of class actions.[32] In consumer class actions, individual consumer damage is usually of such low value that it is pointless for individual claims to be raised. In *Phillips Petroleum Co v Shutts*, the US Supreme Court stated that:

Modern plaintiff class actions follow the same goals, permitting litigation of a suit involving common questions when there are too many plaintiffs for proper joinder. Class actions may permit the plaintiffs to pool claims which would be uneconomical to litigate individually... most of the plaintiffs would have no realistic day in court if a class action were not available.[33]

The US Supreme Court views the class action device as a vehicle which enables these claims to reach the courts, raising the question as to whether such an approach is justified and on what grounds. Commentators have advanced different theories for justifying the existence of this type of action that can be classified under either a compensatory or a deterrence approach. Class action is presented as a means to overcome collective action problems[34] in the sense of providing incentives to affected individuals who suffer minor injuries. The herein termed compensatory approach to consumer

---

Means of Consumer Redress Other than Redress through Ordinary Judicial Proceedings' (Final Report prepared for DG SANCO, 17 January 2007) <http://ec.europa.eu/consumers/redress/reports_studies/comparative_report_en.pdf> accessed 15 October 2014 (Leuven Report), para 449; OECD, 'Consumer Dispute Resolution and Redress in the Global Marketplace' (2006) <http://www.oecd.org/dataoecd/26/61/36456184.pdf> accessed 12 July 2014, 33 stating that actions in the collective consumer interest 'vindicate the general consumer interest without any showing of actual harm to individual consumers...regarded as an important mechanism to correct market failures where the collective harm...is more than the sum of the individual losses involved'. For an attempt to define the collective consumer interest see M Safjan, L Gorywoda, and A Jańczuk, 'Taking Collective Interest of Consumers Seriously: A View from Poland' (2008) EUI Working Papers 2008/26 <http://papers.ssrn.com/sol3/papers.cfm?abstract_id=1330909> accessed 12 July 2014, 8–14.

[32] Here, reference is made to class actions under Rule 23(b)(3) of the Federal Rules of Civil Procedure, and not 'mandatory' class actions under 23(b)(1) and (2). For example, small claims class actions should be distinguished from other mass tort class actions. On mass tort class actions and the distinction with small claims class actions see J Coffee, 'Class Wars: The Dilemma of Mass Tort Class Action' (1995) 95 Colum L Rev 1344, 1351–1352; D Shapiro, 'Class Actions: The Class as Party and Client' (1998) 37 Notre Dame L Rev 913, 923–925, 929. For problems in mass tort cases see S Issacharoff, 'Governance and Legitimacy in the Law of Class Actions' [1999] *Supreme Court Review* 1. See also *Amchem v Windsor Products* 117 SCt 2231 (1997); *Ortiz v Fibreboard* 119 SCt 2295 (1999).

[33] *Phillips Petroleum Co v Shutts* 472 US 797, 809 (1985). See also *Deposit Guarantee Bank v Roper* 445 US 326, 339 (1980).

[34] See M Olson, *The Logic of Collective Action: Public Goods and the Theory of Groups* (Harvard University Press 1971). Discussing Olson's theory in relation to collective actions for competition

collective action treats class actions as a device that permits the enforcement of individual claims.[35] The deterrence approach disregards individual rights, as the victims themselves are indifferent to their own minimal loss. Under this theory, consumer class action is an additional enforcement tool against perpetrators and is primarily concerned with deterrence and the impact on firms' incentives to comply with the law.[36]

Rubenstein advances a very interesting theory to justify small claims class actions.[37] According to him, small claims class actions solve the collective action problem because they permit the pooling of small claims and the creation of a group of claims rather than a group of claimants. This, in turn, allows for the production of positive externalities that exceed the effect of deterrence on firms' behaviour and include, apart from the 'threat effect', wider 'decree', 'institutional', and 'settlement' effects.[38] In essence, based on this theory, small claim class actions promote both the individual and collective consumer interest and encapsulate both deterrence and compensation as their respective functions.

Small claims class actions in the US indeed reflect a combination of the compensation and the deterrence approaches.[39] This can be deduced from the function of the respective actions, as well as the often-adopted innovative methods for the distribution of damages awards. This suggests that small claims class actions in the US are also about enforcing individual rights. At the same time, large awards, or the mere threat of them, may influence firms' behaviour.

The above reference to the US class action system does not suggest that the EU should adopt a similar approach to collective actions, but merely points out that collective actions have the potential to principally promote the collective consumer interest and steer away from the traditional individualistic approach to litigation. This is instructive, as in the context of low value consumer claims, a sterile adherence to the compensatory individualistic approach would negate the very right it seeks to protect. Instead, the remedies appropriate to fulfilling this right in its functional approach need to be devised, thereby drawing a line between the existence

---

claims see A Andreangeli, *Private Enforcement of Antitrust: Regulating Corporate Behaviour through Collective Claims in the EU and the US* (Edward Elgar 2014) 33–54. On collective litigation as a form of collective action see also SC Yeazell, 'Collective Litigation as Collective Action' (1989) 43 U Illinois L Rev 43.

[35] C Lang, 'Class Actions and US Antitrust Laws: Prerequisites and Interdependencies of the Implementation of a Procedural Device for the Aggregation of Low Value Claims' (2001) 24 W Comp 285, 286.

[36] Shapiro (n 32) 924 argues that deterrence is the sole purpose of small claims class actions.

[37] WB Rubenstein, 'Why Enable Litigation? A Positive Externalities Theory of the Small Claims Class Action' (2006) 74 UMKC L Rev 709, 710, 718–719, 723.

[38] Ibid.

[39] See *Blue Shield of Virginia v McCready* 457 US 465 (1982) where, according to the US Supreme Court, 'Congress sought to create a private enforcement mechanism that would deter violators and deprive them of the fruits of their illegal actions, and would provide ample compensation to the victims of antitrust violations'; also *Mitsubishi Motors Corp v Soler Chrysler Plymouth* 473 US 614, 635 (1985), where, according to the US Supreme Court, 'notwithstanding its important incidental policing function, the treble-damages cause of action conferred on private parties by §4 of the Clayton Act...seeks primarily to enable an injured competitor to gain compensation for that injury'; *Brunswick Corp v Pueblo Bowl-O-Mat, Inc* 429 US 477, 485–486 (1977).

of this right and its exercise.⁴⁰ In the light of the maxim *ubi ius ibi remedium* (see Figure 5.1 below), for the protection of the consumer right to damages for competition law violations, the appropriate remedy should be based on the functional enforcement of this right and structured upon the deterrence principle, and pursuing compensation should be a secondary concern. Collective action mechanisms for all other claims, as discussed in the Commission Recommendation, reflect the traditional individualistic approach to litigation, whereas the mechanisms for consumer claims in competition law should embrace a collective approach towards litigation⁴¹ that promotes the collective but also the individual consumer interest.⁴²

'ubi ius, ibi remedium'
Right to Damages → Remedy of compensation

Consumer Right to Damages → Devise an alternative remedy based on the functional enforcement of this right structured upon the deterrence principle; pursuing compensation should be a secondary concern

---

Figure 5.1 Consumer Right to Damages—Corresponding Remedy

3.2 'Access to justice' for consumer claims in competition law

Collective action mechanisms promoting the collective consumer interest and advancing primarily deterrence promote a wider 'access to justice' ideal. This section discusses 'access to justice' with the aim of pointing to its different meanings,⁴³ shedding light on their points of intersection, and also clarifying their important conceptual differences. The exploration of the multifocality of this concept serves to underline the nexus between procedural measures and their respective goals and functions and can act as a justification for the introduction of different mechanisms in the field of competition law.

In competition law 'access to justice' has been associated with the aim of compensating the victims of the respective wrongs, since 'competition law is a field where collective redress mechanisms can significantly enhance the victims' ability to obtain compensation and thus access to justice'.⁴⁴ Access to justice has been linked to obtaining redress for harm sustained.⁴⁵ However, linking and

---

⁴⁰ Distinction also made by the Commission in WP SWP (n 1), paras 308–309.
⁴¹ For the distinction between the individualistic and collective justice approaches see Shapiro (n 32) 916 with further references.
⁴² S Wrbka, S Van Uytsel, and M Siems, 'Access to Justice and Collective Actions—"Florence" and Beyond' in Wrbka, Van Uytsel, and Siems (eds), *Collective Actions: Enhancing Access to Justice and Reconciling Multilayer Interests?* (CUP 2012) 1, 9–10 introducing the notion of multilayer interests.
⁴³ On 'access to justice' see the ambitious four volume project, M Cappelletti (gen ed), *Access to Justice* (4 volumes, Sijthoff and Giuffrè 1978–1979); M Cappelletti 'Alternative Dispute Resolution Processes within the Framework of the World Wide Access to Justice Movement' (1993) 56 MLR 282 provides a concise overview.
⁴⁴ WP SWP (n 1), para 40.
⁴⁵ S Van Uytsel, 'Collective Actions in a Competition Law Context—Reconciling Multilayer Interests to Enhance Access to Justice' in S Wrbka, S Van Uytsel, and M Siems (eds), *Collective Actions: Enhancing Access to Justice and Reconciling Multilayer Interests?* (CUP 2012) 57, 61–3.

equating 'access to justice' with the attainment of compensation as the ultimate aim shows a short-sighted approach. 'Access to justice' not only entails an ultimate aim, it also comprises the necessary procedures through which this aim is achieved.[46] The Recommendation states that 'the possibility of joining claims and pursuing them collectively may constitute a better means of access to justice, in particular when the cost of individual actions would deter the harmed individuals from going to court' and identifies improving access to justice as one of its main aims.[47] Furthermore, in the consumer law field, 'access to justice' encompasses the procedural mechanisms enabling consumers to have recourse to a dispute resolution mechanism as well as the enforcement of substantive consumer rights.[48]

The narrow approach to 'access to justice' entails the mechanisms that allow recourse to dispute resolution, whereas the broad approach encompasses the ultimate aims that these procedures serve. Depending on the ultimate aim, 'access to justice' can be interpreted differently,[49] with the compensatory component being only one of its constituents. The table below (Figure 5.2) depicts this two-pronged approach to the notion of 'access to justice'.

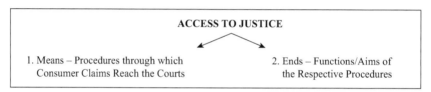

Figure 5.2 Interpreting 'Access to Justice'—Bifurcated Notion (1)

---

[46] Or as Micklitz puts it, 'access to justice comprises two elements: "access" and "justice"'. See HW Micklitz, 'Privatisation of Access to Justice and Soft Law—Lessons from the European Community?' in T Wilhelmsson and S Hurri (eds), *From Dissonance to Sense: Welfare State Expectations, Privatisation and Private Law* (Ashgate 1999) 505. See also M Ioannidou, 'Enhancing Consumers' Role in EU Private Competition Law Enforcement: A Normative and Practical Approach' (2012) 8 Comp L Rev <http://www.clasf.org/CompLRev/Issues/CompLRevVol8Issue1.pdf> accessed 10 June 2014, 59, 71.

[47] Recommendation (n 3), recital 9 and para 1; See also Communication on Collective Redress (n 21) 7.

[48] See, for example, Leuven Report (n 31), para 19; Consumer Redress Memorandum (n 7) 5. For the efforts and different legislative instruments aiming at enhancing access to justice for consumers see I Benoehr, 'Consumer Dispute Resolution after the Lisbon Treaty: Collective Actions and Alternative Procedures' (2013) 36 J Consum P 87, 89–90; I Benoehr, 'Collective Redress in the Field of European Consumer Law' (2014) 41 *Legal Issues of Economic Integration* 243, 247–9; S Wrbka, 'European Consumer Protection Law: Quo Vadis?—Thoughts on the Compensatory Collective Redress Debate' in S Wrbka, S Van Uytsel, and M Siems (eds), *Collective Actions: Enhancing Access to Justice and Reconciling Multilayer Interests?* (CUP 2012) 23, 28–9.

[49] See I Ramsay, 'Consumer Redress and Access to Justice' in C Rickett and T Telfer (eds), *International Perspectives on Consumers' Access to Justice* (CUP 2003) 17, 19 for the distinction between narrow and broad concepts of access to justice. See also R Nordh, 'Group Actions in Sweden: Reflections on the Purpose of Civil Litigation, the Need for Reform and a Forthcoming Proposal' (2001) 11 Duke J Comp & Intl L 381, 387–388 for a broad approach to access to justice.

Collective actions for consumer claims in competition law promote 'access to justice' (see Figure 5.3 below) since they allow the relevant action to reach the courts, even if not every affected consumer receives compensation.[50] The added value of such actions is that they enforce the right to compensation in its functional approach (ie deterrence) and bring moral satisfaction to consumers since the violator is deprived of the anti-competitive gains (disgorgement of profits) and accounts for the competition law infringement.[51]

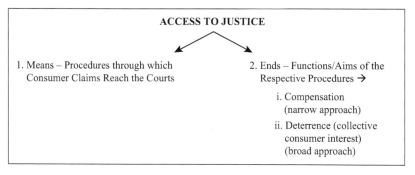

Figure 5.3 Implementing Access to Justice

4. Structural Characteristics of a Model Collective Action

The analysis in section 3 examined the notion of 'access to justice', pointed to its multiple meanings, and employed the 'collective consumer interest' as a demarcation criterion and as a justification for the introduction of different collective action mechanisms for low value consumer claims in competition law, which should aim primarily at deterring competition law violations.[52] Following these normative justifications, different structural characteristics of the collective mechanisms are addressed in this section, with the aim of structuring an aggregation mechanism that alters the claimants' incentives and allows the bringing of otherwise non-viable claims.

In the light of the specific characteristics of consumer claims,[53] aggregation mechanisms that focus on the promotion of procedural efficiency alone would not suffice. Thus, the European Parliament missed the point when it commented on 'the possible benefits of collective judicial actions in terms of lower costs and greater legal certainty for claimants, defendants and the judicial system alike by avoiding parallel litigation of similar claims'.[54] This is not the aim of collective actions for

---

[50] See G Howells and S Weatherill, *Consumer Protection Law* (2nd edn, Ashgate 2005) 606.
[51] H Lindblom, 'National Report: Group Litigation in Sweden' (Report prepared for 'The Globalization of Class Actions') (6 December 2007) <http://globalclassactions.stanford.edu/sites/default/files/documents/Sweden_National_Report.pdf> accessed 15 October 2014, 36.
[52] For a law and economics approach to available group litigation procedures for competition law violations see S Keske, *Group Litigation in European Competition Law: A Law and Economics Perspective* (Intersentia 2010).
[53] See Chapter 4, text to nn 1–20.   [54] See EP Resolution (n 17), para 5.

minimal consumer claims. Collective action mechanisms for non-viable claims allow the bringing of claims that could not be litigated individually, and therefore serve other goals, rather than efficiency of litigation. Thus, they perform a different function and merit a different approach.

Collective actions for low value consumer claims promote the collective consumer interest and advance primarily deterrence against competition law violations. This underlying deterrence rationale is reflected in the structural characteristics of the collective action mechanisms, primarily in the choice between the opt-in or opt-out mechanism.[55] Furthermore, addressing the funding and distribution of the damages awards may point to the underlying rationale of collective actions, and is directly influenced by the adopted opt-in or opt-out model. Finally, awarding standing to a consumer representative impacts upon the viability of collective actions of this type. In structuring the collective action model, reference is made to the US federal system where appropriate, although the analysis moves away from a transplantation of the US system into the EU legal order and advocates the formation of a collective action mechanism that comprises a delicate mix of 'private' incentives coupled with carefully structured and limited 'public' safeguards.

4.1 Structuring the group: Opt in v opt-out

In opt-in collective actions, individual consumers must actively express their desire to be included in the action in order to be bound by the final judgment. In opt-out collective actions, the typical example being the US-type class actions, the victims of a competition law violation are automatically considered to be members of the class unless they expressly state that they want to be excluded. Only in that case will they not be covered by any final judgment.[56] In US small claims class actions, claimants do not actively form a group but, rather, remain inactive; no group of claimants but, rather, a grouping of claims exists, which is made possible by the fact that class members are coerced into joining the group.[57] The 'quasi-mandatory' group formation is realized through the opt-out character of this type of action and, in fact, it has been suggested that the opt-out structure of the class is effectively what permits small claim class actions to reach the courts.[58]

Opt-out collective actions are superior to opt-in actions from a deterrence perspective. The pool of claims covered by an opt-out collective action will far exceed that covered by an opt-in collective action.[59] This is even more the case

---

[55] See R Mulheron, *The Class Action in Common Law Legal Systems: A Comparative Perspective* (Hart Publishing, Oxford 2004) 29–38 for a general overview.
[56] WP SWP (n 1), para 58; On this distinction see also OECD (n 31) 30.
[57] Rubenstein (n 37) 718.
[58] JE Kennedy, 'Class Actions: The Right to Opt out' (1984) 25 Ariz L Rev 3, 20–21.
[59] While this is a logical assumption to make, there are also empirical studies supporting this assertion. See BI Bertelsen, MS Calfee, and GW Connor, 'The Rule 23(b)(3) Class Action: An Empirical Study' (1974) 62 Geo LJ 1123, 1148–1151; T Eisenberg and G Miller, 'The Role of Opt-Out and Objectors in Class Action Litigation: Theoretical and Empirical Issues' (2004) NYU

for low value consumer claims in the light of the consumer rational apathy problem.⁶⁰ In order to overcome this problem a different aggregation mechanism is needed that actually induces consumers to join the action. The legislator should pick an aggregation mechanism capable of affecting consumer behaviour without depriving consumers of their freedom of choice through their right to opt-out.⁶¹

In opt-in cases, a large number of individual consumers will not even bother to declare that they would like to join the action. They may not even be aware of their right to claim.⁶² Subsequently, the possible damages award will be lower rendering it unviable to bring a claim in the light of the litigation costs, and the possible deterrent effect on violators will be fairly insignificant since they are in a position to retain their illicit gains.

Despite being more effective in terms of deterrence, the opt-out structure gives rise to due process concerns both for claimants' and defendants' rights. Claimants do not retain control over the litigation and defendants may face frivolous suits. However, the US class action system suggests that due process rights of class members and defendants can be safeguarded through appropriate certification and notice mechanisms. The US federal courts, when examining the certification requirements ('numerosity', 'commonality', 'typicality', 'adequacy', and 'predominance'),⁶³ have become increasingly scrupulous.⁶⁴

Furthermore, class members can express their decision not to be included in the class, either before the class certification or before the approval of any potential settlement.⁶⁵ In order to express such an intention, they must receive adequate notice. In *Eisen v Carlisle*, the US Supreme Court required notice to be given to individual class members whose conduct details could be found with reasonable effort.⁶⁶ In the light of the low opt-out rates in consumer cases, commentators

---

Law and Economics Research Paper Series Working Paper No 04-004 <http://papers.ssrn.com/sol3/papers.cfm?abstract_id=528146> accessed 1 November 2014, 4 in which they argue that, in the US, the opt-out rate is less than 1% and, in consumer class actions, less than 0.2%. See also R Mulheron, 'Reform of Collective Redress in England and Wales: A Perspective of Need' (2008) (Research Paper for Submission to the CJC).

⁶⁰ On this problem see chapter 4, text to nn 8–11.

⁶¹ This echoes the 'libertarian paternalism' theory articulated by Sunstein and Thaler. CR Sunstein and RH Thaler, 'Libertarian Paternalism is not an Oxymoron' (2003) 70 U Chi L Rev 1159, 1161–1162; CR Thaler and RH Sunstein, *Nudge: Improving Decisions about Health, Wealth and Happiness* (Yale University Press 2008) 5, 6.

⁶² C Hodges, *The Reform of Class and Representative Actions in European Legal Systems* (Hart 2008) 120 with further references to Mulheron (n 55).

⁶³ FRCP, Rule 23(a) and 23(b)(3).

⁶⁴ A Andreangeli, 'A View from Across the Atlantic: Recent Developments in the Case-Law of the US Federal Courts on Class Certification in Antitrust Cases' in B Rodger (ed), *Competition Law Comparative Private Enforcement and Collective Redress Across Europe* (Kluwer 2014) 223, 239; Andreangeli (n 34) 130–132; For the situation in Canada and Australia see R Mulheron, 'The Impetus for Class Action Reform in England Arising From the Competition Law Sector' in S Wrbka, S Van Uytsel, and M Siems (eds), *Collective Actions: Enhancing Access to Justice and Reconciling Multilayer Interests?* (CUP 2012) 385, 409 arguing that in both jurisdictions certification acts as an effective screening mechanism. See also S Rajski, '*In Re: Hydrogen Peroxide*: Reinforcing Rigorous Analysis for Class Action Certification' (2011) 34 Seattle UL Rev 577.

⁶⁵ FRCP, Rule 23(c)(2)(b) and 23(e)(1) and (4).   ⁶⁶ 417 US 156 (1974).

have suggested that this is not an efficient approach, as it creates both social, as well as class, costs. Instead, individual notice should be replaced by publication and/or electronic notice.[67] Indeed, there are examples of court decisions at the state level that adopt this approach, as was the case in *In re Domestic Air Transportation Antitrust Litigation*, in which the court accepted that publication in newspapers and airline magazines sufficed to fulfil the individual notice requirement.[68]

4.2 Standing to bring claims: Consumer representatives

4.2.1 Class counsel

A two-fold criticism that is often aired against small claim class actions is related to the class counsel role, either because it drives defendants into unfair settlements and/or because these settlements are of little benefit to individual class members.[69] Counsel's role is more important for small claims class actions, especially because the individual consumer damage claim is very small, thereby precluding any individual consumer from organizing the collective group action.[70] Therefore, actions of this type would not have been brought if it were not for the efforts of the class counsel acting as an agent for a large number of consumers. However, on closer inspection, the principal-agent relationship in small claim class actions is distorted, since the agent assumes the role of the principal.[71] Given that, in small claims consumer class actions, consumers are indifferent to their trivial individual damages, which is also evident in the low opt-out rates, the court should assume a more active managerial role over the class counsel,[72] since there is, in effect, no class representative assuming that role.[73] The court's role with regard to the adequacy of the class counsel is most important at the class certification and approval of a potential settlement phase,[74] especially if one takes into account the

---

[67] Eisenberg and Miller (n 59) 37–38. See also J Bronsteen and O Fisse, 'The Class Action Rule' (2003) 78 Notre Dame L Rev 1419, 1437–1438. ALI, Principles of the Law of Aggregate Litigation (Proposed Final Draft, 1 April 2009) 150–151, 161–162.
[68] S Calkins, 'An Enforcement Official's Reflections on Antitrust Class Actions' (1997) 39 Ariz L Rev 413, 420–421.
[69] EH Cooper, 'Class Action Advice in the Form of Questions' (2001) 11 Duke J Comp Int'l L 215, 235; M Handler, 'The Shift from Substantive to Procedural Innovations in Antitrust Suits' (1971) Colum L Rev 1, 9–10 effectively viewing small claim class actions as not open to trial, resulting in 'legalized blackmail' for defendants and benefiting only the plaintiffs' lawyers. See C Silver, '"We are Scared to Death": Class Certification and Blackmail' (2003) 78 NYU L Rev 1357, who rejects this idea.
[70] S Issacharoff, 'Group Litigation of Consumer Claims: Lessons from the US Experience' (1999) 34 Tex Intl LJ 135, 146–147.
[71] J Coffee, 'Understanding the Plaintiff's Attorney: The Implications of Economic Theory for Private Enforcement of Law through Class and Derivative Actions' (1986) 86 Colum L Rev 669, 678 ('courts...are prone to emphasize that the plaintiff's attorney has no "true" identifiable client'); JR Macey and G Miller, 'The Plaintiff's Attorney's Role in Class Action and Derivatives Litigation: Economic Analysis and Recommendations for Reform' (1991) 58 U Chi L Rev 1, 4.
[72] FRCP, Rule 23(g)(1). [73] Eisenberg and Miller (n 59) 4, 39.
[74] Lang (n 35) 293.

criticism of collusion between the class counsel and the defendant in reaching a settlement, which may disregard the interests of the class.[75]

The role of the class counsel has received criticism in the context of coupon settlements, which appear to be frequent in small claim class actions.[76] The Class Action Fairness Act (CAFA)[77] partly alleviated these concerns, since it aligned the incentives of the plaintiffs' counsel with those of the class in the case of coupon settlements by providing that an attorney's fees are to be calculated based on the percentage of the coupons actually redeemed (and not assessed against those issued, as was the case before).[78]

The fact that the majority of class actions lead to settlements[79] should not exacerbate the principal-agent problem. In other words, the fact that the majority of class actions are settled should not be taken as indicative of a principal-agent problem but, rather, as indicative of the need to formulate an adequate managerial role for the court through legal means. Consumer class actions are usually a win-win situation for consumers, in the sense that they allow for the trial of otherwise non-viable consumer claims. However small the compensation they may bring to consumers, it is better than receiving nothing at all. Whether this small benefit to class members justifies the high litigation costs is a different question, which the US legal system has answered in the affirmative, with the exception of the *Illinois Brick* formulation, which banned indirect purchaser suits before federal courts because final consumers were not regarded as efficient plaintiffs.[80] The active role of the plaintiffs' counsel could effectively rebut this argument.

4.2.2. *Consumer organizations*

Consumer organization involvement on behalf of consumers offers an alternative to the leading plaintiff/class counsel model and is considered preferable since it poses no conflict of interest between the group representative and the group members.[81]

---

[75] Coffee (n 71) 714; RA Nagareda, 'The Preexistence Principle and the Role of the Class Action' (2003) 103 Colum L Rev 149, 163; BL Hay and D Rosenberg, ' "Sweetheart" and "Blackmail" Settlements in Class Actions: Reality and Remedy' (2000) 75 Notre Dame L Rev 1377, 1389. See J Bronsteen, 'Class Action Settlements: An Opt-in Proposal' [2005] U Ill L Rev 903 for an alternative solution.

[76] On coupon settlements see GP Miller and LS Singer, 'Nonpecuniary Class Action Settlements' (1997) 60 LCP 97. For an attempt to rebut this criticism see WB Rubenstein, 'On What a "Private Attorney General" is and Why it Matters' (2004) 57 Vand L Rev 2129, 2159ff. On overcoming the problems posed by coupon settlements see CR Leslie, 'A Market Based Approach to Coupon Settlements in Antitrust and Consumer Class Action Litigation' (2002) 49 UCLA L Rev 991.

[77] Class Action Fairness Act, Pub L 109-2, 119 Stat 4 (18 Feb 2005) (codified in 28 USC).

[78] 28 USC [1712] (a); RD Blaire and CA Piette, 'Coupons and Settlements in Antitrust Class Actions' (2006) 20 Antitrust LJ 32, 33. RD Blaire and CA Piette, 'Coupon Settlements: Compensation and Deterrence' (2006) 51 Antitrust Bulletin 661.

[79] Nagareda (n 75) 151. In fact, economic theory supports the contention that the majority of disputes lead to settlement. See WM Landes, 'An Economic Analysis of the Courts' (1971) 14 JL & Econ 61.

[80] *Illinois Brick Co v Illinois*, 431 US 720, 736 (1977).

[81] C Hodges and A Stadler, 'Introduction' in C Hodges and A Stadler, *Resolving Mass Disputes—ADR and Settlement of Mass Claims* (Edward Elgar 2013) 1, 14.

In addition, the involvement of consumer organizations as intermediary actors in the litigation process contributes to overcoming the rational apathy and information asymmetry problem of individual consumers. Consumer organization involvement on behalf of consumers offers a pragmatic alternative to individual consumer claims that would not otherwise have been brought in the light of their minimal value.

However, consumer organizations should not be viewed as a panacea.[82] First, both the Commission and consumer organizations themselves have recognized that consumer organizations in Europe are under-resourced bodies.[83] Second, empirical research in the field of private enforcement of consumer claims has revealed limited involvement of consumer organizations in litigation.[84] In fact, consumer collective actions represent only 0.4% of the total competition litigation in Europe.[85] There is a record of consumer organization involvement in raising competition law claims only in the UK, France, Spain, and Portugal and, in these cases, the relevant involvement was unsuccessful.[86]

Another example of inadequate involvement of consumer organizations can be drawn from the Injunctions Directive,[87] which has rarely been used in practice.[88] This can be attributed to consumer organizations' lack of funding and expertise.[89]

---

[82] See OD Epstein, 'Representation of Consumer Interest by Consumer Associations—Salvation for the Masses?' (2007) 3 Comp L Rev 209, 222–236, for a concise overview of impediments facing consumer organizations.

[83] Commission (EC), XXXIInd Report on Competition Policy (2002) SEC(2003) 467 final, para 311; BEUC, 'Response to the White Paper' <http://ec.europa.eu/competition/antitrust/actionsdamages/white_paper_comments/beuc_en.pdf> accessed 6 November 2014, 11–12.

[84] The data here is based on D Waelbroeck, D Slater, and G Even-Shoshan, 'Study on the Conditions of Claims for Damages in Case of Infringement of EC Competition Rules' (Comparative Report) (Ashurst Study) (31 August 2004) <http://ec.europa.eu/competition/antitrust/actionsdamages/comparative_report_clean_en.pdf> accessed 17 October 2014; A Renda, J Peysner, A Riley, B Rodger, and others, 'Making Antitrust Damages Actions More Effective in the EU: Welfare Impact and Potential Scenarios' (Report for the European Commission) (December 2007) <http://ec.europa.eu/competition/antitrust/actionsdamages/files_white_paper/impact_study.pdf> accessed 3 July 2014; National Reports submitted for the project 'Globalisation of Class Action' undertaken by Stanford Law School and the Oxford Centre of Socio-Legal Studies <http://globalclassactions.stanford.edu/category/categories/country-reports> accessed 16 October 2014; EU Competition Policy Reports (1971–2009) <http://ec.europa.eu/competition/publications/annual_report/index.html> accessed 16 October 2014. See The ANNALS of the American Academy of Political and Social Science, *The Globalisation of Class Actions*, Contents (March 2009) 622 (The ANNALS) 1 for a wide variety of articles concerning collective actions in different jurisdictions. Civic Consulting, 'Evaluation of the Effectiveness and Efficiency of Collective Redress Mechanisms in the European Union' (26 August 2008) (Report prepared for DG SANCO) (Civic Consulting Study) and also National Reports Submitted under this project (Civic Consulting National Reports) <http://ec.europa.eu/consumers/redress_cons/collective_redress_en.htm> accessed 16 October 2014.

[85] B Rodger, 'Collective Redress Mechanisms and Consumer Case Law' in B Rodger (ed), *Competition Law Comparative Private Enforcement and Collective Redress Across Europe* (Kluwer 2014) 157, 162.

[86] Maybe with the exception of Portugal. For more details see section 5 of this chapter.

[87] Injunctions Directive (n 28).

[88] Commission (EC), 'Report Concerning the Application of Directive 98/27/EC of the European Parliament and of the Council on Injunctions for the Protection of Consumers' Interest' COM(2008) 756 final, paras 13, 32.

[89] Ibid, paras 18, 21; F Cafaggi and H Micklitz, 'Administrative and Judicial Enforcement in Consumer Protection: The Way Forward' (2008) EUI Working Papers Law 2008/29 <http://papers.ssrn.com/sol3/papers.cfm?abstract_id=1317342> accessed 6 November 2014, 7, 18.

This procedure does not apply to competition law violations,[90] but is, rather, indicative of consumer organizations' capacity to act as agents for the consumer interest. This problem might also be exacerbated in the context of competition law; if consumer organizations are reluctant to get involved in 'core' consumer law problems, they will be even more reluctant to engage in the enforcement of competition law. It is evident from the enforcement record to date that consumer organizations are only peripheral players in the competition enforcement field, calling for the adoption of specific procedural measures.

Third, the issue of the representativeness of consumer organizations needs to be addressed. This is related to the issue of whether they are allowed to raise a damages claim only on behalf of their affected members or on behalf of all consumers affected, irrespective of whether they are members of the respective organization. If the policymakers opt for the latter option, necessary safeguards to ensure adequate representativeness need to be devised.[91]

4.2.3 Other public bodies

Public bodies offer an alternative to lawyers and consumer organizations for initiating a collective action in the consumer interest. The nature and role of those public bodies in a legal system is diverse. For example, and in addition to private class actions, the US legal system provides for *parens patriae* actions brought by State Attorneys General on behalf of state residents with the aim of recovering damages caused by an antitrust violation.[92] *Parens patriae* actions were introduced as an antidote to the *Eisen* litigation[93] that, according to some commentators, made consumer class actions theoretically possible but practically infeasible.[94] Interestingly, this fact reveals that US class actions do indeed face problems addressing small consumer claims and some alternative mechanism is called for; a highly topical observation in the light of the current EU efforts.

The requirements for bringing *parens patriae* actions are less stringent than private class actions and it is generally assumed that the State Attorneys General

---

[90] According to Article 1, the Injunctions Directive (n 28) exclusively applies in the case of violation of the Directives included in Annex I.

[91] See section 6.1 below.

[92] Hart Scott Rodino Antitrust Improvements Act of 1976, Pub L No 94–435, 90 Stat 1383 (1976) (codified as amended in scattered sections of 15 USC) USC 15. Calkins (n 68) 433–437. R Lande, 'New Options for State Indirect Purchaser Legislation: Protecting the Real Victims of Antitrust Violations' (2010) 61 Alabama L Rev 447, 461–462; On *parens patriae* actions and AMC proposals for reform see F Cengiz, 'The Role of State Attorneys General in US Antitrust Policy: Public Enforcement through Private Enforcement Methods' (2006) (UEA—CCP Working Paper 06–19) 16ff.

[93] See KW Dam, 'Class Action Notice: Who Needs it?' (1974) *Supreme Court Review* 97, 100–104 for a concise approach to the *Eisen* case.

[94] B DuVal, 'The Class Action as an Antitrust Enforcement Device: The Chicago Experience (II)' (1976) *American Bar Foundation Research Journal* 1273, 1356. See D Shapiro and J Springer, 'Management of Consumer Class Actions after *Eisen*: Notice and Determination of Damages' (1975) 26 Mercer L Rev 851. Also, *parens patriae* were viewed as a solution to combatting the burdens imposed on the judicial system by class actions and reversed *Hawaii v Standard Oil and Co* 405 US 251–254 (1972). See KW Dam, 'Class Actions: Efficiency, Compensation, Deterrence and Conflict

act in the public interest, so these actions are perceived to be capable of addressing the shortcomings of private class actions.[95] No notification to individual victims is required and only aggregate, not individual, damages need be calculated.[96]

Parens patriae actions resemble administrative enforcement since standing is granted to a state official. At the same time, though, they remain a form of private enforcement because they are brought before, and assessed by, civil courts. In addition, they bear similarities to consumer organization actions, given that they are both concerned with addressing the principal-agent problem by granting standing to bodies presumed to be acting in the public interest. The *parens patriae* model is instructive inasmuch as it showcases that public authorities (in the US model, State Attorneys General) may act as a 'public safety valve' addressing concerns in relation to conflicts between legal counsel and group members.

4.3 Funding of actions

The funding of consumer collective actions is influenced by the adopted rules on standing and whether standing is granted to representative bodies, such as consumer organizations. The rules on the funding of actions should essentially allow the bringing of collective claims. This is possible through contingency fees, third party funding, or funding of actions by consumer organizations, provided that the latter have adequate resources.[97]

In the US, another important factor that contributes to the realization of consumer class action litigation are the funding rules, which permit the class counsel to finance the litigation under a contingency fee arrangement,[98] whereby the lawyer's fees are calculated based on a percentage of the successful claim.[99] Contingency fees have been criticized for resulting in lucrative lawyer awards while bringing little benefit to consumers, a concern which the CAFA has tried to address.[100] Also, the fact that each party bears its own costs (and there is no 'loser pays' rule), the so called 'American Rule', incentivizes the bringing of such actions.[101]

---

of Interest' (1975) 4 J Legal Stud 47, 64. SB Farmer, 'More Lessons from the Laboratories: Cy Pres Distributions in Parens Patriae Antitrust Actions Brought by State Attorneys General' (2000) 68 Fordm L Rev 361, 371–376.

[95] Farmer (n 94) 389–391.   [96] 15 USC §15(d).

[97] Other funding rules that incentivize the bringing of claims, such as conditional fee arrangements, but that do not *enable* the bringing of such claims are not covered. Conditional fee arrangements provide that the lawyer receives a reward in the event of successful litigation: see Parliament (n 2) 7.

[98] S Issacharoff and G Miller, 'Will Aggregate Litigation Come to Europe?' (2009) 62 Vand L Rev 179, 199. See D Rubinfeld and S Scotchmer, 'Contingent Fees for Attorneys: An Economic Analysis' (1993) 24 RAND J Econ 343 on the economic justification of contingency fees and their impact on deterrence.

[99] WP SWP (n 1), para 244.

[100] See text to n 77. See also E Helland and A Tabarrok, 'Contingency Fees, Settlement Delays, and Low Quality Litigation: Empirical Evidence from Two Datasets' (2003) 19 JLEO 517 which shows that contingency fees are preferable to hourly fees.

[101] Coffee (n 71) 670.

Similar to contingency fees, third party funding allows the bringing of competition claims, whereby a third party funds the litigation in return for a percentage of the damages award.[102] Devising an intermediary to fund the litigation solves the problem of potential conflict between the interests of the lawyer and those of the group. Another alternative is the assignment of claims to a third party, although this is not possible for minimal consumer claims.

If standing is granted to consumer organizations, the funding rules should be tailored accordingly. This does not preclude the funding of litigation based on contingency fees but suggests that additional rules regulating the funding of consumer organizations are required. If consumer organizations have sufficient funding to bring a claim, then there is less of a need for the adoption of contingency fees.

4.4 Distribution of the damages award

The structure of the group as opt-in or opt-out inevitably influences the calculation and distribution of the damages award. In opt-out collective actions for small consumer claims, it is not possible to strictly adhere to the distribution of the damages award to each consumer. In general, there have been very low claim rates in consumer class actions, given the very small size of individual damages. This calls for distribution mechanisms that also benefit inactive consumers, ranging from discounts on future purchases (coupons) to establishing a trust fund and giving part of the award to a consumer-related cause. All of these mechanisms fall under the general category of cy-près or fluid recovery,[103] with consumer trust funds being viewed as the most appropriate cy-près form for consumer class actions.[104] Reverter mechanisms, which essentially bring unclaimed profits to the defendant, are of no benefit to private or general consumer interests, since they reduce much of the deterrent effect of the respective class actions.[105] The US courts have indeed advanced innovative means for the distribution of damages awards.[106]

---

[102] WP SWP (n 1), para 267. See R Mulheron, 'Third Party Funding: A Changing Landscape' (2008) 27 CJQ 312, 314.

[103] Despite the fact that they are usually used as synonyms they are not the same. Fluid recovery provides relief to future consumers through, for example, discounts on future sales. See A Foer, 'Enhancing Competition through the Cy Pres Remedy: Suggested Best Practices' (2010) 24 Antitrust LJ 86, fn 3. See also G Howells, 'Cy-pres for Consumers: Ensuring Class Action Reforms Deal With "Scattered Damages"' in J Steele and W van Boom, *Mass Justice—Challenges of Representation and Distribution* (Edward Elgar 2011) 58, 60–62. Howells is in favour of the adoption of organizational cy-près trust funds.

[104] See also ALI Principles Draft (n 67), para 3.07, which accepts cy-près as a second best option if further distribution to participating class members is not possible, and which also calls for a close nexus between the proposed recipient and the class. G Hillebrand and D Torrence, 'Claims Procedures in Large Consumer Class Actions and Equitable Distribution of Benefits' (1988) 28 Santa Clara L Rev 747, 748, 756, 762, 766; N DeJarlais, 'Notes—The Consumer Trust Fund: A Cy Pres Solution to Undistributed Funds in Consumer Class Actions' (1987) 38 Hastings LJ 729, 732.

[105] SR Shepherd, 'Damage Distribution in Class Actions: The Cy Pres Remedy' (1972) 39 U Chi L Rev 448.

[106] See DuVal (n 94) 1329–1331 for examples of US cases accepting or rejecting 'fluid class recovery'. See DI Shapiro, 'Processing the Consumer's Claim' (1972) 41 Antitrust LJ 257 for a debate

126   *Improving Consumers' Role: Collective Actions*

Inasmuch as part of the damages award does not reach the consumer beneficiaries, public safety valves need to be devised, either in the form of court supervision of the damages award or legislative provisions allowing the damages award to be given to approved charities.

4.5 Synopsis

Embarking from the particular characteristics of consumer claims resulting from competition law violations that are historically reflected in the distinct discussion of such claims at the EU policy level, section 3 has argued that any collective redress mechanisms for such claims should primarily promote the collective consumer interest, thereby furthering the deterrence against competition law violations. Naturally this underlying deterrence rationale should be reflected in the structural characteristics of the proposed mechanisms. Such structural characteristics have been discussed in section 4 and include the opt-out principle for the group formation, granting standing to representative bodies (private or public), and securing funding for the bringing of such actions as well as mechanisms for the appropriate distribution of the damages award. Opt-out collective actions provide the potential to advance deterrence against competition law violations and improve access to justice for affected consumers. Nonetheless, they should be coupled with specific safety valves in order to protect both the consumers' and the defendants' interests.

5. Structural Characteristics of Member States' Collective Action Mechanisms

Having discussed the desired structure of collective redress mechanisms, we now turn to examine Member States' experiences. Several Member States have sought ways in which to facilitate multi-party litigation. Indeed, the debate on collective action in Europe was first initiated at the Member State level. A vast array of collective actions exists in individual Member States whereas a common characteristic is the opt-in structure of such actions and the role of consumer organizations. The aim here is not to review in detail the different national collective action systems that adopt different public or private models for the enforcement of consumer rights,[107] but to identify certain prevailing characteristics in the European

---

in the light of the antibiotics litigation; contra M Malina, 'Fluid Class Recovery as a Consumer Remedy in Antitrust Cases' (1972) 47 NYU L Rev 477.

[107] For an overview see DG for Internal Policies, 'Overview of Existing Collective Redress Schemes in EU Member State' (July 2011) (IP/A/IMCO/NT/2011-16); Hodges (n 62); D Fairgrieve and G Howells, 'Collective Redress Procedures—European Debates' (2009) 58 ICLQ 379, 383. See also Parliament (n 2) 14–33; Rodger (n 85); F Caffagi and HW Micklitz, 'Administrative and Judicial Collective Enforcement of Consumer Law in the US and the European Community' (2007) EUI Law Working Paper No 2007/22 <http://papers.ssrn.com/sol3/papers.cfm?abstract_id=1024103> accessed 17 October 2014; Leuven Report (n 29). See also n 84.

collective redress procedures, difficult as that may be given the wide variety of different procedures,[108] and to draw general conclusions that could guide the Commission on the design of collective action systems for consumer claims for competition law violations. For example, the role of representative actors, either consumer organizations or representative bodies, should be stressed and these may act as a safety valve against the potential vices of an opt-out procedure.

Collective consumer actions for competition law violations remain very scarce[109] and therefore the focus here is on those actions and their relevant shortcomings. We also discuss models that could possibly be employed in the context of competition law for consumer claims but which lack the necessary structural characteristics to effectively promote claims of this sort. Finally, the discussion singles out those national models that exhibit certain structural themes discussed in section 4 above.

5.1 Furthering individual consumers' interests

In this section a variety of national collective redress mechanisms are examined, all of which serve access to justice, in the sense that their aim is to *compensate* the victims of the respective wrongs, thereby serving the *individual consumer interest*. The compensatory and individualistic nature of those actions can be deduced from their opt-in structure, the active role and participation of individual consumers, and the emphasis placed on the distribution of the damages awards to individual victims. Prominence is given to those mechanisms that alter claimants' incentives to bring an action and not to mechanisms that only improve procedural efficiency.[110]

5.1.1 Opt-in mechanisms

In France, an approved and duly recognized consumer association can sue for damages on behalf of consumers, if asked by two or more consumers suffering damage originating from the acts of the same person.[111] This procedure is structured as opt-in, in the sense that the consumer organization has to secure

---

[108] C Hodges, 'From Class Actions to Collective Redress: A Revolution in Approach to Compensation' [2009] CJQ 41, 45.
[109] See text to n 84.
[110] Mechanisms improving procedural efficiency include joint actions or case management tools, like the English Group Litigation Order. In joint actions, as Lindblom points out, 'the typical representative situation is not present' since 'all the joined plaintiffs are acting for themselves only and they are all parties'; H Lindblom, 'Individual Litigation and Mass Justice: A Swedish Perspective and Proposal on Group Actions in Civil Procedure' (1997) 45 Am J Comp L 805, 820; See also A Stadler, 'Collective Action as an Efficient Means for the Enforcement of European Competition Law' in J Basedow (ed), *Private Enforcement of EC Competition Law* (Kluwer Law International 2007) 195, 201–202; Ashurst Study (n 84) 44.
[111] Article L. 422-1 of the Consumer Code. See V Magnier, 'Class Actions, Group Litigation and Other Forms of Collective Litigation' (Report prepared for 'The Globalization of Class Actions') <http://globalclassactions.stanford.edu/sites/default/files/documents/France_National_Report.pdf>

individual consumer consent, which makes it inappropriate for minimal consumer claims. This is even more so since, as *Cartelmobile* reveals, in order for the case to be admissible, the consumer organization should not actively incite consumers to join the case.[112] The representative organizations can only appeal for consumer mandates through the press and not radio, television, or the Internet[113] and they often criticize the proxy constraints as being too strict.[114] In this case, UFC-Que Choisir brought a follow-on action against three mobile phone operators,[115] but the action was held inadmissible by the first instance court, the Court of Appeal, and the Supreme Court as UFC-Que Choisir had actively solicited consumer mandates via the Internet.[116] UFC-Que Choisir criticized the courts' approach in that it indicates the shortcomings of the French legal system with regard to adequately protecting the consumer interest.[117] However, even if the proxy conditions had been more lax and the action had been held admissible, only a very limited number of consumers joined the case,[118] which proves that its potential to compensate consumers was also limited.

In England, section 47B CA provides for a procedure according to which authorized consumer organizations can bring 'follow-on' damages actions before the Competition Appeal Tribunal (CAT) claiming compensation for consumers who have been affected. The consumers have to expressly declare that they want to be included in the action. The only action brought to date was settled, with judicial proceedings continuing on the matter of cost assessment.[119] In this case very

---

accessed 17 October 2014. V Magnier, 'The French Civil Litigation System, the Increasing Role of Judges, and Influences from Europe' (2009) The ANNALS (n 83) 114; L Idot 'Private Enforcement of Competition Law—Recommendations Flowing from the French Experience' in J Basedow (ed), *Private Enforcement of EC Competition Law* (Kluwer Law International 2007) 85, 97.

[112] Hodges (n 62) 84. The court held that the action was a disguised joint representative action, since the consumer organization in this case chose not to bring a representative action because of its costs (and maybe the strict proxy requirements) but, rather, to appeal to the system of common rules, based on civil action for damages due to unfair practices. See Magnier, Report (n 111) 20; N Jalabert-Doury, 'France' in A Foer and J Cuneo (eds), *The International Handbook of Private Enforcement of Competition Law* (Edward Elgar 2010) 322.

[113] French law does not expressly mention solicitation via the Internet. The issue was decided by Lille First Instance Civil Court in the *Class Action.fr* case. However, in this case it was a company (Class Action.fr) that tried to solicit consumers, and not a consumer organization. Magnier, The ANNALS (n 111) 117.

[114] Magnier, Report (n 111) 12, 14.

[115] See Hodges (n 62) 84; Idot (n 111) 96–98 for more information on this case. See also C Leskinen, 'Collective Antitrust Damages Actions in the EU: The Opt-in v the Opt-out Model' (2010) Working Paper IE Law School 10-03 <http://papers.ssrn.com/sol3/papers.cfm?abstract_id=1612731> accessed 17 October 2014, 13–14, with further references for this case. UFC-Que Choisir, 'Contribution au livre vert de la Commission' (2006) <http://ec.europa.eu/competition/antitrust/actionsdamages/files_green_paper_comments/ufc_fr.pdf> accessed 17 October 2014, 10–12.

[116] Parliament (n 2) 36.

[117] See UFC-Que Choisir, Comments to the Commission Recommendation (2011) <http://ec.europa.eu/competition/consultations/2011_collective_redress/ufc_que_%20choisir_fr.pdf>. For views see <http://www.cartelmobile.org/> accessed 30 September 2014.

[118] UFC-Que Choisir estimated that the infringement affected almost 20 million consumers, with only 12,530 opting in. Ibid 2.

[119] *The Consumers' Association v JJB Sports Plc* (Case No 1078/7/9/07) [2009] CAT 2.

few consumers were compensated, thereby promoting further debate regarding the need to introduce opt-out mechanisms in England.[120]

The Swedish Group Proceedings Act of 2002 provides for collective actions of the opt-in type brought by individuals (private group actions), organizations (organizational group actions), and public bodies (public group actions).[121] The Consumer Ombudsman is the designated public authority for consumer claims,[122] whereas the Swedish Competition Authority has not been designated since, according to the Swedish government, public competition law enforcement suffices.[123] In the light of this, it would appear that public group actions are not available for consumer claims in competition law. However, assuming that the public group action can be employed for consumer claims in competition law, the one precedent suggests that it would not be workable for minimal consumer claims. The Swedish Ombudsman brought an action against an electricity provider for failing to provide electricity at the stated contract price to 7,000 consumers. The consumers sustained individual damage ranging between €100 and €1,000. This case resulted in protracted litigation and was very resource intensive for the Ombudsman, in the light of the difficulties involved in defining the group.[124]

In the three examples above, the failure of the collective action can be attributed mainly to its opt-in nature. This should not be taken to mean, though, that an opt-out structure alone is a sufficient condition for an effective collective action system. However, this bad track record has prompted the legislatures in France and England to change their collective action regimes. However, as will be discussed below, the French model introduces a hybrid representative action that furthers the individual consumer interest and which may prove ill-suited to low value consumer claims.

---

[120] CJC, 'Improving Access to Justice through Collective Actions' (November 2008) (CJC Report) 67–86. OFT, 'Private actions in Competition Law: Effective Redress for Consumers and Business' (Recommendations) (OFT 916resp) (November 2007) <http://webarchive.nationalarchives.gov.uk/20140402142426/http://www.oft.gov.uk/shared_oft/reports/comp_policy/oft916resp.pdf> accessed 17 October 2014, paras 7.11–7.23. See also 'Which' announcement that it does not intend to bring more actions under the current regime in J Pheasant and A Bicarregui, 'Striking the Right Balance towards a "Competition Culture" not a "Litigation Culture"? Comment on the European Commission's White Paper on Damages Actions for Breach of EC Antitrust Rules' (2008) 1 GCLR 98, 102; A Robertson, 'UK Competition Litigation: From Cinderella to Goldilocks?' (2010) 9 Comp Law 275, 288–292; see *The Consumers' Association v JJB Sports Plc* (n 119), paras 31–32 on the extremely disproportionate relationship between damages granted to consumers and the costs incurred by the consumer organization.
[121] See Lindblom (n 51) 10ff, 13. See also M Glader and P Alstergren, 'Sweden' in A Foer and J Cuneo (eds), *The International Handbook of Private Enforcement of Competition Law* (Edward Elgar 2010) 407; A Perrson, 'Collective Enforcement—European Prospects in light of the Swedish Experience' in S Wrbka, S Van Uytsel, and M Siems, *Collective Actions: Enhancing Access to Justice and Reconciling Multilayer Interests?* (CUP 2012) 341.
[122] Perrson (n 121) 347.
[123] D Ashton and D Henry, *Competition Damages Actions in the EU* (Edward Elgar 2013) para 6.139.
[124] Perrson (n 121) 349–350.

5.1.2 Hybrid mechanisms: reverse opt-in mechanisms

This section discusses two stage representative or group actions that allow the courts to pronounce on the liability of the infringer in a judgment that covers all affected consumers, following which the consumers need to take individual actions in order to recover their damages. These mechanisms can be termed 'reverse opt-in' mechanisms, as they are initiated as opt-out since they cover the whole of the affected consumer group but subsequently require consumers to actively 'opt-in' and the infringer pays damages only to the latter group of consumers.

The new French law on consumer representative actions can be given as an example of such a mechanism.[125] This allows authorized consumer organizations to bring an action on behalf of consumers in order to obtain compensation resulting from (amongst other grounds) competition law violations (Article L. 423-1). It is structured as a two stage mechanism.[126] In the first stage the court pronounces on the violation and the liability of the infringer, and defines the group(s) of affected consumers and the value of the individual claims. Then in the second stage consumers need to claim their individual damages within two to six months after the court's judgment in the first phase (Article L. 423-3 to 5).

The law also provides for a simplified procedure that appears to be suitable for consumer claims flowing from competition law violations and provides that when the identity and number of affected consumers are known and those consumers suffer equal damage, then the judge, after pronouncing on liability and the infringement, may ask the perpetrator to compensate consumers directly (Article L. 423-10). Effectively, the simplified procedure merges the two stages and resembles an opt-out procedure that could promote the collective consumer interest. For example, if a company has engaged in a cartel, the judge may use the company's records to identify its customers and ask the company to credit their accounts accordingly. This might not be possible in practice though as the law asks that consumers accept the compensation; if not, the compensation goes to the consumer organization (Article L. 423-10, para 3). Thus, the opt-out structure is retained in essence (if not in form) since the compensation is calculated based on the number of affected consumers. Therefore, the fact that the French Constitutional Court characterized this mechanism as opt-in (and therefore in accordance with the French Constitution) is not entirely accurate. Nonetheless, it boldly shows that it is possible to overcome the resistance against opt-out procedures through cleverly structured mechanisms that advance the collective consumer interest.

---

[125] Law No 2014-344, *French Official Journal* (18 March 2014) No 0065, page 5400 (Loi Hamon). The new law will be incorporated in the French Consumer Code.

[126] Note that for competition law violations, consumer representative action can only be brought as follow-on (Article L. 423.17).

Another example of a reverse opt-in mechanism is the English representative rule. In England, apart from the specific collective action mechanisms for competition law violations, it is possible for a person bearing the same interest in a claim to represent other people, without there being a need for these people to issue their own claim forms.[127] This mechanism, however, possesses limited potential to contribute to the compensation of cartel victims, as *Emerald Supplies Ltd v British Airways plc* (*Emerald Supplies*) indicates.[128] Emerald sued British Airways (BA) on her own behalf as a direct purchaser and on behalf of all indirect purchasers for damage caused to at least 178 further potential claimants, according to Emerald, by British Airways' participation in the air freight cartel.[129] The English High Court, in this case, essentially upheld BA's arguments and struck out the representative part since the claimant failed 'to provide any basis on which "the other persons" with the "same interest in the claim" can be identified' and 'that the class, so far as identifiable, is not a single homogenous class but inherently, at least, two classes with conflicting interests'.[130] The judgment was upheld on appeal.[131]

In addition to the difficulties flowing from the 'same interest' requirement,[132] and the identification of a 'homogeneous class', CPR 19.6 is unlikely to promote consumer claims for the additional reason that individual consumer damages will be small and no individual consumer will have an adequate incentive to bring an action on behalf of others.[133] Moreover, CPR 19.6 does not allow for an award of damages to be made to the represented class since 'a person coming within that class will be entitled to rely on the declarations as res judicata, but will still have to establish damage in a separate action',[134] and this detracts from the procedure's potential to contribute to the raising of consumer claims for competition law violations.

Another example of a reverse opt-in mechanism stems from the amendment[135] to the Greek Consumer Code, which provides consumer organizations that

---

[127] CPR 19.6; M Brealey and N Green (eds), *Competition Litigation—UK Practice and Procedure* (OUP 2010) 35, 40; G Howells, 'Country Report UK' (Report prepared for Civic Consulting to be submitted to DG SANCO) <http://ec.europa.eu/consumers/redress_cons/uk-country-report-final.pdf> accessed 17 October 2014.

[128] [2009] EWHC 741 (Ch), [2009] 3 WLR 1200. For a criticism see R Mulheron, 'Emerald Supplies Ltd v British Airways Plc: A Century Later the Ghost of Markt Lives On' (2009) 8 Comp Law 159.

[129] *Emerald Supplies* (n 128) paras 1–9. Commission decision of 9 November 2011, Case COMP/39258—*Airfreight* (no public version available).

[130] *Emerald Supplies* (n 128), paras 25–26, 32–36.

[131] *Emerald Supplies Ltd v British Airways Plc* [2010] EWCA Civ 1284, [2011] 2 WLR 203, paras 60–69. For a criticism of the appellate judgment see R Mulheron, 'A Missed Gem of an Opportunity for the Representative Rule' (2012) 23 EBLRev 49.

[132] On the difficulties of overcoming the 'same interest' requirement see R Mulheron, 'From Representative Rule to Class Action: Steps Rather than Leaps' (2005) 24 CJQ 424, 427–431.

[133] A Zuckerman, *Zuckerman on Civil Procedure: Principles of Practice* (2nd edn, Sweet & Maxwell 2006) para 12.30.

[134] *Emerald Supplies* (n 128), para 21 citing *Prudential Assurance Co Ltd v Newman Industries Ltd* [1981] Ch 229, [1980] 2 WLR 339. *Emerald Supplies* (n 131), para 24.

[135] L3587/2007.

fulfil certain conditions with the opportunity to obtain a declaratory action for damages.[136] This mechanism does not seem capable of deterring infringements of competition law and thereby promoting the collective consumer interest of retaining competitive markets. This is because, following the declaratory judgment, consumers themselves would have to prove and claim their individual damage from the infringer, which remains very difficult, despite efforts to assist consumers in proving their claims.[137] Given the low value of consumer claims, and the evidential difficulties in proving their damage, consumers will most likely not act at all, leaving the illegal gains to the infringer.

5.1.3 Financial risk

A further problem, often related to the opt-in structure of the relevant collective action mechanisms, is the funding and implicated financial risk of the respective actions. The financial risk of a collective action is related to the initial funding of the action as well as the obligation to pay the other party's costs. For example, according to the Swedish Group Proceedings Act of 2002 the risk of having to pay both parties' costs should the case fail could act as a strong deterrent to prospective plaintiffs, thereby making Swedish collective action mechanisms possible only for cases involving large individual claims.[138]

Denmark introduced a new law on collective actions, with effect from 2008, which provides for opt-in collective and representative actions as well as opt-out representative actions brought by public authorities (a 'public opt-out' mechanism), eg the Consumer Ombudsman.[139] The problem with the opt-in procedure is the financial risk that it entails for the members of the group, which is unlikely to be accepted for small consumer claims. Due to this problem, an opt-out procedure was introduced as well.[140] This is discussed below.

5.2 Furthering the collective consumer interest

This section focuses on collective action mechanisms that serve the *broad notion of access to justice* and could potentially contribute to deterring anti-competitive practices, thereby promoting the collective consumer interest. The deterrence

---

[136] Article 10(16) L2251/1994; E Alexandridou and M Karipidou, 'Country Report Greece' (Report prepared for Civic Consulting to be submitted to DG SANCO) <http://ec.europa.eu/consumers/redress_cons/gr-country-report-final.pdf> accessed 17 October 2014; E Alexandridou and C Apallagaki, 'Article 10 L. 2251/1994' in Alexandridou (ed), *Consumer Protection Law* (Nomiki Vivliothiki 2008) 555 (in Greek).

[137] Article 10(20) L2251/1994.   [138] Lindblom (n 51) 18.

[139] E Werlauff, 'Class Actions in Denmark—From 2008' (Report prepared for 'The Globalization of Class Actions') <http://globalclassactions.stanford.edu/sites/default/files/documents/Demark_National_Report.pdf> accessed 17 October 2014.

[140] The Report notes that an opt-out procedure is foreign to the Danish legal system. However, in the light of pragmatic considerations, the legislator chose to introduce an opt-out procedure in the end. See Werlauff (n 139) 4.

function of the respective actions is evident given their opt-out elements and the methods employed for the distribution of the damages awards.

The Dutch collective settlement mechanism[141] can be employed as a procedural tool in the collective consumer interest. It is based on an opt-out system and applies only to out-of-court settlements with representative organizations that then need to be approved by the Amsterdam Court of Appeal. It does not provide for litigation in opt-out collective actions, so no pressure can be exerted on a defendant who is reluctant to settle, as is the case under the US class action regime.[142] This settlement mechanism appears very interesting as it succeeds in the reconciliation of a compensatory approach with the protection of the collective interest, since it can influence the future behaviour of potential infringers.

At its inception, the Dutch Act on collective settlements was meant to apply to the resolution of mass-scale personal injury claims (the *DES* case).[143] The *Dexia* case, which concerned damages caused to retail investors by misleading bank information, showed that it could be used for other purposes as well.[144] Moreover, this procedure is not confined to the Netherlands, which thereby raises questions as to whether it could serve as an alternative to US class actions. Cases to date (none in the field of competition law) have pointed to its potential to cater for the interests of foreign parties.[145] Nonetheless, the application of the Dutch collective settlement procedure to foreign parties has been criticized from a private international law perspective and the application and interpretation of the Brussels I Regulation.[146] In addition, courts in other Member States may be reluctant to recognize the Dutch judgment approving the settlement.[147] It exemplifies though the need for similar instruments in other Member States.

Since 1995, Portuguese law has provided for 'popular actions' to be brought by any citizen who enjoys civil and political rights, and by associations and foundations, irrespective of whether they have an interest in the claim or not, with the

---

[141] I Tzankova, 'Class Actions, Group Litigation and Other Forms of Collective Litigation—Dutch Report' (24 September 2007) (Report prepared for 'The Globalization of Class Actions') <http://globalclassactions.stanford.edu/category/categories/country-reports> accessed 16 October 2014; I Tzankova and DL Scheurleer, 'The Netherlands' (2009) The ANNALS (n 84) 149; DL Scheurleer, H Speyart, F Wijers, and J Fanoy, 'Netherlands' in A Foer and J Cuneo (eds), *The International Handbook of Private Enforcement of Competition Law* (Edward Elgar 2010) 375–377.

[142] Tzankova, Report (n 141), para 13.

[143] B Allemeersch, 'Transnational Class Settlements—Lessons from *Converium*' in S Wrbka, S Van Uytsel, and M Siems, *Collective Actions: Enhancing Access to Justice and Reconciling Multilayer Interests?* (CUP 2012) 364, 366–367.

[144] Tzankova, Report (n 141) para 15.

[145] The *Royal Dutch Shell* settlement included members from many European countries in addition to the Netherlands. The application of the Dutch settlement procedure to include foreign members has been more recently reaffirmed in *Converium*, a case that can be distinguished from the former in that it had no connection with the Netherlands. See Allemeersch (n 143).

[146] Council Regulation (EC) No 44/2001 of 22 December 2000 on Jurisdiction and the Recognition and Enforcement of Judgments in Civil and Commercial Matters [2001] L12/1 as amended by Regulation (EU) No 1215/2012 on Jurisdiction and the Recognition and Enforcement of Judgments in Civil and Commercial Matters [2012] L351/1.

[147] Allemeersch (n 143) 371–376.

Public Prosecutor being responsible for protecting legality.[148] Furthermore, the fact that this procedure is of an opt-out character,[149] and that any unclaimed funds go to the Ministry of Justice and towards support for the holders of the right of popular action who seek this justifiably after a period of three years from the date of the judgment,[150] indicates the potential of this procedure to bring compensation to individuals, but, most importantly, to impact on the behaviour of potential infringers.[151]

DECO, the Portuguese consumer association, has brought three actions to date;[152] one ended in a settlement and the other two were withdrawn.[153] In *DECO v Portugal Telecom*,[154] DECO challenged the 'activation charge' imposed on its customers by Portugal Telecom in 1998 and 1999 and asked for this unlawful charge to be returned to consumers. This action covered more than 2 million consumers and only five opted out. One of the legal bases invoked was the abuse of dominance on the part of Portugal Telecom. However, the action succeeded on other grounds and the issue was not discussed.[155] This case is indicative of the potential of this mechanism to benefit consumers. DECO reached a settlement with Portugal Telecom amounting to €120 million, according to which Portugal Telecom undertook not to charge its customers for phone calls made on certain specified dates.

The Spanish Civil Procedure Act 2000 provides for actions to be brought by consumer associations on behalf of identified victims. However, it is also possible for a consumer organization that is representative according to the law to bring an action on behalf of identifiable consumers.[156] Furthermore, the law provides that, when consumers cannot be individually determined, 'the judgment shall establish the details, features and requirements necessary to demand payment and, where appropriate, to apply for or take part in the enforcement of the judgment if requested by the claimant association'.[157] This provision, together with the one

---

[148] H Sousa Antunes, 'Class Actions, Group Litigation and Other Forms of Collective Litigation: Portuguese Report' (Report prepared for 'The Globalization of Class Actions') <http://globalclassactions.stanford.edu/sites/default/files/documents/Portugal_National_Report.pdf> accessed 17 October 2014, 6.

[149] Sousa Antunes (n 148) 13.   [150] Sousa Antunes (n 148) 27.

[151] Green Paper on Consumer Collective Redress (n 7), para 12 ('the collective redress scheme that reached the most people in a single case is in Portugal').

[152] Hodges (n 62) 40. The scarce application of the respective law (L. 83/95) can be attributed to the immature stage of the civil society's development, the prohibition of contingency agreements, or to doubts raised in regard to the application of the respective law: see Sousa Antunes (n 147) 20.

[153] Rodger (n 85) 181–182.

[154] On this case see R Mulheron, 'Competition Law Cases under the Opt-out Regimes of Australia, Canada and Portugal' (Research Paper for Submission to BERR, 10 October 2008) 77–78.

[155] Rodger (n 85) 181–182.

[156] On the distinction between multi-party and the collective interest in Spanish law and its impact on the standing requirement see F Gomez and M Gili, 'Country Report Spain' (Report prepared for Civic Consulting to be submitted to DG SANCO) (25 February 2008) <http://ec.europa.eu/consumers/redress_cons/sp-country-report-final.pdf> accessed 17 October 2014, 6.

[157] P Gutiérrez de Cabiedes Hidalgo, 'Group Litigation in Spain' (Report prepared for 'The Globalization of Class Actions') <http://globalclassactions.stanford.edu/sites/default/files/documents/spain_national_report.pdf> accessed 17 October 2014, 9.

providing for *res judicata* to be extended to non-litigants as well,[158] suggests that Spanish representative actions incorporate opt-out elements. Nonetheless, it may be more accurately categorized as reverse opt-in, inasmuch as consumers need to get involved in the process. Currently, following the Commission decision in *Telefonica*,[159] a Spanish consumer association (Ausbanc Consumo) filed a claim for damages against Telefonica for harm suffered by consumers in the Spanish market.[160] This case is still pending and it will be interesting to see the outcome following Telefonica's appeal rejection by the ECJ.

Another example of an opt-out procedure comes from Denmark, where the Danish Consumer Ombudsman can bring an opt-out collective action on behalf of consumers. In 2010 this was extended to include competition law violations.[161] This procedure can be applied for claims up to DKK 2,000 (approximately €270) that cannot be brought individually.[162] Granting standing to the Danish Consumer Ombudsman acts as a public safety valve on the alleged excesses of opt-out class actions.

In the UK, following a long debate over the need to introduce opt-out mechanisms,[163] these have finally been adopted with the Consumer Rights Act that amends the CA 1998.[164] The Consumer Rights Act provides for opt-in and opt-out collective actions before the CAT together with an opt-out settlement procedure. The CAT has also issued Draft Tribunal Rules for the conduct of such proceedings.[165]

The salient points of the proposed collective action regime are as follows: (a) First, an action can be brought by any representative (and thus is not confined to consumer organizations), provided that the CAT authorizes that person to act as a representative (Article 47B(2), (5), and (8));[166] (b) The CAT retains an enhanced role throughout the procedure, since—apart from the authorization of the representative plaintiff—it has to approve that the claims raise similar or

---

[158] Ibid 8.
[159] *Wanadoo España v Telefonica* [Case COMP/38.784] Commission Decision of 4 July 2007. On appeal before the GC, see Case T-336/07 *Telefónica and Telefónica de España v Commission* [2007] OJ C269/55 (judgment delivered on 29 March 2012); on appeal before the CJEU, C-295/12P *Telefónica and Telefónica de España v Commission* (judgment of 10 July 2014).
[160] Commission (EC), 'Annex to the Report on Competition Policy' (Staff Working Document) SEC(2008) 2038, para 19.
[161] Rodger (n 85) 166–167.
[162] Ashton and Henry (n 123) para 6.133 with references to the explanatory notes in the draft Danish legislation.
[163] OFT (n 120); CJC Report (n 120); Ministry of Justice, 'The Government's Response to the Civil Justice Council's Report: "Improving Access to Justice through Collective Actions"' (July 2009); BIS, 'Private Actions in Competition Law: A Consultation on Options for Reform—Government Response' (January 2013).
[164] The Consumer Rights Act received Royal Assent in March 2015. The relevant changes to private competition law enforcement are included in section 81 and Schedule 8.
[165] Draft Competition Appeal Tribunal Rules 2015, Part V <https://www.gov.uk/government/uploads/system/uploads/attachment_data/file/401972/bis-15-76-draft-competition-appeal-tribunal-rules-2015.pdf> accessed 8 May 2015.
[166] References are made to the provisions of the CA 1998, as amended by the Consumer Rights Act.

related factual and legal issues and are suitable for a collective action (Article 47B(6)) and calculate the damages award on a lump sum basis, without having to estimate the damage for each person. Exemplary damages cannot be awarded in collective procedures (Article 47C(2), (3), (5), and (6)). The CAT issues a collective proceedings order, which is akin to certification, that includes authorization of the representative, a description of a class of persons, and the specification of the proceedings as opt-in collective proceedings or opt-out (Article 47B(7)); and (c) The collective action can be brought as opt-in or opt-out, whichever is suitable (Article 47B(7), (10), and (11)). Contrary to the Dutch collective settlement mechanism, the opt-out collective action covers only persons domiciled in the UK, unless they actively opt-in (Article 47B(11)). In addition, it would appear that contingency fees are not available for opt-out proceedings, since 'a damages-based agreement[167] is unenforceable if it relates to opt-out collective proceedings' (Article 47C(8)). The new procedure provides for cy-près distribution, since any unclaimed funds may be paid to the Access to Justice Foundation or to the representative plaintiff (Article 47C(5), and (6)).[168]

The Consumer Rights Act also makes provision for the approval of collective settlements by the CAT provided that the terms of the settlement are just and reasonable (Article 49A and 49B).[169]

5.3 Synopsis

The analysis can be summarized in the following two observations. First, national procedures (despite their respective differences and with a few notable exceptions) are not fit to address low value consumer claims in competition law. At the same time, a bird's eye view of national procedures suggests that functional solutions exist and their functionality relies heavily on the opt-out model. Inasmuch as the opt-out model deprives the group members of control of the litigation, it calls for additional safeguards. These safeguards are primarily related to the nature of the representative plaintiff and the court's role in supervising the procedure.

The second observation reveals the important role of representative plaintiffs, either consumer organizations or public bodies, in raising collective actions, which is intertwined with Member States' legal traditions, unlike the situation in the

---

[167] According to Article 47C(9)b, '"damages-based agreement" has the meaning given in section 58AA(3) of the Courts and Legal Services Act 1990"' that refers to conditional fee agreements between a lawyer and his client.

[168] Article 47C(5) provides that 'subject to subsection (6), where the Tribunal makes an award of damages in opt-out collective proceedings, any damages not claimed by the represented persons within a specified period must be paid to the charity for the time being prescribed by order made by the Lord Chancellor under section 194(8) of the Legal Services Act 2007'. The Access to Justice Foundation is the charity prescribed by the Lord Chancellor. Legal Services Act 2007 (Prescribed Charity) Order 2008, SI 2008/2680.

[169] Article 49C provides for the approval of redress schemes by the CMA. This mechanism is discussed in Chapter 6. Whether the newly introduced collective action proceedings will prove effective depends on the CAT's interpretation of the respective provisions in the light of the respective Tribunal Rules.

US. This has been acknowledged by the Commission in its proposal on representative actions, which emphasizes the role of consumer organizations.[170] Drawing on national mechanisms, the different types of representatives can be located on a spectrum: from purely private, namely lead plaintiffs, to purely public, ie public bodies like the Consumer Ombudsman, with certified consumer organizations occupying the middle ground between public and private. When shifting from public to private on this spectrum, the court's role should be enhanced in order to act as a safety valve for possible excesses of collective actions. The new UK regime can be given here as an example.

When discussing the desirability and feasibility of an EU collective action model, national experiences to date can function as a useful roadmap. At the same time, one should not lose sight of the fact that in this area, namely national procedural rules, it is hard to achieve a common denominator for all Member States; a delicate balancing exercise should take place, on the one hand, between the structural characteristics that are desired in principle (and indeed already in place in certain Member States) and, on the other, their potential to be accommodated under national procedural rules. For example, the role of the class counsel in the US can, under certain safeguards, spur class actions. If Member States oppose the idea of such active lawyer participation, the policymakers need to look at alternatives and come up with modified solutions as to how to spur collective actions. Consumer organizations could provide a valid alternative to the US class counsel model. Inasmuch as opt-out mechanisms are not—completely—alien to national collective action systems, emphasis should be placed on their proliferation coupled with certain public safeguards known to the EU legal traditions. The private/public consumer Ombudsman model can be given here as an example.

6. Structuring the Appropriate EU Collective Action Mechanism

The aim in this section is to structure an effective collective action mechanism that enables the effective enforcement of EU competition law and the enforcement of consumer rights, since, as the Commission concedes:

Effective enforcement of EU law is of utmost importance for citizens and businesses alike...Rights which cannot be enforced in practice are worthless. Where substantive EU rights are infringed, citizens and businesses must be able to enforce the rights granted to them by EU legislation.[171]

The analysis is informed by the historical, normative, and pragmatic arguments discussed above and will show that the Commission Recommendation, while

---

[170] WP SWP (n 1), paras 49–50; Commission (EC), 'Annex to the Green Paper, Damages Actions for Breach of the EC Antitrust Rules' (Staff Working Paper) SEC(2005) 1732, 19 December 2005 (GP SWP), paras 198–200.
[171] Public Consultation (n 4) para 1.

constituting an important development, will fail to introduce effective collective action mechanisms for low value consumer claims.

The Commission, since it acknowledged the wide diversity in the existing national collective redress systems and the impediment this poses to the effective enforcement of EU rights, has aimed at proposing mechanisms that conform to the EU legal tradition while ensuring the effective enforcement of EU law.[172] However, the diverse national approaches to collective redress suggest that, while there are some common recurring characteristics, there is no uniform EU legal tradition. In the light of this observation, the above tour d'horizon of national collective action systems suggests that the Commission can indeed build on the existing approaches and glean those functional characteristics that are fit to address low value consumer claims in competition law. In addition, in line with Member States' approaches, safeguards need to be devised that could take the form of public control elements upon private enforcement procedures, for example, granting standing to bring claims to public bodies, involving public bodies in the management and distribution of the damages awards, and strengthening the courts' role in supervising the proceedings.

Furthermore, despite their differences, the US system has more to offer the current European efforts to devise effective collective redress mechanisms. While it is true that 'the American paradigm is clearly unsuitable for wholesale export to foreign legal systems',[173] the piecemeal adoption of certain features of this system cannot be said to amount to wholesale export,[174] but rather an adjustment to the EU legal environment that calls for increased public control over private litigation in line with the collective redress models already in place in certain Member States.

This section critically discusses and, where necessary, deconstructs the 'basic principles' that, according to the Commission, should be present in national collective redress schemes in order to promote access to justice.[175] The Commission recommendation discussed principles on standing, funding, and the court's role, while aiming at preventing abuses and conflict of interest.

6.1 Standing: Lead plaintiff, public body, or consumer organization

The Commission Recommendation briefly mentioned group actions, ie actions brought jointly by those claiming damages, without delving into the lead plaintiff's role and the counsel's role.[176] The common principles on standing discussed

---

[172] Public Consultation (n 4) paras 10, 12.

[173] R Faulk, 'Armageddon through Aggregation? The Use and Abuse of Class Actions in International Dispute Resolution' in C Rickett and T Telfer (eds), *International Perspectives on Consumers' Access to Justice* (CUP 2003) 330, 353.

[174] Essentially this corresponds to what Gidi terms a 'responsible transplant'. Gidi (n 27) 314, 403. For a similar argument see R O'Donoghue, 'Europe's Long March Towards Antitrust Damages Actions' (April 2011) (2) CPI 1, 5.

[175] Commission Recommendation (n 3), recital 10.

[176] Commission Recommendation (n 3), recital 17.

focused on representative actions and examined three possibilities, namely standing granted to ad hoc certified entities, entities certified by law, or public bodies that can prove their *financial and administrative capacity* to bring the representative action.[177] The principles on standing are in line with both the Commission's past policy documents that, unsurprisingly, favoured collective actions brought by consumer organizations,[178] and national collective action models.[179]

The Commission Recommendation states that Member States afford standing to representative organizations based on clearly defined conditions of eligibility that include: the non-profit making nature of the organization; the aim of the representative organization being related to the protected EU law rights; and the financial and actual capability to bring the action. Representative organizations should be certified prior to bringing the collective action. Alternatively, collective actions can be brought by ad hoc certified entities or public bodies.[180]

This represents a balanced proposal and largely reflects the national procedures in place. Granting standing to consumer organizations and public bodies addresses the principal-agent problem provided that the issue of legitimacy and representation is resolved (standing safety valves).[181] Furthermore, granting standing to public bodies is an option worth exploring inasmuch as collective actions further the collective consumer interest and, historically, in some EU countries public authorities have been entrusted with the protection of the public interest.[182]

However, the Commission Recommendation only refers to general conditions for granting standing to representative organizations, namely their non-profit nature; their relevant aims; and their ability to bring a claim. Thus, the specification of those conditions affords great leeway to Member States and more specific guidelines would have been welcome. In that regard, the Commission's reference to the Aarhus Convention may be instructive.[183] In its previous consultation document, the Commission made reference to certain Member States implementing the Aarhus Convention and requiring representative organizations to fulfil certain criteria in terms of their period of existence, the geographical scope of their activities, and their member base.[184] Regulation 1367/2006 on the application of

---

[177] Commission Recommendation (n 3), recital 18, para 3(d).
[178] GP (n 14), para 2.5; WP (n 14), para 2.1; See Draft Damages Directive (n 15), Article 5.
[179] See section 5 of this chapter. This is also the prevailing approach in EU consumer law. See C Hodges, 'Competition Enforcement, Regulation and Civil Justice: What is the Case?' (2006) 43 CMLRev 1381, 1387. F Cafaggi and HW Micklitz, 'Collective Enforcement of Consumer Law: A Framework for Comparative Assessment' (2008) 16 ERPL 391, 417.
[180] Commission Recommendation (n 3), paras 4–7.
[181] See Hodges (n 179) 1391, discussing the legitimacy of consumer organizations based on the five tests developed by Baldwin, ie legislative mandate, accountability, due process, expertise, and efficiency. See R Baldwin, *Rules and Government* (Clarendon Press 1995). See also OD Epstein, 'Representation of Consumer Interest by Consumer Associations—Salvation for the Masses?' (2007) 3 Comp L Rev 209 on the problems faced by consumer organizations and ways of addressing them. On the criticism against class counsel see text to n 69.
[182] H Koch, 'Non-Class Group Litigation under EU and German Law' (2001) 11 Duke J Comp & Int'l L 355, 358.
[183] Commission Recommendation (n 3), recital 23.
[184] Public Consultation (n 4), para 25.

the Aarhus Convention to EU institutions specifies the conditions that an NGO must satisfy in order to make an application for internal review of an EU act or omission. These criteria, as provided in the Regulation implementing the Aarhus Convention, include the non-profit nature of the representative entity, its primary stated objective (promotion of environmental protection), and its existence for more than two years prior to the date of the action.[185]

Analogous criteria could have been formulated more explicitly by the Commission in its Recommendation and this should be the way forward in any future initiative on collective redress in the field of competition law.[186] Standing can be granted to designated or ad hoc certified consumer organizations. In terms of legal certainty the former is preferable; nonetheless, the courts' supervisory role in the latter should provide adequate safeguards regarding the avoidance of speculative litigation.

Furthermore, the conditions for certification should be harmonized and these can act as guidance for the courts in cases of ad hoc certification. Member States should notify the authorized entities to the Commission, which should maintain a list of all designated organizations EU wide;[187] a list akin to the existing one that lists the entities qualified to bring an action under the Injunctions Directive.[188] Certification of consumer organizations in each Member State based on the EU criteria may further foster informal cooperation and the exchange of information on contemplated collective actions.

To sum up, the Commission's approach to standing in its Recommendation is overall heading in the right direction, since the US model based on the role of the lead plaintiff is alien to Member States' legal systems and approach to legal services and does not present a viable option.[189] While not excluding actions

---

[185] Article 11 of Council Regulation (EC) 1367/2006 of 6 September 2006 on the Application of the Provisions of the Aarhus Convention on Access to Information, Public Participation in Decision Making and Access to Justice in Environmental Matters to Community Institutions and Bodies [2006] OJ L264/13. For a discussion of the Aarhus Convention see B Richardson and J Razzaque, 'Public Participation in Environmental Decision Making' in B Richardson and S Wood (eds), *Environmental Law for Sustainability: A Reader* (Hart 2006) 165, 174–177. See also Eliantonio (n 24) 261 on the national approaches to environmental NGOs.

[186] Cf Article 7 of the Draft Damages Directive (n 15). See also EP Resolution (n 17), para 20, which also asks for the designation of European criteria for designated consumer organizations, but points to Article 3 of Directive 2009/22/EC on injunctions. In favour of adopting EU-wide binding rules on standing for environmental NGOs see Eliantonio (n 24) 270.

[187] Cf Article 7(4) of the Draft Damages Directive (n 15). Other proposals to help national courts with the certification of ad hoc entities and case management include setting up training programmes for judges via the European Judicial Network. See ELI, 'Statement of the European Law Institute on Collective Redress and Competition Damages Claims' (2014) <http://www.europeanlawinstitute.eu/fileadmin/user_upload/p_eli/Projects/S-5-2014_Statement_on_Collective_Redress_and_Competition_Damages_Claims.pdf> accessed 10 April 2015, 15–16, 25–26.

[188] Injunctions Directive (n 28), Article 4(3); Commission (EU), Communication Concerning Article 4(3) of Directive 2009/22/EC of the European Parliament and of the Council on Injunctions for the Protection of Consumers' Interests, which Codifies Directive 98/27/EC, Concerning the Entities Qualified to Bring an Action under Article 2 of this Directive (2014) C115/1.

[189] However, this might change in the near future in the light of the opening of European offices by major US plaintiff firms. See C Cook, 'Private Enforcement of EU Competition Law in Member State Courts: Experience to Date and the Path Ahead' (2008) 4(2) CPI 3, 64.

brought by a lead plaintiff, it focuses on representative actions brought by either private organizations or public bodies that are closer to national collective action mechanisms. In a future binding proposal on collective redress, standing should be afforded both to representative organizations and public bodies with the conditions for authorization being further explored and elaborated upon. In addition, provision should be made for publishing an EU-wide registry of authorized entities.

6.2 Forming the group: Opt-in v opt-out

The basic principles on standing in the Commission Recommendation would have unravelled their potential as 'safety valves' to collective litigation had they been combined with the opt-out principle on group formation. According to the Recommendation, however, the formation of the claimant group is based on the opt-in principle, though the Commission accepts possible exceptions to this basic principle by either law or court order that must 'be duly justified by reasons of sound administration of justice'.[190] Claimants should be able to leave or, conversely, join the group until the issuance of the final judgment (or settlement).[191] The basic principle on group formation is in stark contrast to the Commission proposal in the Draft Damages Directive[192] and can be explained in the light of the criticism that resulted in the withdrawal of this document.[193] However, the experience in national legal systems suggests that opt-in mechanisms are not workable for minor consumer claims.[194] This is supported by a recent study on collective redress in competition law conducted on behalf of the EU Parliament's Committee on Economic and Monetary Affairs.[195] Furthermore, there are examples of opt-out procedures in some Member States,[196] which suggests that 'the dogma of individual litigation control—the "exaggerated individualism"...'[197]—has already begun to crumble.

If the principle of opt-out group formation is combined with certain safety valves, it follows that the risk of speculative litigation is minimized. The safety

---

[190] Commission Recommendation (n 3), para 21.
[191] Commission Recommendation (n 3), paras 22–23.
[192] WP (n 15), para 2.1 on the proposal to introduce actions on behalf of identifiable victims; Draft Damages Directive (n 15), Article 6(4) ('any injured party belonging to the group can exercise its right not to be represented').
[193] See the European People's Party's statements (the leading party in the previous European Parliament) that it would not support any kind of opt-out system. See Tait, 'EU Rules to Ease Burdens on Antitrust Victims', *The Financial Times* (London 26 June 2009). See also EP Resolution (n 17), para 10. ELI (n 187) 13–14.
[194] For the experience in UK and France see text to nn 109–118.
[195] Parliament (n 2) 11.
[196] R Gaudet, 'Turning a Blind Eye: The Commission's Rejection of Opt-out Class Actions Overlooks Swedish, Norwegian, Danish and Dutch Experience' (2009) 30 ECLR 107; J Delatre, 'Beyond the White Paper: Rethinking the Commission's Proposal on Private Antitrust Litigation' (2008) 8 Comp L Rev 29, 30.
[197] R Cappalli and C Consolo, 'Class Actions for Continental Europe? A Preliminary Inquiry' (2001) Temple Int'l & Comp LJ 217, 264.

valves are relevant for the rights of the group members as well as the defendant; some have already been employed in some Member States, such as the nature of the representative (eg a public body) and the role of the court in authorizing the action to proceed as an opt-out collective action.[198] Furthermore, the legislature should be cautious in devising the necessary notice mechanisms, and it would be for the court to decide whether an action proceeds as opt-out provided that notification and due process rights were observed.

The individualistic model of litigation, according to which each claimant retains control of the litigation, may appear irreconcilable with the opt-out principle, which is perceived as amounting to a violation of the due process rights of individual group members.[199] In addition, the opt-out principle may be seen as contrary to Article 6 ECHR and Article 47 of the Charter of Fundamental Rights.[200] Nonetheless, concerns over the rights of individual group members can be disbursed if procedural guarantees, including adequate notice mechanisms, are devised.[201] From a pragmatic perspective and in support of opt-out mechanisms, US empirical studies are particularly instructive and suggest that in the case of very low individual damage, opt-out rates are miniscule.[202] Thus, instead of renouncing the opt-out model, the Commission should have stressed that this represents the only workable mechanism for group formation in the case of minimal consumer claims and provided in the Recommendation that this mechanism may exceptionally be employed for very low value claims under court supervision, if this is the best alternative to the prevailing opt-in model. The supervisory role should ideally be granted to either specialized courts (as is the case with the CAT in England) or higher courts (as is the case with the Amsterdam Court of Appeal under the Dutch model) in the light of their experience and the desirability and potential to develop the necessary expertise. The EU Commission or NCA could also act as *amicus curiae* at the stage of certification.

6.3 Distribution of the damages award

Opt-out collective actions are further criticized as contrary to the compensatory approach to private enforcement, since they may result in individual

---

[198] See, for example, the CAT's role in the certification process under the Consumer Rights Act. Text to nn 163–169. Rule 78 Draft Competition Appeal Tribunal Rules 2015 (n 165).

[199] See Stadler (n 110) 211 in which she accepts though that '[opt-in collective actions] most likely do not constitute a solution to minor and dispersed damages'.

[200] Leuven Report (n 31) 380. See Wrbka (n 48), which rejects this argument, with references to the ECtHR jurisprudence. See Magnier, Report (n 111) 12–13, 17–18 for an account of the French legal system, which in principle rejects the opt-out. However, the new law on collective actions has adopted a model with opt-out elements. See text to nn 125–126.

[201] CJC Report (n 118) 133; J Stuyck, 'Class Actions in Europe? To Opt-In or to Opt-Out, that is the Question' [2009] EBLR 483, 491. Adequate notice is important in US class actions. Interestingly, Dam questions whether the requirement of individual notice rests on FRCP, Rule 23 or the Due Process clause of the Fifth Amendment. Dam (n 91) 109.

[202] See Eisenberg and Miller (n 59) 4. S Issacharoff, 'Preclusion, Due Process and the Right to Opt-out' (2002) 77 Notre Dame L Rev 1057, 1060 where he points out that 'an individual litigant who is unlikely to sue outside an aggregate action is similarly unlikely to exercise a right to opt-out into the domain of unviable individual claims'.

group members remaining uncompensated. The opt-out structure affects the quantification[203] as well as the distribution of the damages award. The collective action model proposed herein (from a normative perspective) furthers the collective consumer interest, while not disregarding the individual consumer interest.

In terms of the quantification of the damages award, the opt-out principle guiding the group formation points towards the employment of alternative models since it is not possible to provide an exhaustive list of all of the members of the group and quantify their individual damage.[204] An alternative approach rests on the calculation of the damages award based on the illegal profits.

Opt-out collective actions have the potential to deliver compensation to a larger number of individual consumers provided that the latter exercise their right to claim compensation from the damages awarded. Therefore, any distribution mechanism should first accord priority to the exercise of the consumer right to damages in the light of the EU courts' case law.[205] In effect, the Draft Damages Directive has taken this approach since it provides that damages should primarily be distributed to individual victims and that a part of the damages award should revert back to the consumer organization bringing the action, in order to cover the litigation expenses.[206]

Thus, in the light of the EU right to damages and the nature and function of opt-out collective actions for minor consumer claims, distribution of damages should combine both individual distribution and cy-près distribution.[207] Cy-près distribution presents a pragmatic solution and is particularly fitted to addressing distribution problems in opt-out collective actions. Mulheron has extensively examined the US and Canadian case law on cy-près and formulated the following conditions under which cy-près distribution would be particularly suitable:

1. Individual recovery should be extremely low;
2. The identities of class members are unknown for the purposes of distribution;
3. It is very likely that some, or all, class members will not come forward;
4. The identity of class members constantly changes; and
5. Distribution is particularly difficult due to the large number of class members.[208]

---

[203] This section does not address the complex issue of damages calculation for competition law violations. On this issue see Commission (EU), 'Staff Working Document—Practical Guide—Quantifying Harm in Actions for Damages Based on Breaches of Article 101 or 102 of the Treaty on the Functioning of the European Union' SWD (2013) (205) (Strasbourg, 11 June 2013).
[204] See HB Schäfer, 'The Bundling of Similar Interests in Litigation. The Incentives for Class Actions and Legal Actions Taken by Associations' (2000) 9 Eur JL & Econ 183, 201 ('it is conceivable to waive the requirement of providing an exhaustive list of the injured persons if this is unreasonable and to calculate the total loss on the basis of probabilities instead').
[205] This excludes skimming off procedures and the reverting of the damages to the State.
[206] Draft Damages Directive (n 15), Article 6(5). On the Commission contemplating alternative distribution mechanisms see WP SWP (n 1), paras 47, 52, 56; GP SWP (n 170), para 199.
[207] See R Mulheron, *The Modern Cy-près Doctrine* (UCL 2006) 1–5 for a definition of 'cy-près'. As Mulheron notes, the cy-près doctrine extends to both the calculation and distribution of damages. Ibid 224.
[208] Ibid 259–263.

The above-mentioned conditions will most likely be present in opt-out consumer collective actions for competition law violations.

The distribution mechanism advocated herein resembles the US approach[209] but has the advantage that it is clearly embedded in legislation and, therefore, addresses the criticism aired against the courts about judicial innovation when devising cy-près solutions for the distribution of damages awards.[210] The court-supervised cy-près distribution established by EU legislation acts as an additional safety valve to opt-out collective actions.

The subsequent question is how damages distribution should be structured in a future EU legislative provision (see Table 5.1 below). The option would be for consumers to claim individually, an amount to cover the litigation expenses of the consumer organization and the remaining amount to go into a fund. In the light of the UK solution, the remaining amount of the award goes to a public service organization. Alternatively, the legislation could provide for the establishment of a consumer fund,[211] but this is a more complex solution and should be left to the discretion of the Member States. The establishment of a consumer fund would aim at furthering the consumer interest by, for example, undertaking consumer education campaigns.[212] This distribution mechanism could also apply in cases of 'public compensation', discussed in Chapter 6.

Table 5.1 Distribution of Damages: The Spectrum Serving Deterrence and Compensation (from Individual to Collective Consumer Interest)

Compensation to consumers (individual interest)	The remaining amount reverts (1) to the consumer organization to cover its litigation expenses and the bringing of similar actions in the future and (2) to a charity or an established consumer fund (collective interest)

6.4 Costs and funding of collective actions

Safety valves should be put in place for the funding of collective consumer actions. These rules will be influenced and dependent upon the adopted rules on standing. If standing is accorded to representative consumer organizations, funding rules should be structured accordingly.[213]

---

[209] In view of the due process clause, individual claimants cannot be precluded from claiming their damages leaving the sum remaining for cy-près distribution. See Dam (n 94) 62.
[210] On the structural and constitutional problems of the cy-près doctrine in the US see M Redish, P Julian, and S Zyontz, 'Cy Pres Relief and the Pathologies of the Modern Class Action: A Normative and Empirical Analysis' (2010) 62 Fla L Rev 617, 641–649.
[211] See K Barnett, 'Equitable Trusts: An Effective Remedy in Consumer Class Actions' (1987) 96 Yale LJ 1591, 1609–1614 for a proposal for an equitable trust upon court discretion.
[212] Howells favours this option. See Howells (n 103) 59.
[213] See BEUC, 'Damages Actions for Breach of EC Antitrust Rules—BEUC Response to the White Paper' <http://ec.europa.eu/competition/antitrust/actionsdamages/white_paper_comments/beuc_en.pdf> 11, accepting that 'financing legal action is also a problem for consumer organisations themselves. This is why at the moment [they] are not able to represent consumers in competition cases'.

In terms of the funding of collective actions, the Commission Recommendation provides that the representative body should have the necessary financial capacity to bring the action.[214] Nonetheless, it does not exclude third party funding, as long as the court is satisfied that there is no conflict of interest between the funder, the representative organization, and its members and that the third party funder can meet its financial obligations.[215] Furthermore, national legislation needs to ensure that if third party funding is available, then the third party does not influence the process, does not engage in litigation that raises a conflict of interest, and does not charge excessive interest on the available funds.[216] However, the Commission Recommendation excludes the funder's remuneration being based on a percentage of the damages awarded, which may defeat the purpose of employing third party funders in the first place.[217]

Furthermore, the Recommendation is negative towards contingency fees, and calls for the Member States that employ such mechanisms to provide the necessary legislation for the control of such mechanisms in the area of collective redress. This is in line with the approach in the Consumer Rights Act.[218] Contingency fees, despite their success in funding class action litigation,[219] are alien to many national legal systems in Europe.[220] In addition, even when contingency fee arrangements are introduced, claimants and their lawyers may appear reluctant to use them due to their complexity.[221]

In the light of the financial constraints facing consumer organizations, if they are afforded standing for consumer collective actions, it does not suffice to state, as the Commission does in its Recommendation, 'that they should have the necessary financial capacity'.[222] If we opt for the exclusion of contingency fees, then we

---

[214] Commission Recommendation (n 3), para 4(c).
[215] Commission Recommendation (n 3), para 15.
[216] Commission Recommendation (n 3), para 16.
[217] Commission Recommendation (n 3), para 32.   [218] See text to n 167.
[219] M Sittenreich, 'The Rocky Path for Private Directors General: Procedures, Politics and the Uncertain Future of EU Antitrust Damages Actions' (2010) 78 Fordm L Rev 2701, 2735 with further references. See also, in the European context, Joined Cases C-94/04 and C-202/04 *Federicco Cipolla v Rosaria Fasari and others* [2006] ECR I-11421, Opinion of AG Maduro, para 94f.
[220] Very few Member States accept contingency fee arrangements. See Ashurst Study (n 84) 93–94, 116. K Viitanen, 'The Crisis of the Welfare State, Privatisation and Consumers' Access to Justice' in T Wilhelmsson and S Hurri (eds), *From Dissonance to Sense: Welfare State Expectations, Privatisation and Private Law* (Ashgate 1999) 549, 562. Contingency fees are permitted in Germany since 2008 following the ruling of the German Constitutional Court (BVerfG, 1 BvR 2576/04 vom 12.12.2006). See also C Hodges, S Vogenauer, and M Tulibacka, 'Part I' in C Hodges, S Vogenauer, and M Tulibacka (eds), *The Costs and Funding of Civil Litigation: A Comparative Perspective* (Hart 2010) 26. Contingency fees are also permitted in Spain. See MA Calzdilla Medina and others, 'Spain' in C Hodges, S Vogenauer, and M Tulibacka (eds), *The Costs and Funding of Civil Litigation: A Comparative Perspective* (Hart 2010) 492. See also C Leskinen, 'Collective Actions: Rethinking Funding and National Cost Rules' (2011) 8 Comp L Rev 87, 98–105.
[221] For the situation in the UK and the limited use of Damages-Based Agreements (DBA) introduced by the Jackson reform see T Bolster, 'The Structure and Funding of Competition Claims Post-Jackson—"All Change" or "Status Quo"?' (2014) Comp Law 202, 206–207. The Consumer Rights Act provides that DBA are unenforceable in opt-out collective actions. See new s 47(c) 8 CA 1998. See also BIS, 'Private Actions in Competition Law: A Consultation on Options for Reform—Government Response' (January 2013), paras 5.62–5.63.
[222] See text to n 214.

need to cater for the need to strengthen the capacity of consumer organizations. As suggested above, this could be done via retaining a portion of the damages award. Another option would be to support recognized consumer organizations through public funding.[223] Restricting funding to consumer organizations that own resources via their membership revenues is not viable, as even consumer organizations with wide membership would still need additional resources. In addition, such a model, even if workable, would result in members subsidizing the compensation of non-members. The other option is for funding to be obtained solely through commercial operations, as the example of the UK consumer organization Which? suggests.[224] However, this would impose a heavy burden on less-developed consumer organizations.

Other options include the creation of a consumer fund aimed at financing consumer organization collective actions and other activities furthering the collective consumer interest.[225] As discussed above, a proportion of damages awards from collective actions could go into this fund.[226] A proportion of public fines could also subsidize this fund.[227] Thus, any future EU legislation should allow for the funding of consumer organizations from different resources (own funds, consumer funds, and public funding).

Apart from securing funding for consumer organizations, their capacity to bring collective actions would be improved if the 'loser pays' rule (that exists in the majority of Member States)[228] were relaxed.[229] This has already been adopted to a limited extent at EU level in the field of enforcement of IP rights and small claims procedures.[230] For example, Article 14 of Directive 2004/48 provides that

---

[223] See, for example, the provision of funding to EU consumer organizations. Council Decision 1926/2006/EC of 18 December 2006 Establishing a Programme of Community Action in the Field of Consumer Policy (2007–2013) [2006] OJ L404/39, Article 4(1)(c), Annex II and Article 5. Regulation (EU) No 254/2014 of the European Parliament and of the Council of 26 February 2014 on a Multiannual Consumer Programme for the Years 2014–20 and repealing Decision No 1926/2006/EC [2014] OJ L84/42, Article 5.

[224] See A Gunn, 'How Which? Chooses What to Campaign On' (Presentation at the CCP Conference 'Problem Markets') (12 June 2014) <http://competitionpolicy.ac.uk/documents/107435/6361808/Ashleye+Gunn+-+CCP+Conference+2014.pdf/5dbb63b4-825e-4419-a91e-49a1307789b0> accessed 28 November 2014.

[225] See A Riley and J Peysner, 'Damages in EC Antitrust Actions: Who Pays the Piper?' (2006) ELRev 748, 756–757, 760–761 in support of a contingency legal aid fund (and ways to collect initial start-up capital).

[226] See text to n 211.

[227] The proposal to establish a European fund financed by fines imposed on companies for infringements of EU competition law is relevant here. See Committee on the Internal Market and Consumer Protection, 'Towards a Coherent European Approach to Collective Redress' (Opinion) (12/10/2011) (2011/2089(INI)), para 28. See also BEUC, 'Litigation Funding in Relation to the Establishment of a European Mechanism of Collective Redress' (2/2/12) <http://www.beuc.org/publications/2012-00074-01-e.pdf> accessed 17 October 2014.

[228] GP SWP (n 170), paras 204, 212. WP SWP (n 1), para 252f.

[229] Lindblom (n 51) 19 stating that this rule, which operates in Sweden, is a crucial factor in the rarity of collective actions. BEUC (n 213) 7. Gidi (n 27) 340 argues that the one-way fee shifting has facilitated collective litigation in Brazil.

[230] See Article 14 of Council Directive 2004/48/EC of 29 April 2004 on the enforcement of intellectual property rights [2004] OJ L195/16; Article 16 of Council Regulation (EC) 861/2007 of 11 July 2007 Establishing a European Small Claims Procedure [2007] OJ L199/1.

'Member States shall ensure that reasonable and proportionate legal costs and other expenses incurred by the successful party shall, as a general rule, be borne by the unsuccessful party, unless equity does not allow this'. A similar provision could be adopted for the enforcement of consumer rights in competition law.

7. Conclusion

The collective action mechanisms proposed herein constitute—strictly speaking—a model of private enforcement, since it relies on raising collective claims before national courts. At the same time though it entails elements of public control from the launching of the action to the distribution of the damages award. Thus, it can be presented as an example of the—often unnoticed—interplay between different public and private enforcement models and thus calls for a closer examination of the respected synergies. The nature of the problem, ie redressing minor consumer damage, calls for tailored enforcement solutions that are located midway between pure private and pure public models of enforcement on the enforcement spectrum, which points to a fused approach to competition law enforcement, which will be explored further in Chapter 6, this time starting from the perspective of public enforcement.

The analysis presented in this chapter examined the question of structuring collective action mechanisms to enable increased consumer involvement in EU competition law enforcement. A critical overview of the Commission's approach towards collective action mechanisms, both in the fields of consumer and competition law, was provided (section 2), in order to introduce the subsequent discussion on the normative justifications for adopting different collective action mechanisms for low value consumer claims in competition law as opposed to a general horizontal approach to collective actions as advocated by the Commission in its Recommendation (section 3). The definition of the 'access to justice' ideal, and the employment of the distinction between the aggregation of individual consumer interests and the collective consumer interest, points to the different goals pursued by each group of claims, a fact that should be reflected in the measures adopted. Aggregation mechanisms are employed in three distinct scenarios: to improve procedural efficiency; to encourage litigation in that they alter claimants' incentives in that direction; and to allow the aggregation of otherwise non-viable claims. Low value consumer claims for competition law violations fall into the third category and this should be reflected in the proposed model.

In sections 4 and 5, the structural characteristics of collective actions for consumer claims in competition law were examined. Different structural characteristics drawn from existing national collective action mechanisms at Member State level were contrasted with the characteristics desired in principle, and those available in the US class action system. The respective procedures were distinguished based on whether they promote the collective, or individual, consumer interest and the narrow, or wide, notion of access to justice. It can be observed that many of the issues permeating the current European debate have troubled (and some continue to trouble) the US legal system. Transplanting the US system into Europe would not be a workable solution and, in any case, this has never been contemplated by EU institutions or individual Member States. However, as Cappelletti pointed out, 'successful transplants do occur, sometimes surprising those aware of the difficulties. And this occurrence is most frequent when the transplant is motivated by a social, economic or political "need" shared in common with the countries involved'.[231]

The analysis in this chapter has revealed that the Commission is, indeed, aware of the difficulties. However, in order for these difficulties to be surmounted, the Commission, as the competition policy-shaping authority in the EU, should be more explicit as to the functions and objectives of the proposed collective actions, build on the common principles, and in the future propose tailored collective action mechanisms for low value consumer claims. Indeed, the need is present since collective consumer actions for competition law violations represent a miniscule percentage of the total competition litigation in Europe.[232]

In section 6, specific suggestions on structuring a collective action mechanism fitted to addressing consumer claims for competition law violations were provided. In so doing, pragmatic considerations and traditional approaches to litigation were balanced and it was shown that there are inherent limits to the measures adopted. However, by employing, at least at this stage of the development of collective redress procedures in Europe, consumer organizations as a distinguishing characteristic, and adopting some 'US class action' elements with structured safety valves, the proposed collective action mechanism appears to be a workable solution. The mechanism proposed has the following characteristics:

1. It focuses on representative actions and grants standing to consumer organizations and public bodies;
2. The representative organizations should be authorized either ad hoc by the court or in advance according to the relevant criteria specified;
3. It adopts an opt-out structure;
4. It discusses an appropriate funding system for consumer organizations whereby funds stem from a combination of the membership, public funds, and an established consumer collective litigation fund; and
5. It proposes distribution of the damages award, whereby priority is granted to consumers filing a claim for their individual damage. The remaining amount reverts back to the consumer organization bringing the action to cover its expenses and to the consumer collective litigation fund or other recognized charity.

Ultimately, the above mechanism would appear to strike a delicate balance between the right to damages and compensation of individual consumers, on the

---

[231] M Cappelletti and B Garth, 'Introduction' in M Cappelletti (ed), *Access to Justice and the Welfare State* (Sijthoff 1981) 6.
[232] See text to n 85.

one hand, and the effective enforcement of competition norms in the consumer interest, on the other. However, as the Commission's efforts so far have shown, it is hard to gain the necessary political support for innovative private enforcement mechanisms.[233] Therefore, alternative public enforcement mechanisms, capable of promoting the consumer interest, are addressed in the next chapter before turning, in the final chapter, to the question of which of these public and private enforcement mechanisms could potentially be adopted at the EU level.

---

[233] Unfortunately the EP Resolution (n 17) points in this direction as well.

6
Consumer Involvement in Public Competition Law Enforcement
Towards Acceptable Alternatives

1. Introduction

The analysis presented in this chapter moves on to explore the possible opportunities for consumer participation and the promotion of the consumer interest in public competition law enforcement. The reasons for the shift from private to public enforcement are twofold: first, it is indicated that, despite the Commission's efforts, consumer involvement in private competition law enforcement is unlikely to be enhanced in the near future; second, it corresponds to a fused approach towards competition law enforcement in which both public and private enforcement share the same objectives of deterrence and compensation, albeit with differing intensities. Consumer participation in public enforcement is viewed as an alternative to private enforcement but it also has an intrinsic value in itself.

Public enforcement encapsulates the avenues open to consumers to alert the competent antitrust authorities of an alleged competition law violation and/or market failure, as well as participation in ongoing proceedings by means of intervention (public enforcement *stricto sensu*).[1] It also covers mixed enforcement mechanisms in which a competition authority provides some form of redress to the affected consumers in the course of public enforcement (public enforcement *lato sensu*).[2]

---

[1] An alternative term to describe these actions is 'privately triggered public enforcement', as employed in F Jacobs and T Deisenhofer, 'Procedural Aspects of the Effective Private Enforcement of EC Competition Rules: A Community Perspective' in CD Ehlerman and I Atanasiu (eds), *European Competition Law Annual 2001: Effective Private Enforcement of EC Antitrust Law* (Hart 2003) 187, 197.

[2] Consultation with consumer organizations prior to the adoption of secondary competition legislation, although very important in increasing the transparency and quality of European policymaking, falls outside the scope of this book. It is true that this input has a significant role to play in defending the consumer interest; however, it is not connected with the actual enforcement of competition law norms. See Commission (EC), 'European Transparency Initiative' (Green Paper) COM(2006) 194 final; Commission (EC), 'Third Strategic Review of Better Regulation in the European Union' (Communication) COM(2009) 15 final, 6–7. See, for example, BEUC, 'Response to the White Paper on Damages Actions' (2008); Commission (EC), XXIXth Report on Competition Policy 1999, SEC(2000) 720 final, 35–36; Commission (EC), 'Staff Working Document Accompanying the Report on Competition Policy 2008', COM(2009) 374 final, paras 19, 26.

The analysis presented in section 2 discusses the fused approach to competition law enforcement and argues that public mechanisms can be structured in a way that promotes the same endemic functions as private enforcement and brings additional institutional benefits. Section 3 assesses the current avenues of consumer participation in public competition law enforcement and suggests ways in which these could be improved (public enforcement *stricto sensu*). Section 4 discusses different mechanisms for the provision of compensation to affected consumers in the course of public enforcement (public enforcement *lato sensu*). Public enforcement *stricto sensu* heavily entails the element of consumer participation whereas the latter mechanism delivers benefits to consumers without the necessary element of consumer participation. However, they both have the capacity to advance the endemic/functional aims of competition law enforcement as well as the ancillary institutional benefits.

2. Fused Approach to Enforcement: The Benefits

2.1 Rethinking the deterrence—Compensation dichotomy

The traditional view of EU competition law enforcement supports a clear distinction between deterrence and compensation, attributing the former to public enforcement and reserving the latter for private enforcement mechanisms.[3] However, in the context of EU competition law, this traditional approach is not supported by either the Court's jurisprudence or by the EU institutions' pronouncements. In Chapter 3 the binary nature of private enforcement was discussed extensively. The aim here is to show that the same holds true for public competition law enforcement as well, and that, despite its primary deterrent role, it may also be used as a compensatory mechanism. In addition, it will be argued that, contrary to the views advanced by commentators, the fact that public enforcement mechanisms could potentially deliver compensation does not negate the need to advance effective private enforcement mechanisms, but functions as a second-best solution in cases in which pragmatic constraints impede effective private enforcement.

---

[3] W Wils, 'The Relationship between Public Antitrust Enforcement and Private Actions for Damages' (2009) 32 W Comp 3, 12. However, Wils does not reject the provision of compensation through public enforcement procedures. Ibid 21. On the deterrence function of public enforcement see Commission (EC), 'Guidelines on the Method of Setting Fines Imposed Pursuant to Article 23(2)(a) of Regulation No 1/2003' [2006] OJ C210/2 (Fine Guidelines), para 4; Joined Cases 100/80 to 103/80 *Musique Diffusion française and others v Commission* [1983] ECR 1825, para 106; Case C-76/06 P *Britannia Alloys & Chemicals v Commission* [2007] ECR I-4405, para 22. On the compensatory potential of private enforcement see Commission (EC), 'Damages Actions for Breach of the EC Antitrust Rules' (White Paper) COM(2008) 165 final, para 1.2; Commission (EC), 'Staff Working Paper Accompanying the White Paper on Damages Actions for Breach of the EC Antitrust Rules' SEC(2008) 404, 2 April 2008, paras 14–15. For a different proposal on a market-based enforcement policy see C Hodges, 'A Market-Based Competition Enforcement Policy' (2011) 22 EBLR 261; C Hodges, 'European Competition Enforcement Policy: Integrating Restitution and Behaviour Control' (2011) 34 W Comp 383.

The Macrory Report on regulatory sanctions supports employing public enforcement mechanisms in delivering redress.[4] Building on the latter report, Hodges advocated a linkage between regulatory sanctions and compensation.[5] The compensation provided in the course of public regulatory enforcement accounts for another type of regulatory sanction, either negotiated with, or imposed by, the public authority. Hodges argues that both public and private enforcement could serve the six penalties principles identified in the Macrory Report,[6] although public enforcement is more effective in attaining them. Therefore, there is no justification for private enforcement. He proposes, instead, a fused approach in which compensation is provided in the course of public enforcement. However, two observations regarding this proposal are warranted. First, it responds to the question on the compatibility of the compensatory function with public enforcement mechanisms in the affirmative by employing an enforcement approach based on wider regulatory theories, in this case the responsive regulation theory that influenced the Macrory Report.[7] Private litigation is seen as contrary to responsive regulation since it increases the regulatory burdens on businesses.[8] However, despite the fact that responsive regulation theory points to the need for less intrusive penalties to ensure compliance, such as, for example, advocacy mechanisms, persuasion, and warning letters, it still does not do away with more severe penalties, such as fines.[9] To the extent that compensation could increase the financial penalty for the incumbents, it could be said to improve the deterrent function of fines. Where fines for competition law violations are beyond the optimal level,[10] additional financial penalties are needed, regardless of the fact that advocacy mechanisms could, indeed, prove to be beneficial.

---

[4] R Macrory, 'Regulating Justice: Making Sanctions Effective' (November 2006) (Final Report) <http://webarchive.nationalarchives.gov.uk/+/http://www.bis.gov.uk/files/file44593.pdf> accessed 13 July 2014 (Macrory Report).

[5] C Hodges, *The Reform of Class and Representative Actions in European Legal Systems* (Hart 2008) 213–216; C Hodges, 'Encouraging Enterprise and Rebalancing Risk: Implications of Economic Policy for Regulation, Enforcement and Compensation' (2009) 20 EBLR 1231, 1261.

[6] Namely that a sanction should aim to: (1) change the offender's behaviour; (2) eliminate any gains resulting from the breach; (3) be responsive; (4) be proportionate; (5) restore the inflicted harm; and (6) deter future non-compliances. Macrory Report (n 4) 10.

[7] See also P Hampton, 'Reducing Administrative Burdens: Effective Inspection and Enforcement' (HM Treasury, March 2005) <http://webarchive.nationalarchives.gov.uk/+/http://www.bis.gov.uk/files/file22988.pdf> accessed 13 July 2014, paras 2.13ff. The Macrory Report (n 4) built upon the findings in the Hampton Report. On responsive regulation see I Ayres and J Braithwaite, *Responsive Regulation—Transcending the Deregulation Debate* (OUP 1992) 4–7, 35–41.

[8] C Hodges, 'Competition, Enforcement, Regulation and Civil Justice: What is the case?' (2006) 43 CMLRev 1381, 1392. Hodges views this approach as contrary to the Commission's 'Better Regulation' agenda. On 'Better Regulation' see Hodges, Encouraging Enterprise (n 5) 1231–1234. Relevant documents available at <http://ec.europa.eu/governance/better_regulation/key_docs_en.htm> accessed 13 July 2014.

[9] See J Braithwaite, *Restorative Justice and Responsive Regulation* (OUP 2002) 29–34, arguing that '[t]his means that consistent punishment and consistent persuasion are foolish strategies. The hard question is to decide when to punish and when to persuade'.

[10] JM Connor and RH Lande, 'How High Do Cartels Raise Prices? Implications for Optimal Cartel Fines' (2006) 80 Tul L Rev 513, 559–564; C Veljanovski, 'Cartel Fines in Europe: Law,

The second observation concerns the public enforcement system's potential to deliver compensation without the concomitant existence of effective private enforcement mechanisms. The compensatory function of public enforcement does not necessarily entail the abandonment of private enforcement mechanisms. If, as Hodges concedes, both enforcement avenues are able to serve these principles, one should look to their complementary relationship rather than disregard one of them completely. The Macrory Report supports this approach, since it upholds the Financial Conduct Authority's point that not all cases should include a restorative element; it may be that the harm is not quantifiable or would be more efficiently and effectively addressed if the individuals were able to directly pursue claims with the firm concerned.[11] As the UK government conceded, 'giving the public authority a role in delivering redress is not a substitute for encouraging private actions [as] all of the burden would fall on the state in a time of increasingly tight public resources and, furthermore, it would not help to tackle anti-competitive behaviour that the OFT has not yet addressed, a key objective of encouraging private actions'.[12] Thus, public enforcement mechanisms may, indeed, adopt a compensatory function, although effective private enforcement mechanisms are still needed.

The complementary nature of public and private enforcement and the compensatory potential of public enforcement mechanisms is supported by the Commission and NCAs as their past practice reveals.[13] Furthermore, in its Resolution on the White Paper, the European Parliament has indirectly taken a positive stance on the compensatory potential of public enforcement by stating that:

in order to encourage undertakings to compensate the victims of illicit behaviour as quickly and effectively as possible, the competition authorities are asked to take account of the compensation paid or to be paid when determining the fine that is to be imposed upon the defendant undertaking;... calls on the Council and the Commission explicitly to incorporate into Regulation (EC) No 1/2003 those fining principles and further improve and specify them in order to comply with the requirements of the general legal principles.[14]

Practice and Deterrence' (2007) 30 W Comp 65, 81, 84. A Stephan, 'The Direct Settlement of EC Cartel Cases' (2009) 58 ICLQ 627, 643.

[11] Macrory Report (n 4), paras 2.5–2.6. See also Hodges, who accepts that 'there is some evidence that enforcement officials may traditionally have been reluctant to assume responsibilities'. Hodges, Encouraging Enterprise (n 5) 1264–1265.

[12] BIS, 'Private Actions in Competition Law: A Consultation on Options for Reform' (April 2012), para 6.33.

[13] On these cases see section 4.1 of this chapter. This practice challenges the statement in Commission (EC), 'Proposal for a Council Directive Governing Actions for Damages for Infringements of Article 81 and 82 of the Treaty' (Draft Damages Directive) (Document withdrawn before publication—on file with the author), Explanatory Memorandum, para 1.2, according to which '[c]ompensation for harm caused by infringements of Articles [101] and [102] of the Treaty cannot be achieved through public enforcement of the competition rules; it is a specific function which is of the domain of courts and of civil law and procedure'. For a similar statement see Commission (EC), 'Staff Working Document—Accompanying Document to the White Paper on Damages Actions for Breach of the EC Antitrust Rules' (Impact Assessment) SEC(2008) 405 (Brussels, 02/04/08), para 1.

[14] European Parliament, Resolution of 26 March 2009 on the White Paper on Damages Actions for Breach of the EC Antitrust Rules (2008/2154(INI)), para 11.

In addition, the UK government has accepted the compensatory function of public enforcement, since it noted that, 'while regulatory aims and objectives are usually strategic and not specifically focused on compensatory objectives, this does not preclude their adaptation for this purpose'.[15] This general approach has been exemplified both in consumer and competition law. In its White Paper entitled 'A Better Deal for Consumers: Delivering Real Help Now and Change for the Future', which focused on consumer policy, it further discussed the option of encouraging businesses to provide voluntary compensation to consumers, while reserving formal public enforcement actions for businesses that refuse to exercise this option.[16] The OFT has also acknowledged the compensatory potential of public competition law enforcement.[17] More recently, in its consultation on reforming private actions, the UK government acknowledged that 'empowering those who have suffered loss to take direct action against those who have caused it is the best way, in general, to increase deterrence and secure redress. However, alongside a strong private actions regime, the Government recognizes that there are some situations where it may be appropriate for the public enforcement body to consider mechanisms for redress, as part of its administrative settlement of cases'.[18] The majority of respondents to the consultation supported this proposal,[19] which now features in the Consumer Rights Act 2015.[20]

2.2 Ancillary institutional benefits

Apart from the potential to deliver redress to affected consumers, public enforcement mechanisms also have the potential to contribute to consumer education and empowerment as well as increase the legitimacy of competition policy.[21] These are promoted not only through public enforcement *lato sensu*,[22] but also

---

[15] Ministry of Justice, 'The Government's Response to the Civil Justice Council's Report: Improving Access to Justice through Collective Actions' (July 2009), para 18.
[16] BIS, 'A Better Deal for Consumers: Delivering Real Help Now and Change for the Future' (July 2009) Cm 7669, 49. The White Paper also discussed the appointment of a Consumer Advocate armed with the power to bring actions on behalf of consumers following a violation of consumer law when no other route to obtain compensation is available and distribute compensation to consumers from illegal funds seized by overseas enforcement authorities. The Consumer Advocate would also be responsible for the administration of voluntary compensation. Ibid 60–61, 63–64.
[17] For the OFT's views regarding redress in the context of administrative settlements see OFT, 'Private Actions in Competition Law: Effective Redress for Consumers and Business' (Recommendations) (OFT 916resp) (November 2007), paras 11.16–11.19.
[18] BIS Consultation (n 12), paras 6.26–6.27. Providing compensation to affected consumers is not specific to competition law. On similar powers of the FCA, OFCOM, and OFGEM see ibid, paras 6.27, 6.38–6.40.
[19] BIS, 'Private Actions in Competition Law: A Consultation on Options for Reform—Government Response' (January 2013), para 6.27.
[20] See Schedule 8 Consumer Rights Act amending CA 1998. On voluntary redress schemes see new ss 49C–49E. CMA, 'Guidance on the CMA's Approval of Voluntary Redress Schemes' (2 March 2015) (Draft, CMA40con).
[21] On these two ancillary benefits as a by-product of effective competition law enforcement see Chapter 3, section 3.
[22] See text to n 2.

by encouraging more active consumer participation. The latter can be achieved through the improvement of the current enforcement avenues discussed below. Consumers can act as informants to the Commission and NCAs and the question addressed is whether the processing of such information and the subsequent case selection could be applied in a more consumer-friendly manner.

Complaints launched by consumer organizations may reveal anti-competitive practices in retail markets and signal the need for articulating a valid consumer harm theory for the finding of an anti-competitive practice. Increased consumer involvement in raising complaints may possibly shift the substantive competition law enforcement standard towards a real consumer welfare standard. In addition, it may offer valuable support to EU competition policymaking, raise consumer awareness, and signpost the linkage between competition and consumer law, and the importance of responsible consumer behaviour in taming market forces.

3. Current Avenues for Consumer Participation: Public Enforcement *Stricto Sensu*

3.1 Complaints to the Commission

The Commission encourages private parties, both undertakings and consumers, to inform public enforcers of alleged competition law violations.[23] Consumers can become involved in public competition law enforcement either by lodging a complaint with the Commission or by providing market information to spur a subsequent sector inquiry.[24] Consumer complaints may contribute to the detection of a competition law violation, thereby increasing the deterrent effect of the enforcement system. Indirectly, they promote the compensatory aim as well, since they are able to incentivize consumer organizations to launch complaints with a view to subsequently raising follow-on damages actions.

In the past, consumers have raised numerous complaints.[25] Their complaints have mainly concerned consumer guarantee systems in the automobile sector, consumer electronics, and perfumes.[26] Complaints filed in the field of motor

---

[23] Commission (EC), 'Notice on the Handling of Complaints by the Commission under Articles 81 and 82 of the EC Treaty' [2004] OJ C101/65 (Notice on Complaints), paras 2–3. See also J Almunia, 'Competition—What's in It for Consumers?' (European Competition and Consumer Day Poznań, 24 November 2011, Speech/11/803).

[24] Notice on Complaints (n 23), paras 3–4.

[25] However, it is questionable as to whether the consumer involvement in raising complaints before competition authorities is indeed satisfactory. See M Hutchings and P Whelan, 'Consumer Interest in Competition Law Cases' (2006) 16 CPR 182, 184–185.

[26] See, for example, complaints by individuals and BEUC regarding the Ford Germany guarantee scheme in Commission (EC), Thirteenth Report on Competition Policy 1983 (Brussels, Luxembourg 1984) <http://bookshop.europa.eu/is-bin/INTERSHOP.enfinity/WFS/EU-Bookshop-Site/en_GB/-/EUR/ViewPublication-Start?PublicationKey=CB3883823> accessed 2 February 2014, paras 104–106; also BEUC complaints on guarantee schemes resulting in the Commission issuing a bulletin warning manufacturers in Commission (EC), Sixteenth Report

vehicle distribution agreements played a role in the adoption of the first Motor Vehicle Block Exemption Regulation.[27] As the Commission points out, there was a significant fall in the number of consumer complaints within one year of the adoption of the Block Exemption Regulation.[28] The Commission recognizes the potential of consumer contribution in revealing competition law violations but also points to the fact that their involvement is minimal. Furthermore, it acknowledges that increased participation on behalf of consumer organizations would be desirable,[29] and in the past such participation has led to the termination of anti-competitive practices, as in the case of an Italian consumer organization (Altroconsumo), which filed a complaint with the Commission regarding an Italian digital broadcasting regulation. This complaint led the Commission to issue a reasoned opinion on its incompatibility with EU competition law.[30] Also, Which?, the UK consumer organization, filed two complaints with the Commission, the first concerning ticket sales arrangements for the 2006 World Cup[31] and the second with regard to an allegedly anti-competitive agreement between Apple and major record companies, which resulted in higher prices for UK consumers than others in the EU when downloading music.[32]

The involvement of individual consumers, not through consumer organizations, can also play a role in the detection and punishment of competition law violations, as *Greek Ferries* reveals.[33] In that case, the Commission fined cartelists

---

on Competition Policy 1987 (Brussels, Luxembourg 1988) <http://bookshop.europa.eu/is-bin/INTERSHOP.enfinity/WFS/EU-Bookshop-Site/en_GB/-/EUR/ViewPublication-Start?PublicationKey=CB4886060> accessed 2 February 2014, para 56.

[27] Commission Regulation (EEC) 123/85 of 12 December 1984 on the Application of Article [101(3)] of the Treaty to Certain Categories of Motor Vehicle Distribution and Servicing Agreements [1985] OJ L15/16.

[28] Commission (EC), Seventeenth Report on Competition Policy 1988 (Brussels, Luxembourg 1989) <http://bookshop.europa.eu/is-bin/INTERSHOP.enfinity/WFS/EU-Bookshop-Site/en_GB/-/EUR/ViewPublication-Start?PublicationKey=CB5087340> accessed 2 February 2014, para 34.

[29] XXIXth Report (n 2) 21–22.

[30] Commission (EC), 'Competition: Commission Formally Requests Italy to Comply with EU Rules on Electronic Communications' (Press Release) IP 07/1114. Altroconsumo has also filed complaints before the Italian Competition Authority. See ECCG, 'Opinion on Private Damages Actions' <http://ec.europa.eu/consumers/empowerment/docs/ECCG_opinion_on_actions_for_damages_18112010.pdf> accessed 30 October 2014, 58. This section addresses only ways to improve the complaints process before the Commission and not NCAs.

[31] Commission (EC), 'Competition: Commission Welcomes Improved Access to Tickets for the 2006 World Cup' (Press Release) IP/05/519.

[32] Commission (EC), 'Annex to the Report on Competition Policy 2007' (Staff Working Document) SEC(2008) 2038, paras 327–328. Commission (EC), 'Antitrust: European Commission Welcomes Apple's Announcement to Equalise Prices for Music Downloads from I-Tunes in Europe' (Press Release) IP/08/22. For more recent complaints raised by consumer associations see ECCG, 'Minutes of the ECCG Competition Subgroup Meeting' (28 June 2011, Brussels) <http://ec.europa.eu/consumers/empowerment/docs/eccg_comp_sub_group_minutes_062011_en.pdf> accessed 30 October 2014, 8, 9.

[33] *Greek Ferries* (Case IV/34.466) Commission Decision 1999/271/EC [1999] OJ L109/24, 1. See also consumer complaints in *Peugeot* (Cases COMP/E2/36623, 36820, and 37275) Commission Decision 2006/431/EC [2006] OJ L173/20, para 27. See C Dussart, 'Parallel Imports of Motor Vehicles: The Peugeot Case' [2006] CPN 49, 51.

following a letter from a single consumer. The fact that consumer organizations and, occasionally, individual consumers raise complaints with the Commission is to be praised, as it reveals awareness on the part of consumers and may increase the wider acceptance of competition policy. Even in cases in which complaints do not actually amount to the finding of a competition law violation, they can still contribute to the development of competition law jurisprudence.[34] Whether this important legitimizing function can be further cultivated rests with the Commission's handling of the respective complaints, to which point attention will now be turned.

3.1.1 The legitimate interest requirement

Consumers/consumer organizations can lodge a complaint before the Commission, provided that they show a 'legitimate interest'.[35] Both the Commission and the GC accept the potential of consumer organizations to lodge complaints as long as they can show that their members are liable to be directly and adversely affected.[36] The same applies to individual consumers whose economic interests are adversely affected when they are the purchasers of goods and services that are the subject of an infringement.[37] This may be considered to be a broad reading of the 'legitimate interest' requirement but the GC has justified it in the light of the EU competition law goals by stating that:

> the ultimate purpose of the rules that seek to ensure that competition is not distorted in the internal market is to increase the well-being of consumers. That purpose can be seen in particular from the wording of Article [101 TFEU]...Competition law and competition policy therefore have an undeniable impact on the specific economic interests of

---

[34] See also *Volkswagen* (Case COMP/F-2/36.693) Commission Decision 2001/711/EC [2001] OJ L262/14, 1. On appeal Case T-208/01 *Volkswagen v Commission* [2003] ECR II–5141, which deals with the notion of 'agreement' in EU competition law; Case C-74/04 P *Commission v Volkswagen* [2006] ECR I-6585.

[35] Council Regulation 1/2003 on the Implementation of the Rules on Competition Laid Down in Articles [81] and [82] of the Treaty [2003] OJ L1/1 (Regulation 1/2003), Article 7(2); Commission Regulation 773/2004 Relating to the Conduct of Proceedings by the Commission [2004] OJ L123/18 (Regulation 773/2004), Article 5(1); Notice on Complaints (n 23), para 40; S Weatherill, 'Public Interest Litigation in EC Competition Law' in HW Micklitz and N Reich (eds), *Public Interest Litigation before European Courts* (Nomos 1996) 169, 173, argues that the Commission adopted a broad approach towards the 'legitimate interest' requirement. See J Stuyck, 'EC Competition Law after Modernisation: More than Ever in the Interest of Consumers' (2005) 28 JCP 1, 14 in the same vein.

[36] Notice on Complaints (n 23), paras 37–38. Cf Case T-114/92 *BEMIM v Commission* [1995] ECR II-147, para 28 regarding the legitimate interest of an association of undertakings. See also Case C-321/95 P *Stichting Greenpeace v Commission* [1998] ECR I-1651 restricting standing for environmental organizations. Arguably, consumer organizations are more privileged compared to environmental organizations because of the competition-specific enforcement mechanism provided by Regulations 1/2003 (n 35) and 773/2004 (n 35).

[37] Ibid. Cf Cases T-213/01 and T-214/01 *Österreichische Postsparkasse AG v Commission of the European Communities* [2006] ECR II-1601, paras 109–110, 113–114. Prior to the adoption of Regulations 1/2003 and 773/2004 it was more difficult for consumers to satisfy the legitimate interest requirement. See Case 246/81 *Lord Bethell v Commission* [1982] ECR 2277.

Public Enforcement Stricto Sensu

final customers who purchase goods or services. Recognition that such customers—who show that they have suffered economic damage as a result of an agreement or conduct liable to restrict or distort competition—have a legitimate interest in seeking from the Commission a declaration that Articles [101 and 102 TFEU] have been infringed contributes to the attainment of the objectives of competition law.[38]

Therefore, the 'legitimate interest' requirement, which is dependent on the direct and adverse effect of the infringement on consumers' economic interests (individually or as members of a consumer association), can be identified as the first condition for the complaint's admissibility.

The legitimate interest requirement is an important prerequisite of the complainant's status, which is further associated with important procedural rights in the event of proceedings being initiated or the rejection of a complaint.[39] However, if the complainant fails to demonstrate its legitimate interest, the Commission is entitled to dismiss the complaint.[40] In the case of complaints raised by consumer organizations, the Commission appears receptive to accepting a lower information threshold. By so doing the Commission seems to recognize the difficulties associated with the gathering of information in cases of complaints by consumer organizations.[41] This should also apply to individual consumer complaints. In addition, even in cases in which the legitimate interest requirement is not fulfilled, the Commission retains the right to initiate proceedings on its own initiative,[42] an option that the Commission should use in the event of consumer complaints in the light of the benefits of consumer involvement.

3.1.2 The Union interest requirement

The Commission may reject a complaint for lack of '[Union] interest'.[43] The complainant's legitimate interest and the nature of the complaint being in the Union's interest may be broadly construed as admissibility requirements, even if the former is technically a prerequisite for allowing the complaint to reach the stage of assessment, regardless of whether or not it is in the Union's interest. In the latter case, the Commission recognizes that the complainant has a legitimate interest; however, it disposes of the complaint because of lack of Union interest after examining the substance of the complaint. Therefore, the end result is the same in both cases. The

---

[38] *Österreichische Postsparkasse AG* (n 37), para 115.
[39] Regulation 773/2004 (n 35), Articles 6–8; Regulation 1/2003 (n 35), Article 27(1). Notice on Complaints (n 23), paras 64–73. Complainants may also challenge the Commission decision. An important procedural right is access to the non-confidential version of the statement of objection. See *Österreichische Postsparkasse* (n 37), paras 106–107.
[40] Notice on Complaints (n 23), para 40.
[41] Regulation 773/2004 (n 35), Article 5(1); Notice on complaints (n 23), para 31; R Wezenbeek, 'Consumers and Competition Policy: The Commission's Perspective and the Example of Transport' [2006] EBLR 73, 78–80.
[42] Notice on Complaints (n 23), para 40. See also *Österreichische Postsparkasse* (n 37), paras 90–92 in which the applicant was granted complainant status, even though the complaint was submitted after the initiation of proceedings on the Commission's initiative.
[43] Notice on Complaints (n 23), paras 41–45.

Commission rejects the complaint and bears an obligation to provide adequate reasons for this rejection, as will be discussed below. However, if a complaint is dismissed for lack of 'Union interest', the complainant retains its procedural rights under Regulation 773/2004.

The review of the Commission's past practice and the EU courts' case law suggests that 'Union interest' affords greater latitude to the Commission with regard to rejecting complaints, as it functions as a case prioritization criterion. This is despite the EU courts having articulated strict conditions regarding the required Commission justifications when rejecting a complaint for lack of 'Union interest'.

The Commission still enjoys discretion regarding case prioritization,[44] especially in the light of the fact that, in assessing the '[Union] interest' condition, it is allowed to apply new criteria not considered before in the light of the factual and legal background of the case presented before it.[45] The 'general supervisory task entrusted to the Commission' does not entail an obligation on its part 'to rule on the existence or otherwise of an infringement' and therefore the Commission can prioritize the cases submitted to it.[46] The Commission should still carefully examine the legal and factual background of a complaint before rejecting it.[47] As an administrative authority, acting in the public interest, the Commission can prioritize its cases based on the criterion of 'Union interest' as long as it provides adequate justifications for its prioritization.[48] The complainant can then challenge the rejection of its complaint under 263(4) TFEU and, in the event that no formal rejection decision is provided, launch an action against the Commission for failure to act under 265 TFEU.[49]

As has been alluded to previously, the 'Union interest' criterion affords the Commission considerable discretion in dealing with the cases brought before it. AG Colomer observed that:

[Union] interest... is no more than an abbreviated formula, a shortcut, to describe, succinctly, the discretion—neither unfettered nor arbitrary, since it is subject to judicial

---

[44] Case T-24/90 *Automec srl v Commission of the European Communities* [1992] ECR I-2223, para 77. On the Commission margin of discretion see W Wils, 'Discretion and Prioritisation in Public Antitrust Enforcement, in Particular EU Antitrust Enforcement' (2011) 34 W Comp 353, 357–360.

[45] Case Case C-117/97 P *Ufex v Commission* [1999] ECR I-1341, paras 79–80. Notice on Complaints (n 23), para 43.

[46] *Automec* (n 44), paras 74–77; Case T-74/92 *Ladbroke Racing v Commission* [1995] ECR II-115 (*Ladbroke I*), para 58; Cf Case 125/78 *Gema v Commission* [1979] ECR 3173, para 18 stating that 'that in no way implies that the applicant within the meaning of [Article 7(2) of Regulation 1/2003] is entitled to require from the Commission a final decision as regards the existence or non-existence of the alleged infringement'; *Ufex* (n 45), paras 88–89; Case C-344/98 *Masterfoods Ltd v HB Ice Cream Ltd* [2000] ECR I-11369, para 46; Case T-229/05 *AEPI v Commission* [2007] ECR II-84 (*T-AEPI*), paras 39–40; Case C-425/07 P *AEPI v Commission* [2009] ECR I-3205, para 31; Case T-306/05 *Scippecercola and Terzakis v Commission* [2008] ECR II-4, para 92. Notice on Complaints (n 23), para 28.

[47] Case T-548/93 *Ladbroke Racing v Commission* [1995] ECR-II 2565, paras 50–51.

[48] *Automec* (n 44), paras 79, 81, 85; *Ladbroke I* (n 46), para 58; *Ufex* (n 45), para 90; Notice on Complaints (n 23), paras 74–75. For a concise depiction of the case law on the Commission's discretion in rejecting complaints see *Scippecercola* (n 46), paras 94–97, 174, 187, 189–190. See also Case T-114/92 *BEMIM v Commission* [1995] ECR II-147. On the notion of '[Union] interest' and its role as a jurisdictional threshold of case allocation see Weatherill (n 35) 177–183.

[49] Notice on Complaints (n 23), para 77. Weatherill (n 35) 172. The other avenue would be to raise the issue before the Ombudsman. See Article 228 TFEU; Article 43 of the Charter of Fundamental Rights of the European Union [2000] OJ C364/1.

review—which the Treaties confer on the Commission for its examination of a complaint alleging the existence of anti-competitive practices. The substance of that concept varies very considerably, to the same extent as the widely differing circumstances which surround cases involving infringements of the competition rules.[50]

Notwithstanding the Commission's discretion, certain patterns can be discerned in the CJEU jurisprudence for assessing the 'Union interest' criterion.[51] In particular, it has been held that the Commission can reject a complaint if the complainant is able to bring an action to assert his right before the national courts.[52] In the event that evidence is adduced to support the fact that the national system does not provide adequate protection for complainants' rights, the Commission cannot reject a complaint based on this argument.[53] However, national systems of civil procedure do not afford adequate protection to consumer rights[54] and, therefore, the Commission should not reject consumer complaints based on this ground.[55] Even if the Commission retains the case, one could question how an individual complainant's rights are to be safeguarded. It is suggested here that the Commission's policy choice of not addressing a complaint because national courts can safeguard individual rights provides a hint of the added value attributed by the Commission to private claims before national courts and of the complementary nature of public and private enforcement.

In the event that the alleged antitrust infringement does not present a threat to the functioning of the internal market the Commission may as well reject the complaint for lack of 'Union interest'.[56] In this case consumers/consumer associations may refer to their national authorities but, given their limited resources, it seems unlikely that they would raise a second complaint, which leaves consumers unprotected.

The GC accepted the above criteria in a case involving an action brought by consumer organizations. *BEUC v Commission*[57] has been listed as an important victory by consumer advocates.[58] The case commenced when BEUC and NCC launched a complaint before the Commission alleging that an agreement between UK and Japanese car manufacturers, which entailed import quotas for Japanese cars in the UK market, was anti-competitive. The Commission did not accept this complaint since the 'Union interest' condition was absent because (i) the

---

[50] C-449/98 P *IECC v Commission* [2001] ECR I-3875, Opinion of AG Colomer, para 57.
[51] See Notice on Complaints (n 23), para 44 for a concise enumeration.
[52] *Automec* (n 44), para 88.
[53] In *Automec*, however, the GC stated that the applicant had not produced any evidence showing that national law (in this case Italian law) provides no satisfactory legal remedies for the protection of the applicant's rights, a fact that was taken into account in order to rule that the Commission did not have an obligation to examine the complaint. *Automec* (n 44), paras 94, 97. See also Case T-575/93 *Koelman v Commission* [1996] ECR II-1, para 79; *T-AEPI* (n 46), paras 44–45.
[54] See Chapter 5, section 5.
[55] In the same vein see C Cseres and J Mendes, 'Consumers' Access to EU Competition Law Procedures: Outer and Inner Limits' (2014) 51 CMLRev 483, 500–501.
[56] *Automec* (n 44), para 86.
[57] Case T-37/92 *BEUC and NCC v Commission* [1994] ECR II-285.
[58] M Goyens, 'A Key Ruling from the ECJ' (1994) 4 CPR 221.

alleged anti-competitive agreement was about to expire; (ii) the agreement was known to, or even encouraged by, UK authorities; and (iii) it did not satisfy the effect on inter-State trade requirements.[59] The complainants brought an action for annulment before the GC. The GC rejected the Commission's arguments and annulled its decision not to investigate the complaint since no proper factual and legal analysis had been conducted before rejecting the complaint.[60] This is an important judgment as it reveals the readiness of the GC to thoroughly review Commission decisions in rejecting the complaint in a case involving consumer organizations acting in the consumer interest. However, the fact remains, ultimately, that it is for the Commission to set its enforcement priorities provided that it gives adequate reasoning for so doing.

3.2 Making complaints to the Commission more effective

3.2.1 Improving standing

The shortcomings encountered by consumers/consumer organizations in launching complaints are, to some extent, alleviated by the rather broad definition given to the 'legitimate interest' requirement and the partial dispensation with the obligation to obtain detailed information on the complaint.[61] However, the latitude for case prioritization afforded to the Commission may inhibit the success of such claims. Even if the Commission is correct in its assessment of 'Union interest', the rejection of a complaint may still have an adverse impact on the consumer interest.

3.2.2 The consumer complaints allocation mechanism

As has been argued in the previous chapter, effective private enforcement mechanisms for consumer claims in the competition field are not to be found in the majority of Member States. There are two options for their implementation: either devise the necessary collective action mechanisms for the additional reason of supplementing the Commission's enforcement efforts or look at alternative public enforcement mechanisms. Given that individual Member States, to a large extent, replicate the EU model of public competition law enforcement,[62] some coordination mechanism

---

[59] See *BEUC v Commission* (n 57), paras 10–11 for the Commission's reasoning.
[60] *BEUC v Commission* (n 57), paras 43–61. For a recent decision of the GC annulling the Commission's decision for lack of proper factual and legal analysis see T-427/08 *CEAHR v Commission* [2011] 4 CMLR 14, paras 49, 176. Following this decision the Commission decided to open formal proceedings, which were subsequently closed. See 'Case AT.39097—Watch Repair: Decision Rejecting a Complaint Pursuant to Article 7(2) of Regulation 773/2004' <http://ec.europa.eu/competition/antitrust/cases/dec_docs/39097/39097_3089_3.pdf> accessed 31 October 2014.
[61] See section 3.1.1 of this chapter.
[62] Regulation 1/2003 (n 35), recitals 8, 15, 18, Article 3, and Article 11. On soft convergence under the auspices of the ECN see R Whish and D Bailey, *Competition Law* (7th edn, OUP 2012) 288–289.

is required for the Commission to allocate these consumer cases to the relevant national competition authority directly, instead of rejecting them outright.

Recital 18 of Regulation 1/2003 provides that 'the Commission [should not be prevented] from rejecting a complaint for lack of [Union] interest...even if no other competition authority has indicated its intention of dealing with the case'. This recital, as well as the Notice on cooperation between the Commission and NCAs,[63] could be amended in order to provide for a 'consumer complaints allocation mechanism'. This would be along the lines that, in the event that the Commission rejects a complaint, it would have to send the file of the case directly to the most appropriate NCA. Following allocation of the complaint, the NCA would then decide how to proceed with it depending on the information supporting the complaint and its own workload. This proposal may require a legislative amendment of Regulation 1/2003 or Regulation 773/2004.[64]

3.3 Sector inquiries

The second participation avenue is the provision of information that falls short of justifying legitimate interest for launching a complaint under Article 7(2) of Regulation 1/2003. However, consumer information can trigger a sector inquiry.[65] In any case, the Commission is committed to treating the information provided in accordance with good administrative practice.[66] Sector inquiries, unlike UK market investigations,[67] do not provide the Commission with powerful enforcement tools. However, information requests from different market players do provide the Commission with the opportunity to form an opinion of the functioning of the respective sector and may also result in the opening of infringement proceedings against specific undertakings.[68] Thus, sector inquiries could potentially

---

[63] Commission (EC), 'Notice on Cooperation within the Network of Competition Authorities' [2004] OJ C101/43.

[64] See Chapter 7, section 4.

[65] Regulation 1/2003 (n 35), Article 17. See, for example, the complaints about electricity price increases that resulted in the energy sector inquiry. P Chauve and M Godfried, 'Modelling Competitive Electricity Markets: Are Consumers Paying for Lack of Competition?' [2007] CPN 18. Commission (EC), 'Report on Competition Policy 2004' (vol II) <http://ec.europa.eu/competition/publications/annual_report/2004/2004_volume2_en.pdf> accessed 3 November 2014, 167.

[66] Notice on complaints (n 23), para 4. See Charter of Fundamental Rights (n 49), Article 41; Ombudsman (EC), 'The European Code of Good Administrative Behaviour' (2005) <http://www.ombudsman.europa.eu/en/resources/code.faces;jsessionid=5DCFB7F16FD3276EF3BFC692DD747792> accessed 3 November 2014.

[67] See P Marsden and P Whelan, 'When Markets are Failing' (2007) 6(2) CLI 6 for a concise account of the differences between the two regimes. It should be noted, though, that sector inquiries can be broader in scope, as they are not restricted to a particular market. In this regard, sector inquiries resemble UK market studies. See G Niels, H Jenkins, and J Casanova, 'The UK Market Investigations Regime: Taking Stock after 5 Years' (2008) 7 Comp Law 346, 347 on sector inquiries as an 'information gathering exercise'.

[68] Commission (EC), 'Citizens' Summary—EU Competition Inquiry into the Pharmaceutical Sector' <http://ec.europa.eu/competition/sectors/pharmaceuticals/inquiry/citizens_summary.pdf> accessed 3 November 2014. A Rosen, 'Sector Inquiries under the Microscope' (2005) 4(14) CLI 9; M Holmes and A Jones, 'Investigating the Business Insurance Industry' (2005) 4(16) CLI 12.

have a deterrent value. The mere opening of sector inquiries may have beneficial effects, as the price reduction in the leased lines sector inquiry reveals.[69] Also, in the context of sector inquiries (even if these do not concern the retail sector) the Commission can take into account the impact of certain business practices on consumers and suggest a certain course of action to businesses.[70] Sector inquiries are not restricted to the competition law field, and they also present a beneficial bridging function between consumer and competition remedies.[71] This is evident in the sector inquiry in the retail banking sector, in which the Commission expressly stated that:

> The sector inquiry into retail banking contributes to this agenda by shedding light on the operation of the market; highlighting possible market failures; and identifying where market failures can be tackled through competition law and, where appropriate, other measures.[72]

The Commission has predicted that the use of the sector inquiries tool will gain pace,[73] following the modernization and decentralization of competition law

---

See also *MasterCard, EuroCommerce and Commercial Cards* (Case COMP/34.579, 36.518, and 38.580) Commission Decision of 17 December 2007 [2009] OJ C264/8. On this case, following the retail banking sector inquiry, see L Repa and others, 'Commission Prohibits MasterCard's Multilateral Interchange Fees for Cross-border Card Payments in the EEA' [2008] CPN 1; Commission (EC), 'Competition: Commission Sector Inquiry Finds Major Competition Barriers in Retail Banking' (IP/07/114) (31.01.2007). The Commission decision was challenged before the European Courts. See Case T-111/08 *MasterCard, Inc. and others v Commission* [2012] 5 CMLR 5; on appeal, Case C-382/12 P *MasterCard Inc and others v Commission* [2014] 5 CMLR 23. On cases following the energy sector inquiry see N Dunne, 'Commitment Decisions in EU Competition Law' (2014) 10 JCLE 399, 408.

[69] M Monti, 'Increasing Competition in Leased Lines—The Benefits for European Businesses and Consumers' (Brussels, 22 September 2000, Speech /00/333); D Wood and N Bavarez, 'Sector Inquiries' (2005) 4(2) CLI 3, 4.

[70] Commission (EC), 'Staff Working Document Accompanying the Communication from the Commission Sector Inquiry under Article 17 of Regulation (EC) No 1/2003 on Business Insurance' (Final Report) SEC(2007) 1231, para 5.4; DG Competition, 'On the Initial Findings of the Sector Inquiry into Mobile Roaming Charges' (Working Document) (13 December 2000) <http://ec.europa.eu/competition/sectors/telecommunications/archive/inquiries/roaming/working_document_on_initial_results.pdf> accessed 3 November 2014, para 6.6 on improving consumer awareness.

[71] For example, the Commission, in its Reports on Sector Inquiries, often refers to the disclosure of information (identified as a widely used remedy in consumer law) as a proposed course of action for businesses. See, for example, Commission (EC), 'Sector Inquiry under Article 17 of Regulation (EC) No 1/2003 on Business Insurance' (Final Report) COM(2007) 556 final, para 22. Commission (EC), 'Sector Inquiry under Article 17 of Regulation (EC) No 1/2003 on Retail Banking' (Final Report) COM(2007) 33 final (Retail Banking Report), para 33. Commission (EC), 'Staff Working Document Accompanying the Communication from the Commission Sector Inquiry under Article 17 of Regulation (EC) No 1/2003 on Retail Banking' (Final Report) SEC(2007) 106 (Retail Banking SWD) 14 (on price transparency), 15 (on information asymmetries and high switching costs).

[72] Retail Banking Report (n 71), para 4.

[73] Commission (EC), 'Modernisation of the Rules Implementing Articles 85 and 86 of the EC Treaty' (White Paper) COM(99) 101 final, para 115; Commission (EC), 'A Pro-active Competition Policy for a Competitive Europe' COM(2004) 293 final, para 4.1. Sector inquiries were available under Article 12 of Regulation 17/1962 as well.

enforcement with Regulation 1/2003, and rightly so, since the Commission has completed five sector inquiries and one is ongoing. The five sector inquiries undertaken by the Commission since the entry into force of Regulation 1/2003 are in the following sectors: media, energy, retail banking, business insurance, and pharmaceuticals. On 6 May 2015, the Commission announced the launch of a sector inquiry into the e-commerce sector. [74] In particular, the Commission acknowledges that:

sector inquiries have become one of its key investigative tools and have enabled it to identify shortcomings in the competitive process of the gas and electricity, retail banking, business insurance and pharmaceutical sectors. They have provided a wealth of factual material that has supported the Commission's enforcement of Articles [101] and [102] in individual cases.[75]

The tool of sector inquiries provides an avenue for consumers and consumer organizations to alert the Commission to possible competition law problems, thereby indicating the potential to legitimize competition policy.[76] Furthermore, the Commission record to date indicates that sector inquiries can be of great value to the Commission in discerning different trends in markets and potential competition law infringements.[77]

3.4 Improvements to sector inquiries: Priorities, structure, and outcome

The Commission could incorporate some changes into its sector inquiries regime so as to increase its relevance for consumers. These changes are related to the choice of sectors and the actual conduct of the sector inquiries. First, the Commission could more actively pursue sector inquiries in retail markets so as to point to the competition law relevance for consumers in the chosen sectors. However, even when Commission sector inquiries concern intermediate markets, they are still conducted in 'key sectors of the EU economy which directly impact consumers'.[78]

---

[74] See Commission (EU), 'Staff Working Document: Ten Years of Antitrust Enforcement under Regulation 1/2003' COM(2014) 453, para 209. Commission (EU), 'Commission Launches E-commerce Sector Inquiry' (6 May 2015) (Press Release, IP/15/4921).

[75] See also Commission (EC), 'Report on the Functioning of Regulation 1/2003' (Communication) COM(2009) 206 final (Report on Regulation 1/2003), para 11. The observation on the rarity of the sector inquiry instrument seems outdated. C Kerse and N Khan, *EC Antitrust Procedure* (5th edn, Sweet and Maxwell 2005), para 1.038.

[76] Dealing with problem markets possesses an important legitimizing function. In problem markets, it is not clear whether a competition law problem exists. See F Ilzkoviitz and A Dierx, 'Problem Markets: The EU Experience' (Presentation at the CCP 10th Annual Conference) (12–13 June 2014) <http://competitionpolicy.ac.uk/documents/107435/6361808/Ilzkovitz+%26+Dierx+Presentation+2014/37775596-5939-45fd-b7ae-b1dfea77566b> accessed 28 November 2014.

[77] For a criticism on this practice see N Dunne, 'Between Competition Law and Regulation: Hybridized Approaches to Market Control' (2014) 2 JAE 225, 245–248.

[78] Report on Regulation 1/2003 (n 75), para 8. This is in line with the most common factors for case selection in relation to market studies according to an ICN report. See ICN, 'Market Studies Project Report' (Prepared by the ICN Advocacy Working Group) (June 2009), para 1.21.

In such cases, the Commission reports should expressly point to the potential benefits of its proposals for consumers. Note, for example, the final Report in the pharmaceutical sector inquiry, in which the benefits for consumers are mentioned throughout the Report although there is not a separate section dedicated to this point.[79]

Furthermore, the design of the conduct of sector inquiries should take consumer interests into account more explicitly. The questionnaires used during sector inquiries should be drafted in a manner that takes into account not only the business but also the consumer perspective.[80] The Commission should, thus, seek consumers' views and not just those of the business community and, indeed, it has done so in the past.[81] Consumers' views can further be encouraged through the introduction of a mechanism akin to the UK super-complaint procedure discussed below.

The third amendment concerns the strengthening of the Commission's remedial powers. Revision of the EU sector investigation regime so as to increase the Commission's remedial powers could prove to be beneficial for the consumer interest and increase consumer organizations' incentives to bring possible competition law violations or market problems to the attention of the Commission. However, Regulation 1/2003 did not grant the Commission such broad enforcement powers. This may suggest that there is no political will to furnish the Commission with more enforcement powers during the course of sector inquiries. In the subsequent section, this proposal is further discussed in relation to the UK markets regime.[82]

3.5 'Super-complaints': The European way

In this section, the possibility of formalizing a communication channel between consumer organizations and the Commission, akin to the UK super-complaints

---

[79] Commission (EC), 'Executive Summary of the Pharmaceutical Sector Inquiry Report' (July 2009) <http://ec.europa.eu/competition/sectors/pharmaceuticals/inquiry/communication_en.pdf> accessed 3 November 2014 (Pharma Report) 2, 7–8.

[80] Marsden and Whelan (n 67) 8.

[81] See Pharma Report (n 79) 6; Retail Banking SWD (n 71) 9.

[82] The UK markets regime has been amended by the Enterprise and Regulatory Reform Act 2013 (ERRA 2013). ERRA 2013 introduced a significant institutional change as it merged the two UK competition authorities (OFT and CC) into a unitary authority (CMA). Reference will be made to the CMA where possible, except, for example, in instances where previous case law, practices, and policy documents are discussed. In relation to the markets regime, ERRA 2013 amended the EA 2002 and any references to sections of the EA 2002 are as amended by ERRA 2013. The main changes concern the cross-market investigations and the reductions in time limits for market investigations. The main guidance on the UK market regime comprises OFT, 'Market Investigation References: Guidance about the Making of References under Part 4 of the Enterprise Act' (OFT 511) (March 2006); OFT, 'Market Studies: Guidance on the OFT Approach' (OFT 519) (2010); CMA, 'Market Studies and Market Investigations: Supplemental Guidance on the CMA's Approach' (January 2014) (CMA3); CC, 'Guidelines for Market Investigations: Their Role, Procedures, Assessment and Remedies' (April 2013) (CC3 revised). On the UK market investigation potential to tackle wider market problems see J Pickering, 'UK Market Investigations: An Economic Perspective' (2006) 5 Comp Law 206, 207–210; H Cartlidge and N Root, 'The UK

procedure, is discussed. Indeed, it has been suggested that the introduction of an 'EU super-complaints procedure', modelled upon the current UK 'super-complaints' regime, could assist with increased consumer involvement in competition law enforcement.[83] As consumer organizations point out, complaints focus on a specific competition law infringement and lack the potential to tackle wider market problems.[84] Since consumer organizations are, indeed, better placed to draw attention to consumer problems in retail markets,[85] a formal procedure of alerting the Commission should be considered as complementary to an efficient complaint-handling process.

The UK markets regime is briefly reviewed with a view to assessing the contribution of super-complaints to a more consumer-friendly competition policy.[86] No detailed account of the UK markets regime and its recent reform is provided in the scope of the present enquiry,[87] since the aim here is to make a much narrower point, namely, to show that the contribution of consumer involvement through super-complaints is beneficial to the functioning of UK markets. This argument is employed to buttress the proposal to introduce a similar mechanism at the EU level.

The EA 2002 provides that designated consumer bodies can make a complaint to the CMA and sectoral regulators when any feature of a market[88] in the UK appears to be significantly harming the interests of consumers.[89] The UK government was considering extending the super-complaint regimes to SMEs as well.[90] This proposal

---

Market Investigations Regime: A Review' (2009) 8 Comp Law 312, 315–316. On the potential of the UK market investigation regime to tackle tacit collusion problems see OFT 511, para 2.5. On the inadequacy of sector inquiries in tackling this problem see B Sufrin and M Furse, 'Market Investigations' (2002) 1 Comp Law 244, 245.

[83] P Evans, 'Making Competition Real: EU Super-Complaints' (2005) 15 CPR 187.

[84] O Dayagi Epstein, 'Representation of Consumer Interest by Consumer Associations—Salvation for the Masses?' (2007) 3 Comp L Rev 209, 237. A Murray, 'Consumers and EU Competition Policy' (Centre for European Reform, September 2005) <http://www.cer.org.uk/sites/default/files/publications/attachments/pdf/2011/policybrief_consumers-839.pdf> accessed 3 November 2014, 4.

[85] Hutchings and Whelan (n 25) 191 with further reference to Evans (n 83).

[86] As Fingleton concedes, 'The super complaints process has given greater impetus to the [consumer] group, often underrepresented in the policy debate': J Fingleton, 'Market Studies: Finding and Fixing Problem Markets' (OFT Market Studies Conference, 4 June 2008).

[87] BIS, 'A Competition Regime for Growth: A Consultation on Options for Reform' (March 2011) (BIS Consultation); BIS, 'Growth, Competition and the Competition Regime' (March 2012) (Government Response to Consultation). For a discussion of the Government's proposal see J Aitken and A Jones, 'Reforming a World Class Competition Regime: The Government's Proposal for the Creation of a Single Competition and Markets Authority' (2011) 10 Comp Law 97; J Lever, 'Fusion of the OFT and the CC: Ask for the Evidence' (2011) 10 Comp Law 126; S Wilks, 'Institutional Reform and the Enforcement of Competition Policy in the UK' (April 2011) 7 Euro CJ 1. On the changes introduced see CMA3 (n 82).

[88] See EA 2002, Section 11(9)(a) and Section 131(2) on the content of this notion.

[89] EA 2002, Section 11(1). See OFT, 'Super-Complaints: Guidance for Designated Consumer Bodies' (July 2003) (OFT 514) (OFT Super-Complaints Guidance). EA 2002, Section 205; The Enterprise Act 2002 (Super-complaints to Regulators) Order 2003 (SI 2003/1368); OFT Super-Complaints Guidance, paras 3.1–3.4; OFT, 'Terms of Reference of the Concurrency Working Party' (OFT 548) (November 2003); CMA, 'Regulated Industries: Guidance on a Concurrent Application of Competition Law to Regulated Industries' (March 2014) (CMA10), paras 4.22 and 4.23.

[90] BIS Consultation (n 87), paras 3.14–3.16.

could possibly detract from the flagship role of the super-complaints procedure, which is correcting market failures in the consumer interest.[91] Therefore, the government dropping this proposal, in the light of the criticism generated, should be viewed as a positive development.[92]

Under the super-complaints regime, the 90-day deadline within which the CMA must publish a response stating how it intends to proceed with the complaints is of particular importance.[93] Thus, the UK super-complaints procedure imposes a tight deadline on the CMA to justify its proposed actions, and so institutionalizes the dialogue between the competition authority and consumer organizations. Following a super-complaint, the options open to the CMA range from taking no action to launching a market study or making a market investigation reference.[94] To date, 14 super-complaints have been raised with the OFT, (the CMA's predecessor) the most recent with regard to travel money, on 21 September 2011.[95] It is striking that, out of these super-complaints, four market studies and three market investigations were undertaken. This data verifies the OFT's pledge to consider possible consumer detriment when choosing to undertake a market study.[96] The remaining super-complaints have also resulted in benefits for consumers, following the solutions negotiated with the industry.

Furthermore, the relationship between super-complaints and market investigations provides an additional argument in favour of consumers' potential to contribute to the well functioning of markets. Interestingly, one of the criticisms

---

[91] M Ioannidou, 'Reforming UK Competition Law Regime: The Consumer Perspective' (2012) 11 Comp Law 28, 34–35.
[92] Government Response to Consultation (n 87), paras 4.8–4.9. The Federation of Small Businesses has been designated as super-complainant to the Financial Conduct Authority (FCA) under s 234C as inserted by s 40 of the Financial Services Act 2012. See 'Financial Services Super-complainants Confirmed by Government' (19 December 2013) <https://www.gov.uk/government/news/financial-services-super-complainants-confirmed-by-government> accessed 4 November 2014; HM Treasury, 'Guidance for Bodies Seeking Designation as Super-complainants to the Financial Conduct Authority' (March 2013).
[93] EA 2002, Section 11(2).
[94] OFT Super-Complaints Guidance (n 89), para 2.25. Market studies undertaken under s 5 of the EA 2002 bear many similarities to Commission sector inquiries. They are not limited to markets in the economic sense. In the course of market studies, the CMA can examine practices across a range of goods and services that are causing adverse effects on competition and that originate either with business and consumer behaviour or government regulation and public policy, with a view to formulating proposals in order to improve the functioning of the markets. See OFT 519 (n 82), paras 2.2–2.3, 2.8. Market investigations are detailed investigations into the possible adverse effects of competition in the relevant markets. Market investigations confer on the CMA significant remedial powers, since they can influence, or even change, the structure of the market (eg divestiture). CC3 (revised) (n 82). On the impact of market investigations and consumer law remedies see C Ahlborn and D Piccinin, 'Between Scylla and Charybdis: Market Investigations and the Consumer Interest' in B Rodger (ed), *Ten Years of UK Competition Law Reform* (Dundee University Press 2010) 169, 181–183, 193–195.
[95] Materials on these super-complaints and the OFT handling of them can be found at <http://webarchive.nationalarchives.gov.uk/20140402142426/http://www.oft.gov.uk/OFTwork/markets-work/super-complaints/> accessed 4 November 2014. On 21 April 2015, Which? made a super-complaint to the CMA about 'grocery retailing in the UK'. See <https://www.gov.uk/cma-cases/groceries-pricing-super-complaint> accessed 11 May 2015.
[96] C Glover and R Owen-Howes, 'The Consumer Face of the OFT: How Does Consumer Protection Fit in with Competition Law?' (2009) 8(6) CLI 3, 5. OFT, 'Market Studies: Guidance on the OFT Approach' (OFT 519) (2010), paras 3.1–3.7.

Public Enforcement Stricto Sensu   169

of the UK markets regime that led to its reform was the low number of market investigations conducted.[97] Thus, it appears striking that out of the 13 market investigation references up until March 2011, three followed a super-complaint.[98] The number of market investigation references has increased quite significantly; during the period 2011–2014, five more market investigations were completed and two are ongoing.[99] This would suggest that super-complaints might have begun to wane. Still though, the track record for market investigations following super-complaints is important and indicates the potential for designated consumer bodies to alert the competent competition authorities to competition problems in retail markets, since market investigations are the instrument for determining whether competition is working effectively in the markets as a whole.[100]

The UK market regime is unique, as it encourages the involvement of designated consumer organizations and provides the competent authorities with powers to implement behavioural and structural remedies.[101] Generally, the UK regime is thought to be successful, and the recent reform concerning the broadening of the scope of market investigations and reductions in timescale[102] could potentially improve it even further.

In the light of this, the Commission could propose the adoption of an EU super-complaints procedure[103] building on the UK model, as well as national super-complaints procedures. In regards to EU super-complaints, the procedures and deadlines within which the Commission must respond could be introduced via an amendment to Regulation 1/2003, whereas the national super-complaint mechanisms could be introduced via emulation of the EU model by the Member States.[104]

The standing of consumer organizations to bring super-complaints should also be regulated. To that end, consumer organizations designated to raise collective

---

[97] BIS Consultation (n 87), para 3.5.
[98] Ibid. The BIS Consultation mentions 11 market investigation references. Following its publication, the OFT made five more market investigation references to the CC; these concerned the markets for aggregates, cement and ready-mix concrete in Great Britain; the market for statutory audit services to large companies in the UK; the private healthcare market; the private motor insurance market; and the payday lending market. On 6 November 2014, the CMA announced its decision to undertake a market investigation into the PCA and banking services for SMEs sectors. In addition, OFGEM made a market investigation reference to the CMA in relation to the energy market. See the list on the OFT's site, <http://webarchive.nationalarchives.gov.uk/20140402142426/http://www.oft.gov.uk/OFTwork/markets-work/references/> accessed 4 November 2014. For the more recent cases see <https://www.gov.uk/cma-cases?keywords=&case_type[]=markets&opened_date[from]=&opened_date[to]=> accessed 3 November 2014.
[99] See n 98.
[100] OFT 511 (n 82), para 2.2. However, see Marsden and Whelan (n 67) 7 who point to the argument that this can be attributed to the tight response deadline and the threat of judicial review of the OFT's decision not to make a market investigation reference. See *The Association of Convenience Stores v OFT* [2005] CAT 36 for a challenge to the OFT's decision not to make a market investigation reference.
[101] In fact, this is only possible in the UK and Israel. See BIS Consultation (n 87), para 3.4.
[102] On the adopted proposals see Government Response to Consultation (n 87) 27–39; ERRA 2013, ss 33–38.
[103] See the proposal made by Evans (n 83) 189. For a similar proposal see Murray (n 84) 4.
[104] See Chapter 7, section 4.

actions will also be entitled to raise super-complaints with the NCAs.[105] In Chapter 5 it is argued that the criteria for the designation of consumer organizations should be regulated by EU legislation.[106] The same criteria could apply to the assessment of the authority of a consumer organization with regard to raising super-complaints.

3.6 Other participation avenues: Intervention

In addition to raising complaints with the Commission, consumers/consumer organizations can apply to be heard by the Commission as third parties provided that they can demonstrate a *sufficient interest*.[107] The Commission Best Practices provide that '[u]pon application, the Commission shall also hear other natural or legal persons which can demonstrate a sufficient interest in the outcome of the procedure in accordance with Article 13 of the Implementing Regulation. The hearing officer takes the decision on whether such third persons are admitted to the proceedings'.[108]

Consumer organizations are expected to take advantage of this option, and have done so in the past,[109] since individual consumers are likely to be unaware of ongoing competition law procedures. In fact, the Commission itself seems to encourage this consumer involvement avenue, since it states that:

> consumer associations that apply to be heard should generally be regarded as having a sufficient interest, where the proceedings concern products or services used by the end-consumer or products or services that constitute a direct input into such products or services.[110]

If the Commission statement above is taken at face value, consumer organizations will be granted authorization to intervene in a large number of competition law cases. Furthermore, consumer organizations can intervene in ongoing proceedings before European courts.[111] Interventions of this kind are beneficial in bringing

---

[105] The UK designation criteria may be informative in that regard. See BERR, 'Super-Complaints: Guidance for Bodies Seeking Designation as Super-Complainants' (March 2009); HM Treasury, 'Guidance for Bodies Seeking Designation as Super-complainants to the Financial Conduct Authority' (March 2013).

[106] See Chapter 5, section 6.1.

[107] Regulation 1/2003 (n 35), Article 27(3); Regulation 773/2004 (n 35), recital 11 and Article 13(1). See also Article 11(c) of Commission Regulation (EC) No 802/2004 of 7 April 2004 implementing Council Regulation (EC) No 139/2004 on the Control of Concentrations between Undertakings [2004] OJ L133/1 on consumer organizations' right to be heard in merger control.

[108] Commission (EU), 'Notice on Best Practices for the Conduct of Proceedings Concerning Articles 101 and 102 TFEU' [2011] OJ C308/6, para 105.

[109] See, for example, consumer organizations' intervention in *Intel* (Case COMP/C-3/37.990) Commission Decision of 13 May 2009 (provisional non-confidential version) <http://ec.europa.eu/competition/antitrust/cases/dec_docs/37990/37990_3581_11.pdf> accessed 6 November 2014, paras 27, 1611.

[110] Regulation 773/2004 (n 35) recital 11. See also Commission (EU), 'Decision of the President of the European Commission on the Function and Terms of Reference of the Hearing Officer in Certain Competition Proceedings' [2011] OJ L275/29, recital 12 and Article 5(2).

[111] CJEU Statute [2008] OJ C115/210, Article 40(2) and 53(1). See, for example, Joined Cases 228 and 229/82 *Ford of Europe Incorporated and Ford Werke AG v Commission* [1984] ECR 1129;

consumer input into consideration and highlighting the consumer interest in competition law analysis. However, despite the positive influence of consumer intervention,[112] as has been shown in Chapter 2, consumer interests bear a sparing and sporadic influence on the competition law enforcement standard employed by the European courts. Hence, they need to be supplemented by additional measures.

Article 13(3) of Regulation 773/2204 provides that '[t]he...Commission may invite any other person to express its views in writing and to attend the oral hearing of the parties to whom a statement of objections has been addressed'. It is suggested that the Commission should interpret the requirement of sufficient interest liberally and actively encourage consumer organizations to intervene in ongoing procedures concerning retail markets.[113]

4. Public Enforcement *Lato Sensu*: Towards a Mixed Approach to Competition Law Enforcement

In this section, mechanisms and instances to date are covered in which compensation or alternative benefits were provided in the course of public enforcement. The employment of public enforcement mechanisms to bring relief to affected parties has been coined as 'public compensation'.[114] Instances where compensation reached the affected parties in the course of public enforcement procedures are analysed first and examples are drawn both from the Commission and Member States' practice, before discussing the potential formalization of such an approach.

Public compensation presents a flexible mechanism that can feed into different existing public enforcement procedures depending on the nature of the competition law infringement (eg Article 102 TFEU and commitment proceedings; Article 101 TFEU and cartel settlement proceedings) and the number of affected parties.[115] Depending on the nature of the violation, public compensation can be

---

T-9/92 *Automobiles Peugeot SA and Peugeot SA v Commission* [1993] ECR II-493; Cases 41/73 R and others, *Suiker Unie v Commission* [1973] ECR 1465 (intervention by Italian consumer organization); also T-336/07 *Telefónica and Telefónica de España v Commission* [2007] OJ C269/55 in which the GC granted Ausbanc Consumo permission to intervene.

[112] In that regard see also *Burgess v OFT* [2005] CAT 25, paras 84, 286–290, 344, in which Which? was granted permission to intervene, causing the CAT to pay increased attention to the consumer choice element. This point raised by Epstein, (n 84) 218.

[113] Cf A Asher, 'Enhancing the Standing of Competition Authorities with Consumers' (ICN Conference Korea, 15 April 2004) <http://www.internationalcompetitionnetwork.org/uploads/library/doc509.pdf> accessed 6 November 2014, 4.

[114] See A Ezrachi and M Ioannidou, 'Access to Justice in European Competition Law—Public Enforcement as a Supplementary Channel for "Corrective Compensation"' (2011) 19 Asia Pac L Rev 195; and A Ezrachi and M Ioannidou, 'Public Compensation as a Complementary Mechanism to Damages Actions: From Policy Justification to Formal Implementation' (2012) 6 JECLAP 536. This section builds on the analysis undertaken therein. Note that the term 'compensation' is used here in the wider sense of bringing benefits to the affected parties, either in the form of compensating their damage (actual compensation) or in the form of ancillary benefits.

[115] Andreas Schwab, the EP Rapporteur for the Directive on Damages Actions has commented that 'a regulatory redress option appears to be a successful mechanism to ensure a fast and

either formal or informal, thereby exhibiting different levels of formalization. In addition, depending on the number of injured parties, it may have a strict compensatory function when, for example, there are few injured parties, or a wider relief function when there is a large number of affected parties, each sustaining very low damage. In the latter case, public compensation possesses the potential to promote the collective consumer interest. In the light of the fused approach to competition law enforcement discussed above and the inadequate development of private enforcement in the consumer interest, public compensation presents the potential to improve this situation.

4.1 Instances of 'public compensation'

4.1.1 EU cases

The Commission's practice suggests that, despite employing public compensation sparingly, it did do so early on. In *General Motors*, the Commission found that General Motors (GM) had abused its dominant position by imposing excessive prices and engaging in price discrimination that impeded parallel trade.[116] GM reimbursed the excessive amount in two instances, a fact that the Commission considered in GM's favour when setting the amount of the fine.[117]

In *Pre-Insulated Pipe Cartel*, the Commission reduced the fine imposed on one of the cartel members (ABB) because it had provided substantial compensation to its damaged competitor. In fact this was the only accepted extenuating circumstance.[118] ABB and its competitor (Powerpipe) reached a settlement that involved a payment of substantial compensation. The parties agreed that the terms and conditions of the settlement would remain confidential.[119]

In *Nintendo*, the Commission found that the respective distribution system had severely restricted intra-brand competition and partitioned the single market and it imposed high fines on the implicated undertakings. Nonetheless, the Commission took into consideration the fact that Nintendo had cooperated with it and at the instigation of the Commission offered substantial financial compensation to the affected parties as an extenuating circumstance. As a result it granted a fine reduction, although compared to the fine imposed, this reduction was rather minimal. In the three cases discussed above, the Commission found an infringement and fined the incumbents. The voluntary compensation provided

---

cost-efficient compensation tool'. See A Schwab, 'Finding the Right Balance—the Deliberations of the European Parliament on the Draft Legislation Regarding Damage Claims' (2014) 5 JECLAP 65, 67.

[116] *General Motors Continental* (Case No IV/28.851) Commission Decision 75/75/EEC [1975] OJ L29/14, paras 8–11.

[117] Ibid, para 18.

[118] *Pre-Insulated Pipe Cartel* (Case No IV/35.691/E-4) Commission Decision 1999/60/EC [1999] OJ L24/1, paras 127, 172. The total amount of the fine imposed on ABB was ECU 70 million and the respective fine reduction was ECU 5 million.

[119] Ibid, para 127. ABB has supplied the Commission with a copy of the respective agreement.

was treated as an extenuating circumstance but ultimately that remains at the discretion of the Commission.[120]

In *Deutsche Bahn*, the Commission accepted the commitments offered by Deutsche Bahn (DB) to dispel its concerns about margin squeeze in relation to DB Energie pricing practices. DB Energie amended its pricing system for traction current (ie electricity used to power locomotives) to apply uniformly to all railway companies and to allow other electricity suppliers to provide traction current to railway companies. In addition, the commitments offered entailed an element of public compensation since DB Energie committed to providing a 4% discount on the traction current supplied to railway companies not belonging to DB based on their preceding year's invoices, thereby ensuring that the latter benefited immediately from the lower prices.[121]

Deutsche Bahn constitutes the first use of public compensation in the context of commitment proceedings. Nonetheless, prior to the official enactment of such proceedings with Article 9 of Regulation 1/2003, there have been instances of public compensation in cases closed informally. In *Macron*, the Commission ended its investigation after Angus Fire pledged to comply with Article 102 TFEU in the future and provided an *ex gratia* payment to the complainant, Macron.[122]

In *Rover*, Rover Group revised its discount scheme and notified the Commission and the OFT.[123] Furthermore, it committed to compensating its dealers and donating £1 million to the Consumer Association (now Which?). This donation was to be overseen by an independent board and spent on consumer information services. In its annual competition report for that year the Commission clarified that the donation did not affect consumers' right to compensation.[124]

In *Sony/Phillips Licensing Agreement*, an amended Standard Licensing Agreement was drafted and cleared by the Commission by means of a comfort letter. Philips also committed to making a payment to each licensee of $10,000 on

---

[120] Case T-59/02 *Archer Daniels Midland Co v Commission* [2006] ECR II-3627, paras 354–355.

[121] Commission (EU), 'Antitrust: Commission Accepts Legally Binding Commitments from Deutsche Bahn Concerning Pricing of Traction Current in Germany' (Press Release, 18 December 2013); Commission Decision of 18 December 2013 (Case COMP/AT.39678/*Deutsche Bahn I*; Case COMP/AT.39731/*Deutsche Bahn II*) (non-confidential version) <http://ec.europa.eu/competition/antitrust/cases/dec_docs/39678/39678_2514_15.pdf> accessed 27 October 2014. See also T Steinvorth, 'Deutsche Bahn: Commitments End Margin Squeeze Investigation' (2014) 5 JECLAP 628.

[122] Reference to this case in PR Beaumont and S Weatherill, *EU Law* (3rd edn, Penguin 1999) 909–910. See also Seventeenth Report on Competition Policy (n 28), para 81.

[123] No official decision was issued on this case. See Commission (EC), XXIIIrd Report on Competition Policy 1993 (1994), para 228. See P Evans, 'Consumer Interest and Supercomplaints' (Consumers' Association Presentation) <http://www.incsoc.net/conf-2ppt5.ppt> accessed 6 November 2014; see also R Mulheron, 'Cy-pres Damages Distribution in England: A New Era for Consumer Redress' (2009) 20 EBLR 307, 320–21 pointing to the lack of information regarding this case; G Howells and R James, 'Litigation in the Consumer Interest' (2003) 9 ILSA J Int'l & Comp L 1, 40; and Nicholson Lord, 'Rover "Pays" 1m Pounds Compensation' (*The Independent*, 17 November 1993).

[124] XXIIIrd Report (n 123).

royalties due.¹²⁵ Therefore, it seems that informal contacts between parties may provide an economic benefit of some sort for the victims. However, the alleged victims should possess bargaining power against the incumbent undertakings, a condition unlikely to be fulfilled by consumer organizations, and even less by individual consumers.

4.1.2 National cases

Competition law enforcement in different Member States depicts some sparse instances of public compensation. One of the most discussed cases at national level is *UK Independent Schools*, concerning an information exchange agreement on future prices between 50 fee-paying independent schools.¹²⁶ Following the issuance of the statement of objections, the implicated schools approached the OFT and voluntarily offered to provide compensation in lieu of a fine. Following discussions, the schools accepted liability for the infringement of Chapter I prohibition (Article 101 TFEU equivalent) and made an *ex gratia* £3 million payment to an educational charitable trust for the benefit of students attending the schools in the relevant period. In return, only nominal fines were imposed.¹²⁷ The treatment of this case represented a pragmatic compromise in the light of the possible effects of any fine leading to an increase in student fees.¹²⁸

Examples of public compensation are also found in the Netherlands. First, in *Interpay*, which concerned an agreement between eight banks to establish Interpay as the single provider of network services for PIN payments, the imposed fines were reduced following the creation of a €10 million fund with the aim of promoting an efficient payment system. This case also had an abusive practice element since Interpay was allegedly charging excessive PIN tariffs. The Dutch Competition Authority discontinued its investigations into this matter since it would have been very complex and time consuming. In addition, a compensatory scheme was reached between the banks and retailers offering PIN payments to consumers.¹²⁹ Second, the Dutch Competition Authority also encouraged the provision of compensation during the settlement procedures in the *construction*

---

¹²⁵ See Commission (EC), XXXIIIrd Report on Competition Policy 2003, SEC(2004) 658 final, 197–200; On this case see MA Pena Castellot, 'Commission Settles Allegations of Abuse and Clears Patent Pools in the CD Market' [2003] 3 CPN 56–59.
¹²⁶ OFT Decision No CA98/05/2006 (*UK Independent Schools*), paras 1–2, 6.
¹²⁷ Ibid, para 36.
¹²⁸ J Lawrence and M Sansom, 'The Increasing Use of Administrative Settlement Procedures in UK and EC Competition Investigations' (2007) 6 Comp Law 163, 168.
¹²⁹ See the Netherlands Competition Authority '*NMa herziet boetes banken en Interpay*' (Press Release, 22 December 2005) <http://www.nma.nl/documenten_en_publicaties/archiefpagina_nieuwsberichten/nieuwsberichten/archief/2005/05_46_interpay.aspx> accessed 6 November 2014 (in Dutch). See also J Bourgeois and S Strievi, 'EU Competition Remedies in Consumer Cases: Thinking Out of the Shopping Bag' (2010) 33 W Comp 241, 250. See also P Kalbfleisch, 'The Dutch Experience with Plea Bargaining/Direct Settlements' in CD Ehlermann and M Marquis (eds), *European Competition Law Annual 2007* (Hart 2008) 481, 483–484; P Bos, 'International Scrutiny for Payment Card Systems' (2006) 73 Antitrust LJ 739, 756–761; M Spoek, 'The Dutch Competition Authority Considers Cooperation and Joint Selling of Network Services for Pin-Transactions To Be

cartel case.[130] A 10% fine reduction was granted provided that the implicated undertakings reached a compensation agreement with the Dutch government, which had been damaged by the respective cartel.

In Germany, examples of public compensation stem from the energy sector. The investigation into alleged excessive gas prices was closed following the commitments offered by 29 gas suppliers to refund €127 million to the affected customers through bonus payments and credits on future accounts. In a similar manner, in *Stadwerke Uelzen*, a local gas supplier was ordered to reimburse its customers, and the remedy was upheld by the German Supreme Court.[131] In the electric heating market, the Bundeskartellamt concluded its abuse proceedings following commitments offered by the incumbents that included, amongst other things, the reimbursement of affected customers. In 2010, 13 providers committed to reimbursing approximately 530,000 electric heating customers the amount of €27.2 million,[132] and in 2012 the Bundeskartellamt issued a ruling on abusive pricing against Entega ordering it to pay out €5 million to 23,000 electric heating customers.[133]

The cases mentioned above indicate that the Commission, as well as NCAs, have in the past employed innovative ways of providing compensation during the course of public enforcement procedures. However, if these procedures are really to be employed in the consumer interest they need to be institutionalized. This possibility is discussed in section 4.3.

4.2 Categorization of cases

The cases of public compensation to date can be categorized according to two criteria: first, the number of injured parties; and, second, the provision of public compensation after a formal infringement decision or informal settlement.

---

an Infringement of the Cartel Prohibiton *(Interpay)*' (e-Competitions) <http://www.concurrences.com/article.php3?id_article=35979&lang=fr> accessed 6 November 2014.

[130] See O Brouwer, 'Antitrust Settlements in the Netherlands: A Useful Source of Inspiration' in Ehlermann and Marquis (n 129) 489, 492–493.

[131] There are references to these two cases in C Canenbley and T Steinvorth, 'Effective Enforcement of Competition Law: Is There a Solution to the Conflict between Leniency Programmes and Private Damages Actions?' (2011) 2 J Eur CL & P 315, 325. See Bundeskartellamt, 'Preismissbrauchsverfahren gegen Gasversorger weitgehend abgeschlossen' (Press Release, 1.12.2008) on the first case. See Stadtwerke Uelzen BGH, Decision of 10 December 2008—KVR 2/08—OLG Celle, on the second case.

[132] Bundeskartellamt, 'Successful Conclusion of Abuse Proceedings Against Electric Heating Providers' (29 September 2010) (Press Release) <http://www.bundeskartellamt.de/SharedDocs/Meldung/EN/Pressemitteilungen/2010/29_09_2010_Heizstrom.html;jsessionid=D5DECDEABC4D4B88530073EB51D637A7.1_cid362?nn=3591568> accessed 23 December 2014.

[133] Bundeskartellamt, 'Bundeskartellamt Issues Ruling on Abusive Practices against Entega' (20 March 2012) (Press Release) <http://www.bundeskartellamt.de/SharedDocs/Meldung/EN/Pressemitteilungen/2012/20_03_2012_Entega.html> accessed 23 December 2014. See also U Scholz and S Purps, 'The Application of EU Competition Law in the Energy Sector' (2013) 4 JECLAP 63, 70.

176   *Consumers and Public Competition Law*

The *first category* includes instances such as the *UK Independent Schools, Rover, Interpay,* and *German energy* cases, in which the injured parties are numerous and cannot be individually identified. This category covers all infringements that affect a large number of consumers. The *second category* concerns cases with a limited number of victims that are direct customers or competitors, where each one suffers a high level of harm. This was the case in *Nintendo, General Motors, Pre-Insulated Pipe Cartel, Macron,* and *Sony/Phillips Licensing Agreement*. With regard to the first category, attainment of the compensatory aim of EU competition law enforcement would be very difficult. This presents a gap that public compensation might fill. As will be discussed below, the economic benefits accruing to affected consumers resemble those flowing from collective actions, as discussed in Chapter 5.

Based on the second criterion, the first category contains cases in which formal infringement procedures were initiated and a fine was imposed (eg *Independent Schools, Nintendo, General Motors, Pre-Insulated Pipe Cartel*) and the second comprises cases that were closed without issuance of an official infringement decision or the imposition of a fine (eg *Deutsche Bahn, Rover, Sony/Phillips Licensing Agreement*). Depending on the level of formality, the approach to public compensation needs to be regulated accordingly; however, for the latter type of cases any approach can only remain informal in the light of the nature of the respective procedures.

4.3 Institutionalizing a public compensation approach

The sparse and sporadic use of public compensation points to the possible institutionalization of the relevant procedure by drawing insights from experience to date.[134] At the same time, public compensation has been employed in a diverse range of cases and in many different forms, which suggests that it is difficult to formalize it with a sufficient degree of accuracy. Arguably, it may not only be difficult but also undesirable, since the very advantage of such an approach lies in its flexibility. However, public compensation could be incorporated into the current enforcement mechanisms in a more formal, structured, and principled manner. This section develops both a formal and an informal approach to public compensation. The former is appropriate in cases where an infringement decision is adopted and a fine imposed while the latter may be applied in the course of more informal proceedings, such as commitment proceedings.

An institutionalized approach to 'public compensation' will increase its visibility, improve legal certainty,[135] and render the functioning of the EU authorities

---

[134] See R Cichowski, *The European Court and Civil Society* (CUP 2007) 5 on the term 'institutionalization', in which she states that 'institutionalisation can be measured in terms of whether the current EU institutions (rules and procedures) governing the legal domain become more binding, precise and enforceable and whether they expand in scope'.

[135] Since Guidelines limit the Commission's discretion and may produce legal effects. See Joined Cases C-189/02 P, C-202/02 P, C-205-208/02 P, and C-213/02 P *Dansk Rørindustri and Others v Commission* [2005] ECR I-5425, 211.

(in this case, the Commission) as well as NCAs more transparent.[136] At the same time, both formal and informal public compensation would signal the potential of competition law to benefit the victims of anti-competitive practices, thereby furthering the ancillary institutional benefits.

Public compensation serves distributive justice as it brings benefits back to the affected parties. However, it does not present an accurate quantification of the damage inflicted and therefore departs from the notion of compensatory damages, correlativity, and corrective justice.[137] Public compensation provides a flexible mechanism that brings benefits back to the injured parties, who are identified on an individual basis, or to the injured class.

The proposed formal mechanism views compensation as a type of behavioural remedy that supplements the fine imposed.[138] It will be structured primarily as a remedy to be considered in cartel cases and alternatively as a less formal remedy where there is some voluntary element of participation by the infringer. Finally, voluntary public compensation in the course of commitment proceedings will be discussed.

Public compensation could be incorporated into existing enforcement mechanisms. Article 7 of Regulation 1/2003 enables the Commission to impose behavioural and structural remedies provided that they are proportionate and necessary in order to end an infringement. Public compensation could thus be seen as a form of behavioural remedy to be imposed in appropriate cases.[139] The discount offered in *Deutsche Bahn* constitutes such a remedy. However, the commitment procedure allows the Commission more leeway to impose remedies, thereby evading the risk of being challenged before the EU courts, which may find the behavioural remedies imposed disproportionate.[140]

---

[136] See Macrory Report (n 4) 10, 33. Macrory asks regulators to enforce in a transparent manner and be transparent in the way they determine administrative penalties.

[137] For a succinct discussion on corrective and distributive justice see I Lianos, 'Competition Law Remedies in Europe: Which Limits for Remedial Discretion?' (January 2013) CLES Research Paper Series 2/2013 <http://papers.ssrn.com/sol3/papers.cfm?abstract_id=2235817> accessed 6 November 2014, 26–33. See also S Perry, 'On the Relationship Between Corrective and Distributive Justice' in J Horder (ed), *Oxford Essays in Jurisprudence* (OUP 2000) 237. On the notions of corrective justice and correlativity as central premises in private law relations see E Weinrib, *Corrective Justice* (OUP 2012); E Weinrib, *The Idea of Private Law* (OUP 2012).

[138] Ezrachi and Ioannidou (n 114). See also Canenbley and Steinvorth (n 131) 324–326 for a similar proposal; however, as a mechanism to avoid conflicts between private enforcement and leniency programmes and as an alternative (not a supplement) to private enforcement.

[139] 'Public compensation' presents characteristics of both sanctions and remedies. The OECD distinguishes between remedies and sanctions in that '[r]emedies cure, correct, or prevent, whereas sanctions penalise or punish. Typically, remedies aim to stop a violator's unlawful conduct, its anticompetitive effects, and their recurrence, as well as to restore competition. Sanctions are usually meant to deter unlawful conduct in the future, to compensate victims, and to force violators to disgorge their illegal gains': OECD, 'Remedies and Sanctions in Abuse of Dominance Cases' (2006) (DAF/COMP (2006)19) 18. Arguably though the objectives of remedies and sanctions intersect.

[140] As happened in Case T-395/94 *Atlantic Container Line AB v Commission* [2002] ECR II-875, para 140. On the limited judicial review of commitment decisions see F Wagner von-Papp, 'Best and Even Better Practices in Commitment Procedures after Alrosa: The Dangers of Abandoning the "Struggle for Competition Law"' (2012) 49 CMLRev 929. See Case C-441/07 P *Commission v Alrosa* [2010] ECR I-5949.

Public compensation could form part of the pecuniary penalties imposed following the finding of an infringement, namely the fine plus the purported economic benefits to the affected parties. The Fine Guidelines could be amended so as to reflect this approach. In particular, the Commission could increase the fine in appropriate cases in order to improve deterrence; the Guidelines provide that 'the Commission will also take into account the need to increase the fine in order to exceed the amount of gains improperly made as a result of the infringement where it is possible to estimate that amount'.[141] This paragraph chimes well with the redistributive aim of public compensation and can be coupled with the consideration that this extra amount should benefit the affected parties. The calculation of public compensation will be decided on a case-by-case basis and should not exceed the maximum permitted level of fines.[142] Public compensation as an addition to the fine can be incorporated in cartel settlement procedures that permit a more efficient approach to cartel cases and may prove to be a very powerful tool in the light of their more frequent use and the Commission's accumulated experience.[143]

In addition and reflecting a voluntary approach to public compensation, the Fine Guidelines could add the provision of voluntary compensation as a mitigating factor for the reduction of the imposed fine.[144] This approach is in line with the Directive on Damages Actions, which stipulates that 'actions for damages are only one element of an effective system of private enforcement of infringements of competition law and are complemented by alternative avenues of redress, such as consensual dispute resolution or public enforcement decisions that give parties an incentive to provide compensation'.[145] Article 18(3) of the

---

[141] Fine Guidelines (n 3), para 31.
[142] See Regulation 1/2003 (n 35), Article 23(2) and (3) on calculating the amount of fines. See Fine Guidelines (n 3), paras 32–33 on the maximum legal levels of fines.
[143] Commission Regulation (EC) No 622/2008 of 30 June 2008 amending Regulation (EC) No 773/2004; as regards the conduct of settlement procedures in cartel cases, [2008] L171/3, recital 4; Commission (EC), 'Notice on the Conduct of Settlement Procedures in View of the Adoption of Decisions Pursuant to Article 7 and Article 23 of Council Regulation (EC) No 1/2003 in Cartel Cases' [2008] 167/1. As at December 2014 the Commission had reached 17 settlements, more recently in Swiss Franc interest rate derivatives and in paper envelopes. See Commission (EU), 'Commission Settles Cartel on Bid-Ask Spreads Charged on Swiss Franc Interest Rate Derivatives' (IP/14/1190) (Press Release, 21 October 2014); Commission (EU), 'Commission Fines Five Envelope Producers over €19.4 million in Cartel Settlement' (IP/14/2583) (Press Release, 11 December 2014).
[144] Mitigating factors are described in the Fine Guidelines (n 3), para 29. Temple Lang also proposed a similar inclusion in the Commission's Leniency Notice. See J Temple Lang, 'European Community Competition Policy: How Far Does it Benefit Consumers?' (2004) 18 *Boletin Latinoamericano de Competencia* 128, 133. See J Lever, 'Whether, and if so How, the EC Commission's 2006 Guidelines on Setting Fines for Infringements of Articles 81 and 82 of the EC Treaty are Fairly Subject to Serious Criticism' (Opinion) <http://www.bdi.eu/download_content/Publikation_BDI_Gutachten__Opinion__zu_EU_Bussgeldleitlinien.pdf> accessed 6 November 2014 for a proposal for a two-step approach on the imposition of fines, the first concerning the finding of liability and the second the imposition of fines and compensation offered by the undertaking. This has already been adopted in the Netherlands and Spain. See NMa Fining Code 2007, para 49 (in Dutch); Spanish Competition Act 15/2007 of 3 July, Article 64(3)(c). In a similar vein in the UK, see Macrory Report (n 4) 49.
[145] Directive 2014/104/EU of the European Parliament and of the Council of 26 November 2014 on Certain Rules Governing Actions for Damages under National Law for Infringements of the Competition Law Provisions of the Member States and of the European Union [2014] OJ L 349/1, recital 5.

Directive on Damages Actions provides that national competition authorities may consider the voluntary provision of compensation prior to a decision imposing a fine as a mitigating factor. Thus, consistency considerations advocate in favour of the Commission adopting such an approach and amending its Fine Guidelines accordingly. The UK Consumer Rights Act goes a step further in blending private and public competition law enforcement as it empowers the CMA to approve redress schemes.[146]

Finally, and as the Commission's recent approach in *Deutsche Bahn* suggests, public compensation can be employed in Article 9 of Regulation 1/2003 commitment proceedings.[147] The flexible nature of commitment decisions allows the Commission to request the provision of innovative remedies.

Public compensation, either formal or informal, should be complementary to private enforcement, so injured parties should not be barred from launching damages actions. This corresponds with the Commission's approach in *Rover*. In cases where public compensation has been offered, the injured parties may still have the incentive to claim damages in court. Where part of the public compensation is paid directly to the injured parties, that sum could be deducted from any future damages that they obtain through the court. However, follow-on actions are unlikely in cases in which victims suffer a low level of damage.

4.4 Serving the collective consumer interest

The collective consumer interest can thus be served both by appropriately structured collective actions and through public compensation, where appropriate. The means of quantification and distribution of damages to affected consumers are similar. Channelling back the economic benefits in cases involving a large number of victims resembles the distribution conundrum in opt-out collective actions.[148] In this case the employment of cy-près distribution through the establishment of a consumer fund may prove workable. The distribution should primarily encourage consumers to claim their individual damage if possible, and employ cy-près as the second best option. The cases discussed above that involve a large number of affected parties suggest that competition authorities have been particularly innovative in the distribution of compensation, either through the establishment of a fund (*UK Independent Schools, Interpay*), donation to a consumer organization (*Rover*), or bonus payments on customers' future accounts (*German gas* cases).

In multiparty consumer cases, in the light of the unsatisfactory approach in the Commission Recommendation[149] and its flexible remedial nature, public compensation may fill the current gap in promoting the collective consumer interest in competition law.

---

[146] See n 20.   [147] See Bourgeois and Strievi (n 129) 246–248.
[148] See Chapter 5, section 6.3.   [149] See the analysis in Chapter 5.

5. Conclusion

In this chapter the current participation avenues open to consumers to become involved in public competition law enforcement, as well as their relevant shortcomings, have been assessed. A normative argument was put forward for suggesting certain changes in the respective public enforcement mechanisms. The proposed changes contribute to the overall deterrence potential of the enforcement system, and simultaneously bring ancillary institutional benefits. Even the proposal regarding the institutionalization of the public compensation approach, and the introduction of compensatory elements to public enforcement, is important, not only for promoting compensation but also for the advancement of deterrence and the ancillary aims as well. The proposals to enhance public participation avenues are mutually reinforcing and complementary.

The system could function such that a consumer or consumer organization complaint is brought first before the Commission or before an NCA. Second, the competition authority should seriously address the complaint and provide reasons for choosing to dismiss it, if it decides to do so. If the Commission rejects the complaint for lack of EU interest, it should forward the complaint to the most relevant NCA. If the complaint is examined and a fine is contemplated, the competition authority could, in addition to the fine, examine the possibility of imposing public compensation. Also, the incumbent undertaking could consider the option of making an offer for compensation with a view to reducing the fine imposed. Consumer participation in public enforcement could, thus, strengthen the functioning of the enforcement system as a whole.

7

Overcoming Institutional and Political Limitations

Appropriate Instruments for the Introduction of European-Wide Measures

1. Introduction

In this concluding chapter, the EU framework and the constitutional division of power between the Union institutions and the Member States is examined with a view to determining whether the proposals encouraging consumer participation and promoting the consumer interest in competition law enforcement articulated in Chapters 4, 5, and 6 could be introduced via an EU legislative instrument. First, the relevant proposals in the fields of private and public enforcement are briefly presented. Emphasis is placed on their common elements in the light of the fused approach to competition law enforcement. The mechanisms discussed point to the potential of private and public enforcement to promote both deterrence and compensation while accounting for additional ancillary benefits. This is reflected in certain common elements of the proposed mechanisms.

Following this, the extent to which the current Treaty framework permits the adoption of the relevant measures is explored. Furthermore, attention is placed on the fact that, even if the legal hurdles involved in finding an adequate legal base were to be overcome, there remain important political limitations that would impede the adoption of the measures. The analysis seeks a solution, *de lege ferenda*, for the introduction of the proposals encouraging consumer involvement. At the same time, it explores workable alternatives in the current political and institutional environment.

2. Enhancing Consumer Participation: Political Obstacles and the Proposed Measures

2.1 Political obstacles and the Directive on Damages Actions

The EU Directive on Damages Actions,[1] together with the Commission Recommendation on common principles for collective redress,[2] have improved certain aspects of private enforcement. Nonetheless, these measures are still unlikely to promote consumer participation. In particular, the proposals on indirect purchaser standing and the passing-on defence, as well as the proposals on access to evidence discussed in Chapter 4, have made it easier to bring claims for competition law violations.

Following the Directive on Damages Actions indirect purchasers are granted standing, and the passing-on defence is permitted with the concomitant alleviation of the burden of proof for indirect purchasers through the adoption of a rebuttable presumption that the overcharge has been passed on.[3] Regarding access to evidence, the Directive on Damages Actions has introduced wider disclosure rules and allowed disclosure for specifically defined categories of documents.[4]

Notwithstanding the above improvements, previous proposals to adopt binding rules on collective redress have been abandoned.[5] The modest Directive on Damages Actions and the non-binding Recommendation on collective redress should be read in the light of the opposition expressed by two main groups of actors, the business lobby and a number of Member States, as their comments on the Green Paper (GP), the White Paper (WP), and the public consultation on collective redress reveal.[6] In particular, businesses and business associations,

---

[1] Directive 2014/104/EU of the European Parliament and of the Council of 26 November 2014 on Certain Rules Governing Actions for Damages Under National Law for Infringements of the Competition Law Provisions of the Member States and of the European Union [2014] OJ L349/1.

[2] Commission (EU), 'Recommendation of 11 June 2013 on Common Principles for Injunctive and Compensatory Collective Redress Mechanisms in the Member States Concerning Violations of Rights Granted under Union Law' [2013] OJ L201/60.

[3] See Articles 12–14 of the Directive on Damages Actions (n 1). See Chapter 4, section 3.3.

[4] See Articles 5–7 of the Directive on Damages Actions (n 1). See Chapter 4, section 4.

[5] For example, on the proposals contained in the Draft Damages Directive see Chapter 5, text to n 15.

[6] See generally comments on the GP <http://ec.europa.eu/competition/antitrust/actionsdamages/green_paper_comments.html> accessed 10 November 2014; Comments on the WP <http://ec.europa.eu/competition/antitrust/actionsdamages/white_paper_comments.html> accessed 10 November 2014; Comments on Public Consultation <http://ec.europa.eu/competition/consultations/2011_collective_redress/index_en.html> accessed 10 November 2014. The comments on the public consultation are summarized in M Mertens and others, 'Detailed Minutes of the Public Hearing "Towards a Coherent European Approach to Collective Redress"' (28/10/2011) <http://ec.europa.eu/competition/consultations/2011_collective_redress/study_heidelberg_hearing_en.pdf> accessed 14 November 2014; H Hess and others, 'Evaluation of the Contributions to the Public Consultation and Hearing: "Towards a Coherent European Approach to Collective Redress"' (28/10/11) <http://ec.europa.eu/competition/consultations/2011_collective_redress/study_heidelberg_contributions_en.pdf> accessed 14 November 2014.

with the exception of SMEs, and certain companies that have been harmed by cartel activity (eg customers in the beer, paper, and elevator cartels) have opposed the Commission's efforts in promoting private competition law enforcement.[7] Further, in the public consultation on collective redress, 15 Member States submitted comments; five Member States favoured a non-binding instrument (Austria, the Czech Republic, France, Germany, and Hungary) whereas 10 were in favour of legislation, but were divided on whether it should be competition law specific or horizontally applicable. Six Member States were in favour of the former (Bulgaria, Greece, Poland, Portugal, Sweden, and the UK) whereas four were in favor of the latter (Austria, the Czech Republic, Denmark, and the Netherlands).[8] However, even the Member States that supported a binding instrument had different views on how collective action mechanisms should be structured.

Member States and business associations depart from different standpoints, but they were both critical of the adoption of private enforcement measures that could act as a deterrent to competition law violations.[9] Member States with a civil law tradition view the formulation of private enforcement measures based on the deterrence principle as contrary to their individualistic approach to litigation.[10] For example, proposals on opt-out collective actions and innovative ways to distribute damages awards cannot be reconciled with these systems' prevailing principle of corrective justice. Thus, Member States' main concern is not to jeopardize their national legal systems. Meanwhile, businesses are driven by their own concerns regarding the dissuasive effects and costs that increased private competition litigation would entail. These concerns voiced by the Member States, as the main actors in the EU, and by businesses with a strong influence, indicate that the future of consumer participation in private competition law enforcement is not promising, despite consumer representatives urging the Commission to adopt measures to improve consumer damages claims by providing both for deterrence and compensation to affected consumers.[11]

---

[7] Commission (EU), 'Damages Actions for Breach of the EU Antitrust Rules' (Impact Assessment Report—Staff Working Document) SWD (2013) 203 final, paras 9–11.
[8] Ibid, para 20.
[9] See, for example, ICC, 'ICC Comments on the Commission Green Paper on Damages Actions for Breach of the EC Antitrust Rules'; also CBI, 'EC Commission Green Paper on Damages Actions—CBI Response' (April 2006) 1. See 'White Paper: Adopts a Conservative Approach' (2008) 1 GCLR R-48; 'French Government Bodies Comment on White Paper on Damages Actions for Breach of EC Antitrust Rules' (2008) 1 GCLR R-51; 'Germany Comments on the Commission's White Paper on Damages Actions for Breach of the EC Antitrust Rules' (2008) 1 GCLR R-52.
[10] See Chapter 3, text to nn 92–93.
[11] Finnish Consumer Ombudsman and others, 'The EC Green Paper on Damages Actions for Breach of the EC Antitrust Rules' (21 April 2006); UFC-Que Choisir, 'Contribution au livre vert de la Commission Europeenne'; Which, 'Consultation Response' (12 April 2006). These contributions are available at <http://ec.europa.eu/competition/antitrust/actionsdamages/green_paper_comments.html> accessed 20 November 2014. Consumer organizations possess limited powers to influence decision-making at EU level. See, for example, H Heinelt and B Meinke-Brandmaier, 'Comparing Civil Society Participation in European Environmental Policy and Consumer Protection' in S Smismans (ed), *Civil Society and Legitimate European Governance* (Edward Elgar 2003) 196, 201–202.

In principle, the EU legal framework allows for the adoption of measures to improve consumer participation and further both deterrence and compensation. The remainder of this chapter discusses the content of these measures and points to their common elements before untangling the legal complexities pertaining to the adoption of such measures and exploring whether the EU has the relevant legislative competence. In effect, EU competence in the field could be used as an argument to overcome the concerns expressed and, if overcoming these were not possible, EU competence could allow the Commission to make the necessary suggestions through appropriate soft law instruments.

2.2 Content of the proposals

Despite the improvements to private competition law enforcement introduced by the Directive on Damages Actions, it remains very difficult to bring consumer damages claims under the existing procedural framework in many Member States. The provisions in the Directive on Damages Actions should be complemented by more enabling provisions for consumer claims as well as provisions on collective redress. Special disclosure rules for consumer damages claims should be introduced, as an exception to the general disclosure rule based on fact pleading. National courts should order disclosure of the relevant documents provided that the claimant has presented a plausible claim concerning the existence of a competition law violation. Rules on access to the competition authority's file should also reflect a more lenient approach allowing disclosure of documents to consumer organizations, provided that these documents are used only for the purposes of private litigation.[12]

The Commission's proposals also failed to introduce a workable collective action mechanism. The analysis in this book has advocated that such a mechanism should have certain characteristics and incorporate elements of public control. In particular, opt-out collective actions need to be introduced allowing standing to representative consumer organizations and public bodies. Consumer organizations need to be recognized prior to the bringing of the action or ad hoc by the court and the respective conditions for authorization should be regulated at EU level. Funding for recognized consumer organizations should be derived from private means, namely their members and public sources, from successful litigation, and possibly through the establishment of a consumer litigation fund. Importantly, distribution of the damages award should place emphasis first on individual distribution and when this is not possible it should opt for cy-près distribution.[13]

Throughout the analysis of measures facilitating consumer involvement in private competition law enforcement, political constraints on the Commission in the light of businesses' and Member States' concerns have often permeated, pointing to a gap between the Commission's aspirations and its actual potential to necessitate change. Therefore, examining available participation avenues in the field of public enforcement was seen as a solution to bridging this gap. To this end, the following proposals

[12] See Chapter 4, section 4.2.
[13] On this proposal see Chapter 5, section 6.

were formulated: first, the introduction of a consumer complaints allocation mechanism. If the Commission rejects a complaint made by a consumer/consumer organization, it should allocate it to the most competent NCA. Second, the Commission should increase the relevance of the sector inquiries regime for consumers by actively seeking consumer input when conducting sector inquiries and expressly pointing to the benefits that consumers derive from them. A proposal worth considering in the future is to amend the sector inquiries regime so that the Commission can propose binding remedies. Third, the introduction of a procedure akin to that of the UK super-complaints procedure at EU level would make consumer interest more explicit in competition law enforcement. An EU super-complaints procedure could then, possibly, inspire the adoption of similar procedures at national level. Fourthly, public compensation should be incorporated into the current mechanisms.[14]

The advocated proposals comprise both private and public enforcement mechanisms and display certain common elements. The first common element is the leading role ascribed to representative bodies (consumer organizations) and public authorities, either in raising private actions or in exercising a supervisory role, for example, by certifying the respective consumer organizations. The supervisory courts' role in private enforcement proceedings and the competition authorities' involvement in public compensation attests the importance given to public authorities. Second, public and private mechanisms, in effect, incorporate very similar distribution mechanisms. Third, both mechanisms promote the collective consumer interest and are not confined to a strict compensatory approach. The following table (Table 7.1) depicts these similarities.

Table 7.1 Proposals Increasing Consumer Participation: Common Elements

	Private enforcement	Public compensation	Public enforcement *stricto sensu*
Role of representatives and public bodies	Certified consumer organizations granted standing	Role of the NCA—imposed remedy (fine plus)	Complaints
	Consumer organizations certified ad hoc—granted standing—managerial role of the court	Role of the NCA—voluntary compensation (fine minus)	Super-complaints
	Public bodies granted standing	Role of the NCA—informal remedies—commitment procedure	Intervention
Group	Opt-out group formation—every affected consumer included	Opt-out group formation—every affected consumer included	
	Safety valves: court's supervisory role over certification and notice	Safety valves: NCAs supervisory role over the remedy	

(*Continued*)

[14] On these proposals see Chapter 6, sections 3 and 4.

Table 7.1 Continued

	Private enforcement	Public compensation	Public enforcement *stricto sensu*
Benefits calculation and distribution	Calculation based on illegal profits	Flexible remedy—part of the inflicted harm	
	Damages primarily distributed to individual victims—portion to consumer organization for litigation expenses—consumer fund	Cy-près	

3. Implementing the Proposals

3.1 Justifying a competition-specific harmonization of procedural rules for consumer claims

The first issue that needs to be addressed is whether, *de lege ferrenda*, the EU legal framework allows for the adoption of specific rules facilitating consumer damages actions for competition law violations, as opposed to the horizontal approach adopted in the Commission Recommendation.[15]

The adoption of the Directive on Damages Actions has already set a precedent for the specific harmonization of procedural rules for competition claims. This is consistent with the policy discussions on private competition law enforcement, since the Commission has repeatedly stressed that its initiative on private competition law enforcement was not about unnecessarily harmonizing national tort and civil procedure rules. The aim was rather to make EU rights more effective. Thus, the harmonization of tort and civil procedure rules was necessary only to the extent that they presented obstacles to the effective enforcement of EU substantive rights in accordance with the principles of subsidiarity and proportionality.[16]

---

[15] Commission Recommendation (n 2).

[16] N Kroes, 'Reinforcing the Fight Against Cartels and Developing Private Antitrust Damages Actions: Two Tools for a More Competitive Europe' (Commission/IBA Joint Conference on Competition Policy, Brussels, 8 March 2007) (Speech/07/128). The issue of subsidiarity and proportionality is also addressed in the Draft Damages Directive. See Commission (EC), 'Proposal for a Council Directive governing actions for damages for infringements of Article 81 and 82 of the Treaty', Draft Damages Directive (Document withdrawn before publication—on file with the author), Explanatory Memorandum, paras 3.2, 3.3 and recital 23. However, inasmuch as Article 103 TFEU was the selected legal base for the Draft Damages Directive and EU competition policy falls under the area of exclusive Union competence, no justification in light of the subsidiarity principle was necessary. Article 5(3) TEU and 'Protocol on the Exercise of Shared Competence' [2007] OJ C306/158. It might, however, be seen as an attempt to persuade the objecting Member States. In addition, at the time the Draft Damages Directive was issued, the nature of EU competition policy as exclusive Union competence was not clarified. Establishing competition rules necessary for the functioning of the internal market has now been listed expressly in the LT (Article 3(1)(b)

The harmonization of certain procedural rules for competition claims preceded the Directive on Damages Actions, being brought about by Regulation 1/2003. This not only changed the administrative enforcement of competition rules by the Commission and NCAs, but also brought about changes that affect the enforcement of private competition law.[17] Regulation 1/2003 harmonizes the burden of proof[18] between undertakings and the public authority, or between private parties, thereby going a step further than the ECJ in *GT Link*, in which it stated that, in the absence of Union rules, national rules on the burden of proof apply, subject to the principles of equivalence and effectiveness.[19] The Directive on Damages Actions constitutes the first considerable attempt to harmonize national rules facilitating damages actions for competition law violations. Thus, a sectoral harmonization of procedural rules in EU competition law has already occurred, pointing to the possible adoption of other harmonized measures, provided that they meet existing need.

The Commission's policy documents and reports issued to date all point to the very large damages flowing from EU competition law violations and to the low number of consumer damages actions, thus calling for a change to the status quo.[20] The Commission opted for a distinct approach to damages claims in EU competition law, without legislatively addressing the thorny issue of collective actions. In principle though, in the realm of competition law, and given the rhetorical importance placed on consumer interest and the identified need for encouraging consumer claims, specific rules are needed in order to ensure the effective enforcement of substantive consumer rights. A harmonized mechanism across Member States would bring benefits both to consumers and defendant

---

TFEU) as an area of exclusive competence, dispensing with the past controversy as to whether EU competition policy constitutes an exclusive or shared competence. See Case 14/68 *Walt Wilhelm and others v Bundeskartellamt* [1969] ECR 1; M Dougan, *National Remedies before the Court of Justice* (Hart 2004) 120–123 argues that competition policy constitutes an area of shared competence, although with characteristics of de facto exclusivity. See also M Dougan, 'The Convention's Draft Constitutional Treaty: Bringing Europe Closer to Its Lawyers' (2003) 28 ELRev 763, 770; T Konstadinides, *Division of Powers in European Union Law* (Kluwer Law International 2009) 170–172, 236–237.

[17] On the changes brought about by Regulation 1/2003 and their respective assessment see Commission (EC), 'Report on the Functioning of Regulation 1/2003' (Communication) COM(2009) 206 final.

[18] See Council Regulation (EC) 1/2003 on the Implementation of the Rules on Competition Laid Down in Articles 81 and 82 of the Treaty [2003] OJ L1/1 (Regulation 1/2003), Article 2 and recital 5. Note, though, that the harmonization concerns only the burden, and not the standard, of proof, which is still subject to national rules as long as they are compatible with the general principles of EU law. On implying that the burden of proof is a procedural issue see M Storme (ed), *Approximation of Judiciary Law in the European Union* (Kluwer Rechtswetenschappen 1994) 65. In this vein see Case C-242/95 *GT-Link A/S v De Danske Statsbaner* [1997] ECR I-4449, paras 22–27. Contra Case C-8/08 *T-Mobile Netherlands BV v Raad van Bestuur van de Nederlandse Mededingingsautoriteit* [2009] ECR I-4529, Opinion of AG Kokott, para 77.

[19] *GT-Link* ibid.

[20] See, for example, Commission (EC), 'Staff Working Document—Accompanying Document to the White Paper on Damages Actions for Breach of the EC Antitrust Rules' (Impact Assessment) SEC(2008) 405 (Brussels, 02/04/08) (WP IAR), paras 31–46.

businesses as well as resulting in substantial cost savings that would outweigh the costs of implementing such a proposal.[21]

In addition, and outside the field of competition law, the EU has also adopted other legislative instruments for the harmonization of specific procedural rules.[22] There are also existing sectoral instruments in the fields of public procurement,[23] consumer law,[24] environmental liability,[25] and intellectual property.[26] If the basic distinction in the European legal systems between the adversarial and inquisitorial models is so deeply embedded in the Member States' legal cultures as to render harmonization very difficult,[27] sectoral harmonization in fields in which there is an existing need presents itself as a more realistic option. In fact, despite the European Parliament being in favour of a horizontal approach to the harmonization of procedural rules, it has itself acknowledged that:

the more advanced analysis of civil competition law redress and the advanced framework for competition authorities, including the European Competition Network, and that, at least in regard to some issues, this justifies moving forward rapidly, taking into account that some of the measures envisaged could be extended to non-competition law sectors; *takes the view that such sectoral measures could already be proposed* with regard to the *particular complexities and difficulties encountered by victims of breaches of the EC competition rules.*[28]

Thus, past experience suggests that the harmonization of specific procedural rules is feasible, whereas when the Commission attempted to carry out more ambitious legislative projects for the possible harmonization of civil procedure rules, the outcome was rather unsatisfactory. Attempts to approximate the procedural rules

---

[21] P Buccirossi et al, *Collective Redress in Antitrust* (2012) (Study—DG for Internal Policies) 12, 42–45.

[22] See, for example, Council Regulation 44/2001 on Jurisdiction and Recognition and Enforcement of Judgments in Civil and Commercial Matters [2001] OJ L12/1; Council Regulation 1206/2001 on Cooperation between Courts of the Member States in the Taking of Evidence in Civil and Commercial Matters [2001] OJ L174/1; Council Directive 2002/8/EC of 27 January 2003 to Improve Access to Justice in Cross-border Disputes by Establishing Minimum Common Rules Relating to Legal Aid for Such Disputes [2003] OJ L26/41; Regulation 861/2007 on the European Small Claims Procedure [2007] OJ L199/1 (European Small Claims Procedure). For an analysis of these instruments see E Storskrubb, *Civil Procedure and EU Law* (OUP 2008) esp 114–152, 169–180, 220–232.

[23] Council Directive 2007/66/EC amending Council Directives 89/665/EEC and 92/13/EEC with Regard to Improving the Effectiveness of Review Procedures Concerning the Award of Public Contracts [2007] OJ L335/31.

[24] Council Directive 1999/34/EC amending Council Directive 85/374/EEC on the Approximation of the Laws, Regulations and Administrative Provisions of the Member States Concerning Liability of Defective Products (Product Liability Directive). Commission (EC), 'Proposal for a Council Directive on Consumer Rights' COM(2008) 614 final.

[25] Council Directive 2004/35 EC on Environmental Liability with Regard to the Prevention and Remedying of Environmental Damage [2004] OJ L143/56 (Environmental Liability Directive).

[26] Council Directive 2004/48 EC on the Enforcement of Intellectual Property Rights [2004] OJ L195/16 (Enforcement of IP Rights Directive).

[27] C Harlow, 'Voice of Difference in a Plural Community' in PR Beaumont, C Lyons, and N Walker (eds), *Convergence and Divergence in European Public Law* (Hart 2001) 217, 202 pointing to this conclusion in Storme (n 19).

[28] EP, 'Non-legislative Resolution on the White Paper on Damages Actions' (2008/2154(INI)) (EP Resolution on WP), para 6, emphasis added.

in the EU that resulted in the mere pronouncement of general principles prove this fact.²⁹ The Recommendation on collective redress can be seen in this light.

Finally, EU competition law constitutes the prime example of an EU law field in which a high degree of substantive harmonization is achieved.³⁰ Many commentators have highlighted this potential sectoral approach, and rightly so, since harmonized substantive competition rules could more easily justify further harmonization of the respective procedural rules.³¹

3.2 In search of an adequate legal base

The analysis presented above suggests that a sectoral harmonization of consumer damages actions for competition law violations is appropriate.³² The concomitant question is whether the EU possesses the necessary legislative competence for the adoption specific procedural rules for consumer damages claims in competition law. The Commission's policy documents on improving private competition law enforcement, while not questioning EU competence to adopt legislative measures on damages actions in the context of EU competition law,³³ have been restricted to making rather Delphic pronouncements regarding the appropriate legal basis in the Treaty.³⁴ The political opposition expressed by the Member States and

---

²⁹ Storme (n 18). By way of analogy, general initiatives in the field of contract and tort law also prove this point. For a concise presentation of other initiatives in the field of private law see T Moellers and A Heinemann (eds), *The Enforcement of Competition Law in Europe* (CUP 2007) 425–429. Marcos and Graells seem to suggest that the fact that these initiatives have not yet yielded results is indicative of the dangers entailed in piecemeal harmonization of procedural rules. However, their argument can run both ways, ie point to the need for this piecemeal harmonization, especially where there is a strong case in favour of such harmonization. F Marcos and AS Graells, 'Towards a European Tort Law? Damages Actions for Breach of the EC Antitrust Rules: Harmonising Tort Law through the Back Door?' (2006) <http://papers.ssrn.com/sol3/papers.cfm?abstract_id=1028963> accessed 21 November 2014, 3–4. Arguing in favour of a sectoral harmonization of national tort laws see W van Boom, 'European Tort Law: An Integrated or Compartmentalized Approach' in A Vaquer (ed), *European Private Law Beyond the Common Frame of Reference* (Europa Law Publishing 2008) 133, 142, 148–149.
³⁰ See Regulation 1/2003 (n 18), Article 3. Cf s 60 CA 1998.
³¹ Dougan (n 16) 202–203; On the sectoral approach to remedies see S Weatherill, 'Addressing Problems of Imbalanced Implementation in EC Law: Remedies in an Institutional Perspective' in C Kilpatrick, T Novitz, and P Skidmore (eds), *The Future of Remedies in Europe* (Hart 2000) 87, 108; D Leczykiewicz, 'Private Party Liability in EU Law: In Search of the General Regime' in C Barnard and O Odudu (eds), *The Cambridge Yearbook of European Legal Studies*, Volume 12, 2009–2010 (Hart Publishing 2010) 257, 280. D Beard and A Jones, 'Co-contractors, Damages and Article 81: The ECJ Finally Speaks' (2002) 23 ECLR 246, 255. For an analogy with public procurement rules in which the EU 'Remedies Directive' reinforces the harmonized substantive public procurement rules see C-15/04 *Koppensteiner GmbH v Bundesimmobiliengesellschaft mbH* [2005] ECR I-4855, Opinion of AG Stix Sackl, para 47.
³² See M Tulibacka, 'Europeanization of Civil Procedures: In search of a Coherent Approach' (2009) 46 CMLRev 1527, 1546–47, for an opposing view, although she acknowledges that Member States may be more prone to accepting sectoral harmonization.
³³ This is how Commission reference to the CJEU having 'indirectly confirmed' EU competence to act should be read. See Commission (EC), 'Staff Working Paper Accompanying the White Paper on Damages Actions for Breach of the EC Antitrust Rules' SEC(2008) 404, 2 April 2008 (WP SWP), fn 164.
³⁴ EP Resolution on WP (n 28), paras 2, 4.

the need to involve the Parliament in the process resulted in the adoption of the Directive on Damages Actions based on two legal bases, namely Article 103 and Article 114 TFEU. These legal bases may not be easily justified in the light of the aims of the Directive, as will be explained below.

The sectoral instruments for improving the enforcement of EU rights mentioned above[35] were all based on Article 114 TFEU (former 95 TEC), with the exception of the Environmental Liability Directive, which was based on Article 192(1) TFEU (former 175(1) TEC). Furthermore, the instruments harmonizing certain procedural rules[36] are all based on Article 81 TFEU (former 65 TEC). Following the measures so far adopted at EU level, as well as the aim of the measures proposed in this book, that is, enhancing the enforcement of consumer rights for competition law violations, the potential legal bases seem to be Articles 81 TFEU, 103 TFEU, 114 TFEU, 169(2) TFEU, and 352 TFEU.

Choosing the correct legal base has political and institutional significance,[37] since the EU enjoys only conferred powers.[38] If a legislative measure is based on an incorrect legal basis, it can be invalidated[39] following a challenge brought by either an EU institution or a Member State.[40] From a practical perspective, the choice between competing legal bases matters only if they entail different methods for adopting legislative measures.[41] The degree of involvement of EU institutions differs according to the adopted legislative procedures. Thus, if Article 81, 114, or 169(2) TFEU is preferred, the ordinary legislative procedure will be followed,[42]

---

[35] See text to nn 23–26.   [36] See text to n 22.

[37] R Barents, 'The Internal Market Unlimited: Some Observations on the Legal Basis Of Community Legislation' (1993) 30 CMLRev 85, 89.

[38] See Article 5(1) and (2) TEU; Article 1(1) TFEU. Opinion 2/94 Accession by the Community to the ECHR [1996] ECR I-1759, paras 23–24; On the division of competence between the EU and the Member States see amongst others G de Búrca and B de Witte, 'The Delimitation of Powers between the EU and its Member States' in A Arnull and D Wincott (eds), *Accountability and Legitimacy in the European Union* (OUP 2002) 201; S Weatherill, 'Better Competence Monitoring' (2005) 30 ELRev 23; S Weatherill, 'Competence Creep and Competence Control' (2004) 23 YEL 1; R Schütze, 'The European Community's Federal Order of Competence—A Retrospective Analysis' in M Dougan and D Currie (eds), *50 Years of the European Treaties* (Hart Publishing 2009) 63; D Wyatt, 'Community Competence to Regulate the Internal Market' in M Dougan and S Currie (eds), *50 Years of the European Treaties* (Hart Publishing 2009) 93; R Schütze, 'Organised Change Towards an "Ever Closer Union": Article 308 EC and the limits of the Community Legislative Competence' (2003) 22 YEL 79. On the Court-imposed limits upon the principle of conferral see the seminal Case C-376/98 *Germany v European Parliament and Council* [2000] ECR I-8419 (*Tobacco Advertising*); cf C-58/08 *Vodafone and others v Secretary of State* [2010] ECR I-4999 (*Vodafone*), Opinion of AG Maduro, para 18. See S Weatherill, 'The Limits of Legislative Harmonisation Ten Years after Tobacco Advertising: How the Court's Case Law has Become a "Drafting Guide"' (2011) 12 *German LJ* 827 for a critical review of the relevant case law, which acts merely as a 'drafting guide' to the legislature rather than imposing limits.

[39] See, for example, Opinion 2/00 (Cartagena Protocol) [2001] ECR I-9713, para 5.

[40] The issue of an incorrect legal base can also be raised in the course of a preliminary ruling. See, for example, Case C-331/88 *FEDESA* [1990] ECR 4023, paras 22–28. See H Cullen and A Charlesworth, 'Diplomacy by Other Means: The Use of Legal Basis Litigation as a Political Strategy by the European Parliament and Member States' (1999) 36 CMLRev 1243.

[41] S Weatherill, *Cases and Materials on EU Law* (11th edn, OUP 2014) 47.

[42] The ordinary legislative procedure provides for the joint adoption of legislative acts by the Parliament and the Council on the Commission's proposal. Articles 289(1) and 294 TFEU. The

thereby preserving the prerogatives of the Union institutions. On the other hand, the EP may object to the choice of Article 352 TFEU as the appropriate legal basis, since this Article provides for measures to be adopted by 'the Council, acting unanimously on a proposal from the Commission and after obtaining the consent of the European Parliament'. Thus, here, instead of the joint adoption of the legislative measure, only the consent of the EP is required.[43]

If measures are based on Article 103 TFEU, the EP's role is diminished to a mere consultative function. Since the EP only has a consultative role for legislative measures adopted under Article 103(1) TFEU, it has urged the Commission to adopt any future collective redress mechanisms according to the ordinary legislative procedure,[44] and the Commission has followed Parliament's request.[45] This is now enshrined in the Directive on Damages Actions thereby obviating the risk of challenge before the ECJ. Equally, the choice of the legal basis matters since the legislative measures may be challenged by an objecting Member State before the Court.[46]

The choice of a legal basis is influenced by the following judge-made rules. First, it should be based on objective factors, amenable to judicial review. These factors include, in particular, the aim and content of the measure.[47] Second, if the adopted measure pursues more than one purpose, the predominance purpose test is to be followed, namely the preferred legal basis should be the one corresponding to the measure's purpose.[48] Third, if no predominant purpose is identified, the measure can be based on more than one legal basis, with the caveat that the procedures laid down by each legal basis should be compatible with each other.[49]

LT also provides for special legislative procedures which distribute powers differently between the Council and the Parliament. Article 289(2) TFEU.

[43] See, for example, Case C-436/03 *Parliament v Council* [2006] ECR I-3733, paras 12–15; See also J Rutgers, 'European Competence and a European Civil Code, a Common Frame of Reference or an Optional Instrument' in A Hartkamp and C von Bar (eds), *Towards a European Civil Code* (4th edn, Kluwer Law International 2011) 311, 316. However, as will be discussed below, the EP's involvement is perhaps a lesser matter. Article 352 TFEU is incapacitated by the proliferation of specific legal bases in the Treaty and emphasis on unanimity. Thus, it is currently used for trivial things.

[44] EP Resolution on WP (n 28), paras 5, 23.

[45] Former Competition Commissioner Almunia, in his confirmation hearing before the Parliament, committed to sending a proposal based on the co-decision procedure. See J Almunia, 'Antitrust Litigation—The Way Ahead' (London, 23 October 2014) (Speech/14/713).

[46] This is not the case for measures adopted following Article 352 TFEU, inasmuch as unanimity in the Council is required.

[47] See, for example, Case 45/86 *Commission v Council* [1987] ECR 1493, para 11; Case C-300/89 *Commission v Council* [1991] ECR I-2867, para 10; Case C-268/94 *Portugal v Council* [1996] ECR I-617, para 22; Opinion 2/00 (n 39), para 22; Case C-338/01 *Commission v Council* [2004] ECR I-4829, para 54; Case C-94/03 *Commission v Council* [2006] ECR I-1, para 34; Case C-436/03 *Parliament v Council* (n 43), para 35.

[48] Case C-36/98 *Spain v Council* [2001] ECR I-779, para 59; Case C-338/01 *Commission v Council* (n 47), para 55; Case C-94/03 *Commission v Council* (n 47) para 35; Case C-155/07 *Parliament v Council* [2008] ECR I-7879, para 68.

[49] Case C-336/00 *Republik Österreich v Martin Huber* [2002] ECR I-7699, para 31; Case C-338/01 *Commission v Council* (n 47), paras 56–57; Case C-94/03 *Commission v Council* (n 47), para 36; Case C-155/07 *Parliament v Council* (n 48), para 75.

The Directive on Damages Actions is based on both Articles 103 and 114 TFEU; since 'the differences in the liability regimes applicable in the Member States may negatively affect both competition and the proper functioning of the internal market, it is appropriate to base this Directive on the dual legal bases of Articles 103 and 114 TFEU'.[50] Since Article 114 TFEU affords greater participation to the Parliament (a co-decision between the Parliament and the Council as opposed to a consultative role), the legislative procedure provided therein was followed. Harmonization measures based on Article 114 TFEU must have, as their object, the establishment and functioning of the internal market (defined in Article 26 TFEU).[51] The choice of Article 114 TFEU is explained in recital 7 of the Directive, which states that:

> There are marked differences between the rules in the Member States governing actions for damages for infringements of Union or national competition law. Those differences lead to uncertainty concerning the conditions under which injured parties can exercise the right to compensation they derive from the TFEU and affect the substantive effectiveness of such right. As injured parties often choose their Member State of establishment as the forum in which to claim damages, the discrepancies between the national rules lead to an uneven playing field as regards actions for damages and may thus affect competition on the markets on which those injured parties, as well as the infringing undertakings, operate.[52]

The choice of Article 114 TFEU for the Directive on Damages Actions may be questionable but can nonetheless be justified in the light of former legal instruments and the Courts' case law. It is submitted that the mere finding of disparities between national laws, and an abstract risk of obstacles to the exercise of fundamental freedoms or of distortions of competition, does not suffice to establish the necessary internal market-making link.[53] Rather, the measures should seek to eliminate obstacles to either the free movement of goods or the freedom to provide services, which either exist or are likely to exist in the future, or seek to remove appreciable distortion of competition.[54]

---

[50] Directive on Damages Actions (n 1), recital 8.   [51] *Vodafone* (n 38), para 32.
[52] Directive on Damages Actions (n 1).
[53] *Tobacco Advertising* (n 38), para 84. See *Tobacco Advertising* (n 38), Opinion of AG Fennelly, para 83 stating that 'the internal market is not a value free synonym of general economic governance'. See also Joined Cases C-154/04 and C-155/04 *The Queen, on the Application of Alliance for Natural Health and Nutri-Link Ltd v Secretary of State for Health and the Queen, on the Application of National Association of Health Stores and Health Food Manufacturers Ltd v Secretary of State for Health and National Assembly for Wales* [2005] ECR I-6451 (*Alliance For Natural Health*), para 28. *Vodafone* (n 38), paras 32–33.
[54] *Tobacco Advertising* (n 38), paras 86, 96, 108; *Alliance for Natural Health* (n 53), para 29; Case C-350/92 *Spain v Council* [1995] ECR I-1985, para 35. *Vodafone* (n 38), paras 32–33. On the possibility of future obstacles to trade from the diverse national approaches to collective redress see Civic Consulting, 'Evaluation of the Effectiveness and Efficiency of Collective Redress Mechanisms in the European Union' (Final Report prepared for DG SANCO, 26 August 2008) <http://ec.europa.eu/consumers/redress_cons/finalreportevaluationstudypart1-final2008-11-26.pdf> accessed 21 November 2014, 134. On the inadequate judicial control over policing the limits of EU competence and the case law's function as a mere 'drafting guide' for the legislature see Weatherill, Drafting Guide (n 38) esp 841–849. See also *Vodafone* (n 38), Opinion of AG Maduro, para 18,

Initially in *Rewe* and *Comet*, and then repeating the same statement in a number of other cases, the ECJ acknowledged that:

in the absence of any relevant [Union] rules, it is for the national legal order of each Member State... to lay down the procedural rules for proceedings designed to ensure the protection of the rights which individuals acquire through the direct effect of [Union] law... [Articles 114–115, 117 and 352 TFEU] enable the appropriate steps to be taken as necessary, to eliminate differences between the provisions laid down in such matters by law... in Member States if these differences are found to be such as to cause distortion or to affect the functioning of the common market.[55]

The ECJ made similar pronouncements in *Courage* and *Manfredi*,[56] although without making any reference to the possible adoption of EU harmonized measures. However, the fact that the ECJ did not mention a legal basis in *Courage* and *Manfredi* to harmonize damages actions in private competition claims does not mean that the EU does not have competence to act in this area. The similar wording of the ECJ's judgments in the abovementioned cases, and the fact that they deal with 'procedural rules',[57] seems to suggest that Article 114 TFEU could be utilized as the appropriate legal basis to harmonize national procedural rules, provided that the conditions set forth in it are fulfilled. So, the question then turns on whether the conditions to be satisfied under Article 114 TFEU are met in the case of the Directive on Damages Actions. Likewise, determining the likelihood of resorting to Article 114 TFEU in the context of private enforcement in competition law would be useful for the framework to increase consumer involvement in private competition law enforcement proposed herein.

The Enforcement of IP Rights Directive based on Article 114 TFEU is illustrative of the manner in which the EU legislature is satisfied that the measures make an adequate contribution to the internal market.[58] In Recital 3 it states that:

It is therefore necessary to ensure that the substantive law on intellectual property, which is nowadays largely part of the *acquis communautaire*, is applied effectively in the Community. In this respect, the means of enforcing intellectual property rights are of paramount importance for the success of the internal market.[59]

---

who, contrary to the ECJ, did not think that the threshold for harmonization based on Article 114 TFEU for eliminating future obstacles to trade was met.

[55] Case 33/76 *Rewe v Landwirtschaftskammer fuer das Saarland* [1976] ECR 1989, para 5; Case 45/76 *Comet v Produktschap voor Siergewassen* [1976] ECR 2043, paras 13–14 (emphasis added).
[56] Case C-453/99 *Courage Ltd v Bernard Crehan and Bernard Crehan v Courage Ltd and Others* [2001] ECR I-6297, para 29; Joined Cases C-295/04 to 298/04 *Vincenzo Manfredi and Others v Lloyd Adriatico Assicurazioni SpA and Others* [2006] ECR I-6619, para 62.
[57] The CJEU attributes a broader meaning to the term 'procedural', as it comprises both procedural and remedial rules. See A Komninos, 'Civil Antitrust Remedies between Community and National Law' in C Barnard and O Odudu (eds), *The Outer Limits of European Union Law* (Hart 2009) 363, 372.
[58] Enforcement of IP Rights Directive (n 26). See Tulibacka (n 32) 1546–1549, 1563 for a criticism of this Directive and selection of Article 114 TFEU as the legal basis.
[59] See also Enforcement of IP Rights Directive (n 26), recitals 8 and 9.

194   *Institutional and Political Limitations*

The same can be said about private competition law enforcement and consumer participation. It has been argued in the previous chapters that the primary aim of the measures seeking to increase consumer involvement in private competition law enforcement should be to deter competition law violations, since this primary aim not only corresponds to the ECJ case law but also allows for the adoption of effective measures to enhance consumer involvement. The Commission's Impact Assessment Report for its WP suggests that there is an existing problem that is causing 'appreciable' distortions to competition.[60] Furthermore, Article 114 TFEU, unlike Article 81 TFEU, is not limited to cross-border situations. However, the ECJ formulated test vis-à-vis the condition for resort to Article 114 TFEU is rather vague, and a more specific legal basis for the adoption of these measures exists, namely Article 103 TFEU, so there is no need to resort to Article 114 TFEU.[61] Resorting to Article 114 TFEU for the Directive on Damages Actions appears to be a political compromise, assuaging the Parliament's fear of the possible introduction of excessive measures. After all, past experience with the Draft Damages Directive demonstrated that the EP's support for the private enforcement initiative was the key to the success of the whole process. After a period of reflection, Article 103 TFEU appeared as the chosen legal basis for the Draft Damages Directive,[62] which was rather surprising in the light of the EP expressly asking to be involved through the co-decision procedure.[63] However, Article 103 TFEU was identified as the sole legal basis for the Draft Directive and the Commission went to great lengths to explain why this was the most appropriate legal basis. In the light of the dual bases of the adopted Directive, no such detailed analysis appears therein.

In the Draft Directive the Commission has suggested that 'the proposal aims at defining the relationship between national rules on civil liability and the application of Articles [101] and [102] of the Treaty', pointing to Article 103(2)(e) TFEU as the category under which the proposed measures fall. However, the Commission's proposal cannot be accommodated by the wording of this provision, which stipulates that the regulatory measures shall be designed to determine the relationship between national laws and the competition provisions. This category refers to substantive national competition laws; including national rules on civil liability seems like a far-fetched reading of the relevant category.[64]

---

[60] WP IAR (n 20), paras 40–46. See F Rizzuto, 'EC Harmonisation of Antitrust National Procedural Rules' [2009] GCLR 29, 45. For a criticism of the Commission Impact Assessment see G Cumming and M Freudenthal, *Civil Procedure in EU Competition Cases before the English and Dutch Courts* (Kluwer Law International 2010) 17–21. On Impact Assessment Reports as a way to check that the Union adopts harmonized measures within the limits of its competence see P Craig and G de Búrca, *EU Law: Text, Cases and Materials* (5th edn, OUP 2011) 93; P Craig, *The Lisbon Treaty: Law, Politics and the Treaty Reform* (OUP 2010) 188–192.

[61] In the same vein, see V Milutinović, *The 'Right to Damages' under EU Competition Law* (Kluwer Law International 2010) 318. On the other hand, the Storme Report suggests that Article 114 TFEU could act as the potential legal basis. See Storme (n 19) 45, 59.

[62] Draft Damages Directive (n 16), Explanatory Memorandum, para 3.1.

[63] EP Resolution on the WP (n 28), paras 5, 23.

[64] This conclusion is also supported by recital 8 and Article 3 of Regulation 1/2003 (n 18), since they refer to substantive competition rules. Contra Rizzuto (n 60) 41.

In addition, the choice of Article 103 TFEU does not fit well with the emphasis on the compensatory objective of damages actions and the proposed measures in the Directive on Damages Actions.[65] In fact, the latter depicts a certain inconsistency between its pursued objectives, oscillating from ensuring the right to full compensation to maintaining the 'full effect of Articles 101 and 102 TFEU'.[66] Raising damages claims and enforcing substantive EU rights cannot be said to be one of the principles of the competition provisions. To the contrary, sustaining competitive markets through the deterrence against competition law violations and promoting consumer welfare serves as a principle of the said provisions.[67]

In principle, Article 103 TFEU can serve as the appropriate legal base for measures facilitating private competition law enforcement, as well as the measures for improving consumer participation in competition law enforcement.[68] The measures herein proposed primarily aim to increase the deterrence against competition law violations and benefit consumers as the ultimate beneficiaries of competition policy. Therefore, it can be said that these measures 'give effect to the principles set out in Articles 101 and 102' as stipulated in Article 103(1) TFEU. Furthermore, the measures for increasing consumer involvement proposed herein do not fall within the subject matter of Article 103(2) TFEU.[69] However, inasmuch as this list is indicative,[70] the relevant measures could fall under a modified Article 103(2)(a)

---

[65] Article 1(1) of the Directive on Damages Actions (n 1) provides that '[t]his Directive sets out certain rules necessary to ensure that anyone who has suffered harm caused by an infringement of competition law by an undertaking or by an association of undertakings, can effectively exercise the right to claim full compensation for that harm from that undertaking or association. It sets out rules fostering undistorted competition in the internal market and removing obstacles to its proper functioning, by ensuring equivalent protection throughout the Union for anyone who has suffered such harm'.

[66] Directive on Damages Actions (n 1), recital 54.

[67] See, for example, Regulation 1/2003 (n 18), recital 9.

[68] See R Whish, 'The Enforcement of EC Competition Law in the Domestic Courts of Member States' in L Gormley (ed), *Current and Future Perspectives on EC Competition Law* (Kluwer Law 1997) 73, 83 for an early account favouring Article 103 TFEU as the appropriate Treaty base for harmonizing national rules for enforcing competition norms. See also W van Gerven, 'Substantive Remedies for the Private Enforcement of EC Antitrust Rules before National Courts' in CD Ehlermann and I Atanasiu (eds), *European Competition Law Annual 2001: Effective Private Enforcement of EC Antitrust Law* (Hart 2003) 53, 81. In the same vein T Eilmansberger, 'The Green Paper on Damages Actions for Breach of the EC Antitrust Rules and Beyond: Reflections on the Utility and Feasibility of Stimulating Private Enforcement through Legislative Action' (2007) 44 CMLRev 431, 440–441.

[69] Article 103(2) TFEU provides that '[t]he regulations or directives referred to in paragraph 1 shall be designed in particular: (a) to ensure compliance with the prohibitions laid down in Article 101(1) and in Article 102 by making provision for fines and periodic penalty payments; (b) to lay down detailed rules for the application of Article 101(3), taking into account the need to ensure effective supervision on the one hand, and to simplify administration to the greatest possible extent on the other; (c) to define, if need be, in the various branches of the economy, the scope of the provisions of Articles 101 and 102; (d) to define the respective functions of the Commission and of the Court of Justice of the European Union in applying the provisions laid down in this paragraph; (e) to determine the relationship between national laws and the provisions contained in this Section or adopted pursuant to this Article'.

[70] This can be deduced from the wording of Article 103(2) TFEU which states that 'the regulations or directives referred to in paragraph 1 shall be designed *in particular*: [...]'.

TFEU category since they seek to ensure compliance with the competition law prohibition by making consumer damages actions available for competition law violations.[71]

The choice of Article 103 TFEU as the legal base for the proposed measures has the additional practical advantage that it permits the adoption of measures not limited to cross-border situations. Yet, reliance on Article 103 TFEU as a legal base does not imply that the adoption of measures at EU level should apply to purely internal situations, that is, situations dealt with solely under national competition law. They should only be invoked when EU competition law applies, that is, in situations in which there is an effect on inter-state trade.

The above discussion has suggested that Article 103 TFEU may act as the preferred legal basis for the measures discussed in this book. Nonetheless, for reasons of completeness, Article 81 TFEU also needs to be discussed here as it may serve as the appropriate legal basis for the adoption of procedural measures enhancing consumer participation in private competition law enforcement if the emphasis is placed on the potential of the proposed measures to increase access to justice. The LT has brought changes in the field of judicial cooperation in civil matters, which could potentially affect EU competence to adopt legislative measures based on Article 81 TFEU.[72] Article 81(2) TFEU now provides that:

For the purposes of paragraph 1,[73] the European Parliament and the Council, acting in accordance with the *ordinary legislative procedure*, shall adopt measures, *particularly when necessary for the proper functioning of the internal market*, aimed at ensuring:... (e) *effective access to justice*; (f) the elimination of obstacles to the proper functioning of civil proceedings, if necessary by promoting the compatibility of the rules on civil procedure applicable in the Member States. (emphasis added)

In Article 81 TFEU the internal market link has been somewhat weakened inasmuch as now the EU shall adopt measures '*particularly when necessary*' and not '*in so far as necessary*'[74] for the proper functioning of the internal market.[75] In addition, the LT has expanded the aims of the adopted measures by including the broad category of measures aiming at ensuring effective access to justice but retained the condition that the measures should alleviate matters having

---

[71] An analogy can be drawn here with the Case C-176/03 *Commission v Council* [2005] ECR I-7879, para 48 where the ECJ accepted the harmonization of national laws in order to render environmental protection fully effective. Thus, the ECJ is prone to accepting EU competence to harmonize the 'means' in order to protect Union 'ends' even in criminal law, where at the time the EU did not have competence to act.

[72] The former Article 65 TEC. For a historical account of the development of Union competence in the field of civil justice as well as the latest changes brought by the LT see E Storskrubb, 'Civil Justice—A Newcomer and an Unstoppable Wave?' in P Craig and G de Búrca, *The Evolution of EU Law* (OUP 2011) 299, 302–307.

[73] That is, the 'development of judicial cooperation in civil matters having cross border implications'.

[74] As was the wording in Article 65 TEC.

[75] Tulibacka explains that this change could be seen in the light of the prominence attributed to fundamental rights, that is, access to justice and due process post LT. See Tulibacka (n 32) 1535.

cross-border implications. Furthermore, Protocol 21 provides that EU legislative measures in the area of freedom, security, and justice (which covers civil judicial cooperation) are not applicable to the UK and Ireland, unless they expressly opt in.[76]

Nonetheless, the Commission Recommendation points to the Union's objective of 'maintaining and developing an area of freedom, security and justice, inter alia, by facilitating access to justice'.[77] However, since Article 81 TFEU seeks to improve 'judicial cooperation in civil matters',[78] it mainly concerns the approximation of procedural and private international law rules.[79] This conclusion is also supported by the fact that all EU measures in the field of remedies were adopted based on Article 114 TFEU,[80] whereas the procedural measures adopted so far have been based on Article 81 TFEU. It follows that Article 81 TFEU is not a valid legal basis for the approximation of remedial EU rules. In principle though, the inclusion of the 'access to justice' category may enable the adoption of wider remedial and substantive rules based on this provision. Having said that, even if this hurdle were to be overcome, the problem with the cross-border nature of the claims remains.

It has been argued that EU collective action measures will not prove to be effective if limited to cross-border claims.[81] This is mainly because the problems of defining the group, notifying possible victims of anti-competitive practices, and distributing damages would be aggravated in the cross–border context. Therefore, it would be even more difficult for consumer organizations to bring cases, thereby rendering any adopted measure redundant. This explains why consumer organizations call for both national and cross-border collective redress procedures.[82] In

---

[76] Protocol (No 21) on the Position of the United Kingdom and Ireland in Respect of the Area of Freedom, Security and Justice [2012] C362/295.
[77] Commission Recommendation (n 2), recital 1.
[78] See Storskrubb (n 72) 309 on this notion.
[79] The private international law aspect falls outside the scope of this book. Van Gerven points to the wide articulation of procedural rules by the CJEU and points out that, following the insertion of competence on civil procedure by the Treaty of Amsterdam, the Court of Justice might have to reconsider which rules could be characterized as procedural, thereby suggesting that Article 81 TFEU encompasses only the approximation of procedural rules *stricto sensu*. See W van Gerven, 'Of rights, Remedies and Procedures' (2000) 37 CMLRev 501, fn 114. However, the fact that projects on possible future harmonization of contract law now fall under the sphere of civil justice could suggest that Article 81 TFEU is not only confined to procedural matters. See <http://ec.europa.eu/justice/contract/index_en.htm> accessed 21 November 2014, on the relevant documents. Craig (n 58) 360. On the scope of Article 81 TFEU see also H Hartnell, 'A Cinderella Story: "Judicial Cooperation in Civil Matters" Meets the Prince. Review of Eva Storskrubb, Civil Procedure and EU Law: A Policy Area Uncovered' (2010) YEL 483, 485–486.
[80] With the exception of the Environmental Liability Directive (n 25). Also, the Product Liability Directive (n 24) was adopted before the Treaty of Amsterdam, which brought civil justice in the area of Community competence.
[81] J Stuyck, 'Class Actions in Europe? To Opt-in or to Opt-out, that is the Question' [2009] EBLR 483, 499.
[82] See 'Summary of Interventions' (15 November 2010, ECOSOC Brussels) (BEUC/Test Achats Joint Conference—Group Action: A Necessity for Consumers). See also Test Achats and Test Aankoop, 'Towards a Coherent Approach to Collective Redress—Response' 4 <http://ec.europa.eu/competition/consultations/2011_collective_redress/testaankoop_en.pdf> accessed 21 November 2014.

effect, as there is a need for the adoption of measures applicable both to national and cross-border procedures, it seems that the textual interpretation of Article 81 TFEU precludes the adoption of these measures.[83]

Finally, Articles 169 and 352 TFEU may serve as the legal bases for measures enhancing consumer participation, although in the light of the 'predominant purpose test', they are less relevant than Article 103 TFEU and possibly Article 81 TFEU. Article 169 TFEU allows the adoption of harmonized measures 'in order to promote the interests of consumers and to ensure a high level of consumer protection' either 'pursuant to Article 114 TFEU' or following the ordinary legislative procedure for measures that 'support, supplement and monitor the policy pursued by Member States'. The analysis on Article 114 TFEU applies equally to the former (Article 169(2)(a) TFEU), whereas it can be said that only the second category comprises pure consumer policy measures, in the sense that no market-making link need be present (Article 169(2)(b) TFEU).

Indeed, it is very unlikely that measures facilitating consumer involvement in private competition law enforcement will be based on Article 169(2)(b) TFEU, given that it has scarcely been employed.[84] In addition, Article 169(2)(b) TFEU cannot serve as the appropriate legal basis for the proposed measures facilitating consumer involvement in private competition law enforcement, since the primary aim of these measures is to enhance the deterrence of violations of EU competition law. Consumer interests in the form of compensation are served incidentally.

Article 352 TFEU constitutes a residual legal base. It provides for the adoption of measures in which 'action by the Union should prove necessary, *within the framework of the policies defined in the Treaties*, to attain one of the *objectives* set out in the Treaties, and *the Treaties have not provided the necessary powers*' (emphasis added). Since the Treaty provides more specific legal bases in the case of consumer involvement in private competition law enforcement, Article 352 TFEU cannot act as the appropriate legal base.[85]

---

[83] In the same vein see Tulibacka (n 32) 1562–1563.
[84] S Weatherill, 'Consumer Policy' in P Craig and G de Búrca, *The Evolution of EU Law* (OUP 2011) 837, 838; S Weatherill, *EU Consumer Law and Policy* (2nd edn, Edward Elgar 2013) 18, 19. Stuyck (n 82) 501 points to only one Directive adopted on this base so far. See Council Directive 98/6 EC on Consumer Protection in the Indication of Prices of Products Offered to Consumers [1998] OJ L80/27.
[85] See Opinion 2/94 (n 38), para 29; Joined Cases C-402/05 P and C-415/05 P *Yassin Abdullah Kadi and Al Barakaat International Foundation v Council of the European Union and Commission of the European Communities* [2008] ECR I-6351, para 211. On the function and risks of Article 352 TFEU as an instrument ensuring 'a continuous process of constitutional adaptation and updating' see Schütze, 'Organised Change' (n 38) 80. On the changes to Article 352 TFEU brought by the LT see Weatherill (n 41) 32; Craig and de Búrca (n 60) 91–92. See also T Konstadinides, 'Drawing the line between Circumvention and Gap-Filling: An Exploration of the Conceptual Limits of the Treaty's Flexibility Clause' (2012) 31 YEL 227.

3.3 In search of the most appropriate legislative instrument

The discussion presented above suggests that the proposed measures to enhance consumer involvement in private competition law enforcement should be adopted based on Article 103 TFEU. This section deals with the most appropriate legislative instrument for the introduction of those measures.

Van Gerven suggested that a Regulation on the substantive law aspects of private remedies before national courts should be introduced.[86] Many of the issues dealt with in his proposed Draft Regulation (the remedies of nullity, restitution, compensation, and interim relief) built on the pronouncements of the ECJ and, since they present a codification of the Court's case law, they could be introduced via a Regulation. In Article 9 he proposes the introduction of a collective claims procedure. The suggestion regarding collective claims could not possibly be introduced via a Regulation given the existing diversity on this issue in national legal orders. As Craig and de Búrca observe 'the direct applicability of Regulations means that they have to be capable of being "parachuted" into the legal systems of all the Member States just as they are'.[87] Therefore, in the light of the multitude of existing national models,[88] it seems that it would be impracticable for the proposed measures on collective actions to be introduced via a Regulation.

The Commission, in its WP IAR, identifies the following factors influencing the choice of the most appropriate legislative instrument(s): the contents of the proposals; the legal, economic, and political environment at the time when the proposal is made;[89] and the desired degree of a level playing field in Europe.[90] Given the diverse national landscapes on collective redress, a level playing field brought about by uniform Regulation rules is not feasible at present.

From a practical perspective, the best way forward would be to adopt the measures proposed herein by means of a Directive that sets common standards and maximum rather than minimum harmonization should be the preferred legislative technique. Minimum harmonization permits the setting of more stringent rules by Member States, thus allowing the preservation of a form of national diversity, whereas the Treaty framework acts as the upper limit.[91] In this case, Member States should conform to the proposed measures but could enact different rules as well, so long as they comply with the general principles of EU law, namely the principles of equivalence and effectiveness. The choice of minimum harmonization as the appropriate technique is also supported by the Commission's documents on private enforcement.[92] Article 103 TFEU is put forward as the

---

[86] Van Gerven (n 68) 90.   [87] Craig and de Búrca (n 60) 106.
[88] See Chapter 5, section 5.   [89] See also Storme (n 18) 61.
[90] WP IAR (n 20), fn 70.
[91] S Prechal, *Directive in EC Law* (2nd edn, OUP 2005) 44. On different methods of harmonization see JP Slot, 'Harmonisation' (1996) 21 ELRev 378, 382–387.
[92] See Draft Damages Directive (n 16), Explanatory Memorandum, para 1.2 stating that 'the Directive is designed to establish...common minimum guarantees on antitrust damages actions'. See also ibid, para 3.4; WP SWP (n 33) para 316 stating that 'the list of suggestions should rather be regarded as what the Commission considers to be the minimum necessary to achieve that objective'.

preferred legal base for a Directive on consumer damages actions in the field of competition law; this provision accords to the EU an exclusive competence and does not contain a minimum harmonization clause, thus excluding the adoption of a measure of minimum harmonization without defeating the very purpose of its adoption in the first place.

Despite the existence of legislative competence, in the light of the Member States' expressed opposition to effective collective action mechanisms, the Commission, as a first step, may issue Recommendations on consumer collective redress in competition law. This would possibly facilitate the exercise of public compensation since the latter constitutes a flexible mechanism that may benefit from the suggested distribution mechanisms in the Recommendation.

4. Implementing Remaining Public Enforcement Proposals

The proposed changes to facilitate consumer participation in public enforcement do not present complex issues with regard to identifying the appropriate legal basis. Some of the proposals related to the Commission practice in sector inquiries, to encouraging consumer intervention in the course of ongoing procedures, and to the provision of compensation to affected consumers in the course of public enforcement procedures could be introduced by a mere change in the Commission's current practice and the issuance of soft law instruments, such as Commission Guidance or a Notice.[93] The remaining proposals can be introduced via harmonized legislative measures. Since they aim to increase compliance with EU competition rules, thereby giving effect to the principles laid down in Articles 101 and 102 TFEU, Article 103 TFEU is the appropriate legal basis. This is supported by the EU legislative instruments adopted in the field of competition law to date. For example, Regulation 1/2003 was based on Article 103 TFEU. Since the Treaty provides a specific legal basis for the adoption of legislative measures giving effect to competition law provisions, adopting Regulation 1/2003 based on Article 103 TFEU would appear to be uncontroversial. This is not the case, however, in regard to the European Merger Regulation (EUMR), which was adopted based on Articles 103 and 352 TFEU.[94]

However, in para 321, the Commission states that 'Depending on the degree to which a level playing field in Europe is required to ensure the effectiveness of antitrust damages actions, a choice will have to be made between the available instruments for Community legislative action. While some of the issues enumerated below could thus be the subject of an EC Regulation, other[s] may be more suited for an EC Directive'.

[93] See Chapter 6, text to nn 77–80, 112–113, 138–147.

[94] Council Regulation (EC) No 139/2004 on the Control of Concentrations between Undertakings [2004] OJ L24/1, recital 7. The fact that the EUMR is based on two legal bases suggests that its purpose is two-fold; giving effect to principles set out in Articles 101 and 102 TFEU, as well as furthering the Treaty objective of ensuring that competition in the internal market is not distorted, as stated in the former Article 3(1)(g). See ibid, recitals 2–3, 5–7. It seems odd that the Regulation itself nominates Article 352 TFEU as its principal legal base. Further to the 'predominant purpose' test, Article 352 TFEU should suffice. See text to n 48.

Article 103 TFEU is the most appropriate legal base for the proposals that enhance consumer participation in public competition law enforcement, in the light of their predominant aim and context. Thus, it could be argued that, given that Regulation 1/2003 is based on 103 TFEU and pursues the same aim, the most effective manner for the introduction of the relevant proposals, namely establishing a consumer complaints allocation mechanism, an EU 'super–complaints' mechanism, and strengthening the Commission's role in sector inquiries by imposing binding remedies, would be through an amendment to Regulation 1/2003 or implementing Regulation 773/2004.

The consumer complaints allocation mechanism could, for example, be included as a separate paragraph in Article 11 of Regulation 1/2003 on the cooperation between the Commission and the NCAs and provide that 'in the event of a rejection of a consumer complaint for lack of Union interest, the Commission shall forward the relevant complaint to the competent competition authorities of the Member States'. Alternatively, it could be added as an amendment to Article 7 of Regulation 773/2004 on the 'Rejection of Complaints'. The latter has the additional advantage that it can be introduced only by a Commission proposal following Article 33 of Regulation 1/2003.[95]

The proposed EU 'super-complaints' mechanism could be inserted as a separate Article in Regulation 1/2003 under chapter IV and provide that:

1. A recognized consumer organization can complain to the Commission that any feature, or combination of features, of a market in the EU for goods or services is, or appears to be, significantly harming the interests of consumers;
2. The Commission shall, within 90 days after the day on which it receives the complaint, publish a response stating how it proposes to deal with the complaint, and in particular:
   i. whether it has decided to take any action or to take no action in response to the complaint,
   ii. if it has decided to take action, the nature of the relevant action, and
   iii. if it has decided to forward the complaint to the competent national competition authority.[96]

A Notice on EU super-complaints needs to be published as well, in order to clarify the function of the respective procedure. For example, the notion of the recognized consumer organization needs clarification, as does the notion of the 'market in the EU' in relation to the 'effect on trade' requirement for the Commission to take action, the possible Commission actions, and the proposed manner in which, following a Commission referral, NCAs are to handle a super-complaint. Devising a super-complaint mechanism at EU level could spur the adoption of

---

[95] This was the case for the cartel settlement procedure introduced as an amendment to Regulation 773/2004 rather to Regulation 1/2003.
[96] This draft Article is modelled upon EA 2002, Section 11(1).

similar national mechanisms, as was the case, for example, with the adoption of leniency programmes in individual Member States.⁹⁷ Finally, the proposal on imposing binding remedies in sector inquiries could be introduced by an amendment to Article 17 of Regulation 1/2003.

5. Conclusion

After briefly alluding to the political concerns voiced against the Commission's efforts in private competition law enforcement, the analysis has shown that the EU possesses competence to adopt both a Directive on consumer involvement in private competition law enforcement and the necessary measures in the field of public enforcement through the amendment of existing legislative instruments (Regulation 1/2003 and Regulation 773/2004).

Despite the existence of EU competence in adopting a Directive on consumer involvement in private competition law enforcement, the political opposition of Member States impedes the adoption of any effective measures. The Directive on consumer involvement could have formed part of a wider legislative package of instruments encouraging private enforcement of EU competition law,⁹⁸ but this opportunity has been missed. The Commission could nonetheless build on the policy discussions to date and complement the adopted Directive with a specific Directive for consumer claims that addresses the special characteristics for this category of claims.

The Commission would have to satisfy the concerns raised by Member States first in order to adopt any meaningful instrument enhancing consumer participation. This means that the Commission needs to undertake a new round of consultations with interested stakeholders and present a separate Impact Assessment on this issue. If it is not possible to adopt a binding legislative instrument, a specific Recommendation for consumer claims in competition law, which complements the general Recommendation, presents a realistic alternative.

This soft law approach, despite its shortcomings, seems, for the time being, to be the only plausible way forward.⁹⁹ 'Soft law acts' have no legally binding force; however, they could potentially produce practical effects.¹⁰⁰ For example, the Commission

---

⁹⁷ On the ECN model leniency programme spurring de facto harmonization see Case C-360/09 *Pfleiderer AG v Bundeskartellamt* [2011] ECR I-5161, Opinion of AG Mazák, paras 26, 33.
⁹⁸ Alternatively, consumer collective redress mechanisms for competition law violations could be introduced as an exception to the horizontal instrument on collective redress.
⁹⁹ In the field of EU competition law, soft law instruments are widely used. See I Maher, 'Competition Law Modernization: An Evolutionary Tale?' in P Craig and G de Búrca, *The Evolution of EU Law* (OUP 2011) 717, 734; H Cosma and R Whish, 'Soft Law in the Field of EU Competition Policy' (2003) 14 EBLR 25.
¹⁰⁰ Article 288 TFEU lists recommendations and opinions as legal acts with no binding force. On soft law instruments as a means of increasing the effectiveness of EU law see F Snyder, 'The Effectiveness of European Community Law: Institutions, Processes, Tools and Techniques' (1993) 56 MLR 19, 32–33; F Beveridge and S Nott, 'A Hard Look at Soft Law' in P Craig and C Harlow, *Lawmaking in the European Union* (Kluwer Law International 1998) 285, 288, 290; G Borchardt and K Wellens, 'Soft Law in European Community Law' (1989) 14 ELRev 267, 285, 320. For a

Conclusion

has issued several notices in the field of competition law, which, despite not being legally binding, affect the Commission's practice and should, therefore, be taken into account by the Commission when dealing with individual cases.[101] However, these soft law instruments cannot impose obligations upon Member States,[102] nor can they convince objecting Member States to adopt the relevant proposals;[103] nonetheless, they remain the only way open to the Commission in order to put forward proposals that are consistent with the CJEU case law on effective competition law enforcement and its own policy pronouncements on the importance of consumer interests in EU competition policy. Furthermore, despite the existing objections by some Member States, other Member States appear to be more open to proposals of this type.[104] A soft law approach may also satisfy those who view national systems of civil procedure as being deeply embedded in national traditions.[105]

So far, the Commission has overlooked the need to devise special collective actions for consumer claims resulting from competition law violations. Specific collective actions for the competition law field could indeed be the first step in the Commission's efforts to enhance collective redress mechanisms for violations of EU law. EU competition law is uniquely placed for the adoption of harmonized measures; not only has the ECJ pronounced on the existence of a directly effective right to damages but a large degree of substantive uniformity exists as well. It is, therefore, suggested, in order for the Commission to attain the necessary political support, a new, more focused, round of discussions is warranted. Furthermore, the Commission could at the same time opt for the adoption of facilitating measures in the field of public enforcement, in which, arguably, it has more latitude to act. Increased consumer involvement in the public enforcement of competition law has the potential to improve the participation rate in private enforcement, for which, at present, the only option open at EU level is the adoption of soft law instruments.

---

definition see L Senden, *Soft Law in European Community Law* (Hart 2004) 112. For a classification of the various soft law instruments see L Senden and S Prechal, 'Differentiation in and through Community Soft Law' in B de Witte, D Hanf, and E Vos (eds), *The Many Faces of Differentiation in EU Law* (Intersentia 2001) 181, 187–190.

[101] Joined Cases C-189/02 P, C-202/02 P, C-205-208/02 P, and C-213/02 P *Dansk Rørindustri and Others v Commission* [2005] ECR I-5425, para 211.
[102] Snyder (n 100) 35–36. See also *Pfleiderer* (n 97), para 23.
[103] Cf Eilmansberger (n 68) 438.
[104] See, for example, the Consumer Rights Act in the UK. See Chapter 5, text to nn 163–169.
[105] See CH van Rhee, 'Civil Procedure: A European Ius Commune?' (2000) 4 ERPL 589, 598–599 with references to proponents of this view. A soft law approach is suitable in areas closely connected with national identity and culture. See Secretariat of the European Convention, 'Coordination of National Policies: The Open Method of Coordination' (Brussels, 26 September 2002) WG VI WD015, 15–16.

8
Concluding Remarks

After a long period of policy deliberations spanning almost 10 years the EU Directive on Damages Actions is now a reality and has been warmly received by EU officials. Former Vice President of the Commission responsible for competition policy, Almunia, has welcomed the Directive on Damages Actions as the most important legal initiative undertaken during his term.[1] The new Competition Commissioner Margrethe Vestager welcomed the adoption of the Directive stating that 'we need a more robust competition culture in Europe…I am very pleased that it will be easier for European citizens and companies to receive effective compensation for harm caused by antitrust violations'.[2] This is true; nonetheless, the Directive failed to enhance consumers' role in private competition law enforcement, which may act as an impediment to the promotion of a competition culture.

The adoption of the Directive can be listed as a major success that has the potential to enhance competition law enforcement and contribute towards the development of uniform procedural rules across Member States on the area of its coverage. However, collective actions were omitted from its scope. This stands at odds with the central consumer role at the inception of this initiative.[3] The consumer role in private competition law enforcement will thus remain largely theoretical in Europe, with the exception of certain Member States that have opted for the adoption of a workable collective redress mechanism. This situation is deplorable, especially in the light of the increased presence of references to the consumer interest in EU competition law rhetoric.

This book has examined the theoretical and practical challenges of realizing consumer participation in EU competition law enforcement and has aspired to unravel EU competition law's relevance for consumers, a topic that often escapes EU policymakers' attention.[4] It embarked from the examination of the consumer interest in competition law enforcement and identified a limited importance

---

[1] J Almunia, 'Antitrust Litigation—The Way Ahead' (23 October 2014) (Speech/14/713).
[2] See Commission (EU), 'Commission Welcomes Council Adoption of Directive on Antitrust Damages Actions' (IP/14/1580) (Brussels, 10 November 2014).
[3] See, for example, Commission (EU), 'Damages Actions for Breach of the EC Antitrust Rules' (Green Paper) COM(2005) 672, final, 8–9; Commission (EU), 'Damages Actions for Breach of the EC Antitrust Rules' (White Paper) COM(2008) 165 final, 4.
[4] See, for example, Commission (EU), 'Consumer Empowerment in the EU' SEC(2011) 469 final, Brussels, 07.04.2011 which focuses only on consumer law issues.

attributed to it. Thus, it sought alternative means to promote consumer interest in EU competition law and argued that this is possible through consumer participation in private competition law enforcement and through certain changes in public enforcement procedures. It promoted a holistic approach to competition law enforcement, whereby private and public enforcement serve the same aims, albeit with different levels of intensity. The mechanisms discussed herein have the potential to further the collective consumer interest and contribute to the deterrence of competition law violations, while not denouncing the compensatory aim of damages claims. The compensatory aim is retained to the extent that it does not prevent the adoption of workable mechanisms. Appropriate mechanisms advancing the collective consumer interest in the field of competition law can serve as pioneers in re-shaping the approach towards the protection of consumer interests in general.

The analysis focused on procedural measures that enhance the consumer role in competition law enforcement. The rules in the EU Directive on Damages Actions on indirect purchaser standing and access to evidence can improve that role. Nonetheless, the analysis has shown that there is still room for improvement in relation to the rules on disclosure and access to evidence. Further, it has been argued that the Recommendation on common principles for collective redress falls short of addressing consumer claims for competition law violations and therefore there is still a need to develop workable collective action mechanisms. Nonetheless, there exists important political limitations for the adoption of such measures at the EU level.

Ultimately, the proposed measures for enhancing the consumer role in competition law enforcement need to strike a delicate balance between the following, sometimes contradictory, elements: first, general principles of tort law pertaining in individual Member States that accord priority to the compensatory rationale of damages actions; second, effective protection of the right to damages as recognized by the ECJ (in the sense of providing compensation to the victims of antitrust infringements); and third, effective enforcement of competition rules, this being the main aim of the right to damages according to the interpretation of the respective CJEU jurisprudence employed herein. From a pragmatic perspective, due account needs to be given to the minor nature of consumer claims in the context of competition law that can tip the balance in favour of the third element identified above.

Regardless of any Commission proposals in this field, in the near or distant future, the practical proposals advanced in this book are theoretically grounded and can serve as useful points of comparison. Throughout the analysis, the objections to the Commission's efforts, raised by the Member States as well as the business community, were underlined. In fact, these objections are of different force and content. They range from an outright rejection of any legislative initiative to supporting the Commission's efforts as long as they are modest and in line with the national traditions. What they do have in common is the fact that they impede the adoption of effective and functional measures in the consumer interest. In this book, it has been argued that shifting away from a competition law-only approach, that even if unsuccessful to date, has at least led to certain concrete proposals, thereby provoking further discussion, to an all inclusive discussion of principles of collective redress could be viewed as the Commission yielding to political pressures and dooms any collective redress initiative to fail.

The expressed opposition to functional private enforcement mechanisms has been very accurately described with regard to effective collective actions as the 'tale of two monsters'.[5] Ultimately, many citizens would prefer the adoption of a US type class action system (being labelled as a Frankenstein monster) to the adoption of an ineffective collective redress mechanism (labelled as a Loch Ness monster), existent in theory but absent in reality. This book submits that neither option is acceptable and puts forward concrete middle ground proposals to steer EU policymakers away from these extremes. The competence of the EU to adopt these proposals is assessed and it is concluded that the Treaty framework does indeed permit the adoption of these measures at the EU level.

At the same time, being aware of the political pressures which impede the adoption of these proposals, as well as the importance of consumer involvement in competition law enforcement, this book examined further alternatives enabling such participation in the field of public competition law enforcement and put forward further proposals that could ameliorate the present situation. Interestingly, the Commission enjoys more latitude to act in the field of public enforcement, and many of the suggested proposals could be adopted by a mere change in the Commission's current practice, without any legislative amendment. In light of the tangible benefits for consumers, the Commission is advised to change its practice in this direction, especially given the difficulties of adopting effective collective redress measures. In light of the current economic crisis, reinvigorating consumer confidence in the internal market is essential. The proposals advanced in this book are a contribution in this direction.

---

[5] R Mulheron, 'The Case for an Opt-Out Class Action for European Member States: A Legal and Empirical Analysis' (2009) 15 Colum J Eur L 409, 452–453.

Selected Bibliography

Adhar R, 'Consumers, Redistribution of Income and the Purpose of Competition Law' (2002) 23 ECLR 341.

Ahlborn C and Grave C, 'Walter Eucken and Ordoliberalism: An Introduction from a Consumer Welfare Perspective' (2006) 2 CPI <https://www.competitionpolicyinternational.com/walter-eucken-and-ordoliberalism-an-introduction-from-a-consumer-welfare-perspective/> accessed 15 June 2014.

Ahlborn C and Piccinin D, 'Between Scylla and Charybdis: Market Investigations and the Consumer Interest' in Rodger B (ed), *Ten Years of UK Competition Law Reform* (Dundee University Press 2010) 169.

Aitken J and Jones A, 'Reforming a World Class Competition Regime: The Government's Proposal for the Creation of a Single Competition and Markets Authority' (2011) 10 Comp Law 97.

Akman P, ' "Consumer" versus "Customer": The Devil in the Detail' (2010) 37 JL & Soc 315.

Akman P, 'Period of Limitations in Follow-on Competition Cases: When Does a "Decision" Become Final?' (2014) 2 JAE 389.

Akman P, 'Searching for the Long-Lost Soul of Article 82 EC' (2009) 29 OJLS 267.

Akman P, 'The Role of Exploitation in Abuse under Article 82 EC' in Barnard C and Odudu O (eds), *Cambridge Yearbook of European Legal Studies*, Volume 11, 2008–2009 (Hart 2009).

Akman P, 'The Role of Freedom in EU Competition Law' (2013) 34 LS 183.

Albors–Llorens A, 'Competition Policy and the Shaping of the Single Market' in Barnard C and Scott J (eds), *The Law of the Single European Market* (Hart 2002) 311.

Albors-Llorens A, 'The Ruling in *Courage v Crehan*: Judicial Activism or Consistent Approach?' (2002) 61 CLJ 38.

Alexandridou E and Apallagaki C, 'Article 10 L. 2251/1994' in Alexandridou E (ed), *Consumer Protection Law* (Nomiki Vivliothiki 2008) 555 (in Greek).

ALI, *Principles of the Law of Aggregate Litigation* (Proposed Final Draft, 1 April 2009).

Allan T, 'Parliamentary Sovereignty: Law, Politics and Revolution' (1997) LQR 443.

Allemeersch B, 'Transnational Class Settlements—Lessons from *Converium*' in Wrbka S, Van Uytsel S, and Siems M, *Collective Actions: Enhancing Access to Justice and Reconciling Multilayer Interests?* (CUP 2012) 364.

Amato G, *Antitrust and the Bounds of Power* (Hart 1997).

AMC, 'Report and Recommendations' (April 2007) <http://govinfo.library.unt.edu/amc/report_recommendation/amc_final_report.pdf> accessed 4 July 2014, 266.

Andreangeli A, 'A View from Across the Atlantic: Recent Developments in the Case-Law of the US Federal Courts on Class Certification in Antitrust Cases' in Rodger B (ed), *Competition Law Comparative Private Enforcement and Collective Redress Across Europe* (Kluwer 2014) 223.

Andreangeli A, 'From Mobile Phones to Cattle: How the Court of Justice Is Reframing the Approach to Article 101 (Formerly 81 EC Treaty) of the EU Treaty' (2011) 34 W Comp 215.

Andreangeli A, *Private Enforcement of Antitrust: Regulating Corporate Behaviour through Collective Claims in the EU and the US* (Edward Elgar 2014).

Andriychuk O, 'Can We Protect Competition Without Protecting Consumers?' (2009) 6 CompLRev <http://www.clasf.org/CompLRev/Issues/Vol6Issue1Article4Andriychuk.pdf> accessed 2 June 2014.

Arkenstette M, 'Reorientation in Consumer Policy—Challenges and Prospects from the Perspective of Practical Consumer Advice Work' (2005) 28 JCP 361.

Armstrong K, 'Rediscovering Civil Society: The European Union and the White Paper on Governance' (2002) 8 ELJ 102.

Armstrong M, 'Interactions Between Competition and Consumer Policy' (2008) 4 CPI 97.

Ashton D and Henry D, *Competition Damages Actions in the EU* (Edward Elgar 2013).

Averitt N and Lande R, 'Consumer Sovereignty: A Unified Theory of Antitrust and Consumer Protection Law' (1997) 65 Antitrust LJ 713.

Averitt N and Lande R, 'Using the "Consumer Choice" Approach to Antitrust Law' (2007) 74 Antitrust LJ 175.

Averitt N, 'Protecting Consumer Choice: Competition and Consumer Protection Together' in Drexl J and others (eds), *More Common Ground for International Competition Law?* (Edward Elgar 2011) 36.

Ayres I and Braithwaite J, *Responsive Regulation—Transcending the Deregulation Debate* (OUP 1992).

Bailey D, 'Restrictions of Competition by Object under Article 101 TFEU' (2012) 49 CMLRev 559.

Baldwin R, *Rules and Government* (Clarendon Press 1995).

Baquero Cruz J, *Between Competition and Free Movement, The Economic Constitutional Law of the European Community* (Hart 2002).

Barber N, 'The Afterlife of Parliamentary Sovereignty' (2011) 9 ICON 144.

Barents R, 'Constitutional Horse Trading: Some Comments on the Protocol on the Internal Market and Competition' in Bulterman M (ed), *Views of European Law from the Mountain: Liber Amicorum for Piet Jan Slot* (Kluwer Law International 2009) 123.

Barents R, 'The Internal Market Unlimited: Some Observations on the Legal Basis Of Community Legislation' (1993) 30 CMLRev 85.

Barnard C and Odudu O (eds), *The Cambridge Yearbook of European Legal Studies*, Volume 12, 2009–2010 (Hart Publishing 2010).

Barnett K, 'Equitable Trusts: An Effective Remedy in Consumer Class Actions' (1987) 96 Yale LJ 1591.

Bartelt S, 'Case T-2/03 *VKI v Commission*' (2006) 43 CMLRev 191.

Basso LJ and Ross RT, 'Measuring the True Harm from Price Fixing to Both Direct and Indirect Purchasers' (Draft, January 2008) <http://www.strategy.sauder.ubc.ca/ross/MeasuringtheTrueHarmfromPriceFixing.pdf> accessed 4 July 2014.

Baumol W and Ordover J, 'Use of Antitrust to Subvert Competition' (1985) 28 JL & Econ 247.

Beard D and Jones A, 'Co-contractors, Damages and Article 81: The ECJ Finally Speaks' (2002) 23 ECLR 246.

Beaumont PR and Weatherill S, *EU Law* (3rd edn, Penguin 1999).

Becker G and Stigler G, 'Law Enforcement, Malfeasance and Compensation of Enforcers' (1974) 3 J Legal Stud 1.

Becker G, 'Crime and Punishment: An Economic Approach' (1968) 76 J Pol Econ 169.

Benoehr I, 'Collective Redress in the Field of European Consumer Law' (2014) 41 *Legal Issues of Economic Integration* 243.

Benoehr I, 'Consumer Dispute Resolution after the Lisbon Treaty: Collective Actions and Alternative Procedures' (2013) 36 J Consum P 87.

Benoehr I, *EU Consumer Law and Human Rights* (OUP 2014).

Bertelsen BI, Calfee MS, and Connor GW, 'The Rule 23(b)(3) Class Action: An Empirical Study' (1974) 62 Geo LJ 1123.

Beveridge F and Nott S, 'A Hard Look at Soft Law' in Craig P and Harlow C, *Lawmaking in the European Union* (Kluwer Law International 1998) 285.

Biondi A, 'C-253/00 Muñoz Cia SA and Superior Fruiticola Ltd and Redbridge Produce Marketing Ltd [2002] ECR I-7289' (2003) 40 CMLRev 1241.

Bishop S and Walker M, *The Economics of EC Competition Law: Concepts, Application and Measurement* (3rd edn, Sweet and Maxwell 2010).

Blair R and Sokol D, 'The Rule of Reason and the Goals of Antitrust: An Economic Approach' (2012) 78 Antitrust LJ 471.

Blaire RD and Piette CA, 'Coupon Settlements: Compensation and Deterrence' (2006) 51 AB 661.

Blaire RD and Piette CA, 'Coupons and Settlements in Antitrust Class Actions' (2006) 20 Antitrust LJ 32.

Block M, Nold FC, and Sidak J, 'The Deterrent Effect of Antitrust Enforcement' (1981) 89 J Pol Econ 429.

Boege U and Ost K, 'Up and Running, or Is It? Private Enforcement—The Situation in Germany and Policy Perspectives' (2006) 27 ECLR 197.

Bolster T, 'The Structure and Funding of Competition Claims Post-Jackson—"All Change" or "Status Quo"?' (2014) Comp Law 202.

Borchardt G and Wellens K, 'Soft Law in European Community Law' (1989) 14 ELRev 267.

Bork R, 'Legislative Intent and the Policy of the Sherman Act' (1966) 9 JL & Econ 7.

Bork R, *The Antitrust Paradox* (2nd edn, Maxwell Macmillan International 1993).

Bos P, 'International Scrutiny for Payment Card Systems' (2006) 73 Antitrust LJ 739.

Bourgeois J and Strievi S, 'EU Competition Remedies in Consumer Cases: Thinking Out of the Shopping Bag' (2010) 33 W Comp 241.

Braithwaite J, *Restorative Justice and Responsive Regulation* (OUP 2002).

Brealey M and Green N (eds), *Competition Litigation: UK Practice and Procedure* (OUP 2010).

Brealy M, 'Adopt *Perma Life*, but Follow *Hannover Shoe* to Illinois?' (2002) 1 Comp Law 127.

Breit W and Elzinga K, 'Private Antitrust Enforcement: The New Learning' (1985) 28 JL & Econ 405.

Brisimi V and Ioannidou M, 'Criminalising Cartels in Greece: A Tale of Hasty Developments and Shaky Grounds' (2011) 34 W Comp 157.

Brisimi V and Ioannidou M, 'Stand-alone Damages Actions: Insights from Greece and Cyprus' (2013) 34 ECLR 654.

Brkan M, 'Procedural Aspects of Private Enforcement of EC Antitrust Law: Heading Toward New Reforms?' (2005) 28 W Comp 479.

Brodley J, 'The Economic Goals of Antitrust: Efficiency, Consumer Welfare and Technological Progress' (1987) 62 NYU L Rev 1020.

Bronsteen J and Fisse O, 'The Class Action Rule' (2003) 78 Notre Dame L Rev 1419.

Bronsteen J, 'Class Action Settlements: An Opt-in Proposal' [2005] U Ill L Rev 903.

Brouwer O, 'Antitrust Settlements in the Netherlands: A Useful Source of Inspiration' in Ehlermann CD and Marquis M (eds), *European Competition Law Annual 2007* (Hart 2008) 489.

Brown C and Ryan D, 'The Judicial Application of European Competition Law' (FIDE Congress Madrid, 2010) <http://www.ukael.org/associates_21_2528442727.pdf> accessed 9 July 2014.

Buccirossi P et al, *Collective Redress in Antitrust* (2012) (Study—DG for Internal Policies) 12.

Bulst F, 'Of Arms and Armour—The European Commission's White Paper on Damages Actions for Breach of EC Antitrust Law' [2008] *Bucerius Law Journal* 81.

Bulst F, 'Private Antitrust Enforcement at a Roundabout' (2006) 7 EBOR 725.

Bulst FW, 'Private Antitrust Enforcement at a Roundabout' (2006) 7 EBOR 725.

Buttigieg E, *Competition Law—Safeguarding the Consumer Interest: A Comparative Analysis of US Antitrust Law and EC Competition Law* (Kluwer Law International 2009).

Buttigieg E, 'Consumer Interests under the EC's Competition Rules on Collusive Practices' [2005] EBLR 643.

Buxbaum H, 'German Legal Culture and the Globalisation of Competition Law: A Historical Perspective on the Expansion of Private Antitrust Enforcement' (2005) 23 Berkley J Int'l L 101.

Cachafeiro F, 'Damages Claims for Breach of Competition Law in Spain' (2014) <http://papers.ssrn.com/sol3/papers.cfm?abstract_id=2456964> accessed 8 July 2014.

Cafaggi F and Micklitz HW, 'Administrative and Judicial Enforcement in Consumer Protection: The Way Forward' (2008) EUI Working Papers Law 2008/29 <http://papers.ssrn.com/sol3/papers.cfm?abstract_id=1317342> accessed 6 November 2014.

Cafaggi F and Micklitz HW, 'Collective Enforcement of Consumer Law: A Framework for Comparative Assessment' (2008) 16 ERPL 391.

Cafaggi F and Muir-Watt H, 'Introduction' in Cafaggi F and Muir-Watt H (eds), *Making European Private Law: Governance Design* (Edward Elgar 2008) 7.

Calabresi G, 'Class Actions in the US Experience: The Legal Perspective' in Backhaus J, Cassone A, and Ramello G (eds), *The Law and Economics of Class Actions in Europe—Lessons from America* (Edward Elgar 2012) 10.

Calkins S, 'An Enforcement Official's Reflections on Antitrust Class Actions' (1997) 39 Ariz L Rev 413.

Calkins S, 'Summary Judgment, Motion to Dismiss, and Other Examples of Equilibrating Tendencies in the Antitrust System' (1986) 74 Geo L J 1065.

Calzdilla Medina MA and others, 'Spain' in Hodges C, Vogenauer S, and Tulibacka M (eds), *The Costs and Funding of Civil Litigation: A Comparative Perspective* (Hart 2010) 492.

Camerer C and others, 'Regulation for Conservatives: Behavioural Economics and the Case for Asymmetric Patternalism' (2003) 151 U Pa L Rev 1211.

Camesasca P and van den Bergh R, 'Irreconcilable Principles? The Court of Justice Exempts Collective Labour Agreements From the Wrath of Antitrust' (2000) 25 ELRev 492.

Cane P, *The Anatomy of Tort Law* (Hart 1997).

Canenbley C and Steinvorth T, 'Effective Enforcement of Competition Law: Is There a Solution to the Conflict between Leniency Programmes and Private Damages Actions?' (2011) 2 J Eur CL & P 315.

Cappalli R and Consolo C, 'Class Actions for Continental Europe? A Preliminary Inquiry' (2001) Temple Int'l & Comp L J 217.

Cappelletti M (gen ed), *Access to Justice* (4 volumes, Sijthoff and Giuffrè 1978–1979).

Cappelletti M and Garth B, 'Access to Justice: The Worldwide Movement to Make Rights More Effective—A General Report' in Cappelletti M and Garth B (eds), *Access to Justice—a World Survey* (Sijthoff 1981).

Cappelletti M and Garth B, 'Introduction' in Cappelletti M (ed), *Access to Justice and the Welfare State* (Sijthoff 1981).

Cappelletti M, 'Alternative Dispute Resolution Processes within the Framework of the World Wide Access to Justice Movement' (1993) 56 MLR 282.

Carpagnano M, 'Private Enforcement of Competition Law Arrives in Italy: Analysis of the Judgment of the European Court of Justice in Joined Cases C-295–289/04 *Manfredi*' (2006) 3 Comp L Rev <http://www.clasf.org/CompLRev/Issues/Vol3Issue1Art3Carpagnano.pdf> accessed 3 July 2014.

Cartlidge H and Root N, 'The UK Market Investigations Regime: A Review' (2009) 8 Comp Law 312.

Cavanagh ED, 'Pleading Rules in Antitrust Cases: A Return to Fact Pleading' (2002) 21 Rev Litigation 1.

Cavanagh ED, 'Twombly, the Federal Rules of Civil Procedure and the Courts' (2008) 82 St John's L Rev 877.

Cengiz F, 'Antitrust Damages Actions: Lessons from American Indirect Purchasers' Litigation' (2010) 59 ICLQ 39.

Cengiz F, 'The Role of State Attorneys General in US Antitrust Policy: Public Enforcement through Private Enforcement Methods' (2006) (UEA—CCP Working Paper 06-19).

Chauve P and Godfried M, 'Modelling Competitive Electricity Markets: Are Consumers Paying for Lack of Competition?' [2007] CPN 18.

Cichowski R, *The European Court and Civil Society* (CUP 2007).

Civic Consulting, 'Evaluation of the Effectiveness and Efficiency of Collective Redress Mechanisms in the European Union' (Final Report prepared for DG SANCO, 26 August 2008) <http://ec.europa.eu/consumers/redress_cons/finalreportevaluationstudypart1-final2008-11-26.pdf> accessed 21 November 2014.

CJC, 'Improving Access to Justice through Collective Actions' (November 2008).

Coffee J, 'Class Wars: The Dilemma of Mass Tort Class Action' (1995) 95 Colum L Rev 1344.

Coffee J, 'Understanding the Plaintiff's Attorney: The Implications of Economic Theory for Private Enforcement of Law through Class and Derivative Actions' (1986) 86 Colum L Rev 669.

Coleman J, 'The Practice of Corrective Justice' in Owen D (ed), *Philosophical Foundations of Tort Law* (Clarendon Press 1995) 54.

Committee on the Internal Market and Consumer Protection, 'Towards a Coherent European Approach to Collective Redress' (Opinion) (12/10/2011) (2011/2089(INI)).

Connor JM and Lande RH, 'How High Do Cartels Raise Prices? Implications for Optimal Cartel Fines' (2006) 80 Tul L Rev 513.

Cook C, 'Private Enforcement of EU Competition Law in Member State Courts: Experience to Date and the Path Ahead' (2008) 4(2) CPI 3.

Cooper EH, 'Class Action Advice in the Form of Questions' (2001) 11 Duke J Comp Int'l L 215.

Cosma H and Whish R, 'Soft Law in the Field of EU Competition Policy' (2003) 14 EBLR 25.

Craig P and de Búrca G, *EU Law: Text, Cases and Materials* (5th edn, OUP 2011).

Craig P, 'Integration, Democracy and Legitimacy' in Craig P and de Burca G (eds), *The Evolution of EU Law* (2nd edn, OUP 2011) 13.

Craig P, 'Once Upon a Time in the West: Direct Effect and the Federalization of EEC Law' (1992) OJLS 453.

Craig P, 'Sovereignty of the United Kingdom Parliament after Factortame' (1991) 11 YEL 221.
Craig P, *The Lisbon Treaty: Law, Politics and the Treaty Reform* (OUP 2010).
Cseres K, 'Competition and Consumer Policies: Starting Points for Better Convergence' (2009) Amsterdam Center for Law & Economics Working Paper No 2009/06 <http://ssrn.com/abstract=1379322> accessed 15 June 2014.
Cseres K, *Competition Law and Consumer Protection* (Kluwer Law International 2005).
Cseres K, 'The Controversies of the Consumer Welfare Standard' (2007) 3 Comp L Rev <http://www.clasf.org/CompLRev/Issues/Vol3Issue2Art1Cseres.pdf> accessed 15 June 2014.
Cseres K, 'What Has Competition Done for Consumers in Liberalised Markets?' (2008) 4 Comp L Rev <http://www.clasf.org/CompLRev/Issues/Vol4Iss2Art1Cseres.pdf> accessed 5 August 2014.
Cullen H and Charlesworth A, 'Diplomacy by Other Means: The Use of Legal Basis Litigation as a Political Strategy by the European Parliament and Member States' (1999) 36 CMLRev 1243.
Cumming G and Freudenthal M, *Civil Procedure in EU Competition Cases before the English and Dutch Courts* (Kluwer Law International 2010)
Dam KW, 'Class Action Notice: Who Needs it?' (1974) *Supreme Court Review* 97.
Dam KW, 'Class Actions: Efficiency, Compensation, Deterrence and Conflict of Interest' (1975) 4 J Legal Stud 47.
Davies J, *The European Consumer Citizen in Law and Policy* (Palgrave Macmillan 2011).
Dayagi Epstein O, 'Representation of Consumer Interest by Consumer Associations—Salvation for the Masses?' (2007) 3 Comp L Rev 209.
Dayagi-Epstein O, 'Furnishing Consumers with a Voice in Competition Policy' (2005) <http://www.luc.edu/media/lucedu/law/centers/antitrust/pdfs/publications/workingpapers/dayagi_epstein_consumers_voice.pdf> accessed 5 August 2014.
De Búrca G and de Witte B, 'The Delimitation of Powers between the EU and its Member States' in Arnull A and Wincott D (eds), *Accountability and Legitimacy in the European Union* (OUP 2002) 201.
De Burca G and Scott J, 'Introduction: New Governance, Law and Constitutionalism' in de Burca G and Scott J (eds), *Law and New Governance in the EU and US* (Hart 2006).
De Leeuw ME, 'The Regulation on Public Access to European Parliament, Council and Commission Documents in the European Union: Are Citizens Better Off?' (2003) 28 ELRev 324.
Deakin S, Johnston A, and Markesinis B, *Markesinis and Deakin's Tort Law* (Clarendon 2008) 50.
DeJarlais N, 'Notes—The Consumer Trust Fund: A Cy Pres Solution to Undistributed Funds in Consumer Class Actions' (1987) 38 Hastings LJ 729.
Delatre J, 'Beyond the White Paper: Rethinking the Commission's Proposal on Private Antitrust Litigation' (2008) 8 Comp L Rev 29.
Delikostopoulos JS, 'Towards European Procedural Primacy in National Legal Systems' (2003) 9 ELJ 599.
DG for Internal Policies, 'Overview of Existing Collective Redress Schemes in EU Member State' (July 2011) (IP/A/IMCO/NT/2011-16).
Dougan M, 'The Convention's Draft Constitutional Treaty: Bringing Europe Closer to Its Lawyers' (2003) 28 ELRev 763.
Dougan M, *National Remedies before the Court of Justice* (Hart 2004).

Drake S, 'Scope of Courage and the Principle of "Individual Liability" for Damages: Further Development of the Principle of Effective Judicial Protection by the Court of Justice' (2006) 31 ELRev 841.

Drexl J, 'Competition Law as Part of the European Constitution' in von Bogdandy A and Bast J (eds), *Principles of European Constitutional Law* (2nd edn, Hart 2009) 659.

DTI, 'Extending Competitive Markets: Empowered Consumers, Successful Business' (June 2005) <http://www.berr.gov.uk/files/file23787.pdf> accessed 14 June 2014.

Dunne N, 'Between Competition Law and Regulation: Hybridized Approaches to Market Control' (2014) 2 JAE 225.

Dunne N, 'Commitment Decisions in EU Competition Law' (2014) 10 JCLE 399.

Dunne N, 'It Never Rains but it Pours? Liability for "Umbrella Effects" under EU Competition Law in Kone' (2014) 51 CMLRev 1813.

Dunne N, 'The Role of Private Enforcement within EU Competition Law' (2014) (University of Cambridge Faculty of Law Research Paper No. 36/2014) <http://papers.ssrn.com/sol3/papers.cfm?abstract_id=2457838> accessed 10 November 2014.

DuVal B, 'The Class Action as an Antitrust Enforcement Device: The Chicago Experience (II)' (1976) *American Bar Foundation Research Journal* 1273.

Easterbrook F, 'The Limits of Antitrust' (1984) 63 Texas Law Review 1.

ECCG, 'Minutes of the ECCG Competition Subgroup Meeting' (28 June 2011, Brussels) <http://www.ec.europa.eu/consumers/empowerment/docs/eccg_comp_sub_group_minutes_062011_en.pdf> accessed 30 October 2014.

ECCG, 'Opinion on Private Damages Actions' <http://www.ec.europa.eu/consumers/empowerment/docs/ECCG_opinion_on_actions_for_damages_18112010.pdf> accessed 30 October 2014.

ECN, 'Protection of Leniency Material in the Context of Civil Damages Actions' (Resolution of the Meeting of Heads of the European Competition Authorities of 23 May 2012) <http://ec.europa.eu/competition/ecn/leniency_material_protection_en.pdf> accessed 20 September 2014.

Edelman J and Odudu O, 'Compensatory Damages for Breach of Article 81' (2002) 27 ELRev 327.

EESC, 'Opinion on the Green Paper on Consumer Collective Redress' [2010] OJ C128/97.

EESC, 'Opinion on Defining the Collective Action System and Its Role in the Context of Community Consumer Law' [2008] OJ C162/1.

EESC, 'Proposal for a Directive of the European Parliament and of the Council on Certain Rules Governing Actions for Damages under National Law for Infringements of the Competition Law Provisions of the Member States and of the European Union' [2014] OJ C67/83.

Ehlermann CD and Laudati L, 'Introduction' in Ehlermann CD and Laudati L (eds) *European Competition Law Annual 1997: The Objectives of Competition Policy* (Hart 1998) x.

Ehlermann CD, 'The Contribution of EC Competition Policy to the Single Market' (1992) 29 CMLRev 257.

Eilmansberger T, 'Dominance-The Lost Child? How Effects-based Rules Could and Should Change Dominance Analysis' (2006) 2 Euro CJ 15.

Eilmansberger T, 'The Green Paper on Damages Actions for Breach of the EC Antitrust Rules and Beyond: Reflections on the Utility and Feasibility of Stimulating Private Enforcement through Legislative Action' (2007) 44 CMLRev 431.

Eilmansberger T, 'The Relationship Between Rights and Remedies in EC Law: In Search of the Missing Link' (2004) 41 CMLRev 1199.

Eisenberg T and Miller G, 'The Role of Opt-Out and Objectors in Class Action Litigation: Theoretical and Empirical Issues' (2004) NYU Law and Economics Research Paper Series Working Paper No 04-004 <http://papers.ssrn.com/sol3/papers.cfm?abstract_id=528146> accessed 1 November 2014.

ELI, 'Statement of the European Law Institute on Collective Redress and Competition Damages Claims' (2014) <http://www.europeanlawinstitute.eu/fileadmin/user_upload/p_eli/Projects/S-5-2014_Statement_on_Collective_Redress_and_Competition_Damages_Claims.pdf> accessed 10 April 2015.

Eliantonio M, 'Collective Redress in Environmental Matters in the EU: A Role Model or a "Problem Child"?' (2014) 41 *Legal Issues of Economic Integration* 257.

Englard I, 'The Idea of Complementarity as a Philosophical Basis for Pluralism in Tort Law' in Owen D (ed), *Philosophical Foundations of Tort Law* (Clarendon Press 1995).

Epstein R, 'Of Pleading and Discovery: Reflections on Twombly and Iqbal with Special Reference to Antitrust' [2011] U Ill L Rev 187.

ESC, 'Opinion on the Thirteenth Report on Competition Policy' [1984] OJ C343/03.

ESC, 'Opinion on the Twenty-second Competition Report' in European Commission, XXIIIrd Report on Competition Policy 1993 (Brussels, Luxembourg 1994) <http://bookshop.europa.eu/is-bin/INTERSHOP.enfinity/WFS/EU-Bookshop-Site/en_GB/-/EUR/ViewPublication-Start?PublicationKey=CM8294650> accessed 15 June 2014.

Estella de Noriega A, *The EU Principle of Subsidiarity and its Critique* (OUP 2002).

European Parliament, *Collective Redress in Antitrust* (2012).

Evans A, 'European Competition Law and Consumers: The Article 85(3) Exemption' (1981) 2 ECLR 425.

Evans D and Padilla J, 'Excessive Prices: Using Economics to Define Administrable Legal Rules' (2005) 1 JCLE 97.

Evans P, 'Consumer Interest and Supercomplaints' (Consumers' Association Presentation) <http://www.incsoc.net/conf-2ppt5.ppt> accessed 6 November 2014.

Evans P, 'Making Competition Real: EU Super-Complaints' (2005) 15 CPR 187.

Everson M, 'The Legacy of the Market Citizen' in Shaw J and More G (eds), *New Legal Dynamics of European Union* (Clarendon Press 1995) 73.

Everson M, 'Legal Constructions of the Consumer' in Trentmann F (ed), *The Making of the Consumer* (Berg 2006) 99.

Ezrachi A and Gilo D, 'Are Excessive Prices Really Self-Correcting?' (2008) 5 JCLE 249.

Ezrachi A and Ioannidou M, 'Access to Justice in European Competition Law—Public Enforcement as a Supplementary Channel for "Corrective Compensation"' (2011) 19 Asia Pac L Rev 195.

Ezrachi A and Ioannidou M, 'Public Compensation as a Complementary Mechanism to Damages Actions: From Policy Justification to Formal Implementation' (2012) 6 JECLAP 536.

Ezrachi A, 'Sponge' (2015) Working Paper CCLP (L) 42 <http://papers.ssrn.com/sol3/papers.cfm?abstract_id=2572028> accessed 5 May 2015.

Ezrachi A, 'The Commission's Guidance on Article 82 EC and the Effects Based Approach—Legal and Practical Challenges' in Ezrachi A (ed), *Article 82 EC: Reflections on its Recent Evolution* (Hart 2009).

Ezrachi A, 'The European Commission Guidance on Article 82 EC—The Way in which Institutional Realities Limit the Potential for Reform' (2009) Oxford Legal Studies Research Paper No 27/2009 <http://ssrn.com/abstract=1463854>, accessed 16 June 2014.

F Caffagi and HW Micklitz, 'Administrative and Judicial Collective Enforcement of Consumer Law in the US and the European Community' (2007) EUI Law Working Paper No 2007/22 <http://papers.ssrn.com/sol3/papers.cfm?abstract_id=1024103> accessed 17 October 2014.

F Cengiz, 'Passing-on Defence and Indirect Purchasers Standing in Actions for Damages against the Violations of Competition Law: What Can the EC Learn from the US' (2007) UEA CCP Working Paper No 07/21 <http://papers.ssrn.com/sol3/papers.cfm?abstract_id=1038521> accessed 4 July 2014.

Fairgrieve D and Howells G, 'Collective Redress Procedures+A434European Debates' (2009) 58 ICLQ 379.

Farmer SB, 'More Lessons from the Laboratories: Cy Pres Distributions in Parens Patriae Antitrust Actions Brought by State Attorneys General' (2000) 68 Fordm L Rev 361.

Faulk R, 'Armageddon through Aggregation? The Use and Abuse of Class Actions in International Dispute Resolution' in Rickett C and Telfer T (eds), *International Perspectives on Consumers' Access to Justice* (CUP 2003) 330.

Fingleton J, 'Market Studies: Finding and Fixing Problem Markets' (OFT Market Studies Conference, 4 June 2008).

Foer A, 'Enhancing Competition through the Cy Pres Remedy: Suggested Best Practices' (2010) 24 Antitrust LJ 86.

Folsom R, 'Indirect Purchasers: State Antitrust Remedies and Roadblocks' (2005) 50 AB 181.

Fox E, 'Monopolization and Dominance in the United States and the European Community: Efficiency, Opportunity and Fairness' (1986) 61 Notre Dame L Rev 981.

Freedland M, 'The Evolving Approach to the Public/Private Distinction in English Law' in Freedland M and Auby JB (eds), *The Public Law/ Private Law Divide* (Hart 2006) 93.

Gal M, 'Abuse of Dominance—Exploitative Abuses' in Lianos I and Geradin D (eds), *Handbook on European Competition Law* (Edward Elgar 2013).

Gans J, 'Protecting Consumers by Protecting Competition: Does Behavioural Economics Support this Contention' 12 (Melbourne Business School, 31 May 2005) <http://www.accc.gov.au/system/files/Joshua%20Gans%20(paper)%20-%20Protecting%20consumers%20by%20protecting%20competition_%20Does%20behavioural%20economics%20support%20this%20contention.pdf> accessed 15 June 2014.

Gaudet R, 'Turning a Blind Eye: The Commission's Rejection of Opt-out Class Actions Overlooks Swedish, Norwegian, Danish and Dutch Experience' (2009) 30 ECLR 107.

Geradin D, 'The Decision of the Commission of 13 May 2009 in the Intel Case: Where is the Foreclosure and Consumer Harm?' (2010) 1 JECLAP 112.

Gerber D, 'Constitutionalising the Economy: German Neo-liberalism, Competition Law and the "New" Europe' (1994) 42 AJCL 25.

Gerber D, *Law and Competition in Twentieth Century Europe: Protecting Prometheus* (OUP 2001).

Gerber D, 'The Transformation of European Community Competition Law?' (1994) 35 Harvard Intl LJ 97.

Gerber D, 'Two Forms of Modernization in European Competition Law' (2008) 31 Fordham Int'l LJ 1235.

Gibbons S, 'Group Litigation, Class Actions and Lord Woolf's Three Objectives—A Critical Analysis' [2008] CJQ 208.

Gidi A, 'Class Actions in Brazil—A Model for Civil Law Countries' (2003) 51 Am J Comp L 311.

Gidi A, 'The Class Action Code: A Model for Civil Law Countries' (2005) 23 Ariz J Intl & Comp L 37.

Ginsburg D, 'Judge Bork, Consumer Welfare, and Antitrust Law' (2008) 31 Harv JL & Pub Pol'y 449.

Giocoli N, 'Competition versus Property Rights: American Antitrust Law, the Freiburg School and the Early Years of EU Competition Policy' (2009) 5 JCLE 747.

Giulietti M, Waddams Price C, and Waterson M, 'Consumer Choice and Competition Policy: A Study of UK Energy Markets' (2005) 115 Econ J 949.

Glader M and Alstergren P, 'Sweden' in Foer A and Cuneo J (eds), *The International Handbook of Private Enforcement of Competition Law* (Edward Elgar 2010) 407.

Glover C and Owen-Howes R, 'The Consumer Face of the OFT: How Does Consumer Protection Fit in with Competition Law?' (2009) 8(6) CLI 3.

Goddin G, 'Recent Judgments Regarding Transparency and Access to Documents in the Field of Competition Law: Where does the Court of Justice of the EU Strike the Balance?' (2011) 2 JECLAP 10.

Gomez F and Gili M, 'Country Report Spain' (Report prepared for Civic Consulting to be submitted to DG SANCO) (25 February 2008) <http://ec.europa.eu/consumers/redress_cons/sp-country-report-final.pdf> accessed 17 October 2014.

Goyder J, 'Consumer Guarantees and Competition Issues' in Lonbay J (ed), *Enhancing the Legal Position of the European Consumer* (BIICL 1996) 80.

Goyens M, 'A Key Ruling from the ECJ' (1994) 4 CPR 221.

Graham C, 'Methods for Determining Whether an Agreement Restricts Competition: Comment on Allianz Hungária' (2013) 38 ELRev 542.

Gubbay I and Maton A, 'Private Enforcement Claims—Are They a Risk for Consumers and Businesses?' (2009) 8(1) CLI 8.

Gutiérrez de Cabiedes Hidalgo P, 'Group Litigation in Spain' (Report prepared for 'The Globalization of Class Actions') <http://globalclassactions.stanford.edu/sites/default/files/documents/spain_national_report.pdf> accessed 17 October 2014.

Gyselen L, 'Comment from the Point of View of EU Competition Law' in Wouters J and Stuyck J (eds), *Principles of Proper Conduct for Supranational, State and Private Actors in the European Union: Towards a Ius Commune, Essays in Honour of Walter van Gerven* (Intersentia 2001) 135.

H Lindblom, 'National Report: Group Litigation in Sweden' (Report prepared for 'The Globalization of Class Actions') (6 December 2007) <http://globalclassactions.stanford.edu/sites/default/files/documents/Sweden_National_Report.pdf> accessed 15 October 2014.

Haapaniemi P, 'Procedural Autonomy: A Misnomer?' in Ervo L, Graens M, and Jokela A (eds), *Europeanization of Procedural Law and the New Challenges to the Fair Trial* (Europa Law Publishing 2009) 87.

Hampton P, 'Reducing Administrative Burdens: Effective Inspection and Enforcement' (HM Treasury, March 2005) <http://webarchive.nationalarchives.gov.uk/+/http://www.bis.gov.uk/files/file22988.pdf> accessed 13 July 2014.

Handler M, 'The Shift from Substantive to Procedural Innovations in Antitrust Suits' (1971) Colum L Rev 1.

Haracoglou I, 'Competition Law, Consumer Policy and the Retail Sector: The Systems' Relation and the Effects of a Strengthened Consumer Protection Policy on Competition Law' (2007) 3 Comp L Rev <http://www.clasf.org/CompLRev/Issues/Vol3Issue2Art2Haracoglou.pdf> accessed 16 June 2014.

Harker M and Hviid M, 'Competition Law Enforcement and Incentives for Revelation of Private Information' (2008) 31 W Comp 297.

Selected Bibliography

Harlow C, 'Voice of Difference in a Plural Community' in Beaumont PR, Lyons C, and Walker N (eds), *Convergence and Divergence in European Public Law* (Hart 2001) 217.

Harris RG and Sullivan LA, 'Passing on the Monopoly Overcharge: A Comprehensive Policy Analysis' (1979) 128 U Pa L Rev 269.

Harris RG and Sullivan LA, 'Passing on the Monopoly Overcharge: A Response to Landes and Posner' (1980) 128 U Pa L Rev 1280.

Harrison P, 'The Court of Justice's Judgment in *Allianz Hungáaria* is Wrong and Needs Correcting' (May 2013) *CPI Antitrust Chronicle* 1.

Hartnell H, 'A Cinderella Story: "Judicial Cooperation in Civil Matters" Meets the Prince. Review of Eva Storskrubb, Civil Procedure and EU Law: A Policy Area Uncovered' (2010) YEL 483.

Hartnell H, 'EUstitia: Institutionalising Justice in the European Union' (2002) 23 Nw J Int'l L & Bus 65.

Hay BL and Rosenberg D, '"Sweetheart" and "Blackmail" Settlements in Class Actions: Reality and Remedy' (2000) 75 Notre Dame L Rev 1377.

Heinelt H and Meinke-Brandmaier B, 'Comparing Civil Society Participation in European Environmental Policy and Consumer Protection' in Smismans S (ed), *Civil Society and Legitimate European Governance* (Edward Elgar 2003) 196.

Helland E and Tabarrok A, 'Contingency Fees, Settlement Delays, and Low Quality Litigation: Empirical Evidence from Two Datasets' (2003) 19 JLEO 517.

Hellwig M, 'Private Damages Claims and the Passing-on Defence in Horizontal Price-Fixing Cases—An Economist's Perspective' in Basedow J (ed), *Private Enforcement of EC Competition Law* (Kluwer Law International 2007).

Hess H and others, 'Evaluation of the Contributions to the Public Consultation and Hearing: "Towards a Coherent European Approach to Collective Redress"' (28/10/11) <http://ec.europa.eu/competition/consultations/2011_collective_redress/study_heidelberg_contributions_en.pdf> accessed 14 November 2014.

Hesselink M, 'European Contract Law: A Matter of Consumer Protection, Citizenship or Justice?' in Grundmann S (ed), *Constitutional Values and European Contract Law* (Kluwer Law International 2008) 241.

Hillebrand G and Torrence D, 'Claims Procedures in Large Consumer Class Actions and Equitable Distribution of Benefits' (1988) 28 Santa Clara L Rev 747.

Hodges C and Stadler A, 'Introduction' in Hodges C and Stadler A, *Resolving Mass Disputes—ADR and Settlement of Mass Claims* (Edward Elgar 2013) 1.

Hodges C, 'A Market-Based Competition Enforcement Policy' (2011) 22 EBLR 261.

Hodges C, 'Competition Enforcement, Regulation and Civil Justice: What is the Case?' (2006) 43 CMLRev 1381.

Hodges C, 'Encouraging Enterprise and Rebalancing Risk: Implications of Economic Policy for Regulation, Enforcement and Compensation' (2009) 20 EBLR 1231.

Hodges C, 'European Competition Enforcement Policy: Integrating Restitution and Behaviour Control' (2011) 34 W Comp 383.

Hodges C, 'From Class Actions to Collective Redress: A Revolution in Approach to Compensation' [2009] CJQ 41.

Hodges C, *Litigating Antitrust Claims in Europe: Proposals and Implications* (National Legal Centre for the Public Interest 2006).

Hodges C, *The Reform of Class and Representative Actions in European Legal Systems* (Hart 2008).

Hodges C, Vogenauer S, and Tulibacka M, 'Part I' in Hodges C, Vogenauer S, and Tulibacka M (eds), *The Costs and Funding of Civil Litigation: A Comparative Perspective* (Hart 2010) 26.

Holmes M and Jones A, 'Investigating the Business Insurance Industry' (2005) 4(16) CLI 12.

Hondius E, 'The Notion of Consumer: European Union versus Member States' (2006) 28 Syd L Rev 89.

Hoskins M, 'Garden Cottage Revisited: The Availability of Damages in the National Courts for Breach of the EEC Competition Rules' (1992) 13 ECLR 257.

Hovenkamp H, 'Book Review—The Rationalisation of Antitrust' (2003) 116 Harv L Rev 917.

Howard A, 'Disclosure of Infringement Decisions in Competition Damages Proceedings: How the UK Courts Are Leading the Way Ahead of the Damages Directive' (2015) 6 JECLAP 256.

Howard A, 'Object and Effect: What's in an Object?' (2009) 8 Comp Law 37.

Howell N and Wilson T, 'The Limits of Competition: Reasserting the Role for Consumer Protection and Fair Trading Regulation in Competitive Markets' in Parry D and others (eds), *Yearbook of Consumer Law 2009* (Ashgate 2009) 147.

Howells G and James R, 'Litigation in the Consumer Interest' (2003) 9 ILSA J Int'l & Comp L 1.

Howells G and Weatherill S, *Consumer Protection Law* (2nd edn, Ashgate 2005).

Howells G, 'Country Report UK' (Report prepared for Civic Consulting to be submitted to DG SANCO) <http://ec.europa.eu/consumers/redress_cons/uk-country-report-final.pdf> accessed 17 October 2014.

Howells G, 'Cy-pres for Consumers: Ensuring Class Action Reforms Deal With "Scattered Damages"' in Steele J and van Boom W, *Mass Justice—Challenges of Representation and Distribution* (Edward Elgar 2011) 58.

Howells G, 'The Potential and Limits of Consumer Empowerment by Information' (2005) 32 JL & Soc 349.

Hutchings M and Whelan P, 'Consumer Interest in Competition Law Cases' (2006) 16 CPR 182.

Idema T and Kelemen D, 'New Modes of Governance, the Open Method of Co-ordination and Other Fashionable Red Herring' (2006) 7 *Perspectives on European Politics and Society* 108.

Idot L, 'Private Enforcement of Competition Law—Recommendations Flowing from the French Experience' in Basedow J (ed), *Private Enforcement of EC Competition Law* (Kluwer Law International 2007) 85.

Incardona R and Poncibo C, 'The Corte di Cassazione takes "Courage". A Recent Ruling Opens Limited Rights for Consumers in Competition Cases' (2005) 26 ECLR 445.

Information Service High Authority of the European Community for Coal and Steel Luxembourg, 'The Brussels Report on the General Common Market' (June 1956) ('Spaak Report').

Ioannidou M, 'Enhancing Consumers' Role in EU Private Competition Law Enforcement: A Normative and Practical Approach' (2012) 8 Comp L Rev <http://www.clasf.org/CompLRev/Issues/CompLRevVol8Issue1.pdf> accessed 10 June 2014.

Ioannidou M, 'Reforming UK Competition Law Regime: The Consumer Perspective' (2012) 11 Comp Law 28.

Issacharoff S and Miller G, 'Will Aggregate Litigation Come to Europe?' (2009) 62 Vand L Rev 179.

Issacharoff S, 'Governance and Legitimacy in the Law of Class Actions' [1999] *Supreme Court Review* 1.

Issacharoff S, 'Group Litigation of Consumer Claims: Lessons from the US Experience' (1999) 34 Tex Intl L J 135.

Issacharoff S, 'Preclusion, Due Process and the Right to Opt-out' (2002) 77 Notre Dame L Rev 1057.

Jacobs F and Deisenhofer T, 'Procedural Aspects of the Effective Private Enforcement of EC Competition Rules: A Community Perspective' in Ehlermann CD and Atanasiu I (eds), *European Competition Law Annual 2001: Effective Private Enforcement of EC Antitrust Law* (Hart 2003).

Jacobs FG and Deisenhofer T, 'Procedural Aspects of the Effective Private Enforcement of EC Competition Rules: A Community Perspective' in Ehlermann CD and Atanasiu I (eds), *European Competition Law Annual 2001: Effective Private Enforcement of EC Antitrust Law* (Hart 2003).

Jalabert-Doury N, 'France' in Foer A and Cuneo J (eds), *The International Handbook of Private Enforcement of Competition Law* (Edward Elgar 2010) 322.

Joliet R, *Monopolisation and Abuse of Dominant Position: a Comparative Study of the American and European Approaches to the Control of Economic Power* (Nijhoff 1970).

Jolls C, Sunstein C, and Thaler R, 'A Behavioral Approach to Law and Economics' (1998) 50 Stan L Rev 1471.

Jolowicz J, *On Civil Procedure* (CUP 2000).

Jones A, 'Left Behind by Modernisation? Restrictions by Object under Article 101(1)' (2010) 6 Euro CJ 649.

Jones C, 'Exporting Antitrust Courtrooms to the World: Private Enforcement in a Global Market' (2004) 16 Loy Con L Rev 409.

Jones C, 'Into the Parallel Universe: Procedural Fairness in Private Litigation after the Damages Directive' (2014, 9th ASCOLA Conference Warsaw) <http://www.ascola-conference-2014.wz.uw.edu.pl/conference_papers/Jonesascola2014.pdf> accessed 22 July 2014.

Jones C, 'Private Antitrust Enforcement in Europe: A Policy Analysis and Reality Check' (2004) 27 W Comp 13.

Jones C, *Private Enforcement of Antitrust Law in the EU, UK and USA* (OUP 1999).

Kagan R, *Adversarial Legalism: The American Way of Law* (Harvard University Press 2001).

Kagan R, 'American and European Ways of Law: Six Entrenched Differences' in Gessner V and Nelken D (eds), *European Ways of Law: Towards a European Sociology of Law* (Hart 2007) 41.

Kakouris C, 'Do the Member States Possess Judicial Procedural "Autonomy"?' (1997) 34 CMLRev 1389.

Kalbfleisch P, 'The Dutch Experience with Plea Bargaining/Direct Settlements' in Ehlermann CD and Marquis M (eds), *European Competition Law Annual 2007* (Hart 2008) 481.

Karipidou M, 'Country Report Greece' (Report prepared for Civic Consulting to be submitted to DG SANCO) <http://ec.europa.eu/consumers/redress_cons/gr-country-report-final.pdf> accessed 17 October 2014.

Karon DR, '"Your Honor, Tear Down that Illinois Brick Wall!" The National Movement towards Indirect Purchaser Antitrust Standing and Consumer Justice' (2004) 30 Wm Mitchell L Rev 1351.

Kauper T and Snyder E, 'An Inquiry into the Efficiency of Private Antitrust Enforcement: Follow-on and Independently Initiated Actions Compared' (1986) Geo LJ 1163.

Kelemen D, 'Americanisation of European Law? Adversarial Legalism à la européenne' (2008) 7 *European Political Science* 32.

Kelemen D, 'Suing for Europe: Adversarial Legalism and European Governance' (2006) 39 *Comparative Political Studies* 101.

Kennedy JE, 'Class Actions: The Right to Opt Out' (1984) 25 Ariz L Rev 3.

Kerameus K, 'Political Integration and Procedural Convergence in the European Union' (1997) 45 Am J Comp L 919.

Kerse C and Khan N, *EC Antitrust Procedure* (5th edn, Sweet and Maxwell 2005).

Kersting C, 'Removing the Tension between Public and Private Enforcement: Disclosure and Privileges for Successful Leniency Applicants' (2014) 5 JECLAP 2.

Keske S, *Group Litigation in European Competition Law: A Law and Economics Perspective* (Intersentia 2010).

King S and Smith R, 'Does Competition Law Adequately Protect Consumers?' (2007) 7 ECLR 412.

King S, 'The Object Box: Law, Policy or Myth?' (2011) 7 Euro CJ 269.

Kingston S, *Greening EU Competition Law and Policy* (CUP 2012).

Kirkwood J and Lande R, 'The Fundamental Goal of Antitrust: Protecting Consumers not Increasing Efficiency' (2008) 84 Notre Dame L Rev 191.

Kjolbye L, 'The New Commission Guidelines on the Application of Article 81(3): An Economic Approach to Article 81' (2004) 25 ECLR 566.

Klees A, 'Breaking the Habits: The German Competition Law after the 7th Amendment to the Act Against Restraints of Competition (GWB)' (2006) 7 *German LJ* 399.

Koch H, 'Non-Class Group Litigation under EU and German Law' (2001) 11 Duke J Comp & Int'l L 355.

Kocher E, 'Collective Rights and Collective Goods: Enforcement as Collective Interest' in Steele J and van Boom WH, *Mass Justice: Challenges of Representation and Distribution* (Edward Elgar 2011).

Komninos A, 'Civil Antitrust Remedies between Community and National Law' in Barnard C and Odudu O (eds), *The Outer Limits of European Union Law* (Hart 2009) 363.

Komninos A, 'Continuity and Change in EU Competition Policy' (February 2010) CPI <https://www.competitionpolicyinternational.com/continuity-and-change-in-eu-competition-policy/> accessed 15 June 2014.

Komninos A, *EC Private Antitrust Enforcement—Decentralised Application of EC Competition Law by National Courts* (Hart 2008).

Komninos A, 'New Prospects for Private Enforcement of EC Competition Law: Courage v Crehan and the Community Right to Damages' (2002) 39 CMLRev 447.

Komninos A, 'Private Enforcement in the EU with Emphasis on Damages Actions' in Lianos I and Gerardin D (eds), *Handbook on EU Competition Law: Enforcement and Procedure* (Edward Elgar 2013) 228.

Komninos A, 'Relationship between Public and Private Enforcement: Quod Dei Deo, Quod Caesaris Caesari' in Lowe P and Marquis M (eds), *European Competition Law Annual 2011* (Hart 2014).

Komninos A, 'The Road to the Commission's White Paper for Damages Actions: Where We Came From' (2008) 4 CPI <https://www.competitionpolicyinternational.com/the-road-to-the-commissions-white-paper-for-damages-actions-where-we-came-from/> accessed 28 July 2014.

Konstadinides T, *Division of Powers in European Union Law* (Kluwer Law International 2009).

Konstadinides T, 'Drawing the line between Circumvention and Gap-Filling: An Exploration of the Conceptual Limits of the Treaty's Flexibility Clause' (2012) 31 YEL 227.

Korah V, 'Judgment of the Court of First Instance in GlaxoSmithKline' (2007) 6 Comp Law 101.

Kortmann J and Swaak C, 'The EC White Paper on Antitrust Damage Actions: Why the Member States are (Right to Be) Less than Enthusiastic' (2009) 30 ECLR 340.

Kortmann J, 'The Tort Law Industry' (2009) 17 ERPL 789.

Kortmann JS and Swaak CR, 'The EC White Paper on Damages Actions: Why the Member States are (Right to Be) Less than Enthusiastic' (2009) 30 ECLR 340.

Kovacic W, 'Competition Policy in the European Union and the United States: Convergence or Divergence?' in X Vives (ed), *Competition Policy in the EU: Fifty Years on from the Treaty of Rome* (OUP 2009) 314.

Kovacic W, 'Private Participation in the Enforcement of Public Competition Laws' in Andenas M, Hutchings M, and Whelan P (eds), *Current Competition Law 2002* (BIICL 2003).

Kovacic W, 'The Intellectual DNA of Modern US Competition Law for Dominant Firm Conduct: The Chicago/Harvard Double Helix' [2007] Colum BLR 1.

Lande R and Davis JP, 'Benefits From Private Antitrust Enforcement: An Analysis of Forty Cases' (2008) *University of San Francisco Law Review* 879.

Lande R and Davis JP, 'Toward an Empirical and Theoretical Assessment of Private Antitrust Enforcement' (2013) University of San Francisco Law Research Paper No 2012-17 <http://papers.ssrn.com/sol3/papers.cfm?abstract_id=2132981> accessed 30 June 2014.

Lande R, 'New Options for State Indirect Purchaser Legislation: Protecting the Real Victims of Antitrust Violations' (2010) 61 Alabama L Rev 447.

Lande R, 'Proving the Obvious: The Antitrust Laws Were Passed to Protect Consumers (Not Just to Increase Efficiency)' (1999) 50 Hastings LJ 959.

Lande R, 'Wealth Transfers as the Original and Primary Concern of Antitrust: The Efficiency Interpretation Challenged' (1982) 34 Hastings LJ 65.

Landes W and Posner R, *The Economic Structure of Tort Law* (Harvard University Press 1987).

Landes W and Posner R, 'The Private Enforcement of Law' (1975) 4 J Legal Stud 1.

Landes W, 'Optimal Sanctions for Antitrust Violations' (1983) 50 U Chi L Rev 652.

Landes WM and Posner RA, 'Should Indirect Purchasers Have Standing to Sue under the Antitrust Laws? An Economic Analysis of the Rule of *Illinois Brick*' (1979) 46 U Chi L Rev 602.

Landes WM and Posner RA, 'The Economics of Passing on: A Reply to Harris and Sullivan' (1980) 128 U Pa L Rev 1274.

Landes WM and Posner RA, 'The Private Enforcement of Law' (1975) 4 J Legal Stud 1.

Landes WM, 'An Economic Analysis of the Courts' (1971) 14 J L & Econ 61.

Lane R, 'EC Competition Law Post Lisbon: A Matter of Protocol' in Bulterman M (ed), *Views of European Law from the Mountain: Liber Amicorum for Piet Jan Slot* (Kluwer Law International 2009) 167.

Lang C, 'Class Actions and US Antitrust Laws: Prerequisites and Interdependencies of the Implementation of a Procedural Device for the Aggregation of Low Value Claims' (2001) 24 W Comp 285.

Lawrence J and Sansom M, 'The Increasing Use of Administrative Settlement Procedures in UK and EC Competition Investigations' (2007) 6 Comp Law 163.

Leczykiewicz D, 'Private Party Liability in EU Law: In Search of the General Regime' in Barnard C and Odudu O (eds), *The Cambridge Yearbook of European Legal Studies*, Volume 12, 2009–2010 (Hart 2010) 257.
Legrand P, 'European Legal Systems are not Converging' (1996) 45 ICLQ 52.
Legrand P, *Fragments on Law as Culture* (W.E.J. Tjeenk Willink 1999).
Legrand P, 'The Impossibility of Legal Transplants' (1997) 4 Maastricht J Eur & Comp L 111.
Leino P, 'Just a Little Sunshine in the Rain: The 2010 Case Law of the European Court of Justice on Access to Documents' (2011) 48 CMLRev 1215.
Lenaerts K, 'Constitutionalism and the Many Faces of Federalism' (1990) 38 AJCL 205.
Leskinen C, 'Collective Actions: Rethinking Funding and National Cost Rules' (2011) 8 Comp L Rev 87.
Leskinen C, 'Collective Antitrust Damages Actions in the EU: The Opt-in v the Opt-out Model' (2010) Working Paper IE Law School 10-03 <http://papers.ssrn.com/sol3/papers.cfm?abstract_id=1612731> accessed 17 October 2014.
Leslie CR, 'A Market Based Approach to Coupon Settlements in Antitrust and Consumer Class Action Litigation' (2002) 49 UCLA L Rev 991.
Leuchts B and Marquis M, 'American Influences on EEC Competition Law—Two Paths, How Much Dependence' in Patel K and Schweitze H (eds), *The Historical Foundations of EU Competition Law* (OUP 2013) 125.
Lever J, 'Fusion of the OFT and the CC: Ask for the Evidence' (2011) 10 Comp Law 126.
Lever J, 'Whether, and if so How, the EC Commission's 2006 Guidelines on Setting Fines for Infringements of Articles 81 and 82 of the EC Treaty are Fairly Subject to Serious Criticism' (Opinion) <http://www.bdi.eu/download_content/Publikation_BDI_Gutachten__Opinion__zu_EU_Bussgeldleitlinien.pdf> accessed 6 November 2014.
Lianos I, 'Competition Law Remedies in Europe: Which Limits for Remedial Discretion?' (January 2013) CLES Research Paper Series 2/2013 <http://papers.ssrn.com/sol3/papers.cfm?abstract_id=2235817> accessed 6 November 2014.
Lianos I, 'Competition Law Remedies in Europe—Which Limits for Remedial Discretion?' (2013) CLES Research Paper Series <https://www.ucl.ac.uk/cles/research-paper-series/index/edit/research-papers/cles-2-2013> accessed 17 August 2014.
Lianos I, 'Some Reflections on the Question of the Goals of EU Competition Law' in Lianos I and Geradin D (eds), *Handbook on European Competition Law* (Edward Elgar 2013) 47.
Lindblom H, 'Individual Litigation and Mass Justice: A Swedish Perspective and Proposal on Group Actions in Civil Procedure' (1997) 45 Am J Comp L 805.
Lovdahl Gormsen L, 'Can Consumer Welfare Convincingly Be Said to Be an Objective of Article 102 When the Methodology Relies on an Inference of Effects?' in Heide-Jorgensen C and others (eds), *Aims and Values in Competition Law* (DJØF 2013).
Lovdahl Gormsen L, 'The Conflict Between Economic Freedom and Consumer Welfare in the Modernisation of Article 82 EC' (2007) 3 Euro CJ 329.
Lovdahl Gormsen L, 'Why the European Commission's Enforcement Priorities on Article 82 EC Should Be Withdrawn' (2010) 31 ECLR 45.
Lowe P, 'Preserving and Promoting Competition: A European Response' [2006] 2 CPN 1.
Lowe P, 'The Design of Competition Policy Institutions for the 21st Century—the Experience of the European Commission and DG COMP' [2008] 3 CPN 1.
Macey JR and Miller G, 'The Plaintiff's Attorney's Role in Class Action and Derivatives Litigation: Economic Analysis and Recommendations for Reform' (1991) 58 U Chi L Rev 1.

Macrory R, 'Regulating Justice: Making Sanctions Effective' (November 2006) (Final Report) <http://webarchive.nationalarchives.gov.uk/+/http://www.bis.gov.uk/files/file44593.pdf> accessed 13 July 2014.

Maduro MP, 'Europe's Social Self: "The Sickness Unto Death"' in Shaw J (ed), *Social Law and Policy in an Evolving European Union* (Hart 2000) 325.

Magnier V, 'Class Actions, Group Litigation and Other Forms of Collective Litigation' <http://globalclassactions.stanford.edu/sites/default/files/documents/France_National_Report.pdf> accessed 17 October 2014.

Magnier V, 'The French Civil Litigation System, the Increasing Role of Judges, and Influences from Europe' (2009) in The ANNALS of the American Academy of Political and Social Science, *The Globalisation of Class Actions*, Contents (March 2009) 114.

Maher I, 'Competition Law Modernization: An Evolutionary Tale?' in Craig P and de Búrca G, *The Evolution of EU Law* (OUP 2011) 717.

Malina M, 'Fluid Class Recovery as a Consumer Remedy in Antitrust Cases' (1972) 47 NYU L Rev 477.

Marco F, 'Damages' Claims in the Spanish Sugar Cartel' (Working Paper IE Law School AJ8-213-I) (2014) <http://papers.ssrn.com/sol3/papers.cfm?abstract_id=2514239> accessed 11 December 2014.

Marcos F and Graells AS, 'Towards a European Tort Law? Damages Actions for Breach of the EC Antitrust Rules: Harmonising Tort Law through the Back Door?' (2006) <http://papers.ssrn.com/sol3/papers.cfm?abstract_id=1028963> accessed 21 November 2014.

Marsden P and Whelan P, '"Consumer Detriment" and its Application in EC and UK Competition Law' (2006) 27 ECLR 569.

Marsden P and Whelan P, 'The "Consumer Welfare" Standard as a Form of Substantive Protection for Consumers under European Competition Law' (2009) in Ezrachi A and Bernitz U (eds), *Private Labels, Brands and Competition Policy* (OUP 2009) 353.

Marsden P and Whelan P, 'When Markets are Failing' (2007) 6(2) CLI 6.

Marsden P, 'Checks and Balances: European Competition Law and the Rule of Law' (2009) 22 Loyola Consumer L Rev 51.

Marsden P, 'Some Outstanding Issues from the European Commission's Guidance on Article 102 TFEU' in Etro F and Kokkoris I (eds), *Competition Law and the Enforcement of Article 102* (OUP 2010).

McAfee P, Mialon H, and Mialon S, 'Private Antitrust Litigation: Procompetitive or Anticompetitive' (2005) Emory Law and Economics Research Paper No 05/18 <http://papers.ssrn.com/sol3/papers.cfm?abstract_id=784805> accessed 5 August 2014.

McAuley I, 'Behavioural Economics and Public Policy: Some Insights' (Working Paper, February 2007) <http://www.home.netspeed.com.au/mcau/academic/bepubpol.pdf> accessed 14 June 2014.

Menon A and Weatherill S, 'Legitimacy, Accountability, and Delegation in the European Union' in Arnull A and Wincott D (eds), *Accountability and Legitimacy in the European Union* (OUP 2002) 113.

Mertens M and others, 'Detailed Minutes of the Public Hearing "Towards a Coherent European Approach to Collective Redress"' (28/10/2011) <http://ec.europa.eu/competition/consultations/2011_collective_redress/study_heidelberg_hearing_en.pdf> accessed 14 November 2014.

Micklitz HW, 'Privatisation of Access to Justice and Soft Law—Lessons from the European Community?' in Wilhelmsson T and Hurri S (eds), *From Dissonance to Sense: Welfare State Expectations, Privatisation and Private Law* (Ashgate 1999) 505.

Miege C, 'Modernisation and Enforcement Pluralism- (2005): The Role of Private Enforcement of Competition Law in the EU and the German Attempts in the 7th Amendment of the GWB' (2005) (Amsterdam Centre for Law and Economics, Workshop on Remedies and Sanctions in Competition Policy).

Miller GP and Singer LS, 'Nonpecuniary Class Action Settlements' (1997) 60 LCP 97.

Milutinović V, 'Private Enforcement' in Amato G and Ehlermann CD (eds), *EC Competition Law—A Critical Assessment* (Hart 2007) 725.

Milutinović V, *The 'Right to Damages' under EU Competition Law: from Courage v. Crehan to the White Paper and Beyond* (Kluwer Law International 2010).

Ministry of Justice, 'The Government's Response to the Civil Justice Council's Report: "Improving Access to Justice through Collective Actions"' (July 2009).

Moellers T and Heinemann A (eds), *The Enforcement of Competition Law in Europe* (CUP 2007).

Monti G, 'Article 81 EC and Public Policy' (2002) 39 CMLRev 1057.

Monti G, 'The Revision of the Consumer Acquis From a Competition Law Perspective' [2007] ERCL 295.

Monti M, 'A New Strategy for the Single Market' (Report to the President of the European Commission, 9 May 2010).

Monti M, 'Effective Private Enforcement of EC Antitrust Law' in Ehlermann CD and Atanasiu I (eds), *European Competition Law Annual 2001: Effective Private Enforcement of EC Antitrust Law* (Hart 2003) 3.

Möschel W, 'The Proper Scope of Government Viewed from an Ordoliberal Perspective: The Example of Competition Policy' (2001) 157 JITE 3.

Motta M and Dde Streel A, 'Excessive Prices and Margin Squeeze under EU Law' in Ehlermann CD and Atanasiu I (eds), *European Competition Law Annual 2003: What is an Abuse of a Dominant Position?* (Hart 2006).

Motta M, *Competition Policy: Theory and Practice* (CUP 2004).

Mulheron R, 'A Missed Gem of an Opportunity for the Representative Rule' (2012) 23 EBLRev 49.

Mulheron R, 'Competition Law Cases under the Opt-out Regimes of Australia, Canada and Portugal' (Research Paper for Submission to BERR, 10 October 2008) 77.

Mulheron R, 'Cy-pres Damages Distribution in England: A New Era for Consumer Redress' (2009) 20 EBLR 307.

Mulheron R, '*Emerald Supplies Ltd v British Airways Plc*: A Century Later the Ghost of Markt Lives On' (2009) 8 Comp Law 159.

Mulheron R, 'From Representative Rule to Class Action: Steps Rather than Leaps' (2005) 24 CJQ 424.

Mulheron R, 'Reform of Collective Redress in England and Wales: A Perspective of Need' (2008) (Research Paper for Submission to the CJC).

Mulheron R, 'The Case for an Opt-out Class Action for European Member States: A Legal and Empirical Analysis' (2009) 15 Colum J Eur L 409.

Mulheron R, *The Class Action in Common Law Legal Systems: A Comparative Perspective* (Hart Publishing, Oxford 2004).

Mulheron R, 'The Impetus for Class Action Reform in England Arising From the Competition Law Sector' in Wrbka S, Van Uytsel S, and Siems M (eds), *Collective Actions: Enhancing Access to Justice and Reconciling Multilayer Interests?* (CUP 2012) 385.

Mulheron R, 'Third Party Funding: A Changing Landscape' (2008) 27 CJQ 312.

Mulheron R, *The Modern Cy-près Doctrine* (UCL 2006).
Murray A, 'Collective Cartel Damages Claims—Practical Financial Considerations for Businesses Bringing an Action in the English High Court' (2008) 7 (12) CLI 14.
Murray A, 'Consumers and EU Competition Policy' (Centre for European Reform, September 2005) <http://www.cer.org.uk/sites/default/files/publications/attachments/pdf/2011/policybrief_consumers-839.pdf> accessed 3 November 2014.
Nagareda RA, 'The Preexistence Principle and the Role of the Class Action' (2003) 103 Colum L Rev 149.
Nagy CI, 'The Distinction between Anti-competitive Object and Effect after Allianz: The End of Coherence in Competition Analysis?' (2013) 36 W Comp 541.
National Commission Staff Papers, 'Scope of Discovery' (1979) 48 Antitrust LJ 1063.
Nazzini R and Nikpay A, 'Private Actions in EC Competition Law' (2008) 4 CPI 107.
Nazzini R, 'Article 81 EC between Time Present and Time Past: A Normative Critique of "Restriction of Competition" in EU Law' (2006) 43 CMLRev 497.
Nazzini R, 'Potency and Act of the Principle of Effectiveness: The Development of Competition Law Remedies and Procedures in Community Law' in Barnard C and Odudu O (eds), *The Outer Limits of the European Union* (Hart 2009) 401.
Nazzini R, *The Foundations of European Union Competition Law* (OUP 2011).
Nazzini R, 'The Wood Begun to Move: An Essay on Consumer Welfare, Evidence and Burden of Proof in Article 82 EC cases' (2006) 31 ELRev 518.
Nazzini R, 'Welfare Objective and Enforcement Standard in Competition Law' (2009) in Ezrachi A and Bernitz U (eds) *Private Labels, Brands and Competition Policy* (OUP 2009) 379
Nebbia P, 'Damages Actions for the Infringement of EC Competition Law: Compensation or Deterrence?' (2008) 33 ELRev 23.
Nebbia P, 'So What Happened to Mr Manfredi? The Italian Decision Following the Ruling of the European Court of Justice' (2007) 28 ECLR 591.
Nebbia P, 'Standard Form Contracts Between Unfair Contract Control and Competition Law' (2006) 31 ELRev 102.
Niels G, Jenkins H, and Casanova J, 'The UK Market Investigations Regime: Taking Stock after 5 Years' (2008) 7 Comp Law 346.
Nihoul P, 'Is Competition Law Part of Consumer Law?' in Drexl J and others (eds), *More Common Ground for International Competition Law?* (Edward Elgar 2011) 46.
Nordh R, 'Group Actions in Sweden: Reflections on the Purpose of Civil Litigation, the Need for Reform and a Forthcoming Proposal' (2001) 11 Duke J Comp & Intl L 381.
O'Connor KJ, 'Is the Illinois Brick Wall Crumbling?' (2001) 15 Antitrust LJ 34.
O'Donoghue R and Padilla J, *The Law and Economics of Article 82 EC* (Hart 2006).
O'Donoghue R, 'Europe's Long March Towards Antitrust Damages Actions' (April 2011) *CPI Antitrust Chronicle* 2.
Odudu O, 'Developing Private Enforcement in the EU: Lessons for the Roberts Court' (2008) 53 Antitrust Bulletin 873.
Odudu O, 'Effective Remedies and Effective Incentives in Community Competition Law' (2006) 5 Comp Law 134.
Odudu O, *The Boundaries of EC Competition Law* (OUP 2006).
Odudu O, 'The Wider Concerns of Competition Law' (2010) OJLS 1.
Olson M, *The Logic of Collective Action: Public Goods and the Theory of Groups* (Harvard University Press 1971).

Ombudsman (EC), 'The European Code of Good Administrative Behaviour' (2005) <http://www.ombudsman.europa.eu/en/resources/code.faces;jsessionid=5DCFB7F16FD3276EF3BFC692DD747792> accessed 3 November 2014.

Orbach B, 'The Antitrust Consumer Welfare Paradox' (2010) JCLE 133.

Osti C, 'Interpreting Convergence: Where Antitrust Meets Consumer Law' (2009) 5 Euro CJ 377.

Owen D (ed), *Philosophical Foundations of Tort Law* (Clarendon Press 1995).

Oxera, 'Quantifying Antitrust Damages: Towards Non-binding Guidance for Courts' (December 2009), Study prepared for the European Commission <http://ec.europa.eu/competition/antitrust/actionsdamages/quantification_study.pdf> accessed 3 July 2014.

Oxera, 'Quantifying Antitrust Damages: Towards Non-binding Guidance for Courts' (December 2009), Study prepared for the European Commission <http://ec.europa.eu/competition/antitrust/actionsdamages/quantification_study.pdf> accessed 26 July 2014.

Page WH, 'Class Certification in the Microsoft Indirect Purchaser Litigation' (2005) 1 J Comp L & Econ 303.

Page WH, 'Class Interpleader: The Antitrust Modernization Commission's Recommendation to Overrule *Illinois Brick*' (2008) 53 *Antitrust Bulletin* 725.

Page WH, 'The Limits of State Indirect Purchaser Suits: Class Certification in the Shadow of *Illinois Brick*' (1999) 67 Antitrust LJ 1.

Parret L, 'Shouldn't we Know what we are Protecting? Yes we Should! A Plea for a Solid and Comprehensive Debate about the Objectives of EU Competition Law and Policy' (2010) 6 Euro CJ 339.

Paulis E, 'Article 82 EC and Exploitative Conduct' in Ehlermann CD and Marquis M (eds), *European Competition Law Annual 2007: A Reformed Approach to Article 82 EC* (Hart 2008).

Paulis E, 'Foreword' in Ashton D and Henry D, *Competition Damages Actions in the EU—Law and Practice* (Edward Elgar 2013).

Pena Castellot MA, 'Commission Settles Allegations of Abuse and Clears Patent Pools in the CD Market' [2003] 3 CPN 56.

Perrson A, 'Collective Enforcement—European Prospects in light of the Swedish Experience' in Wrbka S, Van Uytsel S, and Siems M, *Collective Actions: Enhancing Access to Justice and Reconciling Multilayer Interests?* (CUP 2012) 341.

Perry S, 'On the Relationship Between Corrective and Distributive Justice' in Horder J (ed), *Oxford Essays in Jurisprudence* (OUP 2000) 237.

Pescatore P, 'The Doctrine of "Direct Effect": An Infant Disease of Community Law' (1983) 8 ELRev 155.

Petit N, 'Intel, Leveraging Rebates and the Goals of Article 102 TFEU' (2015) <http://papers.ssrn.com/sol3/papers.cfm?abstract_id=2567628>.

Peyer S, 'Access to Competition Authorities' Files in Private Antitrust Litigation' (2015) 3 *JAE* 58.

Peyer S, 'Myths and Untold Stories—Private Antitrust Enforcement in Germany' (2010) UEA CCP Working Paper 10–12 <http://papers.ssrn.com/sol3/papers.cfm?abstract_id=1672695> accessed 3 July 2014.

Pheasant J and Bicarregui A, 'Striking the Right Balance towards a "Competition Culture" not a "Litigation Culture"? Comment on the European Commission's White Paper on Damages Actions for Breach of EC Antitrust Rules' (2008) 1 GCLR 98.

Pickering J, 'UK Market Investigations: An Economic Perspective' (2006) 5 Comp Law 206.

Popofsky M, 'Defining Exclusionary Conduct' (2006) 73 Antitrust LJ 435.
Posner R, *Antitrust Law* (2nd edn, University of Chicago Press 2001).
Posner R, 'The Chicago School of Antitrust Analysis' (1979) 127 U Pa L Rev 925.
Prechal S, *Directive in EC Law* (2nd edn, OUP 2005).
Prechal S, 'Does Direct Effect Still Matter?' (2000) 37 CMLRev 1047.
Rajski S, '*In Re: Hydrogen Peroxide*: Reinforcing Rigorous Analysis for Class Action Certification' (2011) 34 Seattle UL Rev 577.
Ramirez Perez S and Van de Scheur S, 'The Evolution of the Law on Articles 85 and 86 EEC [Articles 101 and 102 TFEU]—Ordoliberalism and its Keynesian Challenge' in Patel K and Schweitze H (eds), *The Historical Foundations of EU Competition Law* (OUP 2013) 19.
Ramsay I, 'Consumer Redress and Access to Justice' in Rickett C and Telfer T (eds), *International Perspectives on Consumers' Access to Justice* (CUP 2003) 17.
Reding V, Almunia J, and Dalli J, 'Towards a Coherent European Approach to Collective Redress: Next Steps' (Joint Information Note) SEC(2010) 1192.
Redish M, Julian P, and Zyontz S, 'Cy Pres Relief and the Pathologies of the Modern Class Action: A Normative and Empirical Analysis' (2010) 62 Fla L Rev 617.
Reich N, 'Competition Law and the Consumer' in Gormley L (ed), *Current and Future Perspectives in EC on EC Competition Law: A Tribute to Professor M. R. Mok* (Kluwer Law 1997) 126.
Reich N, 'Diverse Approaches to Consumer Protection Philosophy' (1992) 14 JCP 257.
Reich N, 'Protection of Consumers' Economic Interests by the EC' (1992) 14 Syd L Rev 23.
Reich N, 'The "Courage" Doctrine: Encouraging or Discouraging Violations for Antitrust Injuries?' (2005) 42 CMLRev 35.
Reifner U and Volkmer M, 'Neue Formen der Verbraucherrechtsberatung' cited in N Reich, 'Diverse Approaches to Consumer Protection Philosophy' (1992) 14 JCP 257.
Renda A, Peysner J, Riley A, Rodger B, and others, 'Making Antitrust Damages Actions More Effective in the EU: Welfare Impact and Potential Scenarios' (Report for the European Commission) (December 2007) <http://ec.europa.eu/competition/antitrust/actionsdamages/files_white_paper/impact_study.pdf> accessed 3 July 2014.
Repa L and others, 'Commission Prohibits MasterCard's Multilateral Interchange Fees for Cross-border Card Payments in the EEA' [2008] CPN 1.
Rey P and Venit J, 'Parallel Trade and Pharmaceuticals: A Policy in Search of Itself' (2004) 29 ELRev 153.
Richardson B and Razzaque J, 'Public Participation in Environmental Decision Making' in Richardson B and Wood S (eds), *Environmental Law for Sustainability: A Reader* (Hart 2006).
Richman BD and Murray CR, 'Rebuilding *Illinois Brick*: A Functionalist Approach to the Indirect Purchaser Rule' (2007) Duke Law School Legal Studies Paper No 155 <http://ssrn.com/abstract=978968> accessed 4 July 2014.
Riley A and Peysner J, 'Damages in EC Antitrust Actions: Who Pays the Piper?' (2006) ELRev 748.
Riley A, 'The EU Reform Treaty and the Competition Protocol: Undermining EC Competition Law' (2007) 28 ECLR 703.
Rizzuto F, 'EC Harmonisation of Antitrust National Procedural Rules' [2009] GCLR 29.
Robertson A, 'UK Competition Litigation: From Cinderella to Goldilocks?' (2010) 9 Comp Law 275.

Robertson B, 'What is a Restriction of Competition? The Implications of the CFI's Judgment in *O2 Germany* and the Rule of Reason' (2007) 28 ECLR 252.

Rodger B, 'Collective Redress Mechanisms and Consumer Case Law' in Rodger B (ed), *Competition Law Comparative Private Enforcement and Collective Redress Across Europe* (Kluwer 2014) 157.

Rodger B, 'Institutions and Mechanisms to Facilitate Private Enforcement' in Rodger B (ed), *Competition Law, Comparative Private Enforcement and Collective Redress Across Europe* (Kluwer Law International 2014) 23.

Rodger B, 'The Empirical Data Part 1: Methodology, Case Law, Courts and Processes' in Rodger B (ed), *Competition Law, Comparative Private Enforcement and Collective Redress Across Europe* (Kluwer Law International 2014) 83.

Rosen A, 'Sector Inquiries under the Microscope' (2005) 4(14) CLI 9.

Rousseva E, *Rethinking Exclusionary Abuses in EU Competition Law* (Hart 2010).

Rubenstein WB, 'On What a "Private Attorney General" is and Why it Matters' (2004) 57 Vand L Rev 2129.

Rubenstein WB, 'Why Enable Litigation? A Positive Externalities Theory of the Small Claims Class Action' (2006) 74 UMKC L Rev 709.

Rubinfeld D and Scotchmer S, 'Contingent Fees for Attorneys: An Economic Analysis' (1993) 24 RAND J Econ 343.

Ruffert M, 'Rights and Remedies in European Community Law: A Comparative View'(1997) 34 CMLRev 307.

Rutgers J, 'European Competence and a European Civil Code, a Common Frame of Reference or an Optional Instrument' in Hartkamp A and von Bar C (eds), *Towards a European Civil Code* (4th edn, Kluwer Law International 2011) 311.

Safjan M, Gorywoda L, and Jańczuk A, 'Taking Collective Interest of Consumers Seriously: A View from Poland' (2008) EUI Working Papers 2008/26 <http://papers.ssrn.com/sol3/papers.cfm?abstract_id=1330909> accessed 12 July 2014.

Salop SC and White LJ, 'Economic Analysis of Private Antitrust Litigation' (1986) 74 Geo LJ 1001.

Sanchez Graells A, 'Discovery, Confidentiality and Disclosure of Evidence' (2006) IE Working Papers Derecho WPED06-05 <http://papers.ssrn.com/sol3/papers.cfm?abstract_id=952504> accessed 9 July 2014.

Sarra A and Marra A, 'Are Monetary Incentives Enough to Boost Actions for Damages in the European Union? On the Relevance of Incompleteness of Laws and Evidentiary Requirements' (2008) 31 W Comp 369.

Sauter W, *Competition Law and Industrial Policy in the EU* (Clarendon Press 1997).

Schaefer HB, 'The Bundling of Similar Interests in Litigation. The Incentives for Class Actions and Legal Actions Taken by Associations' (2000) 9 Eur J L & Econ 183.

Scharpf F, 'Economic Integration, Democracy and the Welfare State' (1997) JEPP 18.

Scheurleer DL, Speyart H, Wijers F, and Fanoy J, 'Netherlands' in Foer A and Cuneo J (eds), *The International Handbook of Private Enforcement of Competition Law* (Edward Elgar 2010) 375.

Schinkel MP, Tuinstra J, and Rueggeberg J, 'Illinois Walls: How Barring Indirect Purchaser Suits Facilitates Collusion' (2008) 39 RAND J Econ 683.

Scholz U and Purps S, 'The Application of EU Competition Law in the Energy Sector' (2013) 4 JECLAP 63.

Schütze R, 'Organised Change Towards an "Ever Closer Union": Article 308 EC and the limits of the Community Legislative Competence' (2003) 22 YEL 79.

Schütze R, 'The European Community's Federal Order of Competence—A Retrospective Analysis' in Dougan M and Currie S (eds), *50 Years of the European Treaties* (Hart Publishing 2009) 63.

Schwab A, 'Finding the Right Balance—the Deliberations of the European Parliament on the Draft Legislation Regarding Damage Claims' (2014) 5 JECLAP 65.

Schwartz G, 'Mixed Theories of Tort Law: Affirming Both Deterrence and Corrective Justice' (1997) 75 Texas L Rev 1801.

Schwartz W, 'An Overview of the Economics of Antitrust Enforcement' (1980) 68 Geo LJ 1075.

Schwartz W, *Private Enforcement of Antitrust Laws: An Economic Critique* (American Enterprise Institute for Public Policy Research 1981).

Schweitzer H, 'Competition Law and Public Policy: Reconsidering an Uneasy Relationship: The Example of Art. 81' (2007) (EUI WP Law 2007/30) <http://papers.ssrn.com/sol3/papers.cfm?abstract_id=1092883> accessed 15 June 2014.

Schweitzer H, 'The History, Interpretation and Underlying Principles of Section 2 Sherman Act and Article 82 EC' in Ehlermann CD and Marquis M (eds), *European Competition Law Annual 2007: A Reformed Approach to Article 82 EC* (Hart 2008) 119.

Secrétariat Général des Affaires Européennes, République Française, 'Note à la Commission Européenne'.

Secretariat of the European Convention, 'Coordination of National Policies: The Open Method of Coordination' (Brussels, 26 September 2002) WG VI WD015.

Semmelman C, 'The European Union's Economic Constitution under the Lisbon Treaty: Soul-Searching Shifts the Focus of Procedure' (2010) 35 ELRev 516.

Semmelman C, 'The Future of the Non-competition Goals in the Interpretation of Article 81 EC' (2008) 1 Global Antitrust Rev 15.

Senden L and Prechal S, 'Differentiation in and through Community Soft Law' in de Witte B, Hanf D, and Vos E (eds), *The Many Faces of Differentiation in EU Law* (Intersentia 2001) 181.

Senden L, *Soft Law in European Community Law* (Hart 2004).

Shapiro D and Springer J, 'Management of Consumer Class Actions after *Eisen*: Notice and Determination of Damages' (1975) 26 Mercer L Rev 851.

Shapiro D, 'Consumer Class Actions Made Easy' (2008) 7 Comp Law 203.

Shapiro D, 'Processing the Consumer's Claim' (1972) 41 Antitrust LJ 257.

Shepherd SR, 'Damage Distribution in Class Actions: The Cy Pres Remedy' (1972) 39 U Chi L Rev 448.

Shuibhne NN, 'The Resilience of EU Market Citizenship' (2010) 47 CMLRev 1597.

Silver C, '"We are Scared to Death": Class Certification and Blackmail' (2003) 78 NYU L Rev 1357.

Sinclair J, 'Damages in Private Antitrust Actions in Europe' (2002) 14 Loyola Consumer L Rev 547.

Siragusa M, 'The Application of Article 86 to the Pricing Policy of Dominant Companies: Discriminatory and Unfair Prices' (1979) 16 CMLRev 179.

Sittenreich M, 'The Rocky Path for Private Directors General: Procedures, Politics and the Uncertain Future of EU Antitrust Damages Actions' (2010) 78 Fordm L Rev 2701.

Slot JP, 'Harmonisation' (1996) 21 ELRev 378.

Smismans S, 'Civil Society and European Governance: From Concepts to Research Agenda', in Smismans S (ed), *Civil Society and Legitimate European Governance* (Edward Elgar 2006) 3.

Smith H, 'The Francovich Case: State Liability and the Individual's Right in Damages' (1992) 13 ECLR 129.

Snyder E and Kauper T, 'Misuse of the Antitrust Laws: The Competitor Plaintiff' (1991) 90 Mich L Rev 551.

Snyder F, 'The Effectiveness of European Community Law: Institutions, Processes, Tools and Techniques' (1993) 56 MLR 19.

Sousa Antunes H, 'Class Actions, Group Litigation and Other Forms of Collective Litigation: Portuguese Report' (Report prepared for 'The Globalization of Class Actions') <http://globalclassactions.stanford.edu/sites/default/files/documents/Portugal_National_Report.pdf> accessed 17 October 2014.

Spoek M, 'The Dutch Competition Authority Considers Cooperation and Joint Selling of Network Services for Pin-Transactions To Be an Infringement of the Cartel Prohibiton (*Interpay*)' <http://www.concurrences.com/article.php3?id_article=35979&lang=fr> accessed 6 November 2014.

Stadler A, 'Collective Action as an Efficient Means for the Enforcement of European Competition Law' in Basedow J (ed), *Private Enforcement of EC Competition Law* (Kluwer Law International 2007) 195.

Statewatch Observatory: The Regulation on Access to EU Documents: 2008–ongoing <http://www.statewatch.org/foi/observatory-access-reg-2008-2009.htm> accessed 7 May 2015.

Steinvorth T, 'Deutsche Bahn: Commitments End Margin Squeeze Investigation' (2014) 5 JECLAP 628.

Stephan A, 'Survey of Public Attitudes to Price Fixing and Cartel Enforcement in Britain' (2008) 5 Comp L Rev 123.

Stephan A, 'The Direct Settlement of EC Cartel Cases' (2009) 58 ICLQ 627.

Storme M (ed), *Approximation of Judiciary Law in the European Union* (Kluwer Rechtswetenschappen 1994).

Storskrubb E, 'Civil Justice—A Newcomer and an Unstoppable Wave?' in Craig P and de Búrca G, *The Evolution of EU Law* (OUP 2011) 299.

Storskrubb E, *Civil Procedure and EU Law* (OUP 2008).

Stucke M, 'Am I a Price Fixer? A Behavioral Economic Analysis of Cartels' in Beaton-Wells C and Ezrachi A (eds), *Criminalising Cartels: A Critical Interdisciplinary Study of an International Regulatory Movement* (Hart 2011) 263.

Stucke M, 'Behavioral Economics at the Gate: Antitrust in the Twenty-First Century' (2007) 38 Loyola U Chi LJ 513.

Stucke M, 'Reconsidering Antitrust Goals' (2012) 53 *Boston College Law Review* 551.

Stuerner V, 'Duties of Disclosure and Burden of Proof in the Private Enforcement of European Competition Law' in Basedow J (ed), *Private Enforcement of EC Competition Law* (Kluwer Law International 2007) 163.

Stuyck J, 'Class Actions in Europe? To Opt-in or to Opt-out, that is the Question' [2009] EBLR 483.

Stuyck J, 'EC Competition Law after Modernisation: More than Ever in the Interest of Consumers' (2005) 28 JCP 1.

Stuyck J, 'European Consumer Law After the Treaty of Amsterdam: Consumer Policy in or Beyond the Internal Market?' (2000) 37 CMLRev 367.

Stuyck J, 'The Notion of Empowered and Informed Consumer in Consumer Policy and How to Protect the Vulnerable Under Such a Regime' in Howells G and others (eds), *Yearbook of Consumer Law 2007* (Ashgate 2007) 167.

Suffrin B, 'The Evolution of Article 81(3) of the EC Treaty' (2006) 51 AB 915.

Sufrin B and Furse M, 'Market Investigations' (2002) 1 Comp Law 244.
Sunstein CR and Thaler RH, 'Libertarian Paternalism is not an Oxymoron' (2003) 70 U Chi L Rev 1159.
Sutherland P, 'Internal Market after 2002: Meeting the Challenge' (Sutherland Report) SEC(92) 2044.
Sylvan L, 'Activating Competition: The Consumer Protection-Competition Interface' (Speech delivered at the University of South Australia Trade Practices Workshop, 29 October 2004) <http://www.accc.gov.au/system/files/20041029%20SA%20Uni%20Trade%20Practices%20Workshop.pdf> accessed 14 June 2014.
Temple Lang J, 'European Community Competition Policy: How Far Does it Benefit Consumers?' (2004) 18 *Boletin Latinoamericano de Competencia* 128.
Temple Lang J, 'How Can the Problems of Exclusionary Abuses Under Article 102 TFEU be Resolved?' (2012) 37 ELRev 136.
Temple Lang J, 'The Principle of Effective Protection of Community Law Rights' in O'Keeffe D and Bavasso R (eds), *Judicial Review in European Union Law—Liber Amicorum in Honour of Lord Slynn of Hadley* (Kluwer Law International 2000) 235.
Tesauro C and Ruggiero D, 'Private Damage Actions Related to European Competition Law in Italy' (2010) JECLAP 514.
Teubner G, 'Legal Irritants: Good Faith in British Law or How Unifying Law Ends Up in New Divergencies' (1998) 61 MLR 11.
Thaler CR and Sunstein RH, *Nudge: Improving Decisions about Health, Wealth and Happiness* (Yale University Press 2008).
The ANNALS of the American Academy of Political and Social Science, *The Globalisation of Class Actions*, Contents (March 2009).
The Study Centre for Consumer Law—Centre for European Economic Law, Katholieke Universiteit Leuven, 'An Analysis and Evaluation of Alternative Means of Consumer Redress Other than Redress through Ordinary Judicial Proceedings' (Final Report prepared for DG SANCO, 17 January 2007) <http://ec.europa.eu/consumers/redress/reports_studies/comparative_report_en.pdf> accessed 15 October 2014.
Tor A, 'A Behavioural Approach to Antitrust Law and Economics' (2004) 14 CPRev 18.
Townley C, *Article 81 and Public Policy* (Hart 2009).
Townley C, 'Inter-generational Impacts in Competition Analysis: Remembering Those Not Yet Born' (2011) ECLR 580.
Townley C, 'Is There (Still) Room for Non-Economic Arguments in Article 101 TFEU Cases?' in Heide-Jorgensen C and others (eds), *Aims and Values in Competition Law* (DJØF 2013) 115.
Tridimas T, 'Enforcing Community Rights in National Courts: Some Recent Developments' in O'Keeffe D and Bavasso A (eds), *Judicial Review in European Union Law—Liber Amicorum in Honour of Lord Slynn of Hadley* (Kluwer Law International 2000) 465.
Tridimas T, *The General Principles of EU Law* (2nd edn, OUP 2006).
Tulibacka M, 'Europeanization of Civil Procedures: In search of a Coherent Approach' (2009) 46 CMLRev 1527.
Twigg-Flesner C, 'UK and EU Consumer Law' in Twigg-Flesner C and others (eds) *Yearbook of Consumer Law 2008* (Ashgate 2008) 365.
Tzakas DP, 'Collective Redress in the Field of EU Competition Law: The Need for an EU Remedy and the Impact of the Recent Commission Recommendation' (2014) 41 *Legal Issues of Economic Integration* 225.

Tzankova I and Scheurleer DL, 'The Netherlands' (2009) in The ANNALS of the American Academy of Political and Social Science, *The Globalisation of Class Actions*, Contents (March 2009) 149.

Tzankova I, 'Class Actions, Group Litigation and Other Forms of Collective Litigation—Dutch Report' (24 September 2007) (Report prepared for 'The Globalization of Class Actions') <http://globalclassactions.stanford.edu/category/categories/country-reports> accessed 16 October 2014.

Ulen T, 'Information in the Market Economy—Cognitive Errors and Legal Correctives' in Grundmann S, Kerber W, and Weatherill S (eds), *Party Autonomy and the Role of Information in the Internal Market* (De Gruyter 2001) 98.

Utzschneider Y and Parmentier H, 'The New Frontiers of Antitrust: Damages Actions by Indirect Purchasers and the Passing-On Defence in France and California' (2011) 32 ECLR 266.

Van Boom W, 'European Tort Law: An Integrated or Compartmentalized Approach' in Vaquer A (ed), *European Private Law Beyond the Common Frame of Reference* (Europa Law Publishing 2008) 133.

Van den Bergh R and Visscher L, 'The Preventive Function of Collective Actions for Damages in Consumer Law' (2008) 1 Erasmus L Rev 55.

Van den Bergh R, 'Private Enforcement of European Competition Law and the Persisting Collective Action Problem' (2013) 20 *Maastricht Journal of European and Comparative Law* 12.

Van Dijk T and Verboven F, 'Cartel Damages Claims and the Passing-on Defence' (2007) CEPR Discussion Paper No DP6329 <http://papers.ssrn.com/sol3/papers.cfm?abstract_id=1136655> accessed 30 January 2015.

Van Gerven W, 'Harmonisation of Private Law: Do We Need It?' (2004) 41 CMLRev 505.

Van Gerven W, Lever J, and Larouche P, *Tort Law* (Hart 2000).

Van Gerven W, 'Of Rights, Remedies and Procedures' (2000) 37 CMLRev 501.

Van Gerven W, 'Private Enforcement of EC Competition Rules in the ECJ—*Courage v Crehan* and the Way Ahead' in Basedow J (ed), *Private Enforcement of EC Competition Law* (Kluwer Law International 2007) 19.

Van Gerven W, 'Substantive Remedies for the Private Enforcement of EC Antitrust Rules before National Courts' in Ehlermann CD and Atanasiu I (eds), *European Competition Law Annual 2001: Effective Private Enforcement of EC Antitrust Law* (Hart 2003) 53.

Van Gerven W, *The European Union. A Polity of States and People* (Hart 2005).

Van Rhee CH, 'Civil Procedure: A European Ius Commune?' (2000) 4 ERPL 589.

Van Rompuy B, *Economic Efficiency: The Sole Concern of Modern Antitrust Policy? Non-efficiency Considerations under 101 TFEU* (Kluwer Law International 2012).

Van Uytsel S, 'Collective Actions in a Competition Law Context—Reconciling Multilayer Interests to Enhance Access to Justice' in Wrbka S, Van Uytsel S, and Siems M (eds), *Collective Actions: Enhancing Access to Justice and Reconciling Multilayer Interests?* (CUP 2012) 57.

Vedder H, 'Competition Law and Consumer Protection: How Competition Law Can Be Used to Protect Consumers Even Better—Or Not?' (2006) 17 EBLR 83.

Vedder H, 'Of Jurisdiction and Justification. Why Competition is Good for "Non-Economic Goals" but May Need to be Restricted' (2009) 6 Comp L Rev <http://www.clasf.org/CompLRev/Issues/Vol6Issue1Article3Vedder.pdf> accessed 15 June 2014.

Veljanovski C, 'Cartel Fines in Europe: Law, Practice and Deterrence' (2007) 30 W Comp 65.

Venit J, 'Brave New World: The Modernization and Decentralization of Enforcement Under Articles 81 and 82 of the EC Treaty' (2003) 40 CMLRev 545.

Vickers J, 'Healthy Competition and its Consumer Wins' (2002) 12 CPRev 142.

Viitanen K, 'The Crisis of the Welfare State, Privatisation and Consumers' Access to Justice' in Wilhelmsson T and Hurri S (eds), *From Dissonance to Sense: Welfare State Expectations, Privatisation and Private Law* (Ashgate 1999) 549.

Waektare E, 'Private Enforcement: Antitrust Damage Settlement between Claimant CDC and Hydrogen Peroxide Cartellist Kemira (Finland)' (2014) 5 JECLAP 701.

Waelbroeck D, Slater D, and Even-Shoshan G, 'Study on the Conditions of Claims for Damages in Case of Infringement of EC Competition Rules' (Comparative Report) (Ashurst Study) (31 August 2004) <http://ec.europa.eu/competition/antitrust/actionsdamages/comparative_report_clean_en.pdf> accessed 17 October 2014.

Wagner von-Papp F, 'Best and Even Better Practices in Commitment Procedures after Alrosa: The Dangers of Abandoning the "Struggle for Competition Law"' (2012) 49 CMLRev 929.

Waller S, 'In Search of Economic Justice: Considering Competition and Consumer Protection Law' (2005) 36 Loyola U Chi LJ 631.

Waterson M, 'The Role of Consumers in Competition and Competition Policy' (2001) Warwick Economic Research Papers No 607 <http://www2.warwick.ac.uk/fac/soc/economics/research/workingpapers/publications/twerp607.pdf> accessed 5 August 2014.

Watson A, *Legal Transplants: An Approach to Comparative Law* (2nd edn, University of Georgia Press 1993).

Weatherill S, 'Addressing Problems of Imbalanced Implementation in EC Law: Remedies in an Institutional Perspective' in Kilpatrick C, Novitz T, and Skidmore P (eds), *The Future of Remedies in Europe* (Hart 2000) 87.

Weatherill S, 'Article 38—Consumer Protection' in Peers S and others (eds), *The EU Charter of Fundamental Rights—A Commentary* (Hart 2014) 1005.

Weatherill S, 'Better Competence Monitoring' (2005) 30 ELRev 23.

Weatherill S, *Cases and Materials on EU Law* (11th edn, OUP 2014).

Weatherill S, 'Competence Creep and Competence Control' (2004) 23 YEL 1.

Weatherill S, 'Consumer Policy' in Craig P and de Búrca G, *The Evolution of EU Law* (OUP 2011) 837.

Weatherill S, *EU Consumer Law and Policy* (2nd edn, Edward Elgar 2013).

Weatherill S, 'Public Interest Litigation in EC Competition Law' in Micklitz HW and Reich N (eds), *Public Interest Litigation before European Courts* (Nomos 1996) 169.

Weatherill S, 'The Limits of Legislative Harmonisation Ten Years after Tobacco Advertising: How the Court's Case Law has Become a "Drafting Guide"' (2011) 12 German LJ 827.

Weatherill S, 'The Links between Competition Policy and Consumer Protection' in Howells G and others (eds), *Yearbook of Consumer Law 2007* (Ashgate 2007).

Weatherill S, 'Who is the Average Consumer?' in Weatherill S and Bernitz U (eds), *The Regulation of Unfair Commercial Practices under EC Directive 2005/29: New Rules and New Techniques* (Hart 2007) 115.

Weinrib E (ed), *Tort Law* (Ashgate 2002).

Weinrib E, *Corrective Justice* (OUP 2012).

Weinrib E, *The Idea of Private Law* (Harvard University Press 1995).

Weinrib E, *The Idea of Private Law* (OUP 2012).

Weitbrecht A, 'From Freiburg to Chicago and Beyond: The First 50 Years of European Competition Law' (2008) 29 ECLR 81.

Werlauff E, 'Class Actions in Denmark—From 2008' (Report prepared for 'The Globalization of Class Actions') <http://globalclassactions.stanford.edu/sites/default/files/documents/Demark_National_Report.pdf> accessed 17 October 2014.

Wezenbeek R, 'Consumers and Competition Policy: The Commission's Perspective and the Example of Transport' [2006] EBLR 73.

Whish R and Bailey D, *Competition Law* (7th edn, OUP 2012).

Whish R, 'The Enforcement of EC Competition Law in the Domestic Courts of Member States' in Gormley L (ed), *Current and Future Perspectives on EC Competition Law* (Kluwer Law 1997) 73.

Wilks S, 'Institutional Reform and the Enforcement of Competition Policy in the UK' (April 2011) 7 Eur Comp J 1.

Wils W, 'Discretion and Prioritisation in Public Antitrust Enforcement, in Particular EU Antitrust Enforcement' (2011) 34 W Comp 353.

Wils W, *Efficiency and Justice in European Antitrust Enforcement* (Hart 2008).

Wils W, 'Should Private Antitrust Enforcement Be Encouraged in Europe?' (2003) 26 W Comp 473.

Wils W, 'The Judgment of the EU General Court in Intel and the So-called More Economic Approach to Abuse of Dominance' (2014) 37 W Comp 405.

Wils W, 'The Relationship Between Public Antitrust Enforcement and Private Actions for Damages' (2009) 32 W Comp 3.

Wincott D, 'The Governance White Paper, the Commission and the Search for Legitimacy' in Arnull A and Wincott D (eds), *Accountability and Legitimacy in the European Union* (OUP 2002) 379.

Witt A, 'Public Policy Goals under EU Competition Law-Now is the Time to Set the House in Order' (2012) 8 Euro CJ 443.

Wood D and Bavarez N, 'Sector Inquiries' (2005) 4(2) CLI 3.

Wrbka S, 'European Consumer Protection Law: Quo Vadis?—Thoughts on the Compensatory Collective Redress Debate' in Wrbka S, Van Uytsel S, and Siems M (eds), *Collective Actions: Enhancing Access to Justice and Reconciling Multilayer Interests?* (CUP 2012) 23.

Wrbka S, Van Uytsel S, and Siems M, 'Access to Justice and Collective Actions—"Florence" and Beyond' in Wrbka S, Van Uytsel S, and Siems M (eds), *Collective Actions: Enhancing Access to Justice and Reconciling Multilayer Interests?* (CUP 2012) 1.

Wright J, 'Nudging Antitrust? Commissioner's Rosch's Weak Case for Behavioral Antitrust' (July 2010) <http://truthonthemarket.com/2010/07/12/nudging-antitrust-commissioner-roschs-weak-case-for-behavioral-antitrust-part-1/> accessed 15 June 2014.

Wurmnest W, 'A New Era for Private Antitrust Litigation in Germany? A Critical Appraisal of the Modernized Law against Restraints of Competition' (2005) 6 German LJ 1173.

Wyatt D, 'Community Competence to Regulate the Internal Market' in Dougan M and Currie S (eds), *50 Years of the European Treaties* (Hart Publishing 2009) 93.

Yeazell SC, 'Collective Litigation as Collective Action' (1989) 43 U Illinois L Rev 43.

Zakrzewski R, *Remedies Reclassified* (OUP 2005).

Zuckerman A, *Zuckerman on Civil Procedure: Principles of Practice* (2nd edn, Sweet & Maxwell 2006).

POLICY DOCUMENTS

European Union

DG Competition, 'Discussion Paper on the Application of Article 82 of the Treaty to Exclusionary Abuses' (December 2005).

DG Competition, 'The Application of Articles 85 and 86 of the EC Treaty by National Courts in the Member States' (Brussels, July 1997) ('Braakman Report').

European Commission, 'Annex to the Report on Competition Policy 2007' (Staff Working Document) SEC(2008) 2038.

European Commission, 'Commission Work Programme 2010' (Communication) COM(2010) 135 final.

European Commission, 'Commission Work Programme 2011' (Communication) COM(2010) 623 final.

European Commission, 'Consultation on Proposed Modifications to Regulation 773/2004 and the Notices on Access to the File, Leniency, Settlements and Cooperation with National Courts' <http://ec.europa.eu/competition/consultations/2014_regulation_773_2004/index_en.html> accessed 20 December 2014.

European Commission, 'Consumer Empowerment in the EU' (Staff Working Paper) SEC(2011) 469 final, Brussels, 07.04.2011.

European Commission, 'Consumer Policy Action Plan 1999–2001' (Communication) COM(1998) 696 final.

European Commission, 'Consumer Policy Strategy 2002–2006' (Communication) COM(2002) 208 final.

European Commission, 'Consumer Policy Strategy 2007–2013' (Communication) COM(2007) 99 final.

European Commission, 'Consumer Redress' (Memorandum) COM(1984) 629 final.

European Commission, 'Decision of the President of the European Commission on the Function and Terms of Reference of the Hearing Officer in Certain Competition Proceedings' [2011] OJ L275/29.

European Commission, 'EU Consumer Policy Strategy 2007–2013' (Communication) COM(2007) 99 final.

European Commission, 'European Governance' (White Paper) COM(2001) 428 final.

European Commission, 'European Transparency Initiative' (Green Paper) COM(2006) 194 final.

European Commission, 'Follow-up to the Green Paper on Consumer Collective Redress' <http://ec.europa.eu/consumers/redress_cons/docs/consultation_paper2009.pdf> accessed 11 July 2014.

European Commission, 'Green Paper on Consumer Collective Redress' (Green Paper) COM(2008) 794 final, 27 November 2008.

European Commission, 'Green Paper on Vertical Restraints in EC Competition Policy' COM(96) 721 final.

European Commission, 'Green Paper—Liability for Defective Products' (Green Paper) COM(1999) 396 final.

European Commission, 'Interchange Fee Litigation before the Judiciary of England and Wales: Wm. Morrison Supermarkets plc and Others v MasterCard Incorporated and Others (Claim Nos 2012/699; 2012/1305–1311)' (Commission Opinion) C(2014) 3066 final.

European Commission, 'La Reparation des Consequences Dommageables d' une Violation des Articles 85 et 86 du Traite Instituant la CEE' (Brussels, 1966) Série Concurrence No 1, 5.

European Commission, 'Report Concerning the Application of Directive 98/27/EC of the European Parliament and of the Council on Injunctions for the Protection of Consumers' Interest' COM(2008) 756 final.

European Commission, 'Report on Competition Policy 2004' (vol II) <http://ec.europa.eu/competition/publications/annual_report/2004/2004_volume2_en.pdf> accessed 3 November 2014.

European Commission, Report on Competition Policy 2006 (2007) <http://ec.europa.eu/competition/publications/annual_report/2006/en.pdf> accessed 15 June 2014.

European Commission, 'Report on Competition Policy 2008' COM(2009) 374 final.

European Commission, 'Report on the Application in 2009 of Regulation No 1049/2001 Regarding Public Access to European Parliament, Council and Commission Documents' COM(2010) 351 final.

European Commission, 'Report on the Functioning of Regulation 1/2003' (Communication) COM(2009) 206 final.

European Commission, 'Sector Inquiry under Article 17 of Regulation (EC) No 1/2003 on Business Insurance' (Final Report) COM(2007) 556 final.

European Commission, 'Sector Inquiry under Article 17 of Regulation (EC) No 1/2003 on Retail Banking' (Final Report) COM(2007) 33 final.

European Commission, 'Single Market Act—Twelve Levers to Boost Growth and Strengthen Confidence' (Communication) COM(2011) 206 final.

European Commission, 'Staff Working Document Accompanying the Communication from the Commission Sector Inquiry under Article 17 of Regulation (EC) No 1/2003 on Business Insurance' (Final Report) SEC(2007) 1231.

European Commission, 'Staff Working Document Accompanying the Communication from the Commission Sector Inquiry under Article 17 of Regulation (EC) No 1/2003 on Retail Banking' (Final Report) SEC(2007) 106.

European Commission, 'Staff Working Document Accompanying the Report on Competition Policy 2008', COM(2009) 374 final.

European Commission, 'Staff Working Paper Accompanying the Report from the Commission on Competition Policy 2008' COM(2009) 374 final.

European Commission, 'Staff Working Document: Ten Years of Antitrust Enforcement under Regulation 1/2003' COM(2014) 453.

European Commission, 'Third Strategic Review of Better Regulation in the European Union' (Communication) COM(2009) 15 final.

European Commission, 'Three Year Action Plan of Consumer Policy in the EEC (1990–1992)' COM(1990) 98 final.

European Commission, First Report on Competition Policy (Brussels, Luxembourg 1972) <http://ec.europa.eu/competition/publications/annual_report/ar_1971_en.pdf> accessed 15 June 2014.

European Commission, Second Report on Competition Policy (Brussels, Luxembourg 1973) <http://ec.europa.eu/competition/publications/annual_report/ar_1972_en.pdf> accessed 15 June 2014.

European Commission, Fifth Report on Competition Policy (Brussels, Luxembourg 1976) <http://ec.europa.eu/competition/publications/annual_report/ar_1975_en.pdf> accessed 16 June 2014.

European Commission, Thirteenth Report on Competition Policy 1983 (Brussels, Luxembourg 1984) <http://bookshop.europa.eu/is-bin/INTERSHOP.enfinity/WFS/EU-

Bookshop-Site/en_GB/-/EUR/ViewPublication-Start?PublicationKey=CB3883823> accessed 17 June 2014.

European Commission, Fourteenth Report on Competition Policy (Brussels, Luxembourg 1985), <http://bookshop.europa.eu/is-bin/INTERSHOP.enfinity/WFS/EU-Bookshop-Site/en_GB/-/EUR/ViewPublication-Start?PublicationKey=CB4184822> accessed 17 June 2014.

European Commission, Fifteenth Report on Competition Policy (Brussels, Luxembourg 1986) <http://bookshop.europa.eu/is-bin/INTERSHOP.enfinity/WFS/EU-Bookshop-Site/en_GB/-/EUR/ViewPublication-Start?PublicationKey=CB4585430> accessed 17 June 2014.

European Commission, Sixteenth Report on Competition Policy 1987 (Brussels, Luxembourg 1988) <http://bookshop.europa.eu/is-bin/INTERSHOP.enfinity/WFS/EU-Bookshop-Site/en_GB/-/EUR/ViewPublication-Start?PublicationKey=CB4886060> accessed 2 February 2012.

European Commission, Seventeenth Report on Competition Policy 1988 (Brussels, Luxembourg 1989) <http://bookshop.europa.eu/is-bin/INTERSHOP.enfinity/WFS/EU-Bookshop-Site/en_GB/-/EUR/ViewPublication-Start?PublicationKey=CB5087340> accessed 2 February 2012.

European Commission, XXth Report on Competition Policy (Brussels, Luxembourg 1991) <http://bookshop.europa.eu/is-bin/INTERSHOP.enfinity/WFS/EU-Bookshop-Site/en_GB/-/EUR/ViewPublication-Start?PublicationKey=CM6091410> accessed 15 June 2014.

European Commission, XXIst Report on Competition Policy 1991 (Brussels, Luxembourg 1992) <http://bookshop.europa.eu/is-bin/INTERSHOP.enfinity/WFS/EU-Bookshop-Site/en_GB/-/EUR/ViewPublication-Start?PublicationKey=CM7392247> accessed 15 June 2012.

European Commission, XXIInd Report on Competition Policy 1992 (Brussels, Luxembourg 1993) <http://bookshop.europa.eu/is-bin/INTERSHOP.enfinity/WFS/EU-Bookshop-Site/en_GB/-/EUR/ViewPublication-Start?PublicationKey=CM7693689> accessed 15 June 2014.

European Commission, XXIIIrd Report on Competition Policy 1993 (Brussels, Luxembourg 1994) <http://bookshop.europa.eu/is-bin/INTERSHOP.enfinity/WFS/EU-Bookshop-Site/en_GB/-/EUR/ViewPublication-Start?PublicationKey=CM8294650> accessed 3 July 2014.

European Commission, XXIVth Report on Competition Policy 1994 (Brussels, Luxembourg 1995) <http://bookshop.europa.eu/is-bin/INTERSHOP.enfinity/WFS/EU-Bookshop-Site/en_GB/-/EUR/ViewPublication-Start?PublicationKey=CM9095283> accessed 16 June 2014.

European Commission, XXIXth Report on Competition Policy 1999, SEC(2000) 720 final.

European Commission, XXXth Report on Competition Policy 2000 SEC(2001) 694 final <http://ec.europa.eu/competition/publications/annual_report/2000/en.pdf> accessed 15 June 2014.

European Commission, XXXIst Report on Competition Policy 2001 (Brussels, Luxembourg 2002) <http://ec.europa.eu/competition/publications/annual_report/2001/en.pdf> accessed 15 June 2014.

European Commission, XXXIInd Report on Competition Policy (2002) SEC(2003) 467 final.

European Commission, XXXIIIrd Report on Competition Policy 2003, SEC(2004) 658 final.
European Commission, 'White Paper on the Completion of the Internal Market' COM(85) 310 final.
European Commission, 'A Pro-active Competition Policy for a Competitive Europe' COM(2004) 293 final.
European Commission, 'Accompanying Document to the White Paper on Damages Actions for Breach of the EC Antitrust Rules—Impact Assessment' SEC(2008) 405.
European Commission, 'Annex to the Green Paper, Damages Actions for Breach of the EC Antitrust Rules' (Staff Working Paper) SEC(2005) 1732, 19 December 2005.
European Commission, 'Commission Notice on the Conduct of Settlement Procedures in View of the Adoption of Decision Pursuant to Article 7 and Article 23 of Council Regulation (EC) No 1/2003 in Cartel Cases' [2008] OJ C167/1.
European Commission, 'Damages Actions for Breach of the EC Antitrust Rules' (Green Paper) COM(2005) 672 final.
European Commission, 'Damages Actions for Breach of the EC Antitrust Rules' (White Paper) COM(2008) 165 final.
European Commission, 'Damages Actions for Breach of the EU Antitrust Rules' (Impact Assessment Report—Staff Working Document) SWD (2013) 203 final, COM(2013) 404 final.
European Commission, 'Detailed Rules for the Application of Regulation (EC) No 1049/2001 of the European Parliament and of the Council Regarding Public Access to European Parliament, Council and Commission Documents' (Decision) [2001] OJ L345/94.
European Commission, 'Guidance on the Commission's Enforcement Priorities in Applying Article 82 EC of the EC Treaty to Abusive Exclusionary Conduct by Dominant Undertakings' [2009] OJ C45/7.
European Commission, 'Guidelines on the Applicability of Article 101 of the Treaty on the Functioning of the European Union to Horizontal Co-operation Agreements' [2011] OJ C 11/1.
European Commission, 'Guidelines on the Application of Article 101 of the Treaty on the Functioning of the European Union to Technology Transfer Agreements' [2014] C 89/3.
European Commission, 'Guidelines on the Application of Article 81 of the EC Treaty to Technology Transfer Agreements' [2004] C101/02.
European Commission, 'Guidelines on the Application of Article 81(3) of the Treaty' [2004] OJ C101/08.
European Commission, 'Guidelines on the Assessment of Horizontal Mergers under the Council Regulation on the Control of Concentrations between Undertakings' [2004] OJ C 31/5.
European Commission, 'Guidelines on the Method of Setting Fines Imposed Pursuant to Article 23(2)(a) of Regulation No 1/2003' [2006] OJ C210/2.
European Commission, 'Guidelines on Vertical Restraints' [2010] OJ C 130/1.
European Commission, 'Modernisation of the Rules Implementing Articles 85 and 86 of the EC Treaty' (White Paper) COM(99) 101 final.
European Commission, 'Notice on Best Practices for the Conduct of Proceedings Concerning Articles 101 and 102 TFEU' [2011] OJ C308/6.
European Commission, 'Notice on Cooperation between National Courts and the Commission in Applying Articles 85 and 86 of the EEC Treaty' [1993] OJ C39/6.

European Commission, 'Notice on Cooperation within the Network of Competition Authorities' [2004] OJ C101/43.
European Commission, 'Notice on Immunity from Fines and Reduction of Fines in Cartel Cases' [2006] OJ C298/17.
European Commission, 'Notice on the Conduct of Settlement Procedures in View of the Adoption of Decisions Pursuant to Article 7 and Article 23 of Council Regulation (EC) No 1/2003 in Cartel Cases' [2008] 167/1.
European Commission, 'Notice on the Cooperation between the Commission and the Courts of the EU Member States in the Application of Articles 81 and 82 EC' [2004] OJ C101/54.
European Commission, Notice on the Rules for Access to the Commission File [2005] C325/7.
European Commission, 'Notice on the Handling of Complaints by the Commission under Articles 81 and 82 of the EC Treaty' [2004] OJ C101/65.
European Commission, 'Proposal for a Council Directive Governing Actions for Damages for Infringements of Article 81 and 82 of the Treaty' (document withdrawn).
European Commission, 'Proposal for a Directive of the European Parliament and of the Council on Certain Rules Governing Actions for Damages under National Law for Infringements of the Competition Law Provisions of the Member States and of the European Union' COM(2013) 404, 11 June 2013.
European Commission, 'Proposal for a Directive of the European Parliament and of the Council on Consumer Rights' COM(2008) 614 final.
European Commission, 'Proposal for a Regulation of the European Parliament and of the Council Regarding Public Access to European Parliament, Council and Commission Documents' COM(2008) 229 final.
European Commission, 'Public Consultation: Towards a Coherent European Approach to Collective Redress' (Staff Working Document) SEC(2011) 173 final.
European Commission, 'Recommendation of 11 June 2013 on Common Principles for Injunctive and Compensatory Collective Redress Mechanisms in the Member States Concerning Violations of Rights Granted under Union Law' [2013] OJ L201/60.
European Commission, 'Report on the Functioning of Regulation 1/2003' (Communication) COM(2009) 206 final.
European Commission, 'Staff Working Document—Accompanying Document to the White Paper on Damages Actions for Breach of the EC Antitrust Rules' (Impact Assessment) SEC(2008) 405 (Brussels, 02/04/08).
European Commission, 'Staff Working Document—Practical Guide—Quantifying Harm in Actions for Damages Based on Breaches of Article 101 or 102 of the Treaty on the Functioning of the European Union' SWD (2013) (205) (Strasbourg, 11 June 2013).
European Commission, 'Towards a European Horizontal Framework for Collective Redress' (Communication) COM(2013) 401 final.
European Parliament, 'Non-legislative Resolution on the White Paper on Damages Actions' (2008/2154(INI)).
European Parliament, 'Resolution of 26 March 2009 on the White Paper on Damages Actions for Breach of the EC Antitrust Rules' (2008/2154(INI)).
European Parliament, Resolution on 'Towards a Coherent European Approach to Collective Redress' (2011/2089(INI)) (2 February 2012).

United Kingdom

BERR, 'Super-Complaints: Guidance for Bodies Seeking Designation as Super-Complainants' (March 2009).

BIS, 'A Better Deal for Consumers: Delivering Real Help Now and Change for the Future' (July 2009) Cm 7669.

BIS, 'A Competition Regime for Growth: A Consultation on Options for Reform' (March 2011).

BIS, 'Growth, Competition and the Competition Regime' (March 2012) A655.

BIS, 'Private Actions in Competition Law: A Consultation on Options for Reform' (April 2012).

BIS, 'Private Actions in Competition Law: A Consultation on Options for Reform—Government Response' (January 2013).

CC, 'Guidelines for Market Investigations: Their Role, Procedures, Assessment and Remedies' (April 2013).

CMA, 'Guidance on the CMA's Approval of Voluntary Redress Schemes' (2 March 2015) (Draft, CMA40con).

CMA, 'Market Studies and Market Investigations: Supplemental Guidance on the CMA's Approach' (January 2014).

CMA, 'Regulated Industries: Guidance on a Concurrent Application of Competition Law to Regulated Industries' (March 2014).

HM Treasury, 'Guidance for Bodies Seeking Designation as Super-complainants to the Financial Conduct Authority' (March 2013).

OFT, 'Article 101(3)-A Discussion of Narrow Versus Broad Definition of Benefits' (Discussion Note for OFT Breakfast Roundtable, London, May 2010).

OFT, 'Assessing the Effectiveness of Potential Remedies in Consumer Markets' (OFT 994) (April 2008).

OFT, 'Interactions between Competition and Consumer Policy' (OFT 991) (April 2008).

OFT, 'Joining up Competition and Consumer Policy' (OFT 1151) (December 2009).

OFT, 'Market Investigation References: Guidance about the Making of References under Part 4 of the Enterprise Act' (OFT 511) (March 2006).

OFT, 'Market Studies: Guidance on the OFT Approach' (OFT 519) (2010).

OFT, 'Private Actions in Competition Law: Effective Redress for Consumers and Business' (Recommendations) (OFT 916resp, November 2007) <http://webarchive.nationalarchives.gov.uk/20140402142426/http://www.oft.gov.uk/shared_oft/reports/comp_policy/oft916resp.pdf> accessed 17 October 2014.

OFT, 'Private Actions in Competition Law: Effective Redress for Consumers and Businesses' (OFT 916) (Discussion Paper, April 2007).

OFT, 'Super-Complaints: Guidance for Designated Consumer Bodies' (OFT 514) (July 2003).

OFT, 'Terms of Reference of the Concurrency Working Party' (OFT 548) (November 2003).

Other

ICN, 'Competition Enforcement and Consumer Welfare' (2011) <http://www.icn-thehague.org/page.php?id=78> accessed 28 May 2014.

ICN, 'Market Studies Project Report' (Prepared by the ICN Advocacy Working Group) (June 2009).

ICN, Report on the Objectives of Unilateral Conduct Laws, Assessment of Dominance/ Substantial Market Power, and State Created Monopolies (May 2007) <http://internationalcompetitionnetwork.org/uploads/library/doc353.pdf> accessed 15 June 2014.

ICN, Unilateral Conduct Workbook, Chapter 1: 'The Objectives and Principles of Unilateral Conduct Laws' (April 2012).

OECD, 'Consumer Dispute Resolution and Redress in the Global Marketplace' (2006) <http://www.oecd.org/dataoecd/26/61/36456184.pdf> accessed 12 July 2014.

OECD, 'Private Remedies' (2009) *OECD Journal: Competition Law and Policy* 7.

OECD, 'Remedies and Sanctions in Abuse of Dominance Cases' (2006) (DAF/COMP (2006)19) 18.

OECD, 'Remedies Available to Private Parties under Competition Laws' (Report) COM/DAFFE/CLP/TD(2000)24/Final.

OECD, 'Roundtable on Demand-side Economics for Consumer Policy: Summary Report' DSTI/CP(2006)3/FINAL (20 April 2006).

OECD, 'The Interface Between Competition and Consumer Policies' (Policy Roundtables) DAF/COMP/GF(2008) 10.

OECD, 'The Objectives of Competition Law and Policy' (29 January 2003) CCNM/GF/COMP(2003) 3 <http://www.oecd.org/dataoecd/57/39/2486329.pdf> accessed 15 June 2014.

Index

Aarhus Convention
  representative organisations 139–40
abuse of dominant position 35–41
access to evidence
  Commission file 95–101
  Competition Authority's file 101–4
  disclosure 90–4
  follow-on claims 94–104
  introduction 90
  national courts, disclosure before 101–4
  preserving effectiveness of public enforcement 94–104
  stand-alone claims 90–4
access to justice
  collective actions 115–17
  narrow and broad approach 116
aims of competition law
  competitive process, promotion of 16
  consumer welfare 17, 22–4
    Commission rhetoric 26–8
    narrow approach 25
  core EU competition objectives 16–18
  grey zone objectives 21–2
  market integration 17
  multiplicity of aims 15–22
  ordoliberalism 16
  public interest objectives 18–21
aims of private enforcement
  Commission approach 52–3, 60–1
  compensatory function 56, 66–7
  deterrent function
    generally 56–62, 66–7
    scepticism of 62–5
  ECJ approach 53–60
  effective enforcement 56–61
  EU institutions approach to 52–62
  principle of effectiveness 56–9
  protection of individual's rights 55–7
  ranking 66–7
  standing to invoke breach of EU law 55–6
  uniform application of EU law 54
anti-competitive agreements 28–34
apathy
  consumer claims, characteristics of 77

burden of proof
  indirect purchasers 87

class actions
  collective actions, and 113–14
  opt out character 118–20
  SCOTUS approach 113–14, 119
  standing 120–1

class counsel
  standing
    collective actions 120–1
collective actions
  access to justice 115–17
  class actions, and 113–14
  conclusion 147–9
  consumer claims, characteristics of 78
  damages, distribution of
    model collective action 125–6
    proposed mechanism 142–4
  EU development of 108–11
  financial risk 132
  funding
    model collective action 124–5
    proposed mechanism 144–7
  hybrid mechanisms (reverse opt-in) 130–2
  individual v collective consumer interest 111–15
  introduction 107–8
  Members States' mechanisms
    collective consumer interest 132–6
    Denmark 132, 135
    England 131, 135–6
    financial risk 132
    France 130
    generally 126–7
    Greece 131–2
    hybrid mechanisms 130–2
    individual consumers' interests 127–32
    Netherlands 133
    opt-in mechanisms 127–9
    Portugal 133–4
    reverse opt-in mechanisms 130–2
    Spain 134–5
    Sweden 129, 132
    synopsis 136–7
  model collective action, structural characteristics of
    distribution of damages award 125–6
    funding 124–5
    generally 117–18
    opt in v opt out 118–20
    standing 120–4
    synopsis 126
  opt in/opt out
    model collective action 118–20
    opt-in mechanisms 127–9
    proposed mechanism 141–2
    reverse opt-in mechanisms 130–2
  proposed mechanism, structuring
    costs 144–7
    distribution of damages award 142–4

246 Index

collective actions (cont.):
  proposed mechanism, structuring (cont.):
    forming the group 141–2
    funding 144–7
    generally 137–8
    opt in v opt out 141–2
    standing 138–41
  standing
    model collective action 120–4
    proposed mechanism 138–41
collective consumer interest
  collective actions, and 118
  furthering 132–6
  individual contrasted 111–15
  public compensation 179
collective redress
  see also collective actions
  definition 107
  EU developments 108–11
Commission
  access to files of 95–101
  complaints to
    allocation mechanism 162–3
    generally 156–8
    legitimate interest requirements 158–9
    standing 162
    Union interest requirement 159–62
Commission Quantification Guidance
  rebutting passing-on presumption 87–8
compensation
  aims of private enforcement 56, 66–7
  deterrence-compensation dichotomy 152–5
  Directive on Damages Actions 86
Competition Authority's file
  national courts, disclosure before 101–4
competition law enforcement
  background 1–2
  consumer's role in 3–4
  fused approach to 3
  harmonisation 4–5
  terminology 5–7
  tort law, and 4
complaints to Commission
  complaints allocation mechanism 162–3
  generally 156–8
  legitimate interest requirements 158–9
  standing 162
  Union interest requirement 159–62
consumer claims
  see also class actions, collective actions
  characteristics of 75–9
  low value consumer claims
    collective actions 108, 111–4, 117–8
    consumer claims, characteristics of 76–9
    court supervision of 142
    evidential burden 132
    hybrid actions 129
    national procedures and 136–7
  stand-alone claims 90–4

consumer interest
  abuse of dominant position 35–41
  anti-competitive agreements 28–34
  collective
    collective actions, and 118
    furthering 132–6
    individual contrasted 111–15
    public compensation 179
  Commission rhetoric 26–8
  conclusion 44–5
  effect restrictions 33
  embracing 42–4
  EU competition law, and 24–5
  exclusionary abuses 37–41
  exploitative abuses 35–7
  individual
    collective contrasted 111–15
    opt-in mechanisms 127–9
    reverse opt-in mechanisms 130–2
  interplay between competition and consumer laws 12–15
  introduction 11–12
  narrow consumer welfare 25
  object restrictions 29–33
  role of
    Commission rhetoric 26–8
    EU jurisprudence 28–41
    introduction 25
consumer organisations
  funding 125, 145–6
  standing 121–3, 139–41
consumer participation
  access to evidence 90–104
  collective actions 137–49
  consumer claims, characteristics of 75–9
  justifications for increasing
    aims of competition law 44–5
    aims of private enforcement 48–67
    conclusion 72
    institutional benefits 67–72
    introduction 47–8
    legitimisation of EU policies 68–72
    proliferation of information 67–8
  passing on 79–89
  standing 79–89
consumer representatives
  see also consumer organisations
  role of 185
consumer welfare
  consumer interest 24–5
  EU competition law, and 22–4
  EU core competition aims 17
  narrow approach 25
contingency fees
  class actions 124
  collective actions 145
cy-près
  distribution of damages award 125, 143–4
  proposals for increasing consumer participation 185

damages awards, distribution of
  collective actions
    model collective action 125–6
    proposed mechanism 142–4
  proposals for increasing consumer participation 185
defensive passing-on
  see also passing-on defence
  meaning 79
Denmark
  opt out mechanisms 135
  reverse opt in mechanisms 132
deterrence
  deterrence-compensation dichotomy 152–5
  generally 56–62, 66–7
  scepticism of 62–5
Directive on Damages Actions
  adoption of 205
  collective redress 110–11
  disclosure of evidence 91–3
  passing-on 86, 88
  political obstacles 182–4
  standing 84, 86
disclosure
  costs 91
  Directive on Damages Actions 91–3
  information asymmetry 93–4
  leniency material
    access to Commission file 97–9
    access to NCA file 101–4
    damages actions and leniency programmes, interplay between 64, 101–3, 110
    non-disclosure 102–5
  national courts 101–4

England
  collective action mechanisms 135–6
  reverse opt in mechanisms 131

follow-on claims
  Commission file, access to 95–101
  Competition Authority's file, access to 101–4
  deterrent function of 62–5
  national courts, disclosure before 101–4
France
  reverse opt in mechanisms 130
funding
  collective actions
    model collective action 124–5
    proposed mechanism 144–7

Greece
  reverse opt in mechanisms 131–2
group formation
  see also opt in, opt out

harmonisation of procedural rules
  appropriate legal instrument 199–200
  justifying 186–9
  legal basis for 189–98

in pari delicto
  right to damages 54
indirect purchasers
  burden of proof 87
  SCOTUS approach 80–3
  standing 86–7
individual consumer interest
  collective contrasted 111–15
  opt-in mechanisms 127–9
  reverse opt-in mechanisms 130–2
information asymmetry
  consumer claims, characteristics of 77
  disclosure orders 93–4
intervention
  public enforcement, consumer involvement in 170–1

leniency material
  access to Commission file 97–9
  access to NCA file 101–4
  damages actions and leniency programmes, interplay between 64, 101–3, 110
  non-disclosure 102–5
limitations, overcoming
  conclusion 202–3
  Directive on Damages Actions 182–6
  harmonisation of procedural rules
    appropriate legal instrument 199–200
    justifying 186–9
    legal basis for 189–98
  introduction 181
  political obstacles 182–4
  proposals, content of 184–6
  public enforcement proposals, implementing 200–2
low value consumer claims
  see also consumer claims
  collective actions 108, 111–4, 117–8
  consumer claims, characteristics of 76–9
  court supervision of 142
  evidential burden 132
  hybrid actions 129
  national procedures and 136–7

Macrory Report
  deterrence-compensation dichotomy 153–4
model collective action
  see also collective actions
  structural characteristics of
    distribution of damages award 125–6
    funding 124–5
    generally 117–18
    opt in v opt out 118–20
    standing 120–4
    synopsis 126

Index

National Competition Authority
  disclosure of files 101–4
  proposals for increasing consumer participation 185
national procedural autonomy 50
Netherlands
  collective settlement mechanism 133
normative justifications for increasing consumer participation
  aims of private enforcement
    Commission approach 52–3, 60–1
    compensatory function 56, 66–7
    deterrent function 56–67
    ECJ approach 53–60
    effective enforcement 56–61
    EU institutions approach to 52–62
    principle of effectiveness 56–9
    protection of individual's rights 55–7
    ranking 66–7
    standing to invoke breach of EU law 55–6
    uniform application of EU law 54
  conclusion 72
  institutional benefits
    legitimisation of EU policies 68–72
    proliferation of information 67–8
  introduction 47–8

offensive passing-on
  see also passing-on defence
  meaning 79
opt-in mechanism
  EU mechanism 141–2
  financial risk 132
  model collective action 118–20
  opt-in mechanisms 127–9
  reverse opt-in mechanisms 130–2
opt-out
  distribution of damages award 142–3
  model collective action 118–20
  proposals for increasing consumer participation 185
  proposed mechanism 141–2

parens patriae actions
  standing of public bodies 123–4
passing-on
  EU approach 84–6
  generally 79–80
  legislative solution 86–9
  multiple liability 88–9
  quantifying passing-on rate 87–8
  SCOTUS approach 80–3
Portugal
  collective action mechanisms 133–4
private enforcement
  aims of
    EU institutions approach to 52–62
    generally 48–52

    ranking 66–7
    scepticism of deterrent function 62–5
  proposals for increasing consumer participation
    generally 184–6
    implementing 186–98
procedural rules, harmonisation of
  appropriate legal instrument 199–200
  justifying 186–9
  legal basis for 189–98
public bodies
  proposals for increasing consumer participation 185
  standing in collective actions 123–4
public compensation
  categorisation of cases 175–6
  collective consumer interest 179
  EU cases 172–4
  generally 171–2
  institutionalising approach 176–9
  meaning 171
  national cases 174–5
public enforcement
  collective consumer interest 179
  complaints to Commission 156–63
  conclusion 180
  deterrence-compensation dichotomy 152–5
  institutional benefits 155–6
  intervention 170–1
  introduction 151–2
  proposals for increasing consumer participation
    generally 184–6
    implementing 200–2
  public compensation 171–9
  sector inquiries 163–6
  super-complaints 166–70

rational apathy
  consumer claims, characteristics of 77
  opt in v opt out 119

sector inquiries
  generally 163–5
  improvements to 165–6
Spain
  collective actions mechanisms 134–5
stand-alone claims
  distinction, from follow-on 62–4
  promotion of 90–4
standing
  collective actions
    class counsel 120–1
    consumer organisations 121–3
    model collective action 120–4
    proposed mechanism 138–41
    public bodies 123–4
  EU approach 83–4
  generally 79–80

indirect purchasers 80–4, 86–7
legislative solution 86–9
SCOTUS approach 80–3
super-complaints
proposals for increasing consumer participation 185
use of 166–70
Sweden
opt in mechanisms 129
reverse opt in mechanisms 132

third party funding
class actions 125

United States
class actions 113–14, 119
passing-on 80–3
standing 80–3
unjust enrichment
passing-on 85–6

Printed and bound by CPI Group (UK) Ltd, Croydon, CR0 4YY